ANCIENT WEST MEXICO

ART AND ARCHAEOLOGY
OF THE UNKNOWN PAST

ANCIENT WEST MEXICO

ART AND ARCHAEOLOGY OF THE
UNKNOWN PAST

RICHARD F. TOWNSEND
GENERAL EDITOR

WITH ESSAYS BY

Patricia Rieff Anawalt, Christopher S. Beekman,

Barbara Braun, Kristi Butterwick,

Maria Teresa Cabrero, Jane Stevenson Day,

Peter T. Furst, Mark Miller Graham,

Lorenza López Mestas Camberos,

Joseph B. Mountjoy, Robert B. Pickering,

Jorge Ramos de la Vega, Otto Schöndube,

Richard F. Townsend, Francisco Valdez,

Phil C. Weigand, and Christopher L. Witmore

THAMES AND HUDSON

THE ART INSTITUTE OF CHICAGO

This book was published in conjunction with the exhibition "Ancient West Mexico: Art of the Unknown Past," organized by The Art Institute of Chicago and presented in the museum's Regenstein Hall from September 5 to November 22, 1998. The exhibition was also presented at the Los Angeles County Museum of Art from December 20 to March 29, 1999.

This book and the exhibition it accompanied were sponsored by First Chicago NBD Corporation.

Additional support was provided by:
the National Endowment for the Humanities,
the National Endowment for the Arts,
the John D. and Catherine T. MacArthur Foundation,
and the U.S.–Mexico Fund for Culture.

Transportation assistance was provided by American Airlines.

First published in hardcover in the United States of America in 1998 by Thames and Hudson Inc., 500 Fifth Avenue, New York, New York 10110

First published in Great Britain in 1998 by Thames and Hudson Ltd, London

Produced by the Publications Department of The Art Institute of Chicago, Susan F. Rossen, Executive Director
Edited by Robert V. Sharp, Associate Director of Publications, and Catherine A. Steinmann, Assistant Editor
Production by Sarah E. Guernsey, Assistant Production Manager

Unless otherwise noted, all photographs were produced by the Department of Imaging, Alan B. Newman, Executive Director.

Designed and typeset by Marquand Books, Inc., Seattle, Washington
Separations by Professional Graphics, Inc., Rockford, Illinois
Printed and bound by Arnoldo Mondadori Editore, Verona, Italy

Contributions by Lorenza López and Jorge Ramos and by Francisco Valdez were translated from the Spanish by L. Adriana Rosado-Bonewitz.

First Edition

Library of Congress Catalog Card Number 98–60252

British Library Cataloguing-in-Publication data
A catalogue record for this book is available from the British Library

ISBN 0-500-05092-9 (hardcover edition)
ISBN 0-86559-171-7 (softcover edition)

Frontispiece: Seated chieftain; Ameca-Etzatlán style; Jalisco; earthenware. M.G.N. Collection, Vandoeuvres, Switzerland (cat. no. 125).

CONTENTS

LENDERS TO THE EXHIBITION

INSTITUTIONS

American Museum of Natural History,
New York

Appleton Museum of Art, Ocala, Florida

Art Gallery of Ontario, Toronto

The Art Institute of Chicago

Barbier Mueller Museum, Barcelona

The Cleveland Museum of Art

Denver Art Museum

Denver Museum of Natural History

The Detroit Institute of Arts

DeYoung Memorial Museum, The Fine
Arts Museums of San Francisco

Fowler Museum of Cultural History,
University of California, Los Angeles

Hudson Museum, University of Maine,
Orono

The University of Iowa Museum of Art,
Iowa City

Los Angeles County Museum of Art,
Los Angeles

The Metropolitan Museum of Art, New York

The Minneapolis Institute of Arts

Mint Museum of Art, Charlotte, North
Carolina

Staatliche Museen zu Berlin–Preussischer
Kulturbesitz/Museum für Volkerkunde,
Berlin

Natural History Museum of Los Angeles
County, Los Angeles

The Art Museum, Princeton University,
Princeton, New Jersey

Rijksmuseum voor Volkenkunde, Leiden,
The Netherlands

The Saint Louis Art Museum

Utah Museum of Fine Arts, University
of Utah, Salt Lake City

Worcester Art Museum, Massachusetts

Yale University Art Gallery, New Haven

PRIVATE COLLECTIONS

Mr. and Mrs. Alvin Abrams, Greenwich,
Connecticut

Charles and Marjorie Benton, Evanston,
Illinois

Galerie Mermoz, Paris

Mr. and Mrs. Joseph Goldenberg,
Los Angeles

Barbara and Justin Kerr, New York

The Kistermann Collection, Aachen,
Germany

Mr. and Mrs. Morris A. Long, Castle Rock,
Colorado

The Miller Family Collection, Chicago

Herbert and Paula Molner, Chicago

M.G.N. Collection, Vandoeuvres, Switzerland

Anthony Patano, Oak Lawn, Illinois

Bonnie and David Ross, Indianapolis

Alan and Marianne Schwartz, Bloomfield
Hills, Michigan

Mr. and Mrs. Edwin Silver, Los Angeles

Saul and Marsha Stanoff, Tarzana, California

Stokes Family Collection, Upper Nyack,
New York

Twenty-four anonymous lenders

FOREWORD

Anyone traveling across the United States from Okracoke to Chicago, or along the Mississippi and through the Dakotas past Wenatchee to Seattle, or southwest between Acoma and Tehachapi Pass, will be naming the names of Amerindian peoples and the titles they gave to the landscape. From Central Mexico southward to Guatemala, the memory of early peoples and places is marked by the ruins of cities, pyramids, and processional ways at Teotihuacan, Monte Albán, Uxmal, Tikal, and scores of other ancient sites. We now understand that Mesoamerica was one of four primary regions—including Mesopotamia and the Nile, the Huang Ho valley in China, and the Andean region of South America—where civilization evolved independently. Clearly, the enduring presence of Amerindian communities and their creative adjustments and resistance to cultural patterns imposed by dominant governments and tides of immigrating peoples form a deep-seated part of the history shared by our modern nations.

Amerindian life past and present offers sources that touch the imagination of those who have arrived here from Europe, Africa, or Asia. For many there may only be an impression barely noted, as when the long-accepted name of a familiar location is spoken. But for others, there may be deeper resonances that affect an entire pattern of thought. There is a growing perception that the experience of modernity may not be as closely tied to the idea of limitless expansion and progress as we once believed, and that earlier societies in the Americas were much more closely attuned to the notion of cyclic renewal than we are. On another level, the concept of national identity in a country such as Mexico has been shaped in great measure by the ongoing discovery of its own antiquity, and similar considerations are coming to our attention in the United States, as plans for a national museum of Native American art and culture go forward in Washington, D.C.

At The Art Institute of Chicago we are seeking to broaden an understanding of this unique and varied cultural endowment. During the course of this century, thousands of archaeological excavations and intensive art historical and anthropological inquiries have been conducted in many regions. Yet there remain scores of sites and large geographical areas where the record of early life is only tenuously described and is largely unknown to the public. Ancient West Mexico is one such area. Thus, when curator Richard Townsend discussed with me the possibility of forming an exhibition on this still largely unfamiliar art and culture, it was with the idea of finding the finest examples of ancient sculptures, vessels, and related forms—long separated from their original settings—and bringing them back into the context of what is presently understood and what stands to be known about the peoples who made them some two thousand years ago. This catalogue represents a collaborative effort by individuals of different disciplines and nationalities engaged in an innovative project of recovery, designed to bring an unfamiliar chapter of the Amerindian achievement into a larger framework of collective memory and history.

James N. Wood
Director and President
The Art Institute of Chicago

ACKNOWLEDGMENTS

During the course of the twentieth century a cultural movement has been evolving in the Americas, aimed at identifying and restoring a range of settings and landscapes: national preserves, historic towns and urban districts, battlefield sites, migration routes, and the ruins of early civilizations. This process has accelerated as the environment becomes ever more rapidly and permanently changed by industrial development, burgeoning cities, and mechanized cultivation. In *The Necessity for Ruins,* landscape historian J. B. Jackson explained this phenomenon as one that happens after long periods of neglect and discontinuity, followed by times of rediscovering the past and times of preservation. While this may be seen as an expression of a deep-seated psychic impulse aimed at recovering an "original" time of simplicity, the incorporation of the past is also part of imagining the future: we are in the midst of recognizing the patterns of migration, settlement, conflict, and exchange that have characterized life in the Americas for thousands of years and that continue to inform our lives with new forms of cultural encounter and synthesis. In this process we are discovering and acknowledging the achievements of peoples who founded the earliest civilizations in our hemisphere. This book and its accompanying exhibition are part of this ongoing discovery. For West Mexico, this is an especially significant time in which long-buried or dispersed archaeological and artistic evidence is revealing hitherto unknown patterns of the ancient history of the region.

Among those to whom we owe special thanks are the public institutions and individual collectors who have generously allowed their splendid works to be included in the traveling exhibition. I am also deeply grateful for the thoughtful contributions made by the authors whose essays form this volume. I particularly want to thank Hasso von Winning, whose pioneering work in West Mexican art is universally acknowledged.

It is especially important to note our appreciation and thanks to those funders without whom this project would not have been possible: First Chicago NBD Corporation, the exhibition's corporate sponsor; the National Endowment for the Humanities, dedicated to expanding American understanding of human experience and cultural heritage; the National Endowment for the Arts; and The John D. and Catherine T. MacArthur Foundation. The U.S.–Mexico Fund for Culture (funded by The Rockefeller Foundation, Bancomer Cultural Foundation, and Mexico's Fund for Culture and the Arts) supported the publication of this book, and American Airlines provided vital transportation assistance.

Ancient West Mexico would not have been possible without the invaluable assistance of many in the United States, Europe, and Mexico: Isabella Hutchinson, Maria Gualdoni, Wille Fatma, and Stacey Goodman of Sotheby's; Laurence Mattet of the Barbier Mueller Museum, Geneva; Gaston Bernand, Gerard Geiger, Francis Wahl, Phillippe Nordmann, and Samuel Josefowitz in Switzerland; Baron and Baronne Paul Janssen, Jean Cambier, and Emile and Lin Deletaille in Belgium; Melinda and Santo Micali in Paris; Stephen Wittington of the Hudson Museum, University of Maine, Orono; Dr. Phyllis Pitluga of the Adler Planetarium, Chicago; Thomas Cummins of the University of Chicago; Spencer Throckmorton, Alphonse Jax, John Menser, Claudia Giangola, and Mary Anne Martin for their effective help in

New York; Julie Jones at the Metropolitan Museum of Art, New York; Michael Kan at the Detroit Institute of Arts; Berta Cea for her assistance in the U.S. Embassy in Mexico City; Marcela S. Madariaga, Program Coordinator, Cultura Mexico/USA; Ing. Federico A. Solórzano Barreto, Curator of Paleontology, and Lic. Yolanda Carvajal Enríquez, Director, Museo Regional de Guadalajara; Barbara Belle Sloane of the Fowler Museum of Cultural History; John Watson and Mac, Kristin, and Jesse Watson for their hospitality in Los Angeles and Santa Fe; Thomas Holien of Santa Fe; Roger and Tony Johnston in Los Angeles; and Virginia Fields of the Los Angeles County Museum of Art.

At the Art Institute, the staff of the Department of African and Amerindian Art must be at the head of the list of those I wish to thank. Their spirit of cooperation and ability to orchestrate complex tasks under pressure were crucial to the successful outcome of the project. My deepest thanks are given to Anne King, Charmaine Picard, and Julio Sims for all of their efforts on behalf of this undertaking.

There are also many to thank on the extraordinary staff of the Publications Department. The editors of this volume, Robert V. Sharp and Catherine Steinmann, worked devotedly on this challenging project, bringing their intelligence and professional expertise to every aspect of its preparation. Their efforts were complemented by the remarkable ingenuity and meticulous craftsmanship of Sarah Guernsey, who ensured the high quality of the book's production. They were assisted ably by Simone Juter. The excellent translations of original Spanish-language manuscripts by L. Adriana Rosado-Bonewitz allowed the editorial work to go on unimpeded. I am extremely grateful to Michael Guran, Project Architect, for the reconstruction drawing of the Teuchitlán ceremonial center. Thanks also go to Gigi Bayliss for the numerous drawings she created for this book. The elegant design of this volume is a tribute to Ed Marquand and his staff, especially Melanie Milkie, Marie Weiler, and John Hubbard.

I am particularly grateful to James N. Wood, Director and President of The Art Institute of Chicago, for his friendship and unwavering encouragement during the preparation and presentation of *Ancient West Mexico*. Similarly, this project could never have been realized without the involvement and support of many in this museum too numerous to name here. I warmly appreciate the expertise of Deputy Director Teri J. Edelstein; Dorothy Schroeder, Assistant Director for Exhibitions and Budget; Christine O'Neill Singer, Vice President for Development; Ed Horner, Executive Vice President for Development and Public Affairs; Karin Victoria, Director of Government Relations; Eileen Harakal, Executive Director of Public Affairs; and all the members of their respective staffs. Special thanks also go to Reynold Bailey and his art installation crew; to Barbara Hall, Suzie Schnepp, and Emily Dunn of the Conservation Department; in the Department of Imaging, to Robert Hashimoto, Christopher Gallagher, Josh Mosley, and Alan B. Newman, Executive Director; and, in Museum Registration, to John Molini, Mary Mulhern, Darrell Green, and Mary Solt, Executive Director. In the Department of Museum Education I gratefully thank Executive Director Ronne Hartfield and Clare Kunny, Associate Director, who provided the link to a large and enthusiastic staff and, through them, to programs that reach diverse audiences within and without the museum. Celia Marriott and her staff prepared excellent audiovisual materials; and Lyn DelliQuadri and her talented assistants, including Senior Graphic Designer Ann Wassmann, designed the fine exhibition graphics. My thanks go also to William Caddick, Director of Physical Plant, and all his dedicated personnel. The opportunity to work with architects John Vinci and Ward Miller in designing the installation in Chicago was a rewarding pleasure.

In conclusion, I give heartfelt thanks to my wife, Pala, for her strong personal and artistic support while the vision of *Ancient West Mexico* was being transformed into reality.

Richard F. Townsend
Curator, Department of African and Amerindian Art
The Art Institute of Chicago

CHRONOLOGICAL CHART OF ANCIENT WEST MEXICO | OTHER EARLY CULTURES

DATE	JALISCO	COLIMA (AND ADJACENT PARTS OF SOUTHERN JALISCO)	NAYARIT	CENTRAL AND SOUTHERN MEXICO	NORTHERN MEXICO	SOUTH-WESTERN U.S.	SOUTH-EASTERN U.S.
1500–800 B.C. EARLY FORMATIVE PERIOD	The base from which the Teuchitlán tradition began: El Opeño (Michoacán) Citala San Marcos Teuchitlán San Juanito Ancestor worship, ballplaying, Olmec-related figurines	Capacha-style ceramics, some related to Central Mexico		OLMEC			POVERTY POINT (LOUISIANA)
800–300 B.C. MIDDLE FORMATIVE PERIOD SAN FELIPE PHASE	First large ceremonial architecture: circular or oval burial mounds, averaging 28 m dia. × 2 m high Development of shaft tombs			TLATILCO			
300 B.C.–A.D. 200 LATE FORMATIVE PERIOD ARENAL PHASE	Monumental shaft tombs culminate Diverse sculptural styles: San Sebastián, Arenal, Ameca-Etzatlán, Tala-Tonalá	SAYULA USMAJAC / TUXCACUESCO PHASE / ORTICES PHASE / COMALA PHASE	Ixtlán del Río style in S. Nayarit Lagunillas style in Central and S. Nayarit: Las Cebollas, San Pedro Lagunillas, Tequilita, Compostela, etc.	MAYA / CUICUILCO / CHUPICUARO / ZAPOTEC			
A.D. 200–400 EARLY CLASSIC PERIOD AHUALULCO PHASE	Decline of monumental shaft tombs as large circular ceremonial centers evolve at Teuchitlán, Ahualulco, Santa Quiteria, etc. Population implosion, expansion of political and religious ideas and symbols	VERDIA PHASE		El Mirador / TEOTIHUACAN / Kaminaljuyú	ALTA VISTA / LA QUEMADA		
A.D. 400–700 MIDDLE CLASSIC PERIOD TEUCHITLÁN I PHASE	Continuation of monumental ritual centers in Teuchitlán and peripheral areas			Tikal			
A.D. 700–900 LATE CLASSIC PERIOD TEUCHITLÁN II PHASE	Disintegration of Teuchitlán tradition			Copán / Uxmal / TOLTEC	CASAS GRANDES (PAQUIME)	HOHOKAM / ANASAZI	CAHOKIA (ILLINOIS)
A.D. 900 EARLY POSTCLASSIC PERIOD				Chichén Itzá / MIXTEC			ETOWAH (GEORGIA)
A.D. 1100							MOUNDVILLE (ALABAMA)
A.D. 1200 LATE POST-CLASSIC PERIOD				AZTEC		MESA VERDE	
1521–32	Spanish conquest of West Mexico 1528–32			Spanish conquest of Aztecs 1521			

Note: Although the dates given here represent generally accepted parameters for the early cultures included, certain authors have chosen to use slightly different chronological schemes that derive from their own research.

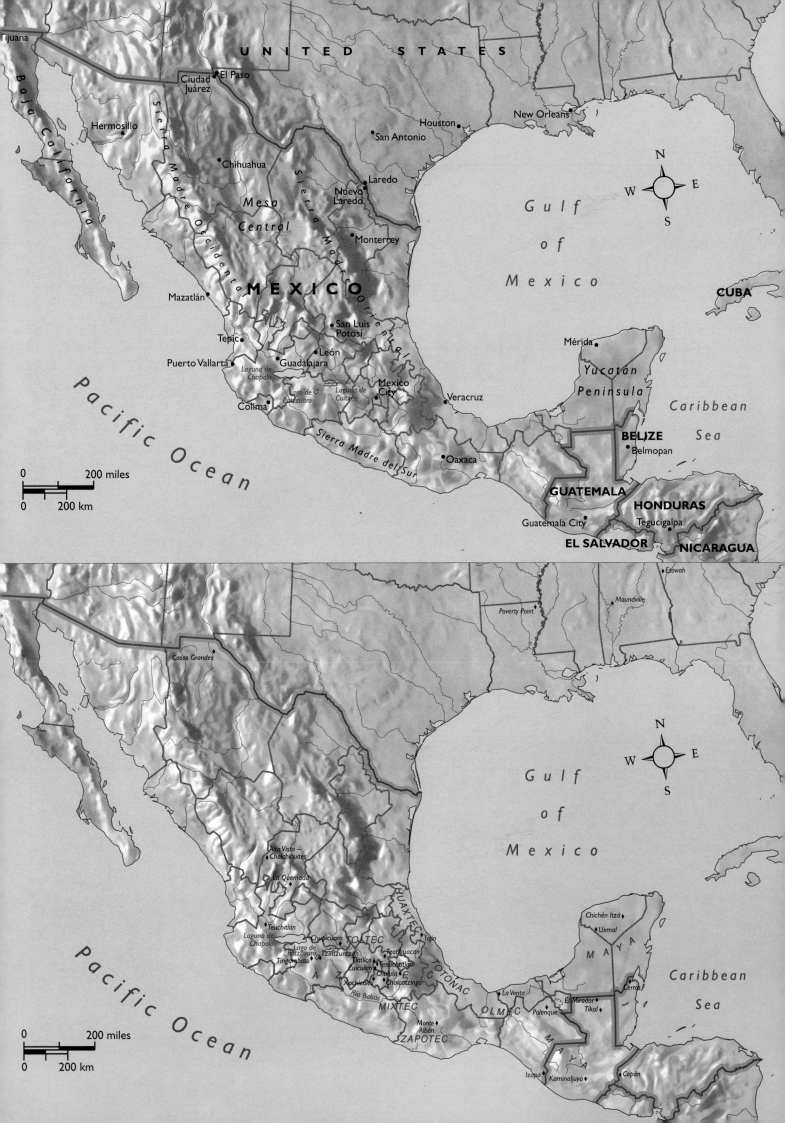

Top map:

UNITED STATES

Tijuana

Ciudad Juárez   El Paso

Hermosillo

Chihuahua

Houston

New Orleans

San Antonio

Mazatlán

Laredo
Nuevo Laredo

Monterrey

Gulf
of
Mexico

CUBA

Baja California

Sierra Madre Occidental

Sierra Madre Oriental

Mesa Central

M E X I C O

San Luis Potosí

Mérida

Tepic

León

Yucatán Peninsula

Puerto Vallarta   Guadalajara
Laguna de Chapala

Caribbean Sea

Colima

Lago de Pátzcuaro   Laguna de Cuitzeo

Mexico City

Veracruz

BELIZE
Belmopan

Sierra Madre del Sur

Oaxaca

GUATEMALA

HONDURAS

Pacific Ocean

Guatemala City

Tegucigalpa

EL SALVADOR   NICARAGUA

0   200 miles
0   200 km

Bottom map:

Etowah

Poverty Point   Moundville

Casas Grandes

Gulf
of
Mexico

Alta Vista – Chalchihuites

La Quemada

Chichén Itzá
Uxmal

Teuchitlán
Laguna de Chapala   Chupícuaro
TOLTEC
Lago de Pátzcuaro   Tzintzuntzan
Tingambato   Tlatilco   Teotihuacán
Cuicuilco   Tenochtitlán
Xochicalco   Cholula   Chalcatzingo

M A Y A

Caribbean Sea

Cerros

Tajín

HUAXTEC

TOTONAC

MIXTEC

Río Balsas

La Venta

OLMEC   El Mirador   Palenque   Tikal

Monte Albán

ZAPOTEC

Izapa   Kaminaljuyú   Copán

Pacific Ocean

0   200 miles
0   200 km

NAYARIT

Tuxpan ◆Peñitas
  ◆Coamiles
Amapa ◆ ◆Santiago
  Ixcuintla
San Blas
Santa Cruz ◆
  Tepic Cerro
  Jalisco ◆ Sangangüey ▲
  Santa Maria del Oro
Chacala Compostela Corral
  Falso ◆Ocotillo
San Pedro Lagunillas ◆Tetitlan ▲Volcán
  Céboruco
Tequilita ◆Las Cebollas

Guaynamota

Totuate

Bolaños

Río Bolaños

ZACATECAS

Jalpa ◆

Téul ◆
  Cerro
  Juchipila ◆ Encantado
  Teocaltiche ◆ Nochistlan ◆

Río Grande de Santiago

Camotlan
  Ixtlán del Río
Río Ameca Magdalena
  Huitzilapa Tequila
  San Sebastián ◆San Juanito Santa Quiteria
  Antonio Escobedo Amatitán Tabachines
  Etzatlán El Arenal
Llano Grande Ahualulco ▲Volcán de
  Teuchitlán Tequila Guadalajara
  La Vega Tala Atemajac
  Cuspala Valley
Ameca
  Acatlán de Juárez Laguna de Zapotlanejo
  Cajititlán Río Santiago
  Laguna de Atotonilco
  Atotonilco Ixtlahuacán
Banderas San Ajijic Chapala Río Lerma
Valley Tenamaxtlán Marcos Laguna de Chapala
  Tecolotlán Laguna Zacoalco San Gregorio
Puerto Vallarta Zacoalco San Pedro Caro
  JALISCO Laguna de Tizapán Cojumatlán
  Talpa Sayula Citala
  Ayutla Techaluta Teocuitatlán El Opeño ◆
  Tuxcacuesco Amacueca Jiquilpan Zamora
Tomatlán Atoyac Jacona
  Río Tomatlán Armería Caseta ◆
  Río San Nicolas Sayula Zapotlán
  San Miguel Tonaya (Ciudad Guzmán)
  Río Purificación Autlán Tuxcacuesco
Purificación Zapotiltic
  Nevado de Zapotlán Tamazula
  Colima ▲
  Zapotitlán ▲Volcán de
  Colima
  Tuxpan
  Río El Naranjo
  Comala Capacha ◆
  La Campaña Pihuamo
Cihuatlán Río Marabasco COLIMA Colima
  Morett Los Ortices ◆ Corralitos ◆
Barra de Navidad Playa del Tesoro Copales ◆
  Río Ameria Apatzingán
Pacific Ocean Manzanillo Río Salado Las Trancas ◆
  Periquillo ◆ MICHOACAN
  Armería Río Coahuayana
  Tecomán
  Chanchopa
  (Alima)
  Coahuayana

N
W   E
S

Legend:
● Major cities
• Other towns
◆ Archaeological sites
▲ Volcanoes
▨ Lake basins

0   25   50 miles
0   25   50 km

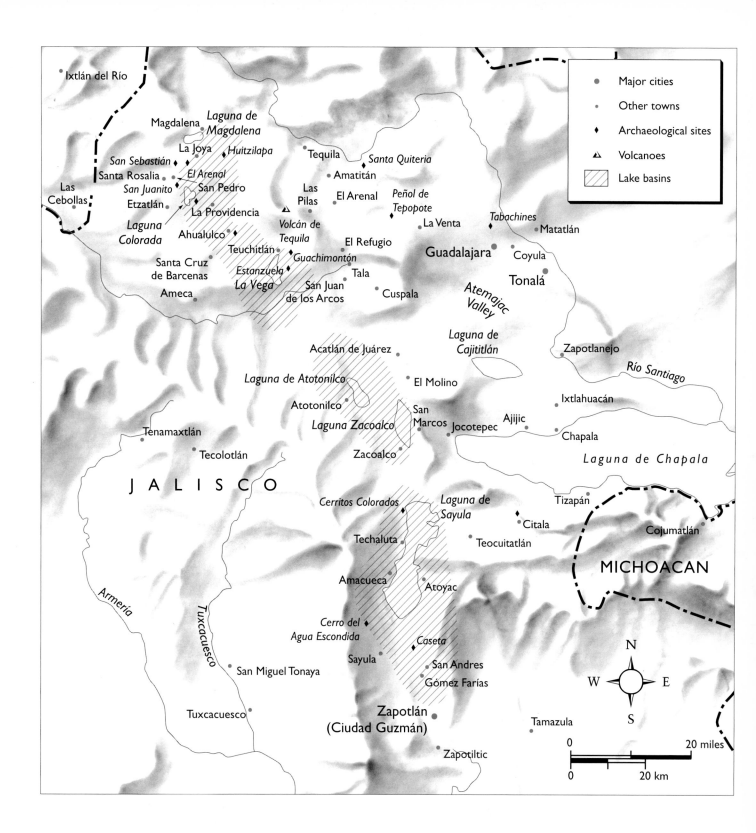

Ixtlán del Río

Magdalena
Laguna de Magdalena
La Joya ◆ *Huitzilapa*
San Sebastián ◆
Santa Rosalia ◆ *El Arenal*
San Juanito ◆ San Pedro
Etzatlán
La Providencia
Las Cebollas
Laguna Colorada
Ahualulco ◆
Santa Cruz de Barcenas
Teuchitlán ◆ *Guachimontón*
Estanzuela ◆
Ameca
La Vega
San Juan de los Arcos

Tequila
Santa Quiteria
Amatitán
Las Pilas
El Arenal
Peñol de Tepopote ◆
La Venta
Volcán de Tequila ⟁
El Refugio
Tala
Cuspala

Tabachines ◆
Matatlán

Guadalajara
Coyula
Tonalá

Atemajac Valley

Laguna de Cajititlán
Zapotlanejo
Río Santiago

Acatlán de Juárez

Laguna de Atotonilco
El Molino
Ixtlahuacán

Atotonilco
San Marcos
Ajijic
Laguna Zacoalco
Jocotepec
Chapala

Tenamaxtlán
Zacoalco
Laguna de Chapala

Tecolotlán

J A L I S C O

Cerritos Colorados ◆
Laguna de Sayula
Tizapán

Techaluta
Citala ◆
Cojumatlán

Teocuitatlán

Armería
Tuxcacuesco
Amacueca
Atoyac

MICHOACAN

Cerro del Agua Escondida ◆
Caseta ◆

Sayula
San Andrés

San Miguel Tonaya
Gómez Farías

Tuxcacuesco
Zapotlán
(Ciudad Guzmán)
Tamazula

Zapotiltic

N
W E
S

● Major cities
• Other towns
◆ Archaeological sites
⟁ Volcanoes
▨ Lake basins

0   20 miles
0   20 km

INTRODUCTION RENEWING THE INQUIRY IN ANCIENT WEST MEXICO

When the British artist Adela Breton arrived in the city of Guadalajara, Jalisco, in May 1895, her interest in antiquities was aroused by descriptions of ancient ruins and artifacts in the surrounding region (see fig. 2). An adventurous and experienced traveler, she soon made arrangements to explore this area and boarded a local train heading westward into a country of broad, open basins and dun-colored mountains. The railway ran past the shallow lake of the Teuchitlán *vega,* glittering in the intense sunlight (see fig. 3 and map, p. 12). Descending at the town of Etzatlán, Breton proceeded about four miles to an estate, the Hacienda Guadalupe, where she was taken to see the site of a large earth and masonry tumulus already partly excavated by the landowner. There she made sketches and noted the find of an impressive burial, above which some twenty earthenware figures had been placed. Several of these figures were still kept at the Hacienda: Breton acquired two of them, as well as a jar and several shell bracelets, including one with twenty-six carved frogs, another with frogs and double-headed serpents, and several pieces of worked obsidian (see fig. 4). All of these objects she eventually sent to the Bristol Museum in England. At this same site Breton also observed smaller mounds associated with the principal tumulus. Continuing her journey by horseback around the marshes of the Laguna de Magdalena, she arrived at the town of San Juanito. There she hired a canoe to visit La Otra Banda, an island on which a remarkable outcrop of black obsidian and thousands of sherds mark the site of ancient toolmaking workshops.

Returning southward around the base of the extinct Volcán de Tequila, Breton arrived at the town of Teuchitlán; local guides took her by the shaded pools of a large spring on the outskirts of town and on up the bluff, where another major obsidian-working site is located. On the terraced hillside overlooking the spreading valley, she was shown an extraordinary set of mounds arranged in three circles, each with a large tumulus or pyramid rising in the center. This archaeological site, known as Guachimontón, has since been identified as the largest in the entire region (see the essays by Phil Weigand and Christopher Beekman and by Christopher Witmore in this volume). Breton's observations and sketches were published in two very brief articles in 1903 and 1905. By portraying the association of tumuli, high-status burials, ceramic tomb sculptures, shell jewelry, large obsidian mines and workshops, and the monumental ritual circles at Teuchitlán, Breton pointed to the essential features of what is only now emerging in archaeological investigations as the heartland of an ancient, complex society with a distinctive symbolic and aesthetic system, yet with many social, economic, and cultural forms akin to those of other Mesoamerican peoples. Adela Breton later extended her Mexican travels and deepened her interest in archaeological monuments. As a result of her correspondence with the renowned archaeologist Sir Alfred Maudslay, she went to Chichén Itzá in 1900 to depict the Maya-Toltec buildings, sculptural reliefs, and murals at that site and related ruins in the Yucatán. Later she published an important description of Xochicalco

Fig. 1 Seated turtle-shell drummer; Ixtlán del Río style; Nayarit; earthenware. American Museum of Natural History, New York. Cat. no. 198. Alert posture, lively expression, and portraitlike features characterize figures of high-ranking people from one of the various tomb-sculpture styles in the vicinity of Ixtlán del Río, Nayarit. Careful modeling of the coiffure and jewelry, as well as bold facial painting, denotes the status and office of West Mexican chieftains.

in Central Mexico (1906). Her remarkable watercolors of the Mexican landscape and her views of cities and ruins form an invaluable record of settings and monuments, many of which have since been lost or irretrievably altered. But her descriptions of the first reconnaissance of West Mexican ruins in Jalisco were destined to attract little attention, and not until some eighty years later would her observations begin to seem so telling.

Instead, it was to be the detailed ethnographic reports and books of another explorer, the Norwegian anthropologist Carl Lumholtz, that would attract a larger scholarly and public attention to the region. In 1892 Lumholtz began a long journey on horseback and foot from the United States border in Arizona down the length of the Sierra Madre Occidental into the center of Mexico (see map, p. 11). His primary objective was to visit and describe the various Amerindian tribes inhabiting this great chain of mountains. Lumholtz's travels led in stages from the Tarahumara to the Tepehuan, the Cora, and others. Eventually, he reached the country of the Huichol in the remote Nayarit sierras. After a lengthy stay among the Huichol, Lumholtz departed to the city of Tepic; there his attention was called to ancient ceramic figures and vessels of a type previously unreported in Mexico. Continuing south to

Ixtlán del Río, he was guided to various looted archaeological sites, where he acquired a variety of artifacts and sculptural figures (see fig. 1). His journey proceeded into the lake-basin district seen by Breton, but Lumholtz was apparently unaware of her visit. Once again, he was able to purchase a sampling of archaeological objects, some vessels of which may have been from the vicinity of the Guachimontón complex at Teuchitlán (see Weigand and Beekman, fig. 20). Yet he did not report the site nor the existence of other large circular ruins.

Lumholtz proceeded on his journey through the shallow lake basins of western Jalisco and into the neighboring state of Colima, and continued into the high, forested mountainous country of Michoacán, inhabited by the Tarascans. Returning to Guadalajara, he acquired more archaeological figures and vessels from local dealers, who, to his dismay, were finding a market among foreign travelers in search of unusual curiosities. Lumholtz's collection of objects resides today in the American Museum of Natural History in New York. In his two-volume book *Unknown Mexico*, published in 1902, his chapters on archaeological findings are informative and well illustrated, yet his account does not offer as essential and suggestive a picture as that in the short articles Adela Breton later published. Breton and Lumholtz thus wrote the first notices of early peoples whose domains are now found to have extended across the upland basins, tablelands, river valleys, and coasts of the states of Nayarit, Jalisco, and Colima. Nevertheless, interest in the art and archaeology of this region lapsed until the late 1920s, when earthenware tomb sculptures again provided glimpses into its unknown past.

The area known archaeologically as West Mexico embraces a complex topography with a considerable range of climates and natural resources (see map, p. 12). The Sierra Madre extends from northwest to southeast in long parallel ranges, separating the upland basins of the interior from the warm Pacific coast. Several massive volcanic peaks rise darkly above the ridges and canyons, beginning with the extinct Sanganguey and Ceboruco in Nayarit, the Volcán de Tequila, the snow-covered Nevado de Colima, and the still-smoking Volcán de Colima in Jalisco (see fig. 5). High elevations are covered with oak and pine forests, giving way

to mesquite and acacia brush at lower elevations. A linked series of shallow basins lie at the 5,000-foot level in northwestern Jalisco. These are now mostly drained and converted to agriculture, yet some still held extensive tracts of marshlands and open water in the first half of the twentieth century. Today, only Lake Chapala remains, the largest lake in Mexico (see fig. 6). Southward from Sayula to Zacoalco, during the dry months between January and June, the flat lake beds become deserts, sources of sandstorms and whirlwinds that leach out the last remaining moisture; yet these lake beds were also centers of salt production in antiquity (see Valdez, fig. 8). To the east the high tableland and mountains of Jalisco lead into the central highlands of Mexico. The Río Lerma traverses this rich agricultural landscape flowing from its source just west of Mexico City into Lake Chapala, which in turn is drained by the Santiago river flowing through a great circuitous chasm to reach the Pacific on the coast of Nayarit (see fig. 7). Other rivers drain from the sierras, among which the Ameca, Tomatlán, and Armería are most significant.

In the ancient farming communities as in the agricultural towns of today, life's basic rhythm follows the annual cycle of the dry and wet seasons. The season of drought culminates in the heat of April and May, when tall dust-devil columns move lazily across the parched fields, and the hazy mountains seem to recede in tones of tan and pale violet shadow. The first hints of rain appear at night, when distant cloudbanks beyond the dark mountains far to the south are silently illuminated by flashes of lightning. Soon the winds bring a scent of moisture as immense thunderheads sweep across the valleys in

curtainlike downpours and shattering thunder. Within days, inky masses of frog eggs float in the rising ponds and marshes. Flocks of birds appear in phalanxes with their cacophony of songs, croakings, screams, and trills. Humped and stilted, graceful and awkward, herons move slowly among the rushes. In two weeks the land becomes light green and slowly acquires a deepening verdure. On the terraced alluvial slopes, in lakeside fields, and on the open lands of the basins, a new round of cultivation begins.

Ancient sculptural figures from West Mexican tombs attracted curiosity during the cultural renaissance taking place in Mexico City after the revolution of 1910–20. Diego Rivera, Frida Kahlo, and other painters with a profound interest in the archaeological past began collecting works of art from many early indigenous cultures, among which the

Fig. 3 View of the Ameca-Etzatlán valley with the town of Teuchitlán below. In the foreground, an unexcavated mound of the ritual precinct at Teuchitlán.

Fig. 4 Adela Breton's watercolor drawing of a figure from the Hacienda Guadalupe tumulus excavation near Etzatlán, Jalisco, c. 1895. City of Bristol Museum and Art Gallery.

Fig. 5 Volcán de Colima, Jalisco. The Nevado de Colima rises to the left; both peaks are in the state of Jalisco.

Fig. 6 Lake Chapala basin, Jalisco. The town of Ajijic lies in the foreground; settlements around this and other highland basins date from before 1000 B.C.

earthenware figures of people, animals, and plants from Nayarit, Jalisco, and Colima were especially appreciated. While made in a variety of styles and substyles in seemingly endless permutations, these ceramic sculptures share a predilection for the representation of figures with lively, naturalistic gestures and expressions (see figs. 8 and 9), and sometimes display an extraordinary abstraction (see fig. 10). Human forms are rarely encumbered by the elaborate ritual attire depicted on rulers and priests in the monuments of other Mesoamerican traditions. Only in exceptional instances do they portray masked performers and elaborate ritual paraphernalia (see figs. 11–13). Yet even in these cases, the figures are never inert mannequins, but are invested with a strong sense of motion, immediacy, and emotion.

It was this warm, expressive appeal that made these earthenware figures so attractive to the artists and intellectuals of the Left who found them to be ideologically significant because they seemed to speak of an ideal, communal way of life, far from the regimented coercion and economic exploitation of warlike fascist or imperialistic states. In diverse ways, the ancient tomb figures began to be quoted in new paintings reflecting poetic and intensely political dialogues about a national cultural identity rooted in Mexico's still unknown past (see the essay by Barbara Braun in this volume). In part stemming from this enthusiastic recognition, the first official archaeological explorations of West Mexico were launched in the 1930s. Hans-Dietrich Disselhoff published plans of a looted shaft-and-chamber tomb in Colima; Eduardo Noguera excavated an important early tomb site in El Opeño, Michoacán; and the American Isabel Kelly also began explorations and surveys to map the distribution of ancient ceramic typologies—the "ceramic provinces" of the region. In 1946 Edward Gifford of the University of California conducted a surface survey of the Ixtlán del Río area in southern Nayarit. That same year the first public exhibition of ancient tomb sculptures was held in the Palacio de Bellas Artes in Mexico City, mainly featuring pieces from Diego Rivera's extensive collection and an exhibition catalogue with essays by art historian Salvador Toscano and anthropologists Paul Kirchhoff and Daniel Rubín de la Borbolla. Kirchhoff noted that various figurines seemed to represent high-status people, while others were clearly religious performers and some were bearers of burdens—all of which suggested the existence of a stratified society. He also remarked on a curious affinity between these figures from Nayarit, Jalisco, and Colima, and others from the coast of Ecuador and Colombia. Yet in West Mexico the seeming absence of monuments such as grand pyramids, plazas, and processional avenues, impressive stone stelae, or other imposing urban constructions comparable to those of central and southern Mesoamerican peoples led archaeologists and art historians to a general perception that West Mexico had remained an isolated region where a primitive, "formative" way of life persisted while complex societies were evolving elsewhere. At that time the materials from the West Mexican sites were beginning to be dated to the first centuries A.D., contemporaneous with the rise of the great city of Teotihuacan in the central basin of Mexico; Monte Albán, the Zapotec capital in Oaxaca; and the Maya capitals of southern Mexico and Guatemala. The "village farming" assumption was to have long-lasting effects. As late as 1969, the eminent Mexican archaeologist Ignacio Bernal remarked that "not having had the civilizing influence of the Olmecs, Western Mexico remained permanently in a state of backwardness." The *Archaeological Map of Middle America,* published by the National Geographic Society in 1968, began at a point some sixty miles north of Mexico City, entirely omitting West Mexico. Thus the region seemed to many to have remained beyond the pale of Mesoamerican civilization. Nevertheless, throughout the 1950s, 1960s, and early 1970s, a handful of archaeologists—Corona Núñez, Stanley Long, Betty Bell, Isabel Kelly, Clement Meighan, Otto Schöndube, and others—patiently continued to map the ceramic provinces, establish chronologies, and record what might be learned of the shaft-and-chamber tombs that by then were everywhere subject to looting on an unprecedented scale.

In 1969 an important monograph on the ceramics of Chupícuaro by Muriel Porter Weaver and others was published by UCLA. The homeland of this key Late Formative–period society is located along the Lerma river and around Lake Cuitzeo in Michoacán and neighboring Guanajuato (see map, p. 11). Chupícuaro is known to have had long-lasting cultural and trade connections with the Valley of Mexico between the second century B.C. and the first century A.D., and its influence reached northwest as far as the mineral-rich area around La Quemada in Zacatecas. It had already been speculated by the leading Mexican archaeologist Jimenez Moreno that Chupícuaro played a unifying role in a cultural tradition spreading from Central Mexico westward. At present, the possible connection between Chupícuaro and the areas of Jalisco, Nayarit, and Colima with which this book is primarily concerned, remains to be archaeologically explored. There can be little doubt, however, from the character of figurines and vessels found in the burials, that deep cultural affinities once linked these regions in Formative times.

In 1970 the Proctor Stafford Collection of West Mexican art was exhibited at the Los Angeles County Museum of Art with a landmark catalogue, *Sculpture of Ancient West Mexico.* In this publication, anthropologists Henry Nicholson and Clement Meighan wrote insightful articles summarizing the

current archaeological picture. Another catalogue essay by art historian Michael Kan offered a meticulous description of the dominant styles of figurative sculpture and related vessels in a study that remains one of the standard references in the field.

As the custom of furnishing the tombs of dominant families with elaborate offerings flourished between 200 B.C. and A.D. 250, a series of well-defined styles were developed by groups of workshops within particular areas, each workshop producing variations of the dominant local style. For example, the large hollow figures from the vicinity of Ixtlán del Río, Nayarit, portray men and women in energetic poses and with exaggerated, even grotesque caricature-like expressions and brightly polychromed attire (see fig. 14). Others of the Ixtlán style are more naturalistically modeled, especially in the facial features and markings and in the coiffure (see fig. 1). Still other Ixtlán varieties are known, some of exceptional detail and refinement (see Townsend essay, fig. 29; Weigand and Beekman, fig. 13). Clay models of ceremonial places, houses, and ritual scenes were also made in the vicinity of Ixtlán, providing a remarkable index to the ritualized patterns of ancient life (see Townsend essay, figs. 2, 27, and 38). Further to the west in southern Nayarit, around the area of San Pedro Lagunillas, another stylistic group includes a range of figures with burnished, ivory-slipped surfaces (see figs. 15 and 16). Popularly known as "Chinescos," these Lagunillas-style figures communicate a sense of introspection and reserve, while variant types may be brilliantly polychromed with masklike faces and painted torsos (see fig. 17). Nearby in northwest Jalisco, figures in the Arenal and San Sebastián styles include

Fig. 7 Canyon of the Río Santiago, near Guadalajara, Jalisco.

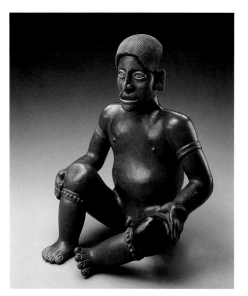

naturalistic, monumental male and female effigies of commanding presence, with implements and attire of high office; some show intentions of portraiture (see Townsend essay, figs. 6 and 12). Between Ameca and Etzatlán, a wide range of forms tend towards long faces and full, rounded limbs and torsos in dynamic poses (see figs. 8, 9, 18, and 19). Others may stress emblematic ornamentation (see fig. 4). Figures of the widely distributed Tala-Tonalá style (popularly known as "sheep-faced") have sharply pointed faces, wide-set eyes, and bold patterns of white-on-red textile decoration (see figs. 20 and 21). The highly abstract Zacatecas-style figures from northwestern Jalisco are fashioned with flattened bodies, tubular limbs, and geometric facial features (see Butterwick, fig. 9). In central Colima, burnished figures from the highly varied Comala style portray chieftains, ladies, warriors, acrobats, shamans, musicians, and many other human types (see figs. 22–26). Dogs, turtles, iguanas, armadillos, migratory birds, and other animals are also represented in profusion, as are elegant vessels modeled with foodstuffs (see the essay by Otto Schöndube in this volume). At their highest level of artistic accomplishment, Comala vessels attain remarkable simplicity (see figs. 27 and 29).

The complex Comala tradition also includes a range of small, solid figurines, often modeled with jewel-like precision, deriving from earlier, more primitive figurine traditions (see figs. 25 and 26). Another, separate figurine substyle, flourishing around A.D. 300 in Colima and southern Jalisco features ritu-

alists masked with animal and human forms, and with necklaces, armbands, and elaborately folded loincloths made with rolled pellets, strips, and flat pieces of clay, marked with punctures and lines. Eyes are round pellets with dotted pupils (see figs. 11 and 12). Rattles and fans may be held in hand and headdresses are sometimes removable. Large incense-burners modeled with intertwining serpents as the headdress of a crouching masked figure also belong to this later period; in rare instances, gesturing figures are modeled holding these elaborate symbolic forms (see fig. 13). Still another, very old and long-lasting figurine tradition in Colima produced flat, "gingerbread" forms, which in exceptional instances may be shaped into remarkable abstractions (see fig. 10).

Along the river between Colima and Michoacán, Coahuayana-style seated figures are modeled with rounded torsos and limbs, as if inflated from within; while others have elongated boardlike flattened bodies (see Townsend essay, fig. 33, and Butterwick, fig. 12). These are only among the most well known types of forms; there are many variants and local substyles—some not yet geographically located (see fig. 28, and Butterwick, fig. 16). All attest to the proliferation of workshops, the specialization of craft production, and a range of quality speaking of "courtly" and "popular" levels of artistic accomplishment. As Peter Furst has pointed out, the fact that tomb sculptures and vessels from several different styles turn up in the same tomb suggests that local workshops held a reputation for excellence extending beyond the range of local communities, and that their creations were sought by peoples from different areas. To this may be added that a growing pattern of ritual exchange between 200 B.C. and A.D. 200 was drawing different groups together, and the equipping of important tombs with contributions offered by communities distributed over a large area reflects this tendency towards greater religious and political cohesion.

Yet by the 1970s the only tomb excavations to be completely scientifically and officially conducted were those of Eduardo Noguera at El Opeño in the 1930s. All other known tomb sites were being found by archaeologists in looted or semi-looted condition. For during the 1950s and 1960s the interest in collecting that began in the late 1930s—and that may be traced back to the nineteenth century and undoubtedly had roots in the Spanish colonial period—was reaching unprecedented and expanding proportions. The completion of the highway from Guadalajara to Nogales, Arizona, in the late 1940s rapidly increased tourism and work-related travel, which, coupled with intensifying public interest in Mexico's extraordinary archaeological past, stimulated a great wave of unauthorized digging and pillaging of unprotected archaeological zones. In Nayarit, Jalisco, and Colima, entire sites were left scored by pits, and large mounds were systematically plundered. Local townspeople and highly organized teams of professional looters, national and international runners and dealers, as well as private collectors and museums in Mexico, the United States, and Europe, were drawn into this phenomenon. For many, the reasons were primarily commercial; others were led by their passionate appreciation of works of great aesthetic value. Some entered searching for knowledge and became deeply concerned about the preservation of cultural properties. Often enough these outlooks were intertwined. Diego Rivera, for example, regarded his own interest in collecting as a form of cultural protection. Despite all of this, West Mexico still failed to attract major attention from the great archaeological institutions in Mexico City or in the United States and Europe. For schoolchildren who grew up in Guadalajara during the 1940s and 1950s, as I did, there was only a vague awareness of the local pre-Hispanic heritage, principally through the rare experience of seeing occasional tomb sculptures in a few private homes of people curious about the ancient art and history of the region. The diaspora of West Mexican materials did not begin to subside until international agreements protecting cultural patrimony were signed between the United States and Mexico in 1972.

Meanwhile, scholarly inquiries were continuing: for an exhibition at the Natural History Museum of Los Angeles County in 1972, Hasso von Winning and Olga Hammer produced another important catalogue, *Anecdotal Sculpture of Ancient West Mexico*. Examining a large number of models of festival scenes, processions, dances, houses, and ballcourts, as well as figurines from Colima and Nayarit, von Winning again remarked on the curious absence of recognizable Mesoamerican gods, concluding that this art portrayed a "secular ceremonialism" in a spectrum of everyday activities. Although he continued

Fig. 10 Female figure with hands on knees; Coahuayana area; Colima/Michoacán; earthenware. Private collection. Cat. no. 113.

to suggest the existence of a comparatively simple type of society, by noting funerary scenes and marriage festivals von Winning identified points of departure that would eventually lead to new approaches to this imagery.

A more radical approach to the tomb sculptures was taken by anthropologist Peter Furst in the late 1960s. It was Furst's intention to penetrate the religious world of ancient West Mexico, which he saw—and still sees—in terms of shamanic themes. Drawing analogies from the ethnological literature on the Huichol and other tribes of the Sierra Madre and the southwestern U.S., as well as other groups from South America to the Eskimo, Furst discussed an array of tomb figures from Nayarit, Jalisco, and Colima as shamans—magical healers who, in trances, fight evil spirits, fly through the sky, and descend to the land of the dead. His descriptions of animal and human transformations, initiations by ritual death and rebirth, and shamans who fulfill the role of priests or rulers attracted wide notice and provoked controversial discussion. Furst's use of ethnographic analogy and his writings on shamanism have continued to be the subject of warm debate, yet it cannot be doubted that he succeeded in shifting attention to the religious dimensions of this ancient art by searching for underpinnings in the deep-seated patterns of spiritual experience among Amerindian peoples.

During the 1970s, Isabel Kelly examined archaeological evidence from a series of related sites along the Salado and Colima rivers in northeastern Colima and around Tuxcacuesco in southern Jalisco. Named after the key site of Capacha, these materials yielded the surprising date of c. 1500 B.C., comparable to El Opeño in Michoacán. Vessel types and ornamentation show similarities with early works from Central Mexico. In 1983 another exhibition featured the collection of the Fowler Museum of Cultural History at UCLA. The catalogue *Companions of the Dead: Ceramic Tomb Sculpture from Ancient West Mexico* by Jacki Gallagher summarized the archaeological picture and reviewed stylistic and iconographic issues. Gallagher's essay also called attention to similarities between certain Capacha and Capacha-related ceramics and other types from the Pacific coast areas of Colombia and Ecuador—renewing speculations of ancient contact by sea between these distant regions.

But the most fundamental change in the archaeological picture of West Mexico began to take shape in the 1970s, as archaeologist Phil Weigand and his associates charted different types of regional habitation sites around the Magdalena-Ameca-Etzatlán basins and upon flanks of the Volcán de Tequila. The simplest sites appeared to be hunting stations in the foothills and mountains; but other types were found to have a similar pattern, with a central mound surrounded by others. Over time, such sites increased in size and complexity and were associated with tombs, nearby workshops, and residential areas. The pattern suggested the existence of hierarchically ranked lineages and the growth of large communities. Upon visiting for the first time the obsidian deposits and workshops, and the remarkable circular enclosures at Teuchitlán, Weigand realized that the long-held view of West Mexico as a backwater "village farming" or "eternal formative" cultural region was due for major revision. In 1985 he published a synthesis of the mapping surveys, linking shaft tombs and circular ceremonial centers, showing that ancient ceramic architectural models replicated the circles, and outlining the position of a large number of sites systematically connected in a ranked pattern of settlement. Weigand proposed the development between about 200 B.C. and A.D. 800 of a complex social, economic, and political order named the

Fig. 11 Ritual dancer with a crocodile mask; Colima; Late Comala phase; earthenware. The Miller Family Collection, Chicago. Cat. no. 99.

Fig. 12 Dancer wearing a deity headdress; Colima; Late Comala phase; earthenware. Hudson Museum, University of Maine, Orono, William P. Palmer III Collection. Cat. no. 97.

"Teuchitlán tradition," centered in western Jalisco. This information strongly suggested that the marshy lake basins around the Volcán de Tequila were the setting for another "hearth," the generative center of a statelike society. Similar settings are the Valley of Mexico, where Cuicuilco and Teotihuacan originated; the area of southern Veracruz and Tabasco, location of the Olmec heartland; and the Petén region of Guatemala, where early Maya culture took form.

These discoveries and reassessments opened a new dialogue in the field, presenting fresh prospects to the few archaeologists who were excavating and conducting surveys in West Mexico. There was, however, no sudden or dramatic rush to conduct new projects in the region. The patient work of mapping continued, and it was not until 1993 that a second major breakthrough in West Mexican archaeology occurred with the discovery of an important shaft tomb at the site of Huitzilapa, not far from the town of Magdalena, Jalisco. In this, the first major completely unlooted shaft tomb to be scientifically excavated, archaeologists Lorenza López and Jorge Ramos found two intact chambers containing multiple high-status burials. About eighteen hundred years ago the deceased were covered with textiles and shell jewelry and surrounded by an array of food vessels, obsidian artifacts, and ceramic figures. The richness of the remains and offerings immediately raised questions about connections between residential and ceremonial sites, the religious and political functions of chieftains, and the worship of ancestors in lineage tombs associated with the Teuchitlán tradition. That such questions are now being addressed also reflects changes brought about by interdisciplinary approaches in Mesoamerican studies. Only in the past fifteen years has archaeology broadened from a concentration on ecology and economy to consider evidence leading toward the domain of "ideology" and the functions of religious activity and symbolic systems in the formation and maintenance of ancient societies. In this effort, the contributions of art historians and ethnologists have had a lasting effect.

Today, a hundred years after the travels of Breton and Lumholtz, it is clear that aboriginal communities in West Mexico gave rise to a high socioeconomic, symbolic, and aesthetic achievement with distinctive, even singular features. The availability, manage-

Fig. 13 Standing male holding an *incensario;* vicinity of the Colima volcano; Colima; Late Comala phase; earthenware. Private collection. Cat. no. 106.

ment, and control of natural resources were certainly determining factors in the formation and development of ancient communities; but it is no less important to recognize that such a complex adaptive human experience is never simply an outcome of economic activity or utilitarian purposes. Day-to-day existence and the long process of cultural evolution are much more than relentless competitions for goods and material survival, for there are also other subtle patterns at work. The lift of the mountains, the path of the sun, the rebirth of the seasons, the migration of animals, and the legends of earlier life provide many sources—seen and unseen—that inspire the creation of myths, the invention of symbols, and the rhythm of festivals, giving shape to basic patterns of thought. A sense of order and place is deeply interwoven with the human need to understand the beginning of things, explain the embracing design of nature, and conduct individual and collective activities in accord with the regular, predictable cycle of life, death, and renewal. The pragmatic business of obtaining food went hand in hand with the making of a culturally meaningful habitat. Here as in other pre-literate Amerindian societies, the old stories were told and retold and performed in ritual drama; humans and animals spoke with each other and with the ancestors and heroes, and through them to

Fig. 14 Warrior pair;
Ixtlán del Río style;
Nayarit; earthenware.
Private collection.
Cat. no. 199.

the deified spirits and life-and-death forces
of the sky, the waters, and the mountains.
In this sphere of imagination and expression,
the people and the place became one.

The essays that follow present the descriptions, inquiries, insights, and conjec-
tures of archaeologists, anthropologists, and
art historians seeking new understanding of
a region that seems after all not to have been
an impoverished derivation of the large urban centers of Central Mexico. The themes
explored by the authors of these essays are
interwoven: what are the ecological, economic, and social factors that affected the
dynamic process of cultural change? How
were art, architecture, and ritual drama engaged as determining agents in this process
of cultural transformation? On the basis of
present evidence concerning the geographical extent and complexity of the Teuchitlán
tradition, can this in fact be considered a
"statelike" society holding wide sway across
the region? Or was West Mexico an area of

considerable diversity, with coexisting societies of different complexity? Finally, what
are those aspects of ancient art and culture
that gave the West Mexican communities
their distinct identity? Conversely, what are
the deep structures of ideas, imagery, and
activities that joined these peoples to others
in the larger family of Mesoamerican
civilization?

Part I: The Teuchitlán Tradition:
An Archaeological Prospect
The first set of essays presents an essential
archaeological picture of the Teuchitlán tradition. Phil Weigand and Christopher Beekman
examine the shaft tombs and their associated
ceremonial architecture as evidence of the
growth of local centers of political, religious,
and economic power in the core area of
western Jalisco. The tombs of chieftains
of dominant lineages were an integral part
of ritual centers with platforms and houselike pavilions arranged symmetrically around

a circular patio, with a tiered circular altar or small pyramid rising in the middle. Between 100 B.C. and 200 A.D. such sites grew larger, as certain settlements became dominant. The concentration of these places around the marshy lakes indicates that this entire district was drawing ahead of neighboring areas, in a process of differentiation that was to intensify in succeeding centuries. The importance of the great shaft tombs gradually declined as the circular ritual enclosures increased in size, culminating in the Guachimontón complex at Teuchitlán—a process that Weigand and Beekman see as coinciding with the growth of population, the competitive ascendancy of ever more powerful rulers, and the corresponding need for greater networks of sociopolitical and economic cohesion. In some measure this need was undoubtedly answered by more inclusive and elaborate rituals, drawing local chieftains and their communities into a powerfully centralizing system. Linked to the control of obsidian sources, long-distance trade, and the creation of intensive farming zones, the development of larger circular ceremonial monuments points to the growth of a diversified polity that—in Weigand's estimation—was on the level of an ancient state, with social and economic stratification, increasing specialization of activities, and an elaborate religious, trade, and military organization.

By A.D. 800 great changes were underway here as elsewhere in Mesoamerica, as old social orders disintegrated or were transformed. In West Mexico this process was marked by the disappearance of the circular centers and their replacement by rectangular architectural ensembles and new types of ceramic production. Yet even during this later period, sculpture found in the early shaft tombs may have inspired a "revival" style, as seen in a Colima-like acrobat-juggler highly ornamented with polychrome Mixtec-like painting, a pattern of dots, and gold leaf (see fig. 30).

The essay by López and Ramos describing the newly excavated shaft tomb at Huitzilapa with its offerings and human remains supports Weigand's overview of the rise of a local aristocratic elite and the gradual knitting together of dozens of sites around the Volcán de Tequila in Jalisco. The placement of the tomb within the Huitzilapa settlement, and the materials accompanying the deceased also call attention to the religious relationship between the organization of ancient society and the order they saw in the natural environment, suggesting a system of ritual obligations in which lineage chiefs were responsible for maintaining the cycle of fertility, and the continuation of these functions as revered ancestors after death.

Examining the bones of male and female skeletons found in the Huitzilapa tomb, Robert Pickering and Teresa Cabrero establish their likely family relationships through physical evidence of a congenital deformity present in five of the six remains. In addition, it appears that two of the males were warriors and perhaps ballplayers. In these respects the Huitzilapa remains suggest that the chieftains of West Mexico fulfilled functions similar to those of rulers among the Olmecs, Maya, Teotihuacanos, Toltecs, and others. Pickering and Cabrero also chart a wide range of burial practices in West Mexico, giving account of more than thirty other excavated sites and what their contents have to tell.

Part II: Interpreting the Tomb Sculptures

The second set of essays examines tomb sculpture and ritual architecture to explore the ancient symbolic domain. Kristi Butterwick's detailed examination of tomb sculpture concentrates on models and figures that illustrate the functions of feasts in ancient

Fig. 15 Seated female figure with a "red hand" sign; Lagunillas "E" style; Nayarit; earthenware. Collection of Saul and Marsha Stanoff, Tarzana, Calif. Cat. no. 214.

Fig. 16 Seated female figure with a "red hand" sign; Lagunillas "E" style; Nayarit; earthenware. Private collection. Cat. no. 213.

West Mexican political and economic life. Feasting and the sponsoring of feasts formed a social compact by which chieftains vied to establish personal ascendancy and control of wealth within their communities and in competition with rival leaders from neighboring groups. This "potlatch" aspect of rulership, by which wealth was regularly accumulated and redistributed through festivals, is well known in Mesoamerica and is well documented among the Aztecs, who practiced it on an imperial scale. In the ceramic art of Ixtlán del Río, detailed models of houses, platforms, and pavilions include groups of figures talking, singing, gesticulating, and embracing in the presence of heaped-up bowls and platters of food and vats of corn-beer or *pulque* made from fermented sap of the maguey agave. Large sculptural figures from other regions also hold these containers, and it may be surmised that ritualized drinking was an indispensable part of all festive occasions. Butterwick believes that possession or control of fields of maguey for the production of *pulque* would have been crucial for rising chieftains in sponsoring feasts and developing or maintaining positions of prestige and authority, and that competition for such resources among rivals was a contributing factor in the development of complex society in the region.

In my own essay I have tried to move beyond the notion of "secular ceremonialism" by taking a fresh look at miniature models of houses, ceremonial centers, and lively scenes of feasting and other ritual events, as an expressive index to specific festival themes that are also illustrated by larger hollow sculptural figures. In any society the life of an individual is marked by a series of passages from one age to another and from one occupation to another, and, in ancient West Mexico, many models and larger tomb figures provide evidence of these rites of passage. The initiation of young warriors and the taking of office by major chiefs; the initiation of young women into adulthood and the responsibilities of childbearing; marriage and the biological continuity of the family; and funerary rites and ancestor-worship—these emerge as dominant tomb-sculpture subjects. Seen in this light, a principal purpose of the sculptural works was to testify to the mature rank and status of the ancestors they accompanied. In the domain of the spirits, the ancestors continued to intercede on the part of their people to secure the regular succession of the seasons, the fertility of the soil, and abundant harvests.

The symbolic organization of ceremonial sites is discussed by Christopher Witmore, who draws analogies from diverse archaeological sources, ethnohistorical texts, and ethnographic descriptions to reveal microcosm-macrocosm relationships. The circle replicates the encompassing rim of the horizon; cardinal and intercardinal orientations are established by pyramid stairways along axes related to the path of the sun; and tall masts rising from central pyramids correspond to the *axis mundi* connecting the apex of the sky to the central point of the earth's surface and to the underworld nadir. At the Teuchitlán site, Witmore's discussion focuses on observations and rites on the day of the summer solstice, the annual time of the sun's zenith passage, the beginning of rains and renewal of the earth's fertility.

Throughout the lake-basin heartland of northwestern Jalisco, the major ceremonial sites include long, narrow ballcourt alleys in the shape of a capital I, with flanking stands for viewers and sometimes with end-zone pavilions. Ballcourt models from the Ixtlán

Fig. 17 Seated figure with polychrome face-paint; Lagunillas "C" style; Nayarit; earthenware. Private collection. Cat. no. 208.

tombs, and a variety of figurines and large hollow figures of players, are known in other West Mexican styles. These are described by Jane Day, who traces the history of ballgame imagery in West Mexico leading back to figurines from El Opeño, in a time before formalized courts were constructed and opposing teams met in open fields. As elsewhere in Mesoamerica, games played with a rubber ball between teams were regularly played in important West Mexican festivals events. For prognostication at the inauguration of rulers, for resolving disputes and as a substitute for war, to mark important transitions in the cycle of the seasons, or simply for entertainment and gambling, ballgames provided another arena for activity designed to maintain social integration and cohesion.

Reviewing ideas he initially explored during the late 1960s and 1970s, Peter Furst recalls our attention to the world of medicine-men and magic healers. Among traditional peoples today or in the recent past, the therapeutic functions of shamans may be directed to individuals or to larger congregations; sometimes, shamans may assume roles ordinarily assigned to priests or rulers. In the tomb sculpture, Furst posited that a series of kneeling figures who look to the left and are armed with spears or batons

may not be warriors, but may well be regarded as shamans assuming poses of confrontation with threatening spirits. From this point of view, many warrior figures as well as others who wear single horns strapped to their foreheads or appear to actually grow such "horns of power" from their brows, are manifestations of shamanic "One-Horns" also occurring in ancient Andean art, among the Plains Indians, the Northwest Coast tribes, the Eskimo, and beyond, among peoples of the Asian Circum-Pacific. This speculative, far-reaching use of ethnographic analogy in the interpretation of ancient sculptures has proved a subject of intense and long-lasting argument. Yet, there can be no doubt that as a means of generating hypotheses this approach has much value, for as Furst points out, however one may challenge specific interpretations of individual West Mexican tomb sculptures, there are too many points of engagement in the whole corpus of the tradition to deny the existence of "a very ancient and widely shared shamanic substratum, of which remnants shine through with greater or lesser force in archaeological and contemporary indigenous religions, myths, rituals, and art."

Taking another approach to shamanism, Mark Graham examines the "One-Horn"

Colima figures in the context of Mesoamerican rulership imagery. Pointing out that the "horns" actually appear to be conical spires or protrusions of conch shells, in many cases held in place by a strap-work headdress, he calls attention to the representation of conch shells in the headdresses, ritual attire, and architectural environments of rulers from Olmec, Maya, Teotihuacan, and Aztec symbolic systems. These representations are associated with the religious functions of rulers as sources of fertility and the renewal of vegetal growth. Noting that conch shells appear in symbolic contexts in rites of passage such as a ruler's inauguration into high office, Graham argues that such shells were indicators of cosmic locations, that they signaled wealth and status, and that they were also symbols of mythic creation. Considered in this context, the West Mexican figures of horned personages appear to belong to a widespread, deep-seated tradition of rulership iconography; yet this does not exclude a shamanic dimension, for shamanistic

manipulation of ritual symbols, actions, and works of art was surely used by Mesoamerican rulers in the consolidation of power as complex societies developed.

Part III: Comparative Views

In the third segment of the catalogue, Otto Schöndube and Francisco Valdez consider a variety of evidence—natural resources, settlement patterns, and tomb sculptures—indicating that not all of West Mexico was following the ambitious course of social, economic, and cultural development implied by the Teuchitlán tradition. Schöndube approaches the landscape by "erasing" all those layers of natural products that one sees today but that were imported by the Spaniards from Europe in the sixteenth century, came from other parts of the Americas during the colonial and modern periods, or arrived from Asia. What was there in the original setting? What were those foods that the first Spanish writers described as being *de la tierra*, "of the local land"? The list in fact goes well beyond the often quoted basics: maize, beans, squash, and *chiles*. In addition to colonial texts and minute remains of foods retrieved from archaeological contexts, elegant vessels from Colima representing the fruits of the earth are an important source of information on the ancient diet. These sculptural forms spread a banquet before us, as they once did in the tombs of ancient Colima: tomatoes, *zapotes, guanábanas, chirimoyas, xocotes, tunas,* and other fruits and vegetables, as well as crabs, crayfish, shrimp, fish, armadillos, and dogs. With the exception of the dog, these products were gleaned or hunted in the wild, or were semi-domesticated in orchards. Schöndube notes that these diverse foods come from small ecological niches with a limited production that could not have tolerated exhaustive exploitation: a factor pointing to a general pattern of dispersed village settlements throughout West Mexico. From this point of view, it appears that some communities were undoubtedly larger with a measure of local control over others; yet during the period of the shaft tombs, the region would seem to have had multiple chieftainships, not extensive sociopolitical districts under state-like centralized rule.

Beginning in 1992 and concluding in 1997, the French archaeological mission ORSTOM sponsored an international team

Fig. 20 Female figurine; Tala-Tonalá style; Jalisco; earthenware. Denver Art Museum. Cat. no. 143.

in a survey and excavation of ancient settlements around the Sayula basin. Archaeologist Francisco Valdez has found a pattern quite different from that of the neighboring heartland of the Teuchitlán tradition. Hamlets and small, dispersed village sites appear scattered around the littoral and on the alluvial slopes of the mountains. The lake, flooded to a depth of perhaps two to three feet by the end of the summer rainy season, dries entirely in the winter and spring; yet during the months of drought a salt-making industry thrived. No circular ritual centers have been found in this basin, and local populations seem not to have fallen under direct political and religious sway of the more highly organized and stratified society to the north. Valdez remarks that while the long-held impression of a lack of social complexity in West Mexico has rightly been questioned by evidence associated with the Teuchitlán tradition, "information recently obtained in Sayula does not always correspond with the guidelines of [Weigand's] proposed model. Social complexity has various faces and not all correspond, at a given moment, to the exact notion of a center and periphery at a macroregional level." Valdez underlines the fact that interaction between different communities may not inescapably lead to a pattern of dominance and submission, but rather to complementarity among communities considered to be equal. Thus, Sayula basin chieftainships engaged in the seasonal production of salt might have participated as independent entities in a network of regional trade without being subordinate to a single sociopolitical center in the neighboring Teuchitlán area.

In the catalogue of the first exhibition of ancient West Mexican art, held in Mexico City in 1946, Paul Kirchhoff noted that the sculptural figures and the shaft-and-chamber tombs showed similarities with those of ancient societies in Ecuador. Occasional inquiries have continued to explore the possibility of connections between these distant Pacific coast regions. For the most part comparisons have focused on the shaft tombs, which in northwestern South America are not restricted to Ecuador but also occur in nearby parts of Colombia. It has also been archaeologically established that knowledge of metallurgy reached West Mexico by about A.D. 700, for workshops have been found on the coast of Michoacán with evidence of technologies

that originated in Ecuador and Colombia. But what of the period between c. A.D. 1 and 250, when the shaft-tomb tradition was culminating in Nayarit, Jalisco, and Colima? The question of contacts is explored anew by Patricia Anawalt in the present catalogue. Her novel approach compares certain specific garments, textiles, and emblematic jewelry displayed by West Mexican tomb figures. Anawalt finds that these items enjoyed a long-lasting tradition, surviving among the Tarascans of Michoacán until well into the sixteenth century, yet they were highly distinctive and have not been found elsewhere in Mesoamerica. On the other hand, garments, textiles, and emblems of similar design are seen on Ecuadorian ceramic figures of comparable dates to those from West Mexico. Supporting data concerning Ecuadorian long-distance trade for *Spondylus* shell

Fig. 21 Standing couple; Tala-Tonalá style; Jalisco; earthenware. Private collection. Cat. no. 147.

Fig. 22 Female rasp player seated on a stool; Comala style; Colima; earthenware. Collection of Mr. and Mrs. Joseph Goldenberg, Los Angeles. Cat. no. 25.

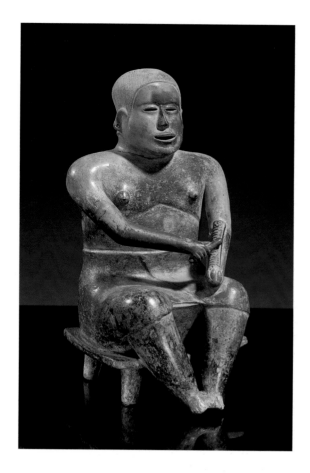

via sea-going balsa rafts is also marshaled in this imaginative thesis.

In the concluding archaeological essay of the catalogue, Joseph Mountjoy reviews the course of cultural evolution in West Mexico, drawing comparisons with other regions of Mesoamerica as well as the southwestern and southeastern areas of the United States. Reminding us that West Mexico in its broadest definition may be extended to include the Pacific coast state of Sinaloa, territories east of the Sierra Madre commanded by the important sites of Alta Vista–Chalchihuites and La Quemada in Zacatecas, as well as parts of Michoacán to the south, Mountjoy focuses on the areas where our attention has concentrated in this book. To what extent does the evidence support the idea of the formation of a statelike society in the lake basins of northwestern Jalisco? Was the Teuchitlán tradition in fact a "hearth," comparable to other well-known generative centers of Mesoamerican civilization between 200 B.C. and A.D. 300? To set this problem in broad historical perspective, Mountjoy begins before 7000 B.C., when tiny bands of hunter-gatherers were gleaning their livelihood in an open terrain of marshes, lakes, mountains, and valleys according to the seasonal availability of animals and plants. It was not until sometime between 1500 and 1200 B.C. that new populations began filtering in,

bringing with them a knowledge of plant cultivation and pottery, and a more sedentary pattern of village life. The cultural remains of these peoples at El Opeño and

Fig. 23 Contortionist; Comala style; Colima; earthenware. Private collection. Cat. no. 22.

Fig. 24 Contortionist; Comala style; Colima; earthenware. Private collection. Cat. no. 23.

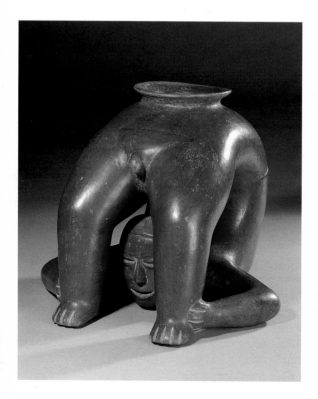

Capacha show traces of connections with archaeological sites in central highland Mexico, and through them to distant Olmec capitals far to the south by the Gulf of Mexico. A thousand years later, between 300 B.C. and A.D. 300 in several locations in Mesoamerica, large towns with ceremonial centers were becoming densely inhabited urban zones with expanded spheres of influence and control as early city-states emerged at Cuicuilco and Teotihuacan in the Valley of Mexico, Monte Albán in Oaxaca, and El Mirador and Kaminaljuyú in Guatemala. The pace of change was growing swiftly in these widespread locations.

In West Mexico this was the period of the great shaft tombs and their associated arts, and the growth of well-defined ceremonial sites with increasing evidence of settlement differentiation, stratified society, economic specializations, and long-distance trade. In the lake-basin area of Jalisco local seats of power took shape where decisions were being made affecting increasingly larger territories. This process appears to have intensified after 300 A.D., as larger circular ceremonial sites were created in response to the need to include and manage polities of greater magnitude. The tendency toward concentration of power also drew together patrons for the inventions and designs of professional craftsmen and artisans. The development of ceremonial architecture and the originality and variety of tomb sculpture in Nayarit, Jalisco, and Colima suggest that peoples of diverse communities and ethnicities were sharing a language of symbols as participants in an *oikoumene* broadly embracing the West Mexican region. These creations were not dutiful reflections at great distances of innovations in the great urban centers of Central or Southern Mexico. Yet Mountjoy underlines the fact that on the basis of actual excavation evidence, it cannot yet be confirmed that the Teuchitlán tradition achieved a complexity comparable to those distant metropolitan cultures. Much more fieldwork will be required to confirm if the circular complexes and ballcourts, terraces, agricultural plantations, and control points along natural routes of travel with neighboring valleys were indeed coeval. Did the large-scale organization and alteration of the landscape in northwestern Jalisco all take place during this period, or may it also be partly attributable to Postclassic developments of which little is pres-

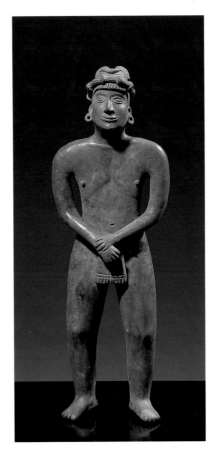

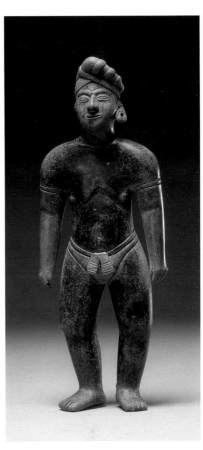

ently known? In conclusion Mountjoy draws insightful comparisons, characterizing "state-like societies" and "complex chiefdoms." He suggests that, as in the examples of ancient peoples who produced the great habitational complexes at Poverty Point, Louisiana, as early as 2000 B.C., or Chaco Canyon, New Mexico, in the eleventh century A.D., or the ceremonial center of Moundville, Alabama, in the twelfth century, or in the early urban zone at Teotihuacan between 200 B.C. and the beginning of the first century A.D., the populations of northwestern Jalisco succeeded in creating a community in which the labor and resources required for major public works were provided primarily through a system of social obligations and feasting, but perhaps not by land ownership or other harsh means of coercion, in a social order more closely identified with chiefdoms than with those of archaic states.

Part IV: A Modernist Perspective

This book and the exhibition it accompanies focus on the art and history of ancient West Mexico to advance the recovery of an important regional cultural tradition and to explore its connections with other Mesoamerican

Fig. 25 Standing male figurine with hands crossed over stomach; Colima/Jalisco; Late Comala phase; earthenware. Private collection. Cat. no. 92.

Fig. 26 Male figurine with a finely modeled coiffure; Colima/Jalisco; Late Comala phase; earthenware. American Museum of Natural History, New York. Cat. no. 91.

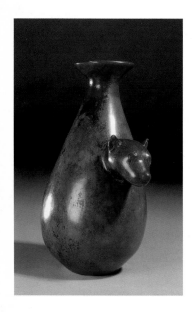

Fig. 27 "Teardrop" bottle with a dog effigy head; Comala style; Colima; earthenware. Hudson Museum, University of Maine, Orono, William P. Palmer III Collection. Cat. no. 65.

Fig. 28 Performer balancing ball on nose; Colima; Comala phase; earthenware. Los Angeles County Museum of Art, The Proctor Stafford Collection, museum purchase with funds provided by Mr. and Mrs. Allan C. Balch. Cat. no. 107.

societies. But it is also important to call attention to the fact that this endeavor also plays against a larger backdrop of issues in the contemporary world. *Ancient West Mexico: Art and Archaeology of the Unknown Past* is part of an ongoing international movement aimed at understanding and acknowledging the reaches of Amerindian cultural heritage in many nations of this continent. This larger framework of issues includes the creation of national identity in modern Mexico, the deepening acknowledgment of Amerindian cultural history in the United States, and the connection between twentieth-century artists and architects and the arts of the pre-Columbian antiquity.

It was in the extraordinary and extensive collections of Diego Rivera and others during the 1930s that West Mexican figurines first began to be prized for their sculptural form and intensity of expression. Painters in Mexico City acknowledged the aesthetic power of these and other Mesoamerican arts, and translated underlying principles of form as they invented new visual languages in the search to define a contemporary but deeply rooted art reflecting Mexico's cultural traditions. Internationally, artists such as Henry

Moore also recognized West Mexican and other important ancient forms as sources for creating an abstract sculptural style. The work of these artists belongs to the larger movement of architects, painters, and sculptors from Frank Lloyd Wright to Jackson Pollock, Max Ernst, Joaquín Torres-García, Michael Heizer, and others who have looked to Amerindian traditions for ideas, forms, and principles in a continuing, ongoing search for a finer cultural adjustment to the land and the peoples who were here long before the voyage of Columbus. Art historian Barbara Braun in *Pre-Columbian Art in the Post-Columbian World* has remarked that "Seeing pre-Columbian art through the eyes of modern masters rather than archaeologically expands our understanding of both pre-Hispanic and modern visual traditions." Continuing to explore this theme in the concluding essay of this catalogue, Braun discusses specific works by Henry Moore, Rufino Tamayo, Diego Rivera, and Frida Kahlo. We are invited to consider the philosophical, aesthetic, and anthropological ways that cross-cultural borrowing can be crucial to the creative efforts of artists as well as scholars and to the general public in understanding how our imagination remains consciously or unconsciously affected by a shared Amerindian culture, past and present.

Conclusion

Acercamiento is a Spanish word corresponding to the English "approach," but allusively it might be also translated as "nearing," carrying the sense of becoming familiar, drawing close, or discovering an inner, emotional or associative meaning to some externally observed phenomenon or historical occurrence. In this sense, the word embraces a wide zone of comprehension ranging from explicit, objective intellectual analysis, to speculative perception and subjective, personal, interpretive finding. I hope that my more scientifically minded colleagues and readers will not be too alarmed if I say that for me at least, the thrust of this book and exhibition project is in a large measure a "nearing." Since the first visits and descriptions by Breton and Lumholtz a hundred years ago, West Mexico has remained the most unknown and neglected of all the major areas where ancient civilization flourished in Mexico. Although the artistic achievements of its peoples touched the imagination of many, the seeming lack of monumental remains contributed to official indifference and intellectual marginalization. Major archaeological programs unfolded elsewhere, sponsored by national and international institutions. At the same time, a rising tide of plundering culminated during the 1950s, 1960s, and early 1970s, leaving many West Mexican archaeological zones in a state of devastation. As recently as December 1997, the National Geographic Society's latest map of Mesoamerica continued to omit the region. Yet as the essays in this volume attest, a handful of scholars from several disciplines have succeeded in establishing an outline of cultural evolution in Jalisco, Colima, and Nayarit. Significantly, several have deep personal connections in the region, as well as long-standing professional interests. The diverse voices heard in this catalogue by no means represent all who are working in West Mexico today: a volume at least twice as large would be required to be truly inclusive.

The present book features some 225 figures, vessels, and related objects from the vast diaspora of West Mexican material. Although separated from their original archaeological settings, they are here brought into a context of information from field surveys, excavations, and iconographic interpretations. The works are at once illuminated by

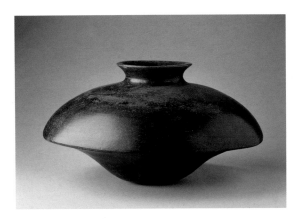

Fig. 29 Vessel; Comala style; Colima; earthenware. Los Angeles County Museum of Art, The Proctor Stafford Collection, museum purchase with funds provided by Mr. and Mrs. Allan C. Balch. Cat. no. 70.

the data and in turn offer informed contributions. In this respect this project has the character of a salvage operation: *rescate,* meaning "rescue" or "recovery" in Spanish. All is not irretrievably lost, and as fieldwork and interpretations progress, an immense body of comparative information may also be brought to bear from elsewhere in Mesoamerica and adjoining areas of the U.S. Southwest and Southeast. The prospects remain open for salvaging the historical record of this singular region.

West Mexico is one of many large and small areas scattered in North, Central, and South America, where the memory of ancient life has not yet fully emerged from the landscape. In some regions the sites may be overshadowed by more spectacular ruins; elsewhere they remain to be charted in remote mountains or forests; more often they are increasingly obscured or lost through mechanized agriculture, ramifying networks of powerlines, highways, and suburban housing developments. Yet their lines, squares, circles, and mounds form part of the great archipelago of settings where life was conducted in concert with nature. Such ruins are integral to our cultural habitat, reminding us that what is best in the new is often that which responds to an ancient aspiration.

Fig. 30 Acrobat-juggler vessel; Colima(?); 11–12 cen.(?); earthenware, gesso, mineral pigments, gold leaf. Private collection. Modeled in a style similar to Comala figures, this acrobat-juggler is ornamented in a manner suggestive of Mixtec tradition from the central and southern highlands of Mexico. Note especially the pictorial decoration around the upper cylinder of the vessel. This hybrid work suggests an effort by new rulers to quote older native artistic traditions in the interest of legitimization.

PHIL C. WEIGAND AND
CHRISTOPHER S. BEEKMAN

THE TEUCHITLAN TRADITION RISE OF A STATELIKE SOCIETY

Prologue

When we began our archaeological research in the area surrounding the sites of Teuchitlán and Etzatlán in Jalisco in 1969, we simply had no idea what we were about to discover. Conventional wisdom concerning the archaeology of this region had always emphasized the presence of shaft tombs and the impressive art objects found within them. Speculations abounded concerning the functions and meanings of the large earthenware figures, the smaller figurines, and the shaft tombs themselves, but these interpretations had very little context in actual field studies. Other than the tombs and figurines, the area had long been characterized as a region that did not have complex cultures or monumental architecture. We accepted these views at the time, without questioning any of them very deeply. The purpose of our research was to examine the simple villages that had been suggested as the source of the shaft tombs. We had planned to spend perhaps a summer, or at most two, in an effort to contextualize the shaft tombs within a regional system of settlements, and, if it existed, in relation to any contemporaneous surface architecture.

We selected as the starting point for our in-depth examination the El Arenal site north of Etzatlán, near the Laguna de Magdalena. There we saw what appeared to be circular compounds that either covered the shaft tombs or were built along with them in antiquity. Since this site had been severely damaged by looting, we were unwilling to make hard-and-fast conclusions regarding the surface architecture. The next site that we examined, Ahualulco, had also been

heavily damaged, but it proved to be far more monumental in scope, and its dominant architectural pattern was still quite visible. The overall circular configuration of the site was immediately clear to us, as was the fact that the constructions there had been complex and very large. Since shaft tombs had been looted at both El Arenal and Ahualulco, we recognized by mid-summer that the traditional characterization of this area was seriously flawed. The first maps we drafted may have been little better than rough drawings, but they nonetheless displayed a type of complex and monumental architecture that had not been reported for pre-Hispanic Mesoamerica prior to these discoveries. This work certainly increased our level of excitement and offered us the beginnings of an entirely new vista on the ancient societies of this region.

During the rest of that summer, and the summers of 1970 and 1971, we continued examining and mapping sites where shaft tombs had been reported, finding at almost all of them indications of the circular architecture we had seen in 1969. In 1970, we acquired our first set of aerial photographs, and the surprise they held for us was nearly overwhelming: hundreds of these circular sites lay scattered across the general region, and some, like those near Teuchitlán and Santa Quiteria, were truly large complexes.

Early in 1972, we visited for the first time the Guachimontón precinct of Teuchitlán, using the aerial photographs as our guide up the hillside to this archaeological site. Years before, during the 1960s, the discovery by Acelia García de Weigand of a large obsidian

Fig. 1 The principal ritual precinct at Teuchitlán, Jalisco. Commandingly placed above the basin, this unexcavated site features a central pyramid-mound surrounded by a circular plaza and an outer ring of platforms that were once surmounted by houselike pavilions. A ballcourt and two smaller unexcavated circular precincts lie to the left; others are found on terraces to the center and to the right. (For a reconstruction view of this important site, see pages 49–50 in this essay).

workshop on the lower slopes of this hillside had given us our first indication of the presence of a complex site in this vicinity. We began our more detailed examination with elevated interest and a sense of anticipation. After several hours of climbing and looking, we finally reached a circular compound whose beauty, symmetry, and monumentality far exceeded the expectations we had formed from the aerial photographs (see fig. 1). Our excitement was intense, and we could barely talk in the ardor of this discovery.

This was, of course, every archaeologist's secret dream: not only had we established a context for the shaft tombs in a system of settlements and surface buildings, but we were also on the verge of describing a totally new building type for the world's architectural repertoire.

Partly from self-doubt, we called in several of our archaeological associates to see this great complex and cross-check our first set of observations. Initially, J. Charles Kelley and Joseph Mountjoy agreed to come and

see the site. Both were as enthusiastic about this discovery as we were. Mountjoy volunteered to help in the first stage of our evaluation of the site, and to spend part of the summer of 1972 examining the buildings and whatever evidence remained of habitation there. Visits by Javier Galván, Jaime Litvak King, James Officer, and Dolores Soto de Arechavaleta, among others, quickly followed. Each archaeologist or anthropologist offered original insights. Some, like Mountjoy, studied the site in a very detailed fashion and focused on the data we had collected, while others, like Officer and Litvak, stressed the need for a completely new view of West Mexico's role in Mesoamerican civilization.

After several more seasons, we realized by 1977 that we were dealing with another hearth, or nucleus, of civilization within ancient Mesoamerica. Since the data we had gathered and our interpretations of it were contrary to received wisdom about West Mexico, we expected that our report would not be received without questions. Indeed, this is how science is expected to operate. Over the past twenty years, we have pursued this documentation at every opportunity. The summary of what we have discovered, while still quite preliminary, nonetheless offers some important insights into Jalisco's ancient past.

Introduction

Our understanding of the archaeology of the highland basins of Jalisco and Nayarit has changed drastically in the last fifty years. A host of research projects aimed at exploring these regions and landscapes have offered us, for the first time, a fundamental knowledge of its settlement patterns and enabled us to identify a hierarchy of sites that includes new architectural styles, zones for terraces and for the small, artificially elevated farm plots called *chinampas*, as well as many newly located mining areas, and more. The purpose of this essay is to examine the current status of archaeology in the vicinity of the Volcán de Tequila, focusing on the Classic period in order to define what we now call the Teuchitlán tradition, and to suggest strategies for enriching our understanding of this area.

The marshy western region of Jalisco has very rich natural ecosystems. Fertile soils and the relative availability of rare resources make this area superior to that of most early

Fig. 2 Drawing of tomb no. 4; Citala area, Teocuitatlán district, Jalisco; El Opeño phase, 1500–800 B.C. The earliest type of tombs in West Mexico—identified with El Opeño and related sites of the Early Formative period—feature a short, stepped entryway leading into a single mortuary chamber.

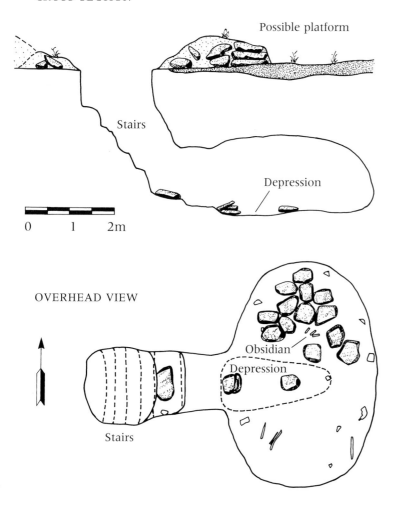

CROSS-SECTION

Possible platform

Stairs

Depression

0   1   2m

OVERHEAD VIEW

Obsidian

Depression

Stairs

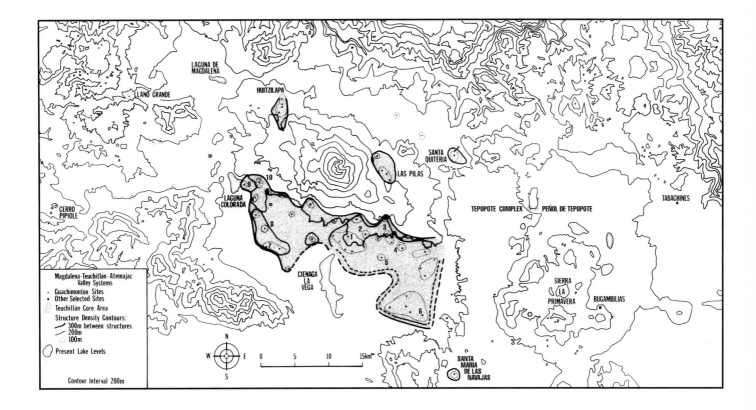

civilizations in Mesoamerica. High-quality obsidian, greenstone, various types of crystals, copper and silver, and salt are among the minerals easily obtained from this region. On the other hand, the semitropical climatic system, alongside irrigation during the dry season, offers the possibility of two harvests per year. Rain precipitation ranges between 900 and 1,600 millimeters each year throughout the area, 85–90% of which falls during the months of June to October.[1]

Contrary to the ideas expressed in some archaeological literature, this area is not strictly divided into small and/or isolated valleys, despite the rugged mountains that extend throughout.[2] There are simply no natural barriers between the middle and lower basin of the Lerma River and the marshy districts, nor is there any type of barrier between the lake valleys themselves, from Sayula on the south, Lake Chapala on the east, and Etzatlán on the north. This enormous system of valleys is, in fact, surrounded by mountains and canyons that do not obstruct the natural flow of communications. Instead, these mountains and ravines increase the variety of resources that are available, especially when compared to other nearby regions. Thus, there is ecological variability in this area, but it does not have a negative impact on the amount of

ideal agricultural land. Instead, the combination of high-quality resources, both rare and strategic, and sufficient arable land provided an excellent setting for the development of complex societies.

Formative Period
Although they were all found looted and devoid of most of their original content, our search produced the discovery of four sites with shaft tombs of the type identified with ones that have been found at El Opeño in northwestern Michoacán and radiocarbon-dated between 1500 and 800 B.C. (see fig. 2).[3] This association could be interpreted to suggest that the cultures (or subcultures) that were responsible for the funerary tradition of El Opeño might also have contributed to the basic cultural stratum of this entire marshy area. But other sites within the area studied have yielded ceramic vessels very similar to those of the Capacha complex, much further south in Colima, so this issue remains unresolved.

The archaeological materials pertaining to the period between 800 and 300 B.C. (often called the San Felipe phase) are poorly understood, although it seems that the idea of creating burial mounds was gradually extending throughout the lake-basin districts. These mounds are round or oval in shape,

Fig. 3 Map of Teuchitlán core area and periphery. The Teuchitlán tradition is located in the Magdalena and Etzatlán basins and smaller valleys surrounding the extinct Volcán de Tequila—the sacred mountain of the region. Population was especially concentrated around the site of Teuchitlán, on the south side of the volcano. A series of outposts guarded the approaches to this central zone from the Atemajac valley to the east.

Among the many archaeological sites in the core area south of the Volcán de Tequila are the following:
1) Guachimontón;
2) Caldera de los Lobos;
3) Las Chivas sites;
4) El Refugio (Mesa Alta and La Mesa);
5) La Noria; 6) San Juan de los Arcos;
7) Ahualulco;
8) Cortacena;
9) La Providencia;
10) Cerro de los Monos.

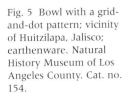

Fig. 4 Shallow bowl with a concentric red and black pattern; vicinity of Etzatlán, Jalisco; earthenware. Private collection. Cat. no. 152. Local distinctive designs were developed for ceramic vessels used by communities in the Ameca-Etzatlán and Magdalena basins during the Late Formative period.

28–30 meters in diameter, and average 2 meters in height. As in the case of the El Opeño–style material, there seem to be at least two distinct levels characterizing the social system that constructed these mounds. Each mound or platform has at least two shaft tombs (some up to eight meters deep), although most burials clearly took place in simple pits. Unfortunately, no burials from this period have been scientifically excavated, so this phase is only superficially understood.

The earthenware figurines and vessels of the Late Formative cultures of West Mexico—which have been the subject of looting since the late nineteenth century and especially between 1930 and 1975—have mostly served as the basis for stylistic and iconographic studies throughout the history of archaeological research in this region. Thanks to recent fieldwork in the lake basins, these objects can now be placed within the context of a more developed anthropological discussion as to their cultural role in societies during the period from 300 B.C. to A.D. 200 (see figs. 4–6 and 10–13). [4] The presence of these shaft tombs in association with the surface architecture that accompanies them indicates the beginnings of the development of a core of complexly organized societies. In fact, this area was beginning to leave its neighbors behind with respect to rhythms of change and complexity (see fig. 3). In other words, a process of differential development was underway, thus marking the origin of a relationship between core and periphery that continued to exist throughout the next thousand years. We have chosen to name this period of expanding differential development, including its pinnacle during the Classic period, the Teuchitlán tradition.

From this same period of roughly 300 B.C. to A.D. 200 (often called the Arenal phase), groups of ceramic figurines and architectural models offer us a very good idea of what ceremonial buildings this culture might have produced.[5] Often, these models, which are almost photographic in detail and ethnographic in quality, reveal that the mounds or platforms surrounded

Fig. 5 Bowl with a grid-and-dot pattern; vicinity of Huitzilapa, Jalisco; earthenware. Natural History Museum of Los Angeles County. Cat. no. 154.

Fig. 6 Bowl with a dotted pattern; vicinity of Huitzilapa, Jalisco; earthenware. Natural History Museum of Los Angeles County. Cat. no. 153.

a circular patio, which in turn wrapped around a central, circular altar (see fig. 7). The altars themselves sometimes served as the focal point for a ceremony featuring an acrobatic performer (called a *volador*) elevated aloft on an erect pole (see the essay by Christopher Witmore in this volume). The architecture represented in these examples can frequently be found in the same configuration in the field, though the circular units are often much more complex: there may be up to eight platforms surrounding the interior concentric elements. Some of these architectural circles are found in groups of as many as three, as in Huitzilapa or El Arenal.[6] Where there are multiple circles and ballcourts, however, one compound is always more elaborate and larger than the others.

Given the fact that most sites from this period do not have multiple circles and ballcourts, the archaeological evidence here suggests that a regional hierarchy of settlements within the Etzatlán-Teuchitlán area was just beginning to emerge. Residential zones continued to be quite small. The one at El Arenal, for instance, is just over two kilometers in diameter and included eighteen compounds or clusters of compounds. The precincts with shaft-tomb chambers found thus far are separated from each other by seven to ten kilometers and are located on the uppermost fossil shores of the lakes.

As is discussed in their essay in this volume, Jorge Ramos and Lorenza López recently excavated one of the compounds at Huitzilapa and discovered a shaft tomb eight meters deep, with two burial chambers, multiple burials, and some 60,000 artifacts, some of which were perishable. This monumental tomb is the only scientifically excavated tomb in the emerging core area.[7] Monumental tombs such as the ones found in El Arenal and in Huitzilapa are extremely rare and are only located within or close to the circular ceremonial structures.[8] Tombs with shafts of a depth less than two meters, such as those in Tabachines, are more common, both within the core and in the adjacent valleys.[9]

The direct association between the concentric circles and the monumental variety of shaft tombs—which are found only within the general Teuchitlán and Volcán de Tequila region—deserves further comment. By monumental, we mean those tombs with multiple chambers that open off shafts four meters or more deep. Shaft tombs of single chambers,

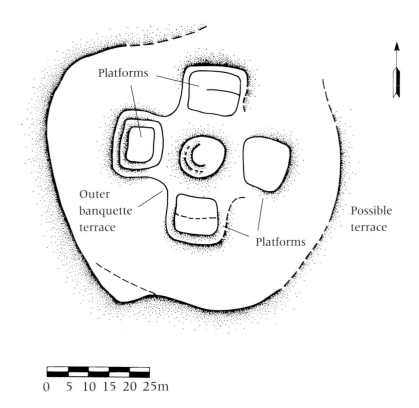

reached by shafts of only two to four meters, are by definition sub-monumental. Those shafts of less than two meters most often end in boot-shaped chambers, and, in the region we are considering, these are classified with the other pit burials. Although the appearance of shaft tombs (both monumental and sub-monumental) in conjunction with the circles does not occur 100% of the time, it is frequent enough to be called a pattern. Even the shaft tombs that are not found under the platforms that constitute an element of the ceremonial circles are nonetheless found in direct association with other types of platforms very near to those circles.

Over the years, from a total sample of 171, we have recorded over 40 instances of monumental and sub-monumental shaft tombs in direct association with circles dating from 300 B.C. to A.D. 200 and from A.D. 200 to 400 (the Arenal and Ahualulco phases, respectively). The shaft tomb at Huitzilapa, with two chambers and a shaft of almost eight meters, is the best-studied monumental shaft tomb that depicts this direct association.[10] The one at El Arenal described by Corona Núñez in 1955 is the most spectacular example to date, although it had been

Fig. 7 Platform complex at La Noria; Tala district, Jalisco. The central circular altar or pyramid surrounded by four platforms supporting houselike pavilions is represented in architectural models that have been found among West Mexican tomb sculptures (see Witmore, fig. 1). This cruciform configuration is the prototype for later, more complex circular ceremonial precincts.

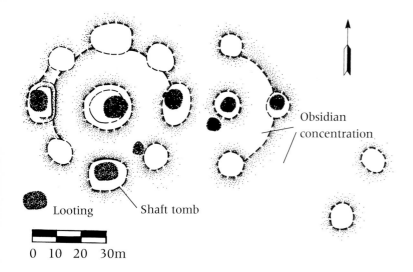

Looting   Shaft tomb

0 10 20 30m

Obsidian concentration

CROSS-SECTION

Possible platform

OVERHEAD VIEW
OF CHAMBERS

Pumice (jal)

0 1 2 3 4m

Shaft

Major
chamber

Major chamber
(looted)

Unlooted or
collapsed chamber

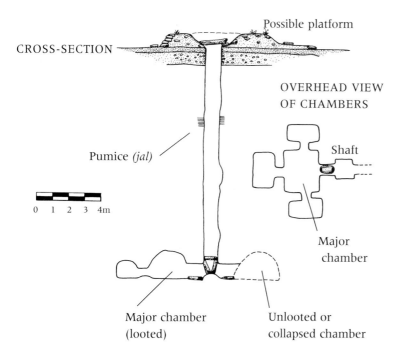

Figs. 8a, b: Remains of circular precincts and plan and elevation of a major shaft tomb at San Andres, Jalisco. Darkened areas represent looters' pits in the platform and mound remains. The plan shows two interlocking ceremonial circles: one circle consists of eight platforms orbiting a central pyramid-mound; a cruciform arrangement of platforms surrounds another mound. The two precincts share a platform on the east-west axis. The interlocking of circles remains a feature of major ceremonial architecture (see fig. 22).

completely looted prior to his examination of the structure.[11] This tomb has three chambers and an eighteen-meter shaft. Two other monumental shaft tombs at El Arenal are located within the major ceremonial circle. Finally, the small circles located near San Andres (see figs. 8a and 8b), which include at least five chambers and a fifteen-meter shaft, and at the Cerro de los Monos, La Providencia (see figs. 9a and 9b), with four chambers and an eleven-meter shaft, constitute two other examples of monumental shaft tombs located in direct association with the ceremonial circles in the Teuchitlán region.

Sub-monumental shaft tombs constitute the majority of shaft tombs that have been discovered within the core area around

Teuchitlán. Almost all of the tombs found outside of this core are non-monumental.[12] In the area beyond the core, monumental shaft tombs simply do not appear to exist. The non-monumental shaft tombs, as mentioned, are often found near or beneath single platforms, behind terraces, or within zones that are unmarked by any visible surface architecture. This last comment, however, should be qualified by the observation that not all studies of shaft tombs outside the Teuchitlán core have made note of any type of surface architecture.

More numerous still are the simple, single-event burials within pits. Thousands of such graves have been looted over the decades, and these clearly represent the burials of the non-elite members of the Teuchitlán tradition's population.

Thus, the association of many monumental shaft tombs with the ceremonial circles, in addition to the restricted distribution of this type of tomb within the Teuchitlán core, strongly implies three important conclusions:

1. The Teuchitlán core area played a special role within the overall burial ceremonialism of the entire region of West Mexico.

2. The monumental shaft tombs were an integral part of the ceremonial nature of the concentric buildings, as were their adjacent structures, such as ballcourts.

3. The use of monumental shaft tombs was restricted to a small element of the overall population, dedicated to ceremonial events and rituals that marked the elite social status of certain individuals within both the local social system and the larger region.

Finally, we should note that fine carvings of obsidian and greenish-blue stone (including small amounts of turquoise and jade), as well as carved seashells and, of course, hollow earthenware figurines and vessels compose the abundant artifacts of this period (see figs. 14 and 15). The various styles of earthenware, obsidian jewelry, and shell artifacts are also proof of the existence of a certain level of craft specialization and artisanship. Quite clearly then, far from lagging behind, the sociocultural developments in West Mexico were progressing at the same rhythm as other emerging complex civilizations in Mesoamerica.

Classic Period

The transition from the era that has just been described—the Arenal phase of the Late Formative period (also commonly known as the Late Preclassic period)—to the Classic period (comprising the Ahualulco and Teuchitlán I phases: A.D. 200–400 and 400–700, respectively) is seen as an process of intensification, which resulted in the emergence of a different type of society, though one that still retained a continuity in expression within the same cultural heritage. For this reason, we have used the term "tradition," instead of culture, to characterize its continuity. At the same time, we wish to emphasize the dramatic differences in the sociocultural characteristics between the Formative and Classic periods. The causes of this intensification of social systems are still unclear, but they might include the growth of neighboring traditions such as the Bajío and the Chalchihuites, because of which the competition for rare resources, which mark one's status, became more pronounced; the expansion of the Teotihuacan system toward the north and west, necessitating more complexity in order to survive culturally; and finally, the entirely local competitive pressures for both rare and strategic resources. None of these possible causes, of course, need be mutually exclusive.

The early portion of the Classic period continues to be poorly defined, even though we now know that it was, in fact, a time of intensification in development and an apparent demographic implosion—by which we mean a rearrangement of population wherein a large percentage becomes concentrated in a relatively small area, leaving neighboring zones with smaller populations. Demographic implosion thus marks the process of nuclearization, or the development of a nucleus within a regional social system. There are several excellent models, the first of which is in evidence at Ahualulco (the site that commonly lends its name to this phase of development), which experienced an enormous demographic implosion that lasted two or three centuries, beginning at approximately A.D. 200 and ending around 400 (see fig. 16).

To a great extent, monumental surface architecture now replaced the shaft tombs as a symbol of sociopolitical power and prestige within the region. Many of the more elegant shaft tombs belong to the early part of the

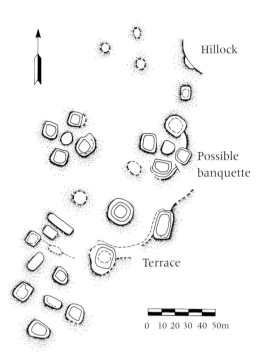

Figs. 9a, b: Plan of the upper complex at Cerro de los Monos, La Providencia, Jalisco, with a cross-section and overhead view of the shaft tomb discovered at this site. Skeletal evidence from the recently excavated tomb at Huitzilapa (see the essay by López and Ramos in this volume) indicates that many-chambered tombs were used to inter members of powerful families and to commemorate their lineage.

Hillock

Possible banquette

Terrace

0 10 20 30 40 50m

CROSS-SECTION

Possible platform

0 1 2 3 4m

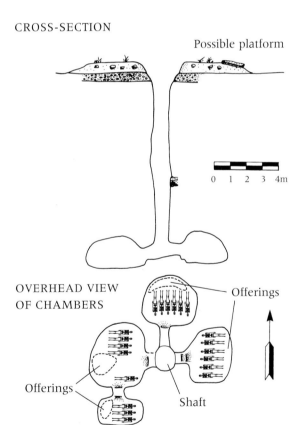

OVERHEAD VIEW OF CHAMBERS

Offerings

Offerings

Shaft

Fig. 10 Seated male figure with an upraised weapon in his hand; Ameca-Etzatlán style; Jalisco; earthenware. Private collection. Cat. no. 127. As complex societies evolved during the Late Formative period, well-defined styles of tomb sculptures were developed. This dynamic seated chieftain shows individual portraitlike features.

Fig. 11 Seated male figure with a shoulder cape; Colima; Late Comala phase; earthenware. Private collection. Cat. no. 104. In Colima there developed a tradition of small solid figurines representing high-ranking personages with highly refined attention to details of dress, coiffure, and jewelry.

Classic period. The later tombs were quite simple, although they continued to be richly supplied with offerings and decorated with murals. The concentration of population in small areas and the contemporaneous changes from monumental funerary architecture to monumental surface forms probably means that it had reached a stratified social order, such as that of a possibly segmentary state within its core.[13] Thus, if the monumental shaft tombs marked a period of veneration of elite ancestors, within societies organized around rigid social ranks that were expressed in part through feasting (see the essay by Kristi Butterwick in this volume), then the shift to monumental surface architecture probably marked not only the de-emphasis on ancestor veneration, but also the rise to prominence of offices and officers within a stratified society. The earthenware figures also changed: they became more formal, losing their portrait characteristics. This change probably denoted the impor-

tance of the positions held, rather than the individuals who held such positions within the social order.

At the time of this continued intensification in development and the implosion of population, the territory immediately adjacent to the core seems to have lost a high percentage of its population. Nothing similar to the monumental structures of the core area of the Classic period (see figs. 17a, 17b, and 22) was built in the adjacent territory, although relatively small circular complexes were sometimes created. In these regions, the number of settlements dramatically decreased, as compared with those of the Late Formative period, and the more important settlements that persisted are found in strategic locations where scarce resources could be obtained, or where fortifications guarded access to the core area.

By around A.D. 400, a series of specialized sites were established at the passes allowing access to the core zone near the

Fig. 12 Two standing male warriors with darts; Ameca-Etzatlán style; Jalisco; earthenware. Private collection. Cat. no. 136. Standardized themes and types appear in Late Formative styles. Warriors are among the most widespread, often shown with protective basketry armor and helmets, crouching with lances or batons held at the ready.

Fig. 13 Marriage pair; Ixtlán del Río style; Nayarit; earthenware. The Cleveland Museum of Art, gift of Clara Taplin Rankin. Cat. no. 191.

it was not until the following Teuchitlán I phase that villages in the less-defensible low-lying terrain were abandoned, leaving the hilltop sites the undisputed centers of activity in the pass.[14]

The extremely low densities of population in the adjacent Atemajac valley and the Atoyac-Sayula valleys would have made those regions incapable of providing defensive buffers for the core, and perhaps the hilltop sites suggest a strategy by the core to protect itself against outside aggressors.[15] But, in truth, there were no other major centers in western Mexico with the demographic clout necessary to form a realistic military threat. On the other hand, when similar patterns of boundary sites are found in ancient states, they tend to delimit the territory directly controlled by the central government. Within boundary sites, territory tends to be directly administered and sectors of the economy like agricultural production tend to be organized and directed from above. Outside the boundary, the state is still quite active and may exercise some authority over others, but it tends to be less dominant. Something similar seems to have been happening in the Teuchitlán tradition core by the Teuchitlán I phase, and we believe that the core had been unified into a single statelike organization.[16]

The delimitation of a boundary, and the population decline in adjacent valleys, does not mean that the Teuchitlán core was isolated from greater West Mexico. Sometime around A.D. 200, complex circular units began to be built in strategic locations, partly to continue to obtain scarce resources (through exchange with the developed societies there) and partly for the sake of communications. Reflecting their overall membership in the Teuchitlán tradition, circular buildings have been found in the Banderas valley, in the Río Bolaños gorge, near Guaynamota in Nayarit, and in the Bajío of Guanajuato.[17] One extraordinary ceremonial circle is also situated near Comala, Colima, along with several other circular buildings.[18] The largest of three circular buildings there measures approximately 120 meters in diameter.

These strategic sites seem to have been "outposts in the surrounding periphery," to use the phrase coined by Guillermo Algaze.[19] According to his analysis, these outposts are common in the early history of civilizations, reflecting the ability to protect the cultural power of the central development and to

Volcán de Tequila: Llano Grande and El Peñol de Santa Rosalia to the northwest, Cerro Pipiole to the west, Santa María de las Navajas and the more distant El Molino to the southeast, and the Tepopote sites to the east. Bugambilias, at the entrance to a particularly rugged pass through the Sierra la Primavera, is potentially a sixth example. Most of these sites are relatively small, in highly defensible locations, have good views of the passes where they appear, and possess one or more examples of the circular architecture in addition to residences, defensive walls, terraces, and other features. Clearly, they appear to have had some function relating to access to the core territory. The eastern pass, overseen by the Tepopote sites, is the best studied of these sites to date. Survey work here discovered that the hilltop sites were founded in the Ahualulco phase, but

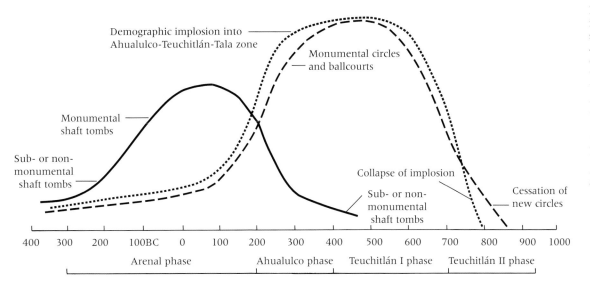

Fig. 16 Diagram showing demographic implosion in the Teuchitlán area. The construction of monumental shaft tombs culminated between 100 B.C. and A.D. 200. Their subsequent decline corresponds with the growth of large circular ritual precincts that include smaller tombs beneath platforms and pyramids. The elaborate sculptures and furnishings of the first monumental type of tombs also declined after A.D. 200–250. The shift from private family or lineage commemorative monuments to more inclusive public forms of ritual architecture suggests the need to incorporate diverse communities in an embracing civic order.

serve their expansionist economies. The direct control of the political systems of the core in regards to these outposts is not a requirement, since they are defined by their cultural affiliation and by their services to an economy dependent upon long-distance commerce and exchange. These remote circular sites cannot be understood in any other way.

As a direct consequence of the increase in demographic implosion in the general region of Teuchitlán, the nuclear area began to feel the strain on its natural resources. A preliminary study by Glenn Stuart of fossil pollen has demonstrated the possibility of a period of massive deforestation associated with the implosion of population that culminated in the Teuchitlán I phase (A.D. 400–700).[20] The climate became somewhat warmer, perhaps reflecting a lower level of water in the lakes and marshes within the core area. The closed canopy of pines and oaks, which had erased the botanical differences between the plant communities on the upper edge of the lakes and those of the hillsides, was replaced by a landscape of mesquite and acacia. This botanical process is obviously related to the sociocultural intensification within the same area. The human impact on the natural environment was severe.

The implosion of population and its resulting ecological transformation required some kind of strategy for increasing food production. The solution was to intensify agricultural production by building what appears to be an integrated system of terraces and *chinampas* (see fig. 21). The latter are quite regular and geometrical, and they give every appearance of having been planned and developed by the state. As examples of landscape engineering, the terraces and *chinampas* joined various sub-basins, diverted streams, and yielded more than thirty square kilometers of gardens. But even this estimate may represent only a fraction of the actual benefit of such cultivation, since the much more recent leveling of land to create sugarcane fields has destroyed all traces of earlier efforts in many areas.[21] Nonetheless, the potential yield of these *chinampa* fields must have been spectacular. And the contribution of open fields with terraces, which substantially improved other large areas within the core, must be added to the total agricultural productivity.

The cultural symbolism of these concentric architectural circles clearly constituted something very different from any other civilization in the Mesoamerican world during the Classic period, for such buildings simply did not exist elsewhere. There is no doubt that such concentric designs (along with the accompanying monumental ballcourts) represented a formal architectural setting (see figs. 17a, 17b, and 22). These sites may have served as focal points for the cult of a deity, such as, for example, Ehecatl, god of the wind, who has been identified with certain of the *volador* figurines.[22] Though many of them are found in the West, circular buildings in general are difficult to design and build. Furthermore, we must bear in mind that the definition of monumental architecture refers not just to a measure of volume, but also to the complexity of design. The concentric circles were certainly complex: in general, each structure is composed of a circular, terraced, and truncated altar or pyramid, which is surrounded by an elevated circular patio composed of very fine and clean fill. This patio is, in turn, surrounded by an elevated circular banquette, atop which are from four to sixteen square or rectangular platforms or small pyramids. Many of the most elegantly finished constructions, such as the Guachimontón complex at Teuchitlán, were also masonry buildings, made of stone and cement, which was made from a mixture of caliche, adobe clay, and volcanic ash. These masonry structures were able to reach very steep angles of construction. In light of their complexity of design and construction, these building must also be considered spectacular achievements.

In addition to the enormous obsidian workshops, such as the one explored by Soto de Arechavaleta near Teuchitlán, and others near San Juan de los Arcos and Huitzilapa, there is other evidence of regional specialization.[23] Salt from the Atoyac-Sayula valley seems to constitute another scarce resource that was being exploited on a massive scale (see the essay by Francisco Valdez in this volume).[24] But there are no other important architectural complexes from the Classic period in that area.[25] The levels of salt production firmly indicate that production was not just for local consumption. The only intense and well-organized sociopolitical system close to the area capable of consuming such large quantities of salt was the neighboring Teuchitlán valley. The acquisition of high-quality obsidian, the production of salt in enormous quantities, and the shell and pseudo-cloisonné craftsmanship (see figs. 18–20), among others, may have helped the formation of an economic basis for the political systems in the core zone.

To date, then, six circular compounds have been studied in depth through excavation: two in the Bolaños valley (see also the essay by Robert Pickering and Teresa Cabrero in this volume), one on the outskirts of Guadalajara, and three in Huitzilapa, where the area that has been excavated is greater than that of any other site in the high valleys of Jalisco.[26] In addition, there are other studies based on excavations at six other circular spaces. With these, and the hundreds of profiles of looted pits and trenches, we now have a preliminary understanding of how this society built its circles and ballcourts, when they were done, and what their cultural associations were.

The Landscape of the Teuchitlán Core
The landscape of the Teuchitlán tradition within the core was a remarkable achievement. Defined as large-scale organizations

Fig. 17a Unexcavated valley site at Santa Quiteria, districts of Arenal and Amatitlán, Jalisco. Maguey agave fields cover the main circular precinct and pyramid to the lower right. A creek-bed (now a ravine) ran through the middle of the settlement, with the long, narrow ballcourt immediately beyond.

Fig. 17b Plan of the Mesa Alta complex at Santa Quiteria. An unexcavated set of interlocking circular precincts and a ballcourt are placed high on the ridge to the left (north), overlooking the larger site in the valley below.

Fig. 18 Bowl with emblematic pseudo-cloisonné designs; Jalisco; earthenware. Private collection. Cat. no. 155.

Fig. 19 Bowl with emblematic pseudo-cloisonné designs; Jalisco; earthenware. Private collection. Cat. no. 156.

of man-made spaces, designed and created as elements of society, landscapes may be considered to be either vernacular or political, to use the terms of John Jackson.[27] A political landscape is made up of "spaces and structures designed for imposing or preserving unity and order within a territory, or for adjustments on a large-scale and long-term plan"; a vernacular landscape, on the other hand, is composed of spaces that are "usually small, irregular in form, subject to quick changes in use, property [and] dimensions."[28] During what we have termed the Teuchitlán

I phase of the Classic period, we are obviously dealing with a political landscape. It was also clear, from the start of our research, that the size of the residential zones within the core area was impressive.

A subsequent analysis by Michael Ohnersorgen and Mark Varien has refined this work, using our maps of settlements and residential systems.[29] Recognizing the unfinished state of our research and the difficulty of dating and evaluating residential units, we have conservatively estimated the population of the core zone of the Teuchitlán tradition at 40,000 people, in residential clusters that cover approximately 24,000 hectares.[30] Keeping in mind the levels of agricultural productivity that could be expected from the *chinampa* fields, this estimated number of inhabitants seems reasonable.

The study by Ohnersorgen and Varien strongly suggests that there were three levels of ceremonial buildings represented with formal architectural aspects within the residential zone. In view of the regional hierarchy that existed, this is sufficient evidence for proposing a state level of political and social organization in the core zone, or more accu-

Fig. 20a. Olla with a pseudo-cloisonné design; vicinity of Estanzuela; Jalisco; earthenware. American Museum of Natural History, New York.

Fig. 20b. Roll-out view of olla. The technique of pseudo-cloisonné involves incising a design into modeled clay and filling it with a colored slip in a manner akin to the popular art of lacquerware on gourds and trays in Michoacán. The repetitive, elaborately costumed ritual figures, dots, and other decorative motifs suggest the existence of a now-lost pictorial manuscript tradition.

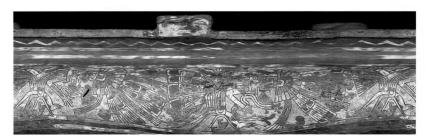

Fig. 21 In the small valley below the Guachimontón complex at Teuchitlán, large springs still supply irrigation ditches between raised fields. These raised fields and irrigation ditches are the remains of an ancient *chinampa* system now covered with sugarcane, but formerly cultivated intensively as horticultural plantations yielding several crops a year.

the presence of the core is marked by ceremonialism and ritual hegemony rather than by political force. Thus, there was clearly a ceremonial architectural hierarchy (including the circles and ballcourts), as well as associated residential areas within the living areas, and the probable organization of residential areas into boroughs.[31] Their research has also posited that the Guachimontón complex of Teuchitlán was clearly the first in importance within the complete system of settlements.

The question regarding the level of urbanization reached in the area of Teuchitlán remains unsolved, and though it seems clear that the processes of urbanization had already begun, we do not know up to which point there already was an urban society. This discussion depends greatly on the manner in which cities are defined. In early Mesoamerica, the system of settlements found in the Teuchitlán area—approximately 24 square kilometers of precincts and residential compounds, 30 square kilometers of *chinampas*,

rately, a segmentary state, as distinct from a territorial one. A segmentary state may be defined as a system that has a fairly compact core and an extensive hinterland wherein

Fig. 22 Reconstruction drawing of the Guachimontón complex at Teuchitlán, Jalisco.

THE GUACHIMONTON COMPLEX AT TEUCHITLAN

High on a bluff, the circular precincts of the Guachimontón complex at Teuchitlán command a westward view across a broad upland basin. Tons of earth and rock were moved to formalize a natural amphitheater and create terraced levels. Floors were made with packed earth and sand. Stone, adobe, and lime were used for the principal buildings. At the center of the largest precinct rises a tiered pyramid with four stairways at intercardinal directions. The small temple above would have been devoted to the cult of a founder-ancestor entombed below. Surrounding the circular floor a banquette supports a ring of platforms, each with a thatched houselike pavilion. These were probably devoted to ancestors of dominant lineages. To the right, a sacred spring supplied water for ritual gardens and related purposes.

A ballcourt runs between the two largest circles at this site (for a plan of the site, see Witmore, fig. 2). A smaller, third circle, interlocked with the second, stands beyond. Small pyramids were surmounted by poles used for *volador* performances as represented by a number of earthenware models (see Witmore, fig. 10). Lesser enclosures are seen to the right and left toward the edge of the bluff. Agricultural plantations cluster around the distant edge of the lake. Marshlands fill the rest of the basin.

The circular enclosures suggest restricted access and exclusive use by ruling families. These West Mexican circular precincts are unique, yet their geometry follows widely understood cosmological principles. Cardinal and intercardinal orientation; a vertical axis connecting the sky, the earth, and the underworld; the surrounding rim corresponding to the encompassing horizon; and sundial-like poles or tall structures that function as markers of the solstitial and equinoctial positions of the sun are motifs shared by all Mesoamerican peoples. In the circular architectural microcosms, theocratic rulers of Teuchitlán conducted a program of cyclic ritual festivals, invoking ancestral spirits as intermediaries to the deified natural forces upon which crops and life depended. Economy, history, and religion were bound in this perception and use of the landscape.

and 300 square kilometers of open terraced fields—appear to be closer to the multicentered (polynuclear) urban experience of the Classic-period Maya, than to such mononuclear urban sites as Teotihuacan.[32] As other historians of the urban phenomenon such as Lewis Mumford have pointed out, however, the highly centralized and mononuclear format is not the only one that can exist.[33] Equally early and perhaps more numerous in pre-Hispanic Mesoamerica were the "green cities," the open, seminuclear cities with a demographic density of close to 800 people per square kilometer. Logically, it would be incorrect to use an exceptional example of urban form, such as Teotihuacan with its density of almost 2,000 people per square kilometer, to characterize every experiment in urbanization in Mesoamerica. The most populated areas within the residential zone of Teuchitlán probably held no more than 700 per square kilometer. The enormous residential area of Teuchitlán, seen as an area with clear hallmarks of urbanization, appears to have evolved toward a type of multicore city in the form of a network or grid of interrelated units.

The Collapse of the Teuchitlán Tradition

By the years A.D. 700 to 900—the phase we call Teuchitlán II—the great residential zone of the Ahualulco–Teuchitlán–Tala valley was beginning to disintegrate. Few circular compounds were being built during this phase, although some were moderately remodeled. Certain variations in the circular architecture are evident: the alignment of the platforms on the banquette frequently changed the symmetry and balance of the older circles. The relocation of the platforms toward the back side of the interior banquette in order to emphasize their size, and other similar variations are common during the Teuchitlán II phase. But above all, the creation of new compounds built next to the residential zone with no circular architecture whatsoever, with only different types of square and rectangular buildings, is most striking. This difference in architecture no doubt reveals that dramatic sociocultural changes were taking place within the core area.

Obviously, the changes that took place within the marshy districts between A.D. 700 and 900 were not unique, but were felt in all Mesoamerica, from the collapse of Classic-period Maya civilization, to the growth of cultural complexity within the Hohokam and Anasazi areas. These changes were profound and often revolutionary. The fact that all Mesoamerica experienced changes within approximately the same time frame, however, does not explain the specific characteristics of the collapse and reorganization in a particular area such as that of West Mexico.

Perhaps the changes in relations for obtaining and exchanging resources or products played an important role in the transition. We know, for example, that metallurgy was beginning to emerge during this Teuchitlán II phase, although it was not popular until sometime after A.D. 900–1000.[34] Looters found little copper in burials belonging to this phase, but the appearance of metallurgy per se undoubtedly introduced entirely new demands on the systems for obtaining scarce resources, and on the distribution networks, to be able to include these new goods. Thus, we might hypothesize that when metals were introduced into the acquisition/distribution equation, the Teuchitlán tradition was not prepared to adapt to the new circumstances, and could have been eclipsed by more flexible societies that were better situated for exploiting the new situation created by the popularity of metal objects.

Whatever actually happened, the core of civilization in ancient West Mexico moved out of the western lake districts, and did not return until the flowering of Guadalajara in the Colonial and modern periods. The activities and traits that had characterized the core Teuchitlán area—monumental architecture, large settlement areas, irrigation systems, high demographic implosion, craft specialization, and more—came to a conclusion in the Volcán de Tequila region. Eventually, a core re-emerged in the eastern lake districts during the Late Postclassic period. The rise of the Tarascan state and empire chronicles this transformation.[35] That expansive and aggressive state played a major role in the cultural histories and social developments that took place in the core of the defunct Teuchitlán tradition from the fourteenth century until the arrival of Europeans.

LORENZA LOPEZ MESTAS CAMBEROS
AND JORGE RAMOS DE LA VEGA

EXCAVATING THE TOMB AT HUITZILAPA

Introduction

West Mexico has long been recognized as a region of shaft tombs and beautiful ceramic sculptures—both of which were manifestations of a reverence of ancestors and a belief in the afterlife. Today, these traits, among many others, are recognized as characteristic of the cultural development of this region during the period from 300 B.C. to A.D. 400 (generally identified as the Late Formative and Early Classic eras). Recent studies have brought to light evidence of complex social systems that found expression through elaborate architectural constructions and ritual practices linked to the shaft tombs, the sculptures, and related offerings. In the pre-Hispanic era, the cult of ancestors represented one of the most important and most fundamental cultural principles for many different Mesoamerican peoples. Various practices reflect a widely shared framework of ideas that are directly related to the experience of death, particularly as the passage into the afterlife was imagined in the collective beliefs of these ancient societies and formed part of their larger vision of the order of the world. Such ideas were deeply rooted in the Mesoamerican tradition and were intricately bound up with the concept of time in their universe. They formed a common creed that was profoundly experienced by all the peoples of early Mesoamerica.

The custom of worshipping ancestors was, of course, the outcome of the long experience of nomadic hunting-and-gathering groups who transmitted to later and more sedentary agricultural peoples an extremely acute understanding of the cycles of nature.

Shaped by an awareness of eternal renewal, their own mythic view of the world gradually evolved, and ritual became increasingly more complex, more sophisticated, and charged with multiple meanings. Within the broad historical development of pre-Hispanic Mexico, therefore, the custom of creating shaft tombs should be understood as a well-defined stage, part of the evolution of concepts and practices concerning death and its meaning. The shaft tomb that was discovered at Huitzilapa in 1993—and that we have been studying for the past five years—provides an excellent opportunity to analyze these funerary beliefs and rituals and consider how they correspond to the social order and complexity of the groups that practiced them.

Cultural Context

The Magdalena basin of upland Jalisco—the intermontane valley in which the Huitzilapa site is located—produced one of the most significant cultural developments of western Mesoamerica: the evolution of a unique architectural form of circular ceremonial centers, one of the hallmarks of a culture that has been given the name the Teuchitlán tradition (see the essay by Phil C. Weigand and Christopher Beekman in this volume). The development of this tradition covered an extensive territory, gradually bringing together other neighboring regions with its core area, which closely circumscribed the now-extinct Volcán de Tequila (fig. 2).

Although this tradition persisted for a long time, it had its beginnings in the Middle Formative period (800–300 B.C.), when the

Fig. 1 Partial view of the burials in the north chamber of the shaft tomb in Huitzilapa, Jalisco. Approximately 2,000 years ago, members of a powerful lineage were interred with rich offerings of foods, ceramic figures, shell jewelry, and textiles as testimony of their status and religious functions.

53

Fig. 2 Rows of maguey agave cactus cover the fields of Huitzilapa, below the Volcán de Tequila.

first architectural manifestations of permanent settlements appeared (see the chronological chart on p. 10). The Arenal phase (300 B.C.–A.D. 200, the last portion of the Late Formative period) marked the formation of a widespread settlement pattern and witnessed the evolution of a cruciform architectural plan that can be observed in its application to both residential settlements and ceremonial sites. During this same time, the common practice of creating shaft tombs achieved a monumental form at Huitzilapa and related sites. Subsequently, the Ahualulco phase (A.D. 200–400, the first phase of the Classic period) can be understood as an important stage of transition, in which the spatial and architectural format of the Arenal phase became modified by a process that produced a new, circular form, as more units were added to the basic cruciform plan. It has also been observed that, during this phase, the practice of interment in shaft tombs apparently declined, with the spaces devoted to these ritual burial practices becoming less elaborate in size and monumen-

tality. This, in brief, is the context in which this essay will examine what we have found at Huitzilapa.

Archaeological examination of the ancient settlements that have been identified in the valley of Huitzilapa confirm that they are directly related to the Arenal phase (300 B.C.–A.D. 200). This bit of chronology is important to keep in mind, since during this period the center or nucleus of the Teuchitlán tradition was restricted to the central area of Jalisco (see Weigand, fig. 3). This nuclear zone has been mainly identified by a spatial and architectural analysis of early settlements, by examination of the largest known shaft tombs, and by concrete evidence of ballcourts as a concurring element that had a parallel development at these sites.[1] Two of these elements—large shaft tombs and ballcourts—have not been reported in areas surrounding the nuclear zone in combination with the circular ensembles. Within the nuclear zone, at a micro-regional level in the valley of Huitzilapa, a series of settlements with different characteristics and functions clearly became established. It is even possible to recognize a hierarchy of such sites based on their size and location within this small geographical area (see fig. 3).

Certain of these differences can be traced to the relationship between settlements and available economic resources, since there were, for example, places of agricultural production such as the site of El Tezontle located within an area of medium-sized terraces. There are also other locations where the mining of obsidian deposits and the manufacturing of obsidian utensils took place, such as the site at La Mina and its associated dwellings in nearby El Zapote. North of the Huitzilapa valley, the sites of La Robleda, El Lienzo, and Los Soles are believed to be dwellings closely linked to the center, located at the main site of Huitzilapa itself. These lesser settlements were made up of residential clusters with a ballcourt, but they are noticeably smaller than the main Huitzilapa settlement. They should, therefore, be understood as peripheral residential units.

Although the sites in the valley of Huitzilapa all developed between 300 B.C. and A.D. 400—spanning the final part of the Formative period and the beginning of the Classic period—and although in neighboring areas around the Volcán de Tequila during this same time the consolidation of the six principal areas of concentrated settlement making up the Teuchitlán tradition took place, development in the Huitzilapa valley itself does not appear to have been sustained through later phases. It is probable that the Huitzilapa valley settlements were abandoned as early as A.D. 400. This contrasts with the evolution of such major sites as Ahualulco, Santa Quiteria, and Teuchitlán (see Weigand and Beekman, figs. 17a, b and 22), which consolidated and lasted until the final decline of the tradition around A.D. 900. The decline of Huitzilapa coincides with the strengthening of other sites in the Teuchitlán area during the period from A.D. 400 to 900 (identified as Teuchitlán I and II phases). Thus, the development of Huitzilapa appears to correspond to an early stage when the Teuchitlán tradition was beginning to establish its specific characteristics.

The Huitzilapa site presents a series of architectural units that demonstrate the formation and evolution of a settlement that lasted approximately three centuries, from

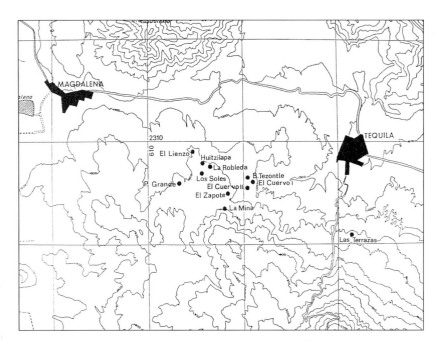

roughly the beginning of this millennium to about A.D. 300. This chronology has been confirmed by radiocarbon dating obtained on samples from the tomb and from other structures at this settlement. During this time the site was formed by the construction of residential units arranged in a basic, cruciform plan (see fig. 4). A limited number of variations or modifications also took place, as can be seen in the circular units and other types of compounds made up of enclosed structures arranged around square courtyards or patios. During this time, as well, the ballcourt was constructed on the southeastern part of the site.

Just as a hierarchy existed between Huitzilapa and its lesser neighbors, so too a hierarchical arrangement can also be seen within the site itself. Upon observing the size of the platforms that composed the residential units and the area that they occupied, we found that the largest units were represented by (1) unit F-4, where the shaft tomb was found; (2) units F-5 and F-1, which exhibit a variation in the square central altar; and (3) the circular unit (A). Distinctly different from these are a series of small residential clusters spread along the length of the slope and at natural levels leading down to the floor of the valley. The small site of Huitzilapa must therefore be considered as the principal civic and ceremonial settlement within the valley, in sharp contrast to other minor settlements. This site represented the focus of political and economic control of the

Fig. 3 Archaeological sites of the Huitzilapa community, between the towns of Magdalena and Tequila, on the lower slopes of the Volcán de Tequila.

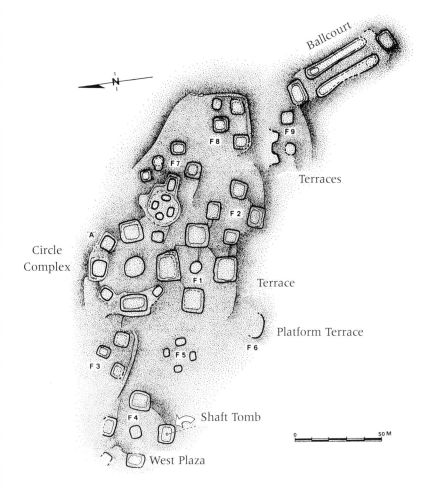

Ballcourt

Terraces

Circle
Complex

F8

F9

F7

F2

A

F1

Terrace

Platform Terrace

F 6

F 5

F3

F4

Shaft Tomb

0   50 M

West Plaza

Fig. 4 Plan of the Hui-
tzilapa site showing the
ballcourt above, the
large ceremonial circle
adjoining the cruciform
platform plaza F-1, and
the smaller west plaza
F-4 where the shaft
tomb is located. The
joining of circles found
at A and F-1 is also seen
in larger scale at the
Guachimontón complex
at Teuchitlán.

area during the Late Formative period within
this sector of the core area of the Teuchitlán
tradition.

Hierarchy and Status

The results obtained from the studies carried
out in this area of West Mexico, together
with those we have conducted in the valley
of Huitzilapa, lead us to believe that the communities that arose around the lake basins
by the Volcán de Tequila between 300 B.C.
and A.D. 200 were in a state of development
that may be called hierarchical societies or
chiefdoms (to use terms in standard archaeological nomenclature). From the point of
view of some investigators, chiefdoms are
understood as societies that tend toward centralization, supported by a political configuration that is well defined, though nevertheless
different from that of a statelike society. In
a chiefdom, the central position is principally
held by means of kinship and political and
religious prestige. Another distinguishing
characteristic of chiefdoms is the absence of
social classes, though there may well be hierarchical strata that are based on personal
status, ritual power, and sumptuary rules.[2]

From an archaeological point of view, the
term chiefdom is applied when there is sufficient evidence of rank: when, for example,
one can identify the existence of contemporaneous sites that are of different size and
architectural complexity; coincident with
this evidence of differentiation in the architectonic units within a given site, one recog-
nizes a chiefdom in the differentiation of
elements present in funerary events, such
as the types of materials, or the quality and
quantity of objects offered.[3]

This process of hierarchical development
at a local level is found among the agricultural communities around the Jalisco lake-
basin region, as they slowly developed their
subsistence base and intensified the diversifi-
cation of their activities. Traces of increasing
complexity can be recognized if one compares the differences between various settlements. The more important communities,
for example, stood out not only because of
their size, as is the case with Huitzilapa, but
also because they contained buildings of a
distinctly ceremonial and political character.
At this time, the division of labor would
have meant that some were occupied in obtaining food, others in producing crafts, as
we can see from the development and specialization in manufacturing obsidian instruments. These important characteristics,
together with other parallel activities, indicate the growing distinction between manual
and intellectual labor.

At least two types of settlements have
been noted as important indicators of Late
Formative–period development: architectural
units arranged in circles that derived from
the earlier cross-shaped pattern with another
element rising in the center; and small, seminuclear plaza units that could have been
seasonal hamlets. In addition to these we
can include two types of ballcourts and the
presence of shaft tombs. The addition of ballcourts and shaft tombs seems to coincide
with the emergence of social hierarchies.
Having considered all of these indicators, we
determined that the upland lake-basin zone
of Jalisco had developed a series of socially
stratified, complex societies.[4] The region of
the valley of Huitzilapa participated in this
development. In this area there is a clear
relation between the pattern of settlements
and the lacustrine resources of the Magdalena
lagoon, where high-yield agricultural systems
appear to have been established.

As archaeologists have frequently observed, agriculture tends to stimulate a sedentary society and allow for the development of new work processes, which in turn produce diversified, and in some cases, specialized goods. This phenomenon at the same time brings about changes within the society, strengthening community links within a region. As is the case with all social processes based on an agricultural economy, a relationship becomes established among culturally related communities that share the same territory—and such was certainly the case in the nuclear area of the Teuchitlán tradition. Under these very conditions, and as a result of the degree of development of the communities settled in the Huitzilapa area, it is certain that one group obtained a more efficient control over certain elements of production. This, in turn, permitted the creation of hierarchical links of dependence among the units within the valley, giving the controlling group greater political power and social prestige. Thus, the communities that had greater possibilities for development were those represented by larger sites, such as Huitzilapa and El Zapote.

By adding architectural information to the data available on settlement patterns, together with the practice of a distinctive funerary tradition as important as that of the shaft tombs, one obtains a much clearer general picture regarding the diverse development with the area and the various levels of settlements. Furthermore, this information helps us understand the interaction of settlements within the different areas of development in the northern lake-basin district.[5]

The Cross-Shaped Residential Units

One way of identifying the ranking or differentiation among the various sectors that constitute a settlement is to start by identifying the cross-shaped residential and domestic ensembles as key elements for analysis. This is where basic production activities and the processes of social reproduction may be inferred, thus enabling us to distinguish the possible functions of their habitations. Within the Teuchitlán tradition, we believe that the residential units, which were part of the cruciform and circular ensembles, followed specific criteria in terms of their spatial arrangement. As we shall see, they were planned according to cosmological principles widespread in Mesoamerica (see also the essay by Christopher Witmore in this volume). This type of layout is fundamental in understanding the character of different areas of activity.

Stylistic studies of these architectural ensembles, as represented by a number of earthenware models that have been found in shaft tombs in the region of Ixtlán del Río, Nayarit, have documented a wide range of activities related to them (see Townsend, fig. 2, and Witmore, fig. 1). The detailed analysis of them conducted by Hasso von Winning identified various forms of labor, domestic tasks, and ritual customs and practices, among other activities.[6] These observations help us recognize and understand the way of life of these communities.

As mentioned above, unit F-4 on the western edge of the Huitzilapa settlement appears from our surveys and excavations to have been one of the main units of the settlement as compared with the other dwelling groups in Huitzilapa. This unit has certain distinguishing characteristics, such as the separation of interior and exterior spaces by means of enclosing walls, which join the front corners of the structures (see fig. 5). These features, and the fact that it was here beneath the southern structure that the shaft tomb was discovered, establish a spatial hierarchy in regards to the other cross-shaped ensembles. It is important to point out that this was the only shaft tomb found within the Huitzilapa settlement, and that it is isolated from the larger community burial grounds. In regard to the question of status and social hierarchy, this evidence indicates that the architectural units composing the western plaza served as the seat of a specific group or sector of the community, which controlled access to the plaza in the middle of the cruciform arrangement. At the same time, the relatively large size of this inner plaza suggests that specific activities, possibly of a political and administrative type or related to special ceremonies, might have been carried out at times when the entire community would assemble, perhaps in order to strengthen its reciprocal communal ties or exercise its collective conscience. All of this would have taken place under the leadership of a specific social group in charge of such activities.

From this perspective, then, the southern structure of the western plaza could be understood as a temple-like place, a sacred

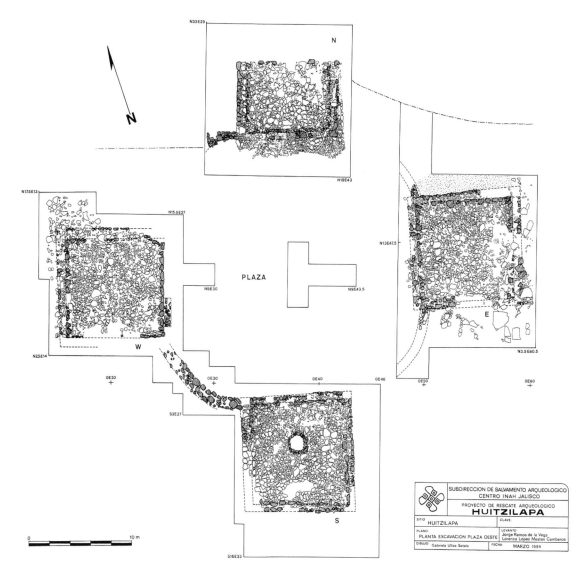

location within the ensemble, a place for contact with the forces of the universe.[7] It was at this temple that an opening was made within the homogeneity of ordinary space, allowing a transition from the profane to the sacred zones above and below, "a link with the three levels of the universe: heaven, earth and the underworld."[8]

The Tomb

The identification of features denoting differences in social status within the community was confirmed by our analysis of the shaft tomb that was unearthed in 1993. This tomb is large in respect to both the depth of its shaft and the size of its chambers. At present, it is acknowledged as the only shaft tomb with these characteristics that has been scientifically studied in detail in West Mexico. The tomb is located beneath the center of the southern structure of unit F-4, with a shaft

7.6 meters deep, excavated through compact volcanic tuff, and leading to two burial chambers (see figs. 1, 6, and 7). The chambers are aligned on a north-south axis. Each chamber held three individuals buried with rich offerings. The burial of a figure we have labeled N1, a male approximately forty-five years old, in the northern chamber, is the most outstanding in its lavish adornment and offerings. Given the nature of these characteristics, we have inferred that the construction of the chamber and the significance of the funeral event itself were dedicated to this individual.

The studies performed on the skeletal remains in the tomb have provided us with information regarding their sex, certain pathologies and traumas they experienced, and other data related to the development of an elaborate funerary treatment of the bodies. The results obtained from the osteo-

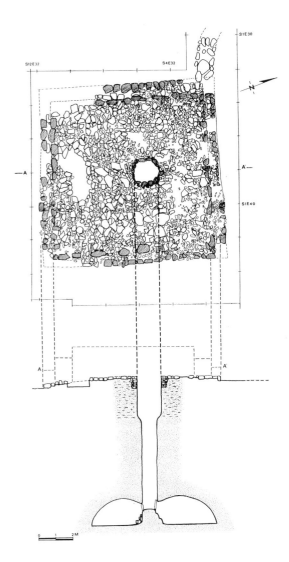

logical analysis have revealed a congenital hereditary defect known as Klippel–Feil syndrome (a fusion of the cervical vertebrae), found in five of the six skeletons. This remarkable information provides evidence of a first degree of blood kinship, and convincingly demonstrates that the tomb was a crypt ·for a group of relatives or members of a specific lineage.[9] Thus, this information proves the inference previously made by other researchers, that certain social spaces defined by architectural units of a residential type corresponded to family units for specific lineages in West Mexico.[10] It should be noted, of course, that this relationship occurs only in special cases, since no other dwellings in Huitzilapa contain funerary chambers under the platforms, lending a mark of exclusivity to the tomb beneath the southern structure of the western plaza.

Another aspect that lends importance to a funerary event governed by consanguinity is the fact that in the type of society we believe existed at Huitzilapa, the social role of an individual—within a regime of communal property—was defined by blood relationship; thus, any particular relationships that may be related to cooperation with other members of a society or to an individual's rights and duties, are determined in a very specific way (i.e., by family relationship), and by social relationships connected with

Fig. 6 Plan and cross-section drawing showing the two-chambered shaft-tomb in relation to the platform in the west plaza F-4 at Huitzilapa.

Fig. 7 The north chamber seen from the shaft entrance. Vessels and figures were originally placed upright around the perimeter of the chamber, but they have since moved or toppled over because of earthquakes.

Fig. 8 Plan of the burials and offerings in the north and south chambers. The shaft is at center. The principal burial figure in the Huitzilapa tomb (figure N1), a male approximately forty-five years of age, shows evidence of a congenital deformity of the neck vertebrae. He was elaborately adorned with jade and shell bracelets, noserings, earrings, greenstone beads, carved jade pendants, and a cloth sewn with shell beads in the thousands. Ornamented conch shells were placed on his loins and at his sides, along with atlatl hooks.

Figure N2, probably a male aged thirty to forty, also wore beaded shell necklaces and other jewelry, and held atlatl hooks in his right hand. Figure N3 was a female at least fifty years of age. Spindle whorls, used in the production of textiles, were placed near her right hand and at the side of her left foot. Earthenware bowls, plates, and cinctured vessels once laden with food offerings lie to her left and at her feet, along with six Arenal-style earthenware sculptures that form part of this offering.

In the south chamber, figure S1, a male approximately forty years of age, was ornamented with noserings, earrings, and necklaces of shell; atlatl hooks were placed in his right hand and a conch shell was positioned upon his pelvis. A female thirty to forty years old (figure S2) was placed upon two metates (rectangular grinding stones) and a semicircular stone in between. She was adorned with simple pendants and shell jewelry. The disarticulated skeleton of this figure and that of a young male approximately sixteen to twenty years of age (figure S3) indicate that they were secondary burials.

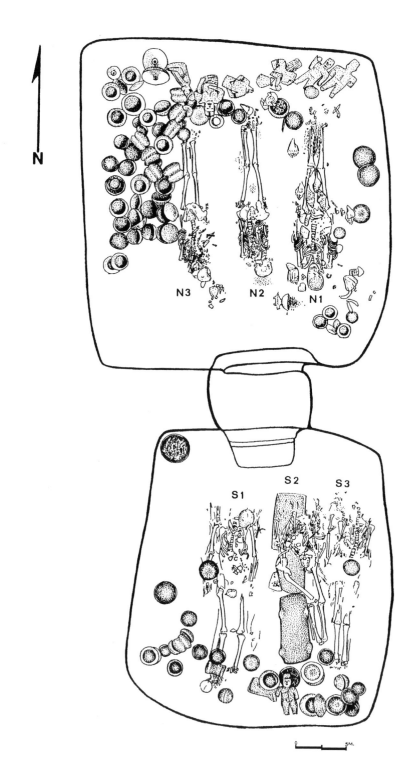

production of certain goods.[11] Now, having identified the existence of family descent groups as essential parts of the inherent social structure, we are able not only to study the possible place they physically occupied within a socioeconomic order, but also to define their status in relation to authority and the exercise of power. What we have discovered in the Huitzilapa tomb will allow us to carry this proposal as far as is possible, given the archaeological evidence necessary to infer types of possible functions and the social status of the deceased.

Naturally, we pay particular attention to lineage since ethnographically it has been recognized that, second only to the domestic family group, lineage is the corporate group that defines relationships regarding cooperation and communal participation with a direct representative. This accords with the well-accepted notion that lineage is identified with descent from a common ancestor historically immediate or with a much older ancestral affiliation that is related to a mythical personage or divinity (possibly even a creator god).[12] This phenomenon permits us to understand why there may exist some lineages that are more important than others, and why they may exercise ideological control, as well as material and economic control, on the rest of society.[13]

In archaeology we frequently speak of social differentiation on the basis of information obtained from burials. In this case, we have been able to identify from the tomb the different use of goods as an example of hierarchy—this in turn enables us to speak of a particular type of social order: the chiefdom. The quantity and quality of the offerings demonstrate quite clearly a distinctive consumption of goods, which tells us something of the importance and social position of the individuals buried there. The tomb at Huitzilapa offers a specific example of social stratification within lineages, as shown by the differences in the burial treatment given to the members of this family group. The number of objects found in the north chamber that are related to the principal figure (N1) confirms the hierarchy. Numerous ceramic pieces; sculptural human figures of very high quality; the presence of quartz, slate, obsidian, and exotic materials such as shell and greenstone—all well represented in the mortuary context—serve to corroborate this inference (see figs. 8 and 9).

In other areas of Mesoamerica at Formative-period sites, the types of luxurious objects found in the Huitzilapa tomb have been understood by scholars to assume a symbolic function, denoting their restricted distribution for a specific social group.[14] Furthermore, these objects are associated with the political and religious activities carried out by the members of the dominant sector of society. They are objects requiring a great deal of craftsmanship with precious raw materials not readily available in the area. In Huitzilapa, for example, there are objects manufactured from shell imported from both the Pacific and the Caribbean (see fig. 10), while the greenstone probably came from areas that are now part of the state of Guerrero. Similar sumptuary goods from looted tombs elsewhere in the Teuchitlán area and neighboring districts underscore the long-distance trade network and widespread use of such exotic materials by the ruling elite

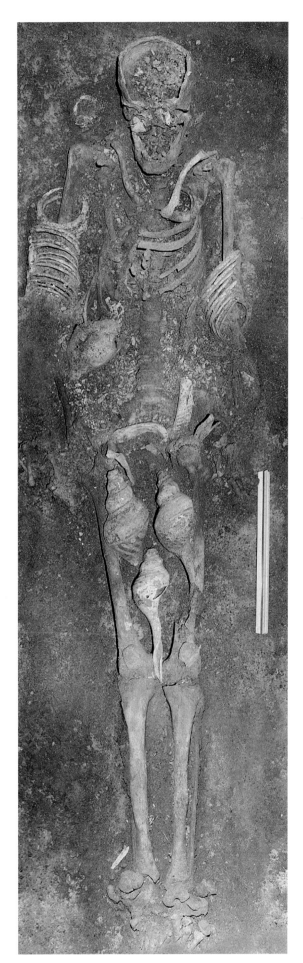

Fig. 9 In the north chamber of the Huitzilapa tomb, remains of the chieftain are shown in the process of archaeological excavation. Note the multiple shell bracelets. The placement of decorated conch shells underscores the religious obligations of rulers and ancestors in promoting and maintaining the natural cycle of fertility.

(see figs. 11–13). Thus, after considering all
of the available evidence and the hypothesis
that correlates space and monumental architectural units with residence and/or the exercise of duties and status by members of the
elite social sector, we confidently assert that
Huitzilapa controlled the series of sites in this
valley.

Ideology and Mortuary Ritual

The discovery of the Huitzilapa tomb offers
an opportunity to explore another important
aspect of ancient West Mexican societies: specifically, their ideological domain, which has
received scant attention, except for the iconographic studies carried out by Peter Furst.[15]
This is true in spite of the fact that the mortuary practices related to the shaft tombs
appear to follow a consistent pattern whose
elements reflect, among other features of the
sociocultural system, the world view of the
peoples who shared this tradition. The tomb
provides plenty of evidence directly related
to mortuary practices, although the lack of
scientific data obtained from other tombs de-
prives us of valuable confirmation. Therefore,
to provide an interpretation based in part

upon a hypothesis, we will make use of ethnological analogies as a tool for analysis. Various authors have expressed their opinion regarding the theoretical validity of such analogies in the case of Mesoamerica, especially in regard to the interpretation of ideological and iconographic systems of the earliest periods before Spanish contact.[16] Methodologically, the use of historical and ethnological analogies is deemed appropriate because Mesoamerica became an area with a common tradition, with a basic religious and cultural unity expressed through shared beliefs and symbolism.[17] This fact leads us to believe that signs and symbols in use by different Mesoamerican groups could have relatively similar meanings, expressed through the particular forms of each region and the specifically historical circumstances of diverse peoples. Therefore, in the analysis presented in regard to this tomb, we will continually make use of other Mesoamerican examples, taking into account the historical moment under study and setting aside any notion of the supposedly marginal significance of West Mexico within the larger Mesoamerican tradition.

First of all, we observe two levels of meaning in analyzing this tomb. The more obvious level concerns the importance attached to the funerary event. We recognize a pattern of ancestor worship, "where the deceased were given a special place from where they could observe or maintain a link with their descendants."[18] Clearly, sustaining a strong link between the living and the dead was critical in this society. In fact, the cult of ancestors, and of the dead in general, has been present in different regions and periods throughout Mesoamerica. It is therefore not strange to find it in West Mexico. The cult of the dead implies the belief that a soul survived corporeal death and that it continued to live, inhabiting other worlds or regions. It also implies the possibility of maintaining a close relationship between the living and the souls of the dead.

As part of their effort to sustain their relationship, the relatives of the deceased offered him or her a series of objects that would assure his survival and comfort in the afterlife, allowing him to enjoy a life similar to the one he had had in this world. In Huitzilapa, evidence of a cult of the dead and a corresponding belief in life after death is supported by the large number of food offerings in ceramic vessels (see fig. 7). By means of this food, the relatives contributed to the continuity of the deceased soul's experience in the underworld, reproducing the material conditions of life on earth. This custom, as mentioned above, replicated the riches and power that the deceased held in this life. This custom also demonstrates why differences in mortuary treatment were consistent with the social position the deceased held within a community.[19]

Such practices appear to have lasted throughout time. If we examine various documented sources from the sixteenth century, numerous descriptions can be found of rituals that prepared the dead for their journey to their next place of dwelling. Among the Tarascans, for example, great importance was given to the burial of rulers, as shown in the following passage from the *Relación de Michoacán:*

> First all the masters present would very diligently bathe him, and the old servants and all who were to follow him would be bathed. And they would dress him in

Fig. 13 Figurine pendant; Colima; jade. Private collection. Cat. no. 11. Jade or greenstone figurines and items of jewelry are found in elite burials throughout Mexico. This figurine, not from Huitzilapa, shows stylistic connections to other stonework from Colima.

the following manner: next to his body they would place a very thin under shirt like the ones used by the masters, and some leather protectors. On his neck, they would place white fish bones, very precious among them; on his legs, golden bells; on his wrists, turquoise gems, and a braid of feathers, and some turquoise necklaces on his neck, and large golden spools on his ears; two golden bracelets on his arms, and a large turquoise ring on his lips. And a very high bed would be prepared for him with many multi-colored coarse cotton cloths; and these cloths would be placed over wide boards; and they would place him on top and would tie him with braids.[20]

The importance of certain members of the community was accentuated, in some cases, by sacrificing servants and relatives who would continue to serve their master in the afterlife. Fray Diego Durán offered the following description of the Aztecs:

> [I]n the case of a ruler or the master of a village, after his death, he would be presented offerings of slaves who were killed to accompany him on his journey and serve him and the women who had ground the corn were also killed to accompany him and supply him with bread for the other world.[21]

Fig. 14 Detail from the *Codex Magliabechiano* depicting a funerary bundle; Aztec; 16th century. Biblioteca Nazionale Centrale di Firenze.

About 1,500 years earlier at Huitzilapa, we find a multiple burial with family members of a chieftain of high status. All five of the other bodies were deposited in different states of desiccation, indicating that they had died before the main individual was interred, and that their remains were preserved and prepared in order to be placed in the tomb later, probably wrapped in straw mats as funerary bundles. Thus far we have uncovered no evidence that indicates any practice of human sacrifice, though it is clear that bodies were preserved to be deposited inside the tomb upon the death of the main individual (N1), during a unique event that led, in addition to the physical preparation of the bodies and the preparation of different offerings, to the carrying out of rituals, implying that the shaft remained opened during a prolonged period of time.[22] The earthenware models from Ixtlán del Río offer examples of funeral processions, indicating that such rites of passage were celebrated by these peoples (see Townsend, figs. 38 and 39).[23]

In various pictorial manuscripts and illustrated ethnohistorical texts pertaining to the Aztecs, such as the Florentine and Magliabechiano codices of the sixteenth century, we can also observe the preparation of funerary bundles in which different offerings were included (see fig. 14). The custom of preparing the dead in reed mats or bundles seems to have lasted for a very long time. For example, in the Huitzilapa tomb, dated A.D. 65, the deceased were wrapped in *otate* (bamboo) mats together with lavish ornaments, and their arms and legs were tied with strings of shells. These funerary bundles might have been decorated with paper, as the rolled-up bark paper found over the head of the principal figure (N1) suggests. Fray Bernardino de Sahagún's account, written in the sixteenth century, also addressed this traditional custom:

> [T]hen the elderly and the officials in charge of cutting up paper, would cut up and adorn and tie the papers in their custody for the deceased and after having made and prepared the papers, they would take the deceased and fold his legs and dress him with the papers and tie him . . . and put him in the shroud and thus they would prepare the deceased with their cloths and papers, and tie him firmly.[24]

Upon further reflection on the elements present in the tomb, it is also possible to recognize a strong symbolic meaning related to basic ideological and religious concepts in the Mesoamerican tradition. Richard Townsend and Alfredo López Austin, for example, have recognized that there was in Mesoamerica an original group of ideas with a common underlying structure that was deeply rooted in time.[25] These ideas were defined throughout the long history of Mesoamerican cultural development and served as a basis for the complex relationships among pre-Hispanic groups. It is possible then to go back in time and search for these common ideas since it is the symbolic traditions that change most slowly. We can make comparisons with other later examples in the Mesoamerican area, even though political and economic structures suffered considerable transformation, because certain ideological concepts remained stable. This essay, accepting this assumption, proposes a symbolic interpretation of the Huitzilapa tomb and its offerings that goes beyond the cult of the ancestors as such.

One of the main elements of the Mesoamerican worldview was the geometric division of the universe. This concept appeared in different regions during the Formative period and lasted through the Classic and Postclassic times. For some, such as the Nahuatl and Maya, the horizontal division of terrestrial space into the four cardinal points was an outstanding feature. The center was considered a sacred area, the place where communication among the earth, heaven, and the underworld occurred; that is, the point where all parts of creation converged.[26]

If we observe the four-sided, cruciform pattern that appears in the residential units of the Middle to Late Formative period in the Teuchitlán tradition, such as that represented by the different units on the western plaza, we can see that they shared the main cosmological principle of spatial geometry with other Mesoamerican cultures. If we then transfer these basic principles to the western plaza where the tomb is located, the architectural unit takes on the form of a cosmogram with its four sides horizontally directed toward the four cardinal points, and a central altar that expresses the vertical axis connecting the earth, heaven, and the underworld. Thus, this space on earth is transformed into a replica of the sacred order that governs the universe: in other words, a cosmic archetype.[27]

On the other hand, it is interesting to observe that the western plaza taken as a whole presents a deviation of approximately 17° from true north with respect to the east. This orientation is shared by various ceremonial centers whose dates range from 500 B.C. to A.D. 1500.[28] It is probable that the buildings that conform to these orientations were locations from which one could observe astronomical phenomena relating to the position of the sun, the Pleiades, and Venus, especially as their movements coincided with the beginning and end of the rainy season.[29] Such features stress the importance of astronomical knowledge in concert with ceremonies and rituals that were dedicated toward propitiating the forces controlling fertility—a concept shared by many societies based mainly on an agricultural economy.

Thus, agricultural fertility is a basic concern manifested in the Huitzilapa tomb. The burials, the offerings, and the tomb itself closely reflect a dual concept of the universe, with the cycle of fertility, life, death, and renewal in which the earth was considered a devourer of people, stars, and seeds, which fall into the underworld to be born again and there undergo a transformation.[30] Shaft tombs were, in fact, the archetype of the underworld, where people were placed in order to be later transformed. The tombs were like caves, considered throughout Mesoamerica as entrances to the sacred dimension, the place of descent into the earth monster.[31] This belief in the cave as an entrance and a means of communication with the supernatural world has been found from very early periods. It seems to have been present in sculptured Olmec altars of the early first millennium B.C., where the niche in which great chieftains or kings were seated was envisioned as a cave.[32] In the cosmic vision of the Nahuatls, the underworld (Mictlán) corresponded not to

> a specific place, but to a dark area underneath the earth, stretching from North to South and limited by the East and West at the solstitial points, being the kingdom of darkness and death.[33]

In West Mexico, there is a marked pattern of north-south orientation for tombs with one or two chambers.[34] This is the case at Huitzilapa as well. Such consistent directional layouts express cosmological concerns intimately connected with the orientation of the site. Furthermore, the underground chambers reproduce that dark space described in the Nahuatl accounts of *Mictlán* as "the place of descent," "the place with no way out and without openings."[35] Both burial chambers of the Huitzilapa tomb were sealed with wedged stone slabs to prevent any penetration of light or dirt from the shaft, and to ensure the preservation of the deceased.[36]

It was within the underworld that transformations took place: here was a realm associated both with death and with fertility, and also with certain water deities. The duality it represents is vividly expressed in the fact that the deities who are depicted as having a skeletal appearance are also those who maintain a close relation with the earth, with maize, and with fertility.[37]

Fertility symbolism is strongly suggested by the treatment of the main body (N1) found in the north chamber. Three conch shells were placed between his thighs to resemble a phallus (see figs. 8, 9, and 15; see also Pickering, fig. 1). Five others were placed at his sides. The conch carries its own associations with fertility, given its obvious connections with water and its deities in the imagery of Formative-period and later Mesoamerican symbolic systems. The conch also represents the female womb: there are repeated images of human beings emerging from a conch.[38] Thus, the phallic symbol formed by these conch shells exhibits both of the basic fertility principles: the masculine and the feminine. It also represents the antagonistic and complementary principle of life-death, since the shells representing birth

form part of a mortuary offering. Furthermore, in the codices where burial rituals are represented, the participants in the celebration appear to be playing trumpets made of conch shells, a motif also seen in models of funerary scenes from Ixtlán del Río.[39]

Within the tradition of shaft tombs, the examples offered in Huitzilapa and San Sebastián, Jalisco, and Las Cebollas, Nayarit, all contemporary sites, show similar shell offerings. *Fasciolaria princeps* and *Strombus peruvians,* originating in the Pacific, were found in the three tombs. *Turbinella angulata* and *Strombus gigas* were also reported in these tombs. Since both *Turbinella angulata* and *Strombus costatus* come from the Caribbean, we are presented with evidence of a well-established pattern of use.[40] Furst has called attention to the fact that the presence of these species in the shaft tombs might indicate certain ideological ties with central Mexico. Several of the *Turbinella* from tomb no. 1 in Las Cebollas were decorated in a manner similar to those at Teotihuacan. In Teotihuacan there is also a mural with conch shells bearing the motif of a flower with four petals, which Furst interpreted as associated with the solar deity (see also the essay by Mark Graham in this volume).[41]

In Huitzilapa, many of the conch-shell trumpets were decorated in pseudo-cloisonné, with alternating schematic designs of two-headed serpents and cross-shaped motifs. Again, since very early times in Mesoamerica, two-headed serpents have been associated with the cult of fertility. At Izapa, far to the south in Chiapas, sculptural reliefs of the Middle Formative period reveal an association between the two-headed serpent and aquatic motifs.[42] There is a possibility as well that the cross-shaped designs accompanying the two-headed serpent at Huitzilapa may be related to symbols of Venus (the morning and evening star), rather than to solar designs. The symbol of Venus as a cross-shaped element was disseminated throughout Mesoamerica from early times. Sprajc has claimed that there was a strong link between these two elements, conceived as the ideological unit of "Venus, rain, corn" and fertility.[43] This association dates from the Middle Formative period.

In addition to two-headed serpents on the conch trumpets, it should be noted that this motif is also one of the most recurrent in the decoration of ceramic vessels made especially for this funerary event. The two-headed serpents appear by themselves or arranged in a cross-shaped design at the bottom of plates, earthenware bowls, and gourds at Huitzilapa (see figs. 16 and 17). This representation is also found in other ceramics from ancient West Mexico, such as on vessels showing a two-headed serpent encircling a human being from the Ortices and Comala phases in Colima, a period contemporary in part with Huitzilapa.

Finally, the importance of maize as a basic nourishment for these societies is also evident: an ear of maize was presented in the tomb not as a prepared food, but rather as an offering in an earthenware bowl next to the principal personage (N1). It was joined with other precious elements: a string of beads made with shells, a large piece of quartz, and a greenstone bead—sufficient indication of its own sacred status.

The Ballcourt

Another architectural feature strongly associated with fertility at Huitzilapa is the ballcourt. There are, in fact, four examples in the residential areas close to the ceremonial center. Although we have not been able to provide dates that absolutely confirm their contemporaneity, a sculpture of a ballplayer among the ceramic figures offered in the tomb offers powerful evidence to this effect (see figs. 18 and 19). Models of ballcourts from tombs in the area of Ixtlán del Río, Nayarit, are also well known (see the essay by Jane Day in this volume and her figs. 1 and 21–23). Ballplayer figurines date from c. 1500 B.C. at El Opeño, but Weigand has proposed that formal ballcourts date from the Late Formative period in western Mesoamerica.[44] As one of the basic features of ritual centers in all regions throughout Mesoamerican history, ballcourts and their associated sculptural monuments and paraphernalia, as well as representations of games on vessels and in pictorial manuscripts, have been the subject of intensive study by many scholars for decades.[45] Even today, versions of the ancient ballgame continue to be played in the state of Sinaloa, immediately north of Nayarit.[46] Ballgames had many functions both practical and symbolic: as a competitive means of resolving conflicts within or between groups; as a place where creation myths were enacted and the idea of regen-

Fig. 16 Plate with serpentine design; Huitzilapa, Jalisco; earthenware. Although the designs have become geometric abstractions, they recall tadpoles or possibly serpents, both of which are creatures traditionally associated in Amerindian ritual context with water or earth and the idea of regeneration.

Fig. 17 Plate with serpentine design; Jalisco, Huitzilapa; earthenware.

eration was expressed; and as entertainment and an activity involved with gambling. The permutations of ballcourt imagery and its functions are many: if there is a dominant, central theme for the ballgame it would be as a means of mediation, an activity connected with the idea of transition and resolution in practical matters as well as in the supernatural frame of reference. Reflecting on these patterns, Florescano has noted that the ritual practice of the ballgame ensured the continuity of the sun's cycle and the fertility of the rainy season, thus linked to the theme of the periodic death and renewal of nature.[47] In the Maya myth of the Popol Vuh, the hero twins descend to the underworld realm and have to play ballgames witnessed by the Lord of the Dead in order to pass through and emerge "reborn" in the world. This mythic motif is also recorded in Mixtec accounts.[48] In other Mesoamerican regions, the imagery of ballgames is strongly linked to sacrificial events and military activity—this is especially remarkable at Chichén Itzá, where on the largest ballcourt of Mesoamerica, relief sculpture depicts the decapitated captain of the losing team, his blood gushing forth to become a great flowering plant.[49] Similarly, at

Fig. 18 In the north chamber of the shaft tomb at Huitzilapa, this ballplayer figure originally stood by the feet of the deceased chieftain (see plan of the north chamber in fig. 8 or Pickering, fig. 1).

Fig. 19 Ballplayer figure; Jalisco, Huitzilapa; earthenware.

Conclusions

Recent archaeology from the Teuchitlán region has convincingly demonstrated that ancient West Mexico reached a level of development and social complexity that is different from the secondary status and cultural lag once attributed to it in relation to neighboring societies of central and southern Mexico. These characteristics identify the region as one that attained an important level of cultural maturity, as shown by the generic features it shared with highly developed Mesoamerican cultures. Studies carried out in the valley of Huitzilapa report the development of organized communities surrounding the main nucleus with its more imposing architectural units. The hierarchy expressed by this pattern of settlement offers an example of complex social development, one of the characteristics of stratified societies. Analysis of the available evidence indicates that this community was of a level similar to that of a hierarchical society or chiefdom.[52] This judgment is corroborated by the presence of public architecture, by the differentiation among dwellings, activity areas, and areas for specialization, as well as by references to special status found in the mortuary treatment of individuals buried in the Huitzilapa tomb. The hierarchy allotted to specific sites certainly suggests that these public spaces possessed some degree of sacredness, attributable to their function

the archaeological site of Bilbao on the Pacific coast of Guatemala, a stela depicts a triumphant ballplayer dismembering a body, while trophy-heads are carried by assistants to the four directions.[50] Many examples of this may be drawn, and it is possible that in West Mexico human figures with trophy-heads and model vessels with such motifs may also prove to be linked to the ballgame.[51] Although hard proof of the various functions of ballgames in West Mexico has yet to be found, circumstantial evidence strongly suggests that the game had similar significance to those well documented elsewhere throughout Mesoamerica history.

in rituals attended by a large part of the community.[53]

The evidence found in the Huitzilapa tomb itself indicates that the funerary event had strong associations with the cult of fertility, involving elements and concepts present in other Mesoamerican areas throughout their cultural development. These characteristics indicate, on the one hand, an early contact with other regions in this large sphere that shared a cultural tradition. On the other hand, it is possible to recognize the existence of original, localized ideas and images that were deeply rooted with beginnings among various groups of early farming populations, who contributed their particular concepts to the larger Mesoamerican tradition. As in all societies, ideological matters were closely linked to other cultural and economic features present during the Late Formative period in West Mexico. Various researchers have also considered the intrinsic function of ritual as a tool for sustaining social stratification and the structure of power within communities.[54]

The Huitzilapa shaft tomb, located within the largest architectural unit of restricted access, contains the remains of a high status individual, probably a ruler. This is a clear example of social differentiation, derived from the mortuary treatment given to a group of blood relatives or to members of a specific lineage related to the ruling group or the elite of the settlement. As indicated by the offerings accompanying the deceased, the central figure served as a symbolic mediator between supernatural forces and the community of which he was a part.

It is a well-known fact that fertility cults developed from very early times among sedentary agricultural people due to the importance that rain and other natural factors had on their survival. As Sprajc has suggested, it may be that this cult had its beginnings with egalitarian bands and tribes, but took on a greater complexity with stratified societies.[55] This religious and social complexity could have developed from interchange systems with other regions, a situation that involved both local materials and foreign products, and that generated a diversity in the flow of ideas and knowledge. In this sense, we should keep in mind that the valley of Huitzilapa is located in a strategic position; the Lerma-Santiago river corridor would certainly have served as a means of communication between West Mexico and the central plateau. Not only would utilitarian objects have circulated through systems of exchange, but so would raw materials and other elements that formed an essential part of ritual, such as greenstone, pyrite mirrors, and sea shells, and almost certainly colorful feathers as well. These objects had clearly symbolic meanings and functions, and very few members of the community had access to them. This exchange of objects and ideas contributed to the development of complexity among the various groups of West Mexico.[56]

Fertility cults involved a deep knowledge of astronomy, most certainly limited to those of privileged status, who took on the responsibility for ritually maintaining the regular function of the universe. The stability of the whole community depended on it.[57] Thus, ritual performance became one of the attributes of the ruling stratum, who not only controlled certain products—whether necessary food and materials or precious goods—but also maintained the sacred relationship with the forces of nature.

In claiming direct descent from the ancestor at the head of the lineage—in this case the main figure to whom the funerary event at Huitzilapa was dedicated, and who served as a sacred mediator between the social and the natural orders—members of the hierarchy who belonged to a specific group of relatives legitimized their authority vis-à-vis other members of the community.

Thus, in the geographical region we have studied, the tradition of shaft tombs reveals a cultural unity in which power and the earthly order of things were venerated, brought to the present, and justified on the basis of ideological principles that were expressed in local terms by the ancient peoples of West Mexico. In terms of its social and political structure, and many other particulars, these principles reveal that the communities of this region indeed belonged to the larger family of Mesoamerican peoples.

ROBERT B. PICKERING
AND MARIA TERESA CABRERO

MORTUARY PRACTICES IN THE SHAFT-TOMB REGION

The shaft-tomb tradition of ancient West Mexico lies within a subtropical region that extends from the west coasts of Colima, Jalisco, and Nayarit through a series of highland valleys and lake basins to Guadalajara and Lake Chapala. Shaft tombs have also been found as far north as western Zacatecas and south into Michoacán. While most of the shaft tombs have been discovered within a small portion of this large area, no one has yet determined the actual extent of this distribution. Nonetheless, much information about mortuary practices can be deduced from extant excavations and the wealth of collections that have been unearthed. In addition, as future surveys illuminate other parts of the region, we can expect that much of what is presented in this essay and discussed throughout this book will be refined and revised—if not dramatically altered.

The Study of Mortuary Practices

For at least a hundred years, the prehistory of West Mexico has been defined almost exclusively by the exploration of shaft tombs and the study of the extraordinary objects, particularly the large, hollow earthenware figurines, that have been found therein. Although the term itself is poorly understood by those outside the field, "shaft-tomb culture" is the designation given to the people or peoples who inhabited this important region around 2,000 years ago. Earlier this century, the shaft tombs were thought to be associated with the Tarascan culture of Michoacán that flourished between 900 and 1500, in what is labeled the Postclassic period. Clearly, the prehistory of West Mexico

is much more complex than the shaft-tomb/ Tarascan dichotomy would imply. In fact, the apparent simplicity of our understanding of West Mexican cultural history is more a product of the limited amount of scientific archaeology that has been done in the area than it is a reflection of the actual situation. Unfortunately, a simplistic and inaccurate analysis of West Mexico is still being voiced by some contemporary scholars. In a recent discussion of New World civilizations, for example, R. E. W. Adams dismisses any evidence of cultural complexity in West Mexican prehistory before the rise of the Tarascan empire.[1] Given the mineral wealth of the region, the early invention of copper metallurgy, and evidence of massive agricultural productivity, all of which would have made this area a desirable trading partner or vassal state, one wonders why West Mexico—if it were such a cultural backwater—was never conquered by Central Mexicans.

In an effort to understand the richness of ancient West Mexican cultures, we need to establish an archaeological baseline of current knowledge regarding the variety of mortuary practices there. With this information we can then determine certain characteristics of social organization and cultural practice that existed in the region. Information gleaned from the analysis of living sites, mining sites, and other locales would ideally be combined with research data from the mortuary sites: regrettably, such opportunities are limited. One might expect that grand burial preparations like those in West Mexico would have been built by people whose living sites were equally imposing and worthy

Fig. 1 In addition to the skeletal remains of three individuals, including a chieftain, at left, who lies surrounded by conch shells, the following offerings and grave goods were discovered in the north chamber of the tomb at Huitzilapa, Jalisco: 1) earthenware vessels; 2) hollow earthenware figures; 3) obsidian points; 4) pendant of carved shell (*Anadara* sp.); 5) beaded conch-shell textile; 6) conch-shell trumpet; 7) slate disc; 8) basalt ax; 9) *incensario*; 10) shell necklaces; and 11) spindle whorls.

of archaeological attention—if not the looter's shovel. Unfortunately, the habitation sites of West Mexico, though some are quite large and sophisticated, have received even less attention than has been given to the shaft tombs. The notable exceptions would include the work of Isabel Kelly more than fifty years ago and the extensive research conducted at the Marismas Nacionales directed by Stuart Scott starting in the late 1960s.[2] Regardless of whether this focus on mortuary sites to the near exclusion of habitation sites has been wise, it is a reality that must be acknowledged. To put the existing work in context, we need to see how mortuary-site archaeology differs from and is complementary to habitation-site archaeology.

The purpose of all anthropological archaeology is to reconstruct human behavior through the material remains left behind. The more complete these remains are and the more detailed our analysis of them, the more precise and insightful will be any effort at reconstruction. Like many other parts of Mexico, the western stretch of the Sierra Madre mountains offers a rich history to be explored. Archaeological surveys conducted by Phil C. Weigand in the Etzatlán region, and by Joseph Mountjoy in the Banderas valley near the West Coast, and the recently completed survey by the French team known as ORSTOM (L'Institut Français de Recherche Scientifique pour le Développement en Coopération) in the Sayula basin south of Guadalajara have revealed large numbers of habitation sites that range from small hamlets to monumental and expansive cities (see the essays by Weigand, Mountjoy, and Francisco Valdez in this volume). In addition, research in the Bolaños canyon has identified 102 sites, of which 11 have been tested archaeologically.[3] The largest of these include living complexes, pyramids, and ballcourts. Surveys have also identified extensive agricultural areas extending for hundreds of hectares that are composed of numerous small raised plots (chinampas). While these have been recognized for at least a decade, they are just now receiving serious study. The ORSTOM group has explored another use of local water resources in the Sayula basin: briny springs were used to extract salt, perhaps producing enough to trade or export. In total, the archaeological evidence reveals that there was human habitation in various parts of West Mexico for a long

period and that the societies that developed there generated large populations at least as early as the third or second century B.C. This trend toward expansive sites, large populations, and large public works constructions— as well as what we can infer about the necessary social and political complexity of such societies—continued until the early entradas of the Spaniards decimated the region's population through new diseases or through warfare.

While the study of habitation sites offers us one view of past cultures, the study of burial sites offers a somewhat different, but complementary, view. The theoretical bases for the study of mortuary practices have been well established by a number of scholars.[4] Central to all such studies are a number of key points that underlie our analysis of available remains:

1. One's status in death reflects one's status in life.

2. The treatment of the body; the size, form, and location of the mortuary structure (whether a shaft tomb, a crypt, shallow grave, etc.); and the type and quantity of grave goods deposited within it are variables that can be used to discern patterns of status and social organization.

3. The human remains and the person they represent are the focus of mortuary practices.

4. Mortuary programs in which all remains are treated in a similar manner tend to represent egalitarian societies, whereas wide differences in the treatment of the body, the contribution of grave goods, and/or the character of mortuary structures indicate stratified societies.

5. By definition, mortuary sites tend to be locations set aside for one purpose— disposal of the dead—whereas in habitation sites a large number of activities and functions and their associated assemblages of artifacts are conducted within the same space.

6. Reconstruction of a mortuary program requires the recovery and analysis of the entire range of practices within a given context.

Shaft-tomb Archaeology

Our knowledge of shaft-tomb archaeology is a pastiche of information gathered from numerous sources. First, and most visible, there are the remarkable objects themselves —most of them from looted sites—that have been collected for the past century (see fig. 2). Contextual information about these objects ranges from limited to non-existent. Second, some occasional, unpublished interviews with looters have yielded creditable information, as have the re-examination and salvage by archaeologists of data from looted tombs. Finally, our understanding has been immensely enriched by a handful of systematic archaeological excavations. This entire database, however, consists more of legend and lore than of reliable information and is not sufficient to create an accurate picture of mortuary behavior as represented by shaft-tomb and non-shaft-tomb interments.

Into this darkness, some rays of light have illuminated ancient West Mexico. From the mid-1950s through the 1980s, several archeologists made substantial contributions to the understanding of shaft-tomb architecture and context. Unfortunately, the study of human remains was mainly limited to noting the number of individuals interred and their positions within the tomb.[5] Since the early 1990s, however, new discoveries of unlooted shaft tombs have provided the most complete contexts from which archaeologists can study such mortuary practices. In most of these projects, detailed examination of the skeletal material has been integral. Over the last ten years, archaeologists have, for the first time, begun to find tombs before the looters. Planned research and uncommon good luck have led investigators to thirty-two unlooted tombs in the Mexican states of Jalisco and Colima. This group constitutes the most reliable and well-documented examinations of the West Mexican shaft tombs. The culture and behavior they reveal will add great detail to the history of this region.

Even from the earlier uncontrolled excavations, certain broad statements can be deduced. The tombs themselves show great diversity. Their depth ranges from no more

Fig. 2 From the 1930s to the mid-1970s scores of archaeological sites in West Mexico were left deeply pitted and destroyed by looters.

than one meter to about nineteen meters. While most consist of a single room off the shaft, others have as many as four. Some were excavated into soil, while other tombs were cut out of soft rock. Some are part of habitation sites, whereas others appear to be cemeteries set aside for mortuary activity only. Observations gleaned from local people who have seen the insides of tombs also suggest great variability. Some have described an orderly tomb with skeletons in supine position on the floor, surrounded by a variety of grave goods. Others have recounted entering tombs in which there were literally piles of jumbled bones and artifacts. Looters themselves have described a wide array of stone, shell, and ceramic artifacts that issued from the tombs. Certainly knowledgeable enough to tell the difference, they have also reported that, at times, figurines of various styles have been found within a single tomb.

Data from controlled excavations now allow archaeologists to record a much wider spectrum of observations and, more importantly, to describe the proximity of human remains and mortuary objects, and the context in which they were found. The range of grave goods varies widely from a few utilitarian earthenware vessels to large quantities of highly decorated vessels and figurines. The spectacular Huitzilapa tomb described in the essay by Lorenza López and Jorge Ramos in this volume included nearly 90 ceramics, 10 conch-shell trumpets painted in pseudo-cloisonné style, and more than 66,000 shell beads (see fig. 1 and López and Ramos, figs. 7, 8, and 15). In addition, there were 12 artifacts of jade, as well as objects of obsidian and quartz, unearthed at Huitzilapa. As a general rule, however, most individuals are entombed with a few ceramic vessels that presumably held food offerings.

At this early stage of analysis, the picture provided by these tombs is not clear. For example, no detailed correlation has yet been done between such biological characteristics as age and sex and the number and types of grave goods deposited within the tombs. Some details from individual sites, however, are notable: Mountjoy's explorations in the Banderas valley of western Jalisco have resulted in the excavation of three tombs. In this region, shaft tombs were only one of a number of burial options, including burial in pits and interment in urns. Offerings were deposited in the shafts themselves as well as in the tombs. Mountjoy has suggested that the shaft-tomb excavators intentionally dug though the soil until they reached a geologic layer of decayed volcanic rhyolite, from which the tomb rooms could then be excavated. Apparently, some tomb sites were abandoned because the subsoil was not suitable. And the poor condition of soil in other locations has also limited the researchers' abilities to analyze skeletal remains. In cases where the bones were greatly decayed, Mountjoy has been fortunate to work with his colleague, physical anthropologist Mary K. Sanford of the University of North Carolina–Greensboro, who has been able to identify basic biological characteristics of the individuals interred and to determine not only that most of the bodies had been cremated, but also that they were at different stages of decomposition before the burning. Nonetheless, based on a sample of only three tombs, it is impossible to know whether this type of mortuary treatment is common throughout the culture or the region.

The most detailed analysis to date has come from the single tomb found at the Huitzilapa site, located slightly northwest of Guadalajara in the Magdalena basin. This site required the salvage efforts of the Instituto Nacional de Antropología y Historia (INAH), and, led by INAH archaeologists Ramos and López, a team has cleared the architecture of the site and tested various structures to determine their construction and age. One of the surprises of the site was the discovery of the opening of a shaft tomb in one of the platforms on the edge of the site (see López and Ramos, fig. 4). Although the site is large, only a single tomb has thus far been discovered. But what a tomb it is: without a doubt, the most spectacular and complex shaft tomb yet discovered by archaeologists. A number of radiocarbon dates derived from the tomb cluster around the first few decades of the first century A.D.

An osteological examination of the skeletal remains at Huitzilapa has revealed that five of the six individuals were adults; the remaining skeleton was that of a woman not twenty years of age. Of the three females and three males, two individuals, one of each sex, displayed evidence of deliberate cranial deformation. In addition, five of the six individuals had similar developmental defects of the spine (see fig. 3), and it is likely that they were genetically related. Only one person, an old female, did not have this spinal abnormality. Whether she married into the group from another lineage or even another village may someday be determined by DNA if enough organic material can be extracted from the bone samples. Analysis of these remains has also uncovered evidence of trauma, illness, or abnormalities that also afflicted these individuals. One of the older males, for example, had a healed fracture of the right elbow that would have been painful and may have resulted in reduced mobility. Interestingly, two rings of jade found at this man's right hand were probably part of the handle of an atlatl, the tool used to hurl spears. Was his injury the result of repetitive stress and hyperextension at the elbow caused by frequent use of the atlatl in hunting or warfare? Does this tomb represent a family crypt under their living site? If so, why was there only one tomb for such a large site? Where and how were the other inhabitants buried? While the Huitzilapa site has yielded an abundance of good information, it has also created these and more questions than can yet be answered. But, then, that is a common archaeological outcome.

The remains from the Bolaños sites excavated by archaeologist Maria Teresa Cabrero of the Instituto de Investigaciones Antropológicas at the Universidad Nacional Autonoma de México tell a story very different from the Huitzilapa example or the tombs in the Banderas valley. Cabrero and her colleague, Carlos López Cruz, have been exploring the remote canyons and mountains of the Bolaños drainage in northern Jalisco. The terrain there is rough; modern conveniences such as electricity and grocery stores are rare; and it can be incredibly hot during the summer months. Not surprisingly, the archaeology of this region is largely unknown and the area has been visited only sporadically by scientists of any kind, except perhaps mineral geologists. Cabrero and López' work has revealed, however, that, although remote to us, this region nearly two thousand years ago had a thriving population with contacts to the outside world. At El Piñon, Cabrero and López identified a large architectural site. During their excavations, three shaft-and-chamber tombs were explored. The dates of the tombs range from about A.D. 135 to 440. Although the site is remote, it has yielded one of the best pieces of temporal evidence to support the radio-

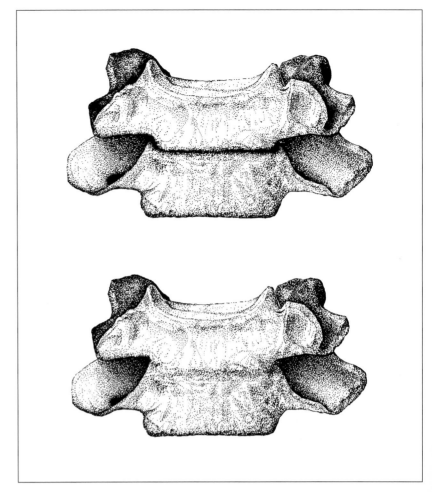

carbon dates: a small, but finely molded, ceramic ear spool of Teotihuacan design.

The Bolaños tombs contained a large quantity of human skeletal material, but unlike the order evident in the Huitzilapa tomb, these excavations revealed tombs that included human remains that were both articulated (that is, complete and in their normal skeletal position) and disarticulated (that is, disjointed or dislocated). Three articulated skeletons were noted in one tomb; two each in the others. Many bones that were not part of the complete remains were broken and most were disarticulated. Part of the damage can be attributed to the fact that the ceiling of the tombs had collapsed, but it is clear that the bones were disjointed at the time they were placed in the tomb. The number of remains recovered, particularly from one tomb, is extraordinary: eighty-six individuals representing all ages and both sexes. Many of these remains represent secondary burials—remains that may have been preserved in a different facility before being moved to this tomb for final disposition. Such secondary burials strongly

Fig. 3 Drawing of a normal cervical vertebra (top) and one of the congenitally deformed vertebrae found in five of the six skeletal remains at Huitzilapa. This physical evidence indicates a close genetic connection among the individuals interred in this tomb.

suggest that the tombs were reused over a period of time.

The artifacts from the Bolaños tombs share some similarities with other West Mexican objects. These include a Lagunillas-style figurine and additional figures that are similar in form but cruder in manufacture (see figs. 4 and 5). Other ceramic figurines are reminiscent of much later styles from Casas Grandes in the state of Chihuahua and elsewhere to the north.

In the Atemajac valley surrounding Guadalajara, some of the most extensive archaeological investigations of shaft tombs have been conducted, principally by archaeologist Javier Galván, who, in the late 1980s, excavated twenty-three tombs.[6] For the most part, the shafts of these tombs are no more than two meters deep, with but a single room in which burials were made. Galván's work comprises the largest such sample to date. He has carefully collected data on the construction of the tombs; the human remains found within them; and the location, type, and quantity of all artifacts. His clear descriptions and comprehensive coverage make this work an invaluable contribution to West Mexican studies.

Variability in mortuary practices can be generally categorized according to three characteristics: treatment of the body; varia-tion in the type and number of grave goods deposited; and the form and location of the mortuary structure in which the remains repose. Burial practices within the Sierra Madre Occidental present wide variation in all of these categories. Within the Occidente (as West Mexico is commonly called), ancient cultures buried their dead in graves as well as tombs of various types. Graves tend to occur in cemeteries, while tombs may either be isolated or arranged in almost cemetery-like clusters. Graves themselves offer some variability in form in that some remains are interred directly in the ground—such as at Chupícuaro and the Marismas Nacionales—while interments also occurred in large ceramic urns—as at Guasave, Culiacán, Chametla, and also within the Marismas Nacionales—all in the Pacific coast state of Sinaloa. Strictly speaking, the term "shaft tomb" describes a situation in which a vertical shaft of varying depth is excavated into the ground (see Weigand, figs. 8b and 9b). At the bottom, one, two, or as many as four rooms lead horizontally from the central shaft. At such sites as El Opeño, Tabachines–El Grillo and Atemajac, a relatively shallow vertical shaft actually intrudes into the tomb. A large step or series of smaller steps may lead from the vertical shaft to the shelf-like portion of the tomb on which the remains

Fig. 4 Seated female figure; Lagunillas style; Bolaños, Jalisco; earthenware. This figure, found near Bolaños in the mountains of extreme northern Jalisco, is stylistically similar to figures of the Lagunillas style in distant southern Nayarit.

Fig. 5 Seated polychrome female figure with tattoos; Lagunillas style; Bolaños, Jalisco; earthenware. Private collection. Cat. no. 200. Similar in form and decoration to figure 5, this figure was probably made in a local Bolaños workshop by artisans linked through trade routes to southern Nayarit communities.

and accoutrements are deposited. Figure 6 identifies the types of mortuary features by site.

Besides differences in the type of the interment facility itself, both tombs and graves vary in form. Depth of the shaft has already been noted as a variable. Part of the explanation for this appears to be connected with the geology of the region, much of which contains a weathered limestone called caliche. The caliche may be exposed on the surface or buried many meters beneath. At some sites, it appears that the ancient inhabitants dug a shaft through the caliche layer and then used that layer to provide structural stability for the roof and sometimes the walls of the tomb. The depth of the caliche determined the depth of the shaft: if the caliche was only two meters deep, for example, then so was the shaft. Similarly, if the caliche layer was ten to fifteen meters deep, then the shaft was excavated to that depth. Mountjoy found essentially the same pattern in the Banderas valley, although the rock material was different. Over forty years ago, Corona Núñez described a spectacular tomb from El Arenal near Etzatlán, Jalisco, which has a shaft of sixteen meters in depth.[7] Two nearly square rooms were accessed from the shaft by short lateral tunnels, and a third room was connected by a lateral shaft leading from one of the other rooms. As has already been noted, the Huitzilapa tomb excavated by Ramos and López had a shaft depth of about eight meters, while at the Tabachines and Atemajac sites, depths were no more than three to three-and-a-half meters, and at the Bolaños sites tombs were only a meter deep.

The location of shaft tombs has been extremely problematic. The best evidence thus far is that archaeologists have not been all that successful in finding them. Looters who live in the area, however, have been more successful. Particularly in the Etzatlán area, tombs appear to occur in circular clusters under habitation sites. In light of Phil Weigand's work on the form and distribution of such sites, many shafts appear to lead from a living area on the surface to a tomb below.[8] The best excavated example of this comes again from Huitzilapa. The mouth of the tomb was in the floor of a house structure and was clearly defined by a circle of stones. Weigand, Otto Schöndube, and others have suggested that the famous ceramic house

SITES	DIRECT	GRAVE	SHAFT TOMB	TOMB	URN
Alta Vista	•	•			
Amapa	•				
Apatzingán (Michoacán)		•			•
Barra de Navidad	•				
Bolaños canyon	•	•	•		•
Capacha		•			•
Chametla (Sinaloa)					•
Cerro Encantado	•				
Cojumatlán	•				
Culiacán (Sinaloa)	•				•
Etzatlán area			•		
Guasave (Sinaloa)	•				•
Huitzilapa			•		
Marismas Nacionales	•				•
Morett	•				
El Opeño				•	
Tabachines–El Grillo		•	•		
Tamazula–Tuxpan–Zapotlán	•	•			•
Tizapán El Alto	•				
Tuxcacuesco	•	•			•
Tzintzuntzan	•				

models that come from this region also may provide evidence (see also the essay by Christopher Witmore in this volume). Many of these models have stairs leading down from the house to a cavelike chamber below —an arrangement that may represent the house above and the house below, and thus reflect the bond between the living family and their entombed ancestors.

In the summer of 1996, Robert Pickering had the opportunity to work with INAH archaeologist Anna Jarkin at the La Campaña site on the edge of Colima, Colima. She and her crew had discovered a tomblike structure in the top of one of the large pyramidal platforms at this site. The form of this chamber was similar to the El Opeño tombs described by Arturo Oliveros.[9] A series of high steps led down into a dome-shaped tomb. Inside were human remains and various artifacts. But these remains did not represent complete skeletons, nor did the deposit of bones appear to be an ossuary. Instead, human remains were represented primarily by the small bones of the body, fingers, toes, vertebrae, and ribs. Almost no long bones were found, and only a portion of a single skull was recovered. The bones appeared to have been scattered in a thin layer across the

Fig. 6 Burial types throughout ancient West Mexico.

floor of the tomb, and none were in anatomical position with any others. In contrast, the artifacts seemed to have been intentionally arranged at the mouth of the tomb and along the sides. Careful excavation also revealed that additional small items and broken artifacts were in the tomb fill.

While this chamber had many of the physical attributes of a tomb—such as shape, size, human remains, and artifacts—neither the placement nor the disposition of the material necessarily makes it one. An alternative hypothesis is that this deposit represents an offering of which remains and artifacts were a part. Further research may reveal that these partial remains are associated with partial skeletons in another deposit.

The variety of material placed within tombs can vary greatly. Items of personal adornment often include ear and nose ornaments made of shells from the Pacific Ocean. Similarly, sets of nested shell armbands have been frequently reported. The Bolaños tombs in northern Jalisco revealed not only items of personal adornment made from various types of shell, but also pieces of black coral. These kinds of body adornments, as well as shell appendages to headdresses and necklaces, are often depicted on the hollow ceramic figurines found within the tombs. In the Huitzilapa tomb, the remains were found with items of shell and jade in situ (see the essays by López and Ramos and by Mountjoy in this volume).

In addition to these objects intended to adorn the human remains, there are other burial items that anthropologists commonly call contributed grave goods. These artifacts can be usefully divided into three categories: utilitarian, symbolic, and ritual. Utilitarian objects are functional tools such as chipped-stone knives and points, stone ax heads, or vessels with food residue inside. An *incensario,* also commonly found in tombs, is by definition a utilitarian object, although its form and possibly the type of material burned in it served some symbolic purpose. In general, however, symbolic artifacts are in the form of utilitarian objects though they are usually made of exotic materials and show no evi-

Fig. 7 Ceremonial spear point; Jalisco; obsidian. Fowler Museum of Cultural History, University of California, Los Angeles. Cat. no. 114.

Fig. 8 Ceremonial club with a human face; Colima; stone. Fowler Museum of Cultural History, University of California, Los Angeles. Cat. no. 13. The haft of this symbolic stone club is wrapped around the carved head of the weapon on which two human faces have been rendered.

Fig. 9 Plate with a lobed rosette pattern; vicinity of Lagunillas, Nayarit; earthenware. Natural History Museum of Los Angeles County. Cat. no. 222. Sets of vessels for different foods were often included in a single tomb.

Fig. 10 Bowl with multiple sets of vertical bands; vicinity of Lagunillas, Nayarit; earthenware. Natural History Museum of Los Angeles County. Cat. no. 220.

Fig. 11 Bowl with four sets of vertical bands; vicinity of Lagunillas, Nayarit; earthenware. Natural History Museum of Los Angeles County. Cat. no. 221.

dence of use (see figs. 7 and 8). For example, a jade atlatl hook and rings, found adjacent to one set of remains at Huitzilapa, might actually have been attached to such a weapon, but their unusual material and lack of wear suggests that they were symbolic representations rather than practical items. Ritual objects serve no mundane function. For example, the presence of thousands of shell beads and their position relative to the body point to the fact that they had been sewn onto a cloth, perhaps a shroud, that was wrapped around the deceased. Of the three categories of artifacts found in tombs, perhaps the most ubiquitous are bowls of varying styles and shapes. Whereas very few bowls may be unearthed with one set of remains, in other cases there appear to be sets of similar vessels, sometimes covered, for each individual (see figs. 9–11). Again, the Huitzilapa tomb provides some of the most spectacular evidence: in two rooms, over seventy vessels were placed with the dead, including redundant groups of covered bowls, ollas, and bi-globular vessels (see figs. 1 and 12). What they contained is currently the object of intensive analysis by Bruce Benz of the Botanical Research Institute, Fort Worth, Texas. His work will provide the first detailed identification of food offerings from a West Mexican tomb. In addition to bowls, incense burners also appear to be quite common. Many are found lying on their sides at the side of the entrance to a tomb. They often have charred residue either within or to one side if the vessel is not upright. Very possibly, the *incensario*s were burning during the entombment process and were toppled as part of the last activity in the tomb.

Perhaps the best-known ceramics to be

recovered from the tombs are the hollow figurines: both anthropomorphic forms and zoomorphic figures representing many kinds of animals. Evidence from the Huitzilapa tomb and the San Sebastián tomb excavated by Stanley Long in the mid-1960s shows that earthenware figures of humans, either individually or in groups, are placed with individual remains.[10] Although few skeletons from West Mexican tombs have ever been examined by a physical anthropologist, human-form figurines appear to be found with skeletons of the same sex. A figurine from the San Sebastián tomb, now in the collection of the Los Angeles County Museum of Art, shows evidence of fabric around its lower portion, suggesting that the figure was either "dressed" or perhaps covered by a cloth or bag. Placement within the tomb of the numerous extant animal figures, however, is not well documented. In her excavations in the Bolaños canyon, Cabrero recovered a dog figurine and two stone axes with dog heads represented. A Colima red dog was also found lying on its side to the left of the entrance in the tomblike facility at La Campaña, Colima. But such examples may not be typical, and our understanding of their significance is, furthermore, far from complete.

The completeness of human remains is directly related to the treatment of the body before entombment. Data from the tombs can reveal aspects of pre-entombment activity, as suggested by ceramic models of funerals and mourning rites (see Townsend, figs. 39–41). While it appears that most remains represent intact bodies, other practices are represented. For example, initial observation of the six remains in the Huitzilapa tomb suggested that they were completely articulated remains. Closer examination, however, demonstrated that five of the six were, in fact, not entirely articulated. In each of the five cases, most portions of the skeleton were in or near anatomical position. Most obviously out of position were adjacent ribs on one side of the body: all out of position, but as a group, and in the same disarticulated position (see fig. 12). This kind of disturbance can best be explained when a body is moved sometime after it has been tightly wrapped and become desiccated. The wrappings hold the body together, as the process of desiccation dries out the soft tissue and reduces the body's weight. Desiccation also makes the joints brittle. Jostling a body may disrupt the joints, and even when the body is bound, bones can move, though they do not move very far out of position. If bodies were lowered into the tomb on the type of pallets often represented in small solid earthenware figurines and models, the binding and movement could result in minor disarticulation. The sixth set of remains at Huitzilapa showed no evidence of disarticulation, and, therefore, likely represents an individual placed directly into the tomb (see fig. 1). In the San Sebastián example, two complete remains were found on the floor near the entrance, while disarticulated remains and associated grave goods had been moved against the walls of the tomb.[11]

Remains from the Bolaños tombs represent an extreme example: of the eighty-six remains identified, only seven were articulated; the rest were either disarticulated or represent partially complete remains. Much remains to be explained here: a high percentage of the bones, for example, showed fractures that had occurred before death. Moreover, of the thousands of bones found in the three Bolaños tombs, many had been burned, although some were only blackened—evidence that they had been exposed to a relatively low temperature fire. Others, calcined and warped, had clearly been exposed to a hot fire for some time. At this point, the most likely explanation is that the bodies had been treated in different ways above ground, before final disposition in the tombs.

Whose Tombs Were They?

Reconstructing the events that surrounded the building and use of tombs is contingent on the amount and quality of the data on which those interpretations are based. Thus, determining when tombs were dug and when people were entombed therein is part of the analysis of a mortuary program. The evidence from a number of tombs suggests that while entombment was performed rarely, people died more frequently than the tombs were opened. The practice of caring for bodies in the form of desiccated remains has been shown to have occurred at Huitzilapa, and periodic disposal of the dead may be inferred from the conditions of the remains discovered by Cabrero and her colleagues in the Bolaños tombs. But if entombments were made periodically, what determined when and why it was done? There are two possible sources for answers: environmental reasons and cultural ones. While we do not yet know enough to comment on possible cultural reasons, there are environmental reasons that might account for episodic entombments. Present-day looters have admitted that their work is restricted to the dry season, first, because agricultural work keeps the men busy until after harvest; and second, because the rainy season increases the possibility that an excavation will collapse. Perhaps the people of ancient West Mexico who were also agriculturists followed a similar yearly schedule. If we consider this interpretation a promising hypothesis, then testing it will have to come from an examination of environmental data inside the tomb. As mentioned earlier, Bruce Benz's examination of the contents of vessels may shed light on this problem. But another set of data also pertains. Some of Pickering's recent work with his associates has focused on remnants of insect puparia that are sometimes found on earthenware vessels from the tombs (see fig. 13).[12] Forensic entomologists Neal Haskell

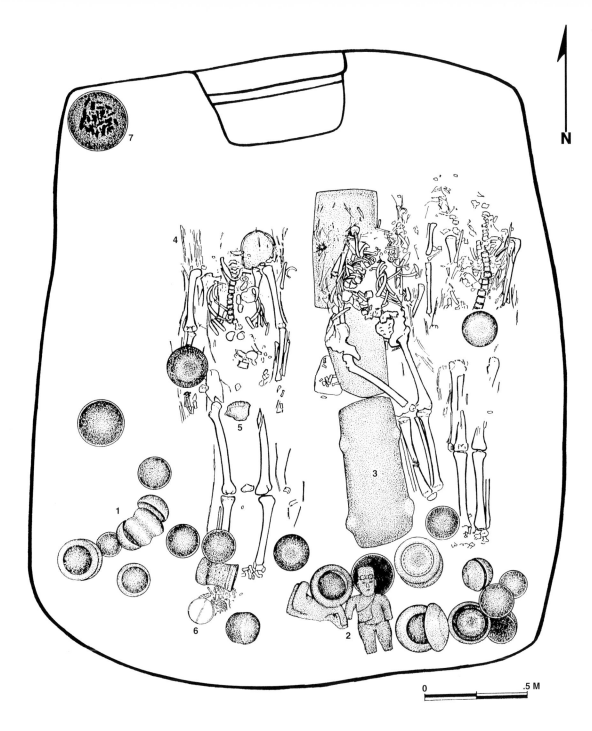

N

Fig. 12 In the second chamber at Huitzilapa the jumbled position of the skeletal remains indicate that these individuals received secondary burial in this tomb.

Among the objects recovered from this chamber are: 1) earthenware vessels; 2) hollow earthenware figures; 3) metate (grinding stones); 4) bamboo matting; 5) conch shell; 6) slate disc; and 7) tripod brazier.

0   .5 M

and Robert Hall have examined examples of puparia from nearly ten vessels and have determined that they represent one of three families of necrophagous flies that must have entered the tomb either with the body or at the time of its burial. Future research on ancient specimens and information from modern entomological researches in West Mexico will provide more specific identifications. If not just the family but the genus and species of the necrophagous flies can be identified, then in fact it may be possible for us to determine the season of the year in which death and entombment occurred.

For a number of decades, art historians, most notably Hasso von Winning, have recognized a large number of similar solid ceramic figurines showing males and females, and sometimes juveniles, reclining on pallets.[13] Alternatively described as people on sleeping beds or sick beds, or women on birthing couches, these sculptures are more accurately identified as pallets for transporting the dead into a tomb. This interpretation is preferable because it accounts for the closed eyes of the bodies on the litter and, more importantly, explains why the bodies are bound to the litter, usually by one or two large straps.

Evidence for the reuse or reopening

of tombs comes, as we have seen, from the disposition of both human remains and contributed grave goods. In many of the tombs, such as Huitzilapa and San Sebastián, the remains and grave goods were laid out in a clear, organized manner. Other tombs, such as those found at Tingambato, Michoacán, present a different pattern: some skeletons and grave goods may be arranged in the central portion of the tomb, while other remains and whole or fragmentary artifacts are clustered against the sides of the tomb. The initial set of remains appears to have been moved to the tomb's periphery in order to make room for the remains occupying the central portion. The extent of such reuse is unknown at present, although reuse of a tomb has important cultural implications that have been studied both ethnographically and archaeologically.[14] Reuse, for example, implies ownership by a closed group such as a lineage, possibly a family or clan, and it requires continual maintenance of a tomb. A tomb may have been built by one generation of a family, and upon their deaths, put to use. Succeeding generations take care of the tomb, performing any required rituals and any necessary maintenance for the sake of their ancestors. When their time comes, they too are entombed.[15] The available evidence suggests that these tombs do house generations of families, but neither the archaeological samples nor the ethnohistoric research from the region is adequate to support such an hypothesis at this point in time.

We are also far from knowing what these people looked like, what kinds of diseases they suffered, and how they modified their bodies. But we can gain a hint by examining the skeletons themselves and the elaborate figurines placed in the tombs. Life expectancy, for example, is a subject of interest to many modern students of the past. There are not large enough groups of skeletons in West Mexico to provide a reliable demographic table, but there are some general statements that can be made. In all pre-industrial eras, infant mortality usually was high, and women in the child-bearing years were vulnerable to death due to birthing complications. In addition, the time of weaning often was a particularly dangerous time for children: the weaning diet was often less nutritious than the mother's milk, and the child lost the antibodies ordinarily received through suckling. Males tended to die at an earlier age, particularly if warfare was a common activity. Life in ancient West Mexico conformed to this general pattern. If one survived to the age of 20, barring severe trauma, there was a good chance that one could live to be 35 to 40 years of age. By age 40, however, people were old, though some did live into their 60s, 70s, and possibly beyond. Two individuals in the Huitzilapa tomb, for example, appear to have been more than 50 years of age.

The physical features of the ancient West Mexicans surely varied, but clearly they were shorter than we are today: the height of most women was within the range of 4' 11" to 5' 3", while that of men was within a range from 5' 5" to 5' 10" as determined by stature estimates based on long-bone lengths. These figures are not very different from those of other Mesoamerican populations. Build and weight, of course, are difficult to ascertain from skeletons, but their remains indicate a robustness that is common among people who do physical work for a living. The shape and morphology of their skulls sometimes tell us an added story. The examination of the skeletons from the Huitzilapa tomb began with an initial examination of the skulls alone. The three females and three males all had robust faces, particularly in the lower face and chin. Not surprisingly, the human figurines from the tombs show that both males and females had broad robust faces. In an earlier study of the skeletons from the Marismas Nacionales, George Gill pointed out that many of the skulls he examined demonstrated types of cranial deformation

Fig. 13 Remnants of insect puparia have adhered to the surface of a ceramic vessel. These puparia would have been deposited shortly after the entombment of the human remains, providing both environmental and seasonal data.

that were reflected in the figurine forms from the same sites.[16]

Other indications that some of the human figurines represent real people have been recognized for years. Von Winning's monograph on the pathologic figures interpreted a number of diseases and physical anomalies that were apparent in many styles of figurines. Hunchbacked figurines are relatively well known (see fig. 14). Their frequent emaciation may be the result of tuberculosis. Other figures have large pustules over most of the body, though specific diagnosis of their disorder is not possible here (see fig. 15). Dwarfism is also represented in a number of figurines, particularly in the Comala style of Colima.

Although some of the human figures are likely to represent real people and, in fact, could be considered idealized portraits strongly reflecting local ethnic types, not all are so personal (see Townsend, fig. 6). Peter Furst has argued that these human forms do not represent vernacular subjects at all.[17] Many styles of the flat figurines, while having considerable variation in personal adornment and clothing, do not have the individualized physical detail to suggest that they represent specific people. For example, flat figurines from Ortices, Tuxcacuesco, and the Late Comala phase represent human figures stylized to different degrees (see figs. 16 and 17). Most styles of large hollow figures also lack individuality. The San Sebastián and Comala figures, particularly the so-called shamans, while finely made, tend to have generalized features (see figs. 18 and 19; see also the essay by Peter Furst in this volume and his figs. 17 and 18). Generalized ethnic types are also portrayed by the Ameca-Etzatlán figures (see fig. 20) and the style popularly known as "sheep-faced," now termed the Tala-Tonalá style (see fig. 21; see also Townsend, "Introduction," fig. 20, and Townsend, fig. 23). Yet some of the Nayarit and Ixtlán del Río pieces occasionally present individualizing details that make them portrait-like (see also the Introduction by Richard Townsend in this volume). This topic is an important one because it is at the center of how to interpret the meaning of the figurines. If a figure is a portrait, then the accoutrements of personal adornment, clothing, and body postures may describe actual events and activities in daily life. However, if the figurines are interpreted

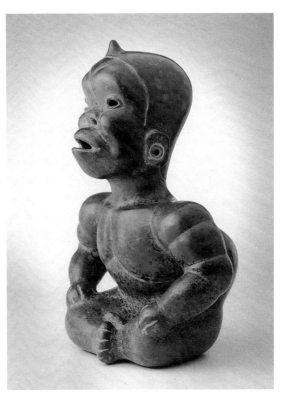

Fig. 14 Seated hunchbacked dwarf; Comala style; Colima; earthenware. The Art Institute of Chicago. Cat. no. 41.

Fig. 15 Male figure covered with sores; Ixtlán del Río style; Nayarit; earthenware. Collection of Charles and Marjorie Benton, Evanston, Ill. Cat. no. 197.

only as abstract or generalized ancestors, deities, or shamans, then their meaning is quite different. Determining if any or all of these interpretations are valid will require detailed examination of complete tomb lots and careful analysis of the human remains with which they are found.

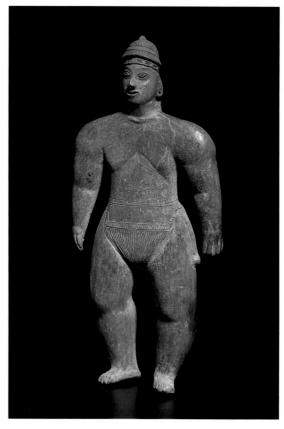

Assessing the state of our knowledge by interpreting the social meaning of shaft tombs is a tenuous undertaking, yet it is important to provide that kind of context in this volume. Clearly, we know that too little good scientific work has been done to really understand the tombs, and that looting has destroyed much of the information upon which detailed analysis and thoughtful inter-pretation could be based. Nevertheless, it is clear that shaft tombs often are located in association with living sites. When associated with such sites, they are clustered under the living floors of houses that are themselves built in clusters, such as the circular pattern of the Teuchitlán tradition defined by Phil Weigand in his essay in this volume. It is also clear that shaft-tomb "cemeteries" may exist, in groups outside habitation areas. Joseph Mountjoy has uncovered the best example of this situation in the Banderas valley, and El Opeño may be another such site. Graves rather than tombs were also a mortuary op-tion, although research has not yet indicated the extent to which graves and tombs co-existed in the same area or which was actu-ally the dominant form of interment. Once again, Huitzilapa is an intriguing example. This large site was completely excavated by

López and Ramos, yet, from it all, only one tomb and no formal graves were located. The unanswered question is, "Where is everyone else buried?" In fact, at no site does the num-ber of tombs seem to be sufficient for the size of the population that is suggested by the size of the habitation site. A possible exception to this statement is represented by the tombs at Atemajac. There Javier Galván found a large number of tombs, all of similar form and most with a relatively small amount and vari-ety of grave goods. Perhaps, in this region within the Occidente, small tombs were the norm. The type and quantity of contributed artifacts also tends to vary less than for large shaft tombs. This would seem to suggest a less stratified social group. Thus, it does not appear that shaft tombs and the smaller El Opeño or Atemajac-style tombs were part of the same mortuary complex of a single cul-ture. Rather, they represent two similar styles of interment by two separate cultures within ancient West Mexico. Where shaft tombs are found, they represent only one type of mor-tuary feature, and the entombment under houses was an option available to only a small segment of society.

Therefore, if only a few people were being buried in shaft tombs, who were they

Fig. 18 Seated male figure wearing a helmet; San Sebastián style; Jalisco; earthenware. Private collection. Cat. no. 141. While West Mexican figures may sometimes display portraitlike features, most, like those found in these illustrations, represent generalized local ethnic types and age groups.

Fig. 19 Seated male figure wearing a beaked helmet; Comala style; Colima; earthenware. The American Museum of Natural History, New York. Cat. no. 21.

Fig. 20 Seated male figure held by a female figure; Ameca-Etzatlán style; Jalisco; earthenware. Private collection. Cat. no. 117.

Fig. 21 Elderly female figurine holding a bowl and cane; Tala-Tonalá style; Jalisco; earthenware. Private collection. Cat. no. 144.

and what segment of society did they represent? The limited number of individuals represented and the wide range and large quantities of contributed grave goods certainly suggest the interment of the elite members of a society. Both males and females are found in the tombs, and all are accompanied by at least some but not necessarily all classes of grave goods. At present, evidence of the entombment of infants or children comes only from the Bolaños canyon. Analysis of the remains at Huitzilapa indicated that five of the six individuals were closely related. This and other data suggest that the tombs were most likely used by families. Yet, with so few people in the tombs, perhaps not everyone in the family had rights to entombment. More than likely, only the senior members, defined by power and status, not necessarily age, could be entombed.

We have determined as well that placement of the artifacts within the tomb is intentional, not random. Male figurines are associated with male skeletons and female figurines with females. In fact, there may be "sets" of figurines with individuals: e.g., a group of like-sexed figures with a single skeleton. Individual figurines may present different body postures and accoutrements, though with similar faces. We believe that these sets represent different important episodes or states of an individual's life. The

states are not clearly defined, but we suggest that for women important ones would include marriage, first pregnancy, or motherhood, and the achievement of particular skill levels at certain domestic activities (see also the essays by Townsend and Mountjoy in this volume). For men, we suggest one's status as a warrior or as a player in a ballgame, as a musician or possibly a shaman or society member (see also the essays by Townsend, Furst, and Jane Day in this volume). For both males and females, achieving a particular advanced age also may be a special status commemorated in figurines (see figs. 21–23). We further suggest that the great similarity of form within sets of figures suggests that they are made around the time of death to be placed in the tomb, rather than being made when the individual achieved the particular status represented. Pairs of male and female figurines in similar postures are known from private and public collections. It is our belief as well that the identification of pairs is a false associate or set. If figurines were made in groups for individuals as we have here proposed, then the so-called "pairs" are individual figurines that have been pulled out of their set and associated with another figurine from a set designed to commemorate a member of the opposite sex.

Similarly, other types of artifacts appear to be placed with purpose. An incense burner at the side of the entrance is one example; clustered groups of pottery vessels are another. In addition, there are items of personal adornment, whether utilitarian or symbolic, that are associated directly with individuals and not part of a cluster or group. These too represent the status of the specific individual. The great quantity and variety of artifacts made from jade, ceramic, shell, and other materials indicates that a few people were the recipients of a great deal of labor in the form of grave goods and exotic materials (not to mention the construction of the tombs themselves).

At a minimum, the people in the shaft tombs probably represent local elite families. Multiple shaft tombs in a habitation site may indicate a multiplicity of important families within larger living sites. Of these, some probably are local chiefs (or caciques). Is there evidence from the tombs that represents more extensive social organization or larger polities? At present, data from known tombs do not support such a statement, but the required evidence may not come from tombs. Answering this question will require not only a better understanding of other kinds of West Mexican sites, but also more intensive comparison of West Mexican mortuary activity with other Mesoamerican cultures, for which higher levels of political organization have been amply demonstrated.

In summation, then, the analysis of mortuary practices across ancient West Mexico is just beginning. Further analysis of scientifically excavated tombs and the discovery of new ones will, for the first time in this region, allow archaeologists to move from anecdote and speculation to serious analysis. Our knowledge to date, incomplete as it is, nonetheless serves as an excellent starting point. We have already recognized a wide diversity of behaviors and activities, and this information—together with what has been presented here—will become the initial hypotheses for critical testing against scientifically recovered data.

KRISTI BUTTERWICK

FOOD FOR THE DEAD
THE WEST MEXICAN ART OF FEASTING

Throughout the Mesoamerican world, feasts were the catalyst for significant ritual, social, and political interchange. We know from historical documents and hieroglyphic texts that pre-Hispanic peoples held over a dozen annual feasts, and that they commemorated life and death events, and brokered political and economic deals, in a milieu of feasting. These occasions were comparable to, or even exceeded, the bounty and significance of present-day state dinners or our own religious and national holidays. For example, the Spanish soldier Bernal Díaz del Castillo, who accompanied Hernán Cortés on the conquest of the Aztec, recorded in his diary a description of one royal feast at which the Aztec king was served "over three hundred plates of the food . . . [consisting of] cooked fowls, turkeys, pheasant, native partridges, quail, tame and wild ducks, venison, wild boar, reed birds, pigeons, hares and rabbits, and many sorts of birds and other things which are bred in this country, . . . [as well as] fruit of all the different kinds that the land produced."[1]

The Mesoamerican calendar of eighteen months attributed cosmic significance to the annual cycle of feasts,[2] and records for the Aztec show that every one of their feasts —some of which lasted for weeks—was a complex ritual devoted to the appropriate seasonal aspects of agriculture and to various deities who were associated with it. Sacred products, such as the fermented sap of agave, called *octli*, and *tzoalli*, a dough made from amaranth seeds, were consumed at certain feasts.[3] At others, when supplies were low, the Aztec lords fed the poor a sweetened

corn gruel called *atole* along with "tamales of maize treated with lime; . . . of fruit; . . . of maize blossoms . . . [in addition to] honey tamales."[4] By harvest time, which occurred toward the end of our month of August, the Aztec held their grandest feast, *Huey Miccaylhuitl*, to honor those ancestors who had become patron deities.[5] On this occasion the people prepared special tamales, chocolates, amaranth cakes, seeds, the meats of turkey and dog, and *octli*. They also decorated a public plaza with a *xocotl* pole, a large tree "twenty-five fathoms long," stripped of its branches and festooned with sashes and garlands of marigolds. At the apex of the pole they placed tamales and images of their deities made of white paper and *tzoalli*. Youths climbed ropes to the top of the pole in a race to claim these prizes. The winner tossed the sacred foods to the people below, and received for his efforts a cape made of feathers. Year after year, pre-Hispanic peoples joined in the ritual of feasting to honor the gods who sustained them and to integrate diverse elements of their societies.

New research indicates that the people of ancient West Mexico held their own ritual feasts and, like the Aztec, hosted the grandest feasts for their ancestors.[6] Fundamental to this position is the belief that the annual cycle of feasting that the Spanish invaders witnessed in the sixteenth century had antecedents dating a millennium or two prior. Thus, it seems reasonable to assume that the Aztec feast for the dead, *Huey Miccaylhuitl*, had roots in the widespread custom of offering the deceased food and drink for the

Fig. 1 Seated male figure holding a bowl and drinking tube; Ameca-Etzatlán style; Jalisco; earthenware. Galerie Mermoz, Paris. Cat. no. 126. The animated posture, the immediacy of facial expression, and the prominence of the vessel and drinking tube suggest the importance of ritualized feasting and drinking in festivals sponsored by the leaders of West Mexican societies.

89

Fig. 2 View of an agave field near Tequila, Jalisco.

journey to the afterlife. Scholars have likewise suggested that the modern celebration in Mexico of All Souls' Day (called Día de los Muertos, or Day of the Dead) acquired its exuberance from a heritage of feeding the dead that dates back to approximately 1000 B.C. Funerary feasts, at which both the living and the dead commune and consume, are a necessity in traditional societies because they allow people to shake off death and begin the processes of social reordering. According to anthropologist Michael Coe, such rituals "deal with the journey of the dead, the voyage of the soul to the underworld, and the reconstituting of society after the ultimate dissolution of the body."[7]

In addition to providing occasions to honor one's ancestors, ritual feasts for the dead are also opportunities to balance the economic interests, debts, and alliances of the deceased with those of the living.[8] Sponsoring any feast, of course, including those for the dead, may be an economic burden beyond the means of any single family. In such cases, kin groups or extended family members may reciprocate responsibilities for each other's feasts, bound in an informal contract of obligations. By exchanging their sponsorship of particular feasts, family members cement their social interactions and extend their mutual economic stability into the future. Thus, beyond its ritual function, feasting becomes a mechanism for the redistribution, reciprocation, or circulation of wealth and food surplus.

Leaders also engage in the competitive aspect of feasting to gain power and build political alliances.[9] They sponsor feasts to promote themselves, using gifts and food to attract a following. In exchange for the feast, followers obligate themselves to the leader, whom they repay with their labor and surplus goods. Prominent leaders expand their network of influence from a local to a regional level by using feasts and gift-giving to publicize their largess and authority. Leaders may also hoard rare objects from afar, display them at feasts, and finally take them to the grave. The burial of such wealth bestows status on the dead and, by association, on other family members. At elaborate mortuary feasts, the surviving kin stand to inherit the status, power, and rights of the newly dead.

The evidence for feasting in ancient West Mexican societies supports the inference that leaders and their families used these occasions of ritual consumption to compete for and maintain their authority. The fertile and diverse environment of West Mexico sustained population growth and facilitated the requisite surplus goods to serve at feasts.[10] In the area surrounding the Volcán de Tequila, leaders of the prosperous Teuchitlán tradition had access to the highly localized and native plant *Agave tequila* Weber (see fig. 2).[11] Cultivation of agave in prehistoric times for food, textiles, and the production of intoxicating beverages made from the fermented juice of the agave offers an explanation of why the land around the Volcán de Tequila was particularly precious to leaders whose power may have been vested in feasting strategies. Indeed, the location, depth, and contents of the shaft tombs in the Teuchitlán region during the period from 300 B.C. to A.D. 200 (the Late Formative period) marked lineage claims to these lands.

The West Mexican Art of Feasting

Like other pre-Hispanic peoples whose histories, poetry, and genealogies were inscribed in books, painted on pots, and etched in stone, the people of ancient West Mexico communicated their beliefs in art. For my study of ritual consumption in early West Mexican societies, I shall examine an extraordinary group of ceramic sculptures whose thematic content is feasting, and whose context is funerary. The placement of these earthenware objects in the shaft tombs of the dead imparts a powerful significance to their depictions of feasting. In addition, the imagery of consumption that pervades the large corpus of art from Nayarit, Jalisco, and Colima suggests that feasting was an entrenched custom throughout the region. The early artists of West Mexico conveyed feasting in three primary ceramic forms: large human figures with vessels; small-scale scenes with groups of figurines shown with food and vessels; and depictions of the actual foods for the feast. The two forms with human figures can tell us a great deal about rituals of consumption in West Mexico, and help us understand the familial and social dimensions of these important events.[12]

Food and Vessels

Several of the large human figures are immediately recognizable as consumers of food or drink because each holds, in one or both hands, a small container shaped like either a bowl or a cup—empty containers of individual serving size (see figs. 1, 3, and 4). Vestiges of original paint still survive on many cups or bowls held by these large figures. Research into pre-Hispanic containers in Mesoamerica supports that such small vessels were multipurpose. The Maya, for example, had only one word for the individual-sized vessels that they used for consuming drinks and stews (rather than the multiplicity of distinctions we make, such as cup, goblet, mug, cereal bowl, etc.).[13] That the small

vessels of the West Mexican figures are empty suggests that they too represent multi-purpose containers, whether they are gourds or earthenware pottery. Gourds were commonly used as containers throughout Meso-america: painted ones, much like decorated ceramic vessels, were reserved for ritual and mortuary events; and undecorated gourds, like plain ceramic vessels, served daily use.[14]

Ceramic models with groups of small figurines shown eating and drinking constitute a second category of the West Mexican art of feasting (see figs. 5 and 6). Food in these models is depicted in a limited range of shapes, making it possible to distinguish four categories: cylindrical food, such as tamales or ears of corn; globular items, such as fruits; discoidal pieces, such as cakes; and lumps of food, such as beans. Except for the cakes, which are served alone, the other food categories are shown in clusters or platefuls, similar to bowls of tamales depicted in Maya art (see fig. 7).[15] Serving platters and shallow bowls hold the tiny shapes of food. In a study of 82 models from West Mexico, I found that platters were the most numerous container depicted, representing nearly 70 percent of the 101 containers for food and drink counted on the models.[16] The model in the collection of the Los Angeles County Museum of Art, for example (fig. 6), exhibits two platters with tamales, and two with cakes. Pre-Hispanic platters were made from

Fig. 3 Standing marriage pair; Ixtlán del Río style; Nayarit; earthenware. Private collection. Cat. no. 195.

Fig. 4 Seated chieftain with female attendants; Ameca-Etzatlán style; Jalisco; earthenware. Private collection. Cat. no. 123. Courtly etiquette is observed by formalized gestures including the presentation of drink. Rank and office are indicated by the relative sizes of the figures.

baked clay, wood, gourd, or maguey leaf. The models also display empty vessels that are but miniature versions of those held by the large-scale figures. Even small figurines are sometimes shown holding tiny cups in their hands. Empty shallow bowls usually occupy the lap or a place adjacent to a small figurine. Large containers of jars and vats, though empty, denote ritual drinking scenes, as will be discussed in detail below.

The Guest List

The portrayal of people attending a feast also gives social meaning to the West Mexican art of consumption. The art itself provides us clues regarding the gender, status, and social grouping of feasting participants in the actual society. Who were these hungry and thirsty souls that the ancient artists chose to depict?

In the shapes of bodies, in the depiction of dress styles, and in the poses of the participants, the early artists captured the feasting participants in idealized forms and in relative degrees of portraiture. The sculptures permit a few basic insights into the social order of West Mexico regarding biological traits and social groups. The primary biological feature unambiguously depicted in human figures is their gender. Males and females are both clearly represented. Males are primarily depicted wearing a belted loincloth or short pants with flaps at front and back; occasionally their genitalia are also evident. Females are identified either by the presence of breasts or by a short skirt to the knees (see fig. 3). But other figures, lacking any gender markings, are essentially indeterminate to us. This is the case in many models where miniaturization may obscure differences. Compare, for instance, figure 8, where skirts on

several figurines designate them as female, although the plainness of several figures on the upper porch makes it impossible to determine their gender. Males and females, however, are almost equally prominent in the modeled scenes of feasting. In my study of available architectural models, females constitute forty percent of the figures whose

Fig. 5 Model of a house on a platform; Ixtlán del Río style; Nayarit; earthenware. The Minneapolis Institute of Arts, the John R. VanDerlip Fund. Cat. no. 175.

Fig. 6 Model of a houselike pavilion on a platform; Ixtlán del Río style; Nayarit; earthenware. Los Angeles County Museum of Art, The Proctor Stafford Collection, museum purchase with funds provided by Mr. and Mrs. Allan C. Balch. Cat. no. 173.

Fig. 7 Cylinder vase roll-out; Guatemala; Maya; c. 683; earthenware. Foundation for the Advancement of Mesoamerican Studies.

Fig. 8 Model of a house on a platform; Ixtlán del Río style; Nayarit; earthenware. Private collection. Cat. no. 176. Houses belonging to ruling families feature first-level adobe platforms, sometimes with inner chambers; the open porches above are for social gatherings. Thatched roofs were covered with mud plaster and painted with geometric designs.

gender can be surmised. Although pre-Hispanic women traditionally governed cooking and all preparations for feasting, the depiction in West Mexican art of females actually attending such events points to the fact that their participation extended beyond the kitchen.[17]

Infrequently, the portrayal of feasting participants includes children. A set of three figures, for example, clearly differentiates ages, as it shows a woman holding a nursing baby (see Braun, fig. 17). An unusual piece shows a large seated female figure whose skirt extends as a feasting platform upon which a pair of figures are seated before a large laden platter. This work undoubtedly represents a sacred theme. The symbolic imbalance in size suggests an artist's rendi-

tion of what some would call a great mother, mother goddess, or food-giving deity (see the essay by Richard Townsend in this volume and his fig. 19).

The adornments that the figures wear, whether painted or modeled in clay, may encode social meaning. Many large figures wear a broad array of adornments, such as headdresses, clothing, body paint, and various forms of jewelry: armbands, leg bands, earrings, nose rings, and necklaces. Headgear ranges from the feather headdress (see Townsend, fig. 2) to plain or long turbans (see Townsend, fig. 32), and conical and horned hats (see Townsend, figs. 10 and 29). While males wear the more elaborate types, only the plain turban is worn by both male and female figures. Earrings, too, vary: they

may be drop style, multiple rings, or earspool style. Such signs of gender, rank, and status are also reflected in miniature form, where feasting figurines in the models wear the same costume styles, although, due to size constraints, they are less elaborately rendered.

The adornments that West Mexican figures wear, given regional and stylistic variations, suggest that membership in a group, rather than individual identities, was the artist's primary social message.[18] Many large figures, as well as those in figurine groupings, illustrate this point. For instance, Ameca-Etzatlán–style figures wear identical and distinctive headdresses, painted and applied armbands, and facial paint (see fig. 4). In like manner, a pair of Zacatecas-style figures show similar earspools and body paint, while clearly distinguishing male and female (see fig. 9). The ceramic models, with numerous figurines, however, offered an even better format for artists to communicate social group membership. The clustering of shared adornments on figurines in modeled feasting scenes shows up in the use of the same types of armbands (see fig. 10) or in hat styles (see Townsend, fig. 27). Shared social emblems are coded prominently in the figurines of the models of ballcourts, dance groups, and other communal meetings (see

Fig. 9 Seated marriage pair; Zacatecas style; vicinity of Teocaltiche, Jalisco; earthenware. Denver Art Museum. Cat. no. 148.

Fig. 10 Model of a house on a platform; Ixtlán del Río style; Nayarit; earthenware. The Art Institute of Chicago, gift of Ethel and Julian R. Goldsmith. Cat. no. 172. Repeated hand-to-cheek gestures may signal the end of a "cheek-piercing" mourning rite.

Townsend, fig. 2; Day, figs. 1 and 21–23; and Witmore, fig. 1).

A close examination of the West Mexican art of feasting reveals three types of social-group messages: male and female pairs; ranked social groups; and leadership. The theme of male and female pairs indicates that family and bloodlines were elemental to social organization in ancient West Mexico (see also the essays by Lorenza López and Jorge Ramos, and Robert Pickering and Teresa Cabrero in this volume). This imagery may represent ancient lineages, whose genealogy was conveyed through traditional types of body paint, armbands, or turban styles. That male and female leaders of dominant lineages may have sponsored great feasts in West Mexico is suggested by the analogy presented by ancient Maya language. The relationship between feasts and lineage is explicit among the Maya whose word for "honored lineage leader" translates into "head of the banquet."[19] The male and female pairs may indicate that siblings headed two lineages and exchanged the burden of sponsoring feasts on an alternating basis. An example of this tradition is found in the Tewa Pueblos of New Mexico, whose dual social organization unifies their society. The summer and winter clans exchange authority seasonally, and each "owns" its namesake

season in which their feasts, harvests, rituals, and chiefs predominate.[20] On a grand, imperial scale, the Inca of South America similarly reckoned social and political power through two royal lineages.[21] This same concept of dual lineage structures deserves further investigation in early West Mexican societies.[22]

The presence or absence of adornments in the West Mexican tomb figures also points to the existence of social-group ranking. In the exhaustive study of architectural models that I previously conducted, a pattern of differentiation in adornment clearly emerged: just under half of the 590 figurines wear recognizable emblems of social rank; the remainder have none. This is surely a deliberate attempt to distinguish members of elite social groups, such as powerful lineages, from members of lower-ranked social groups. Lest there be any confusion, however, it should be noted that even the models with unadorned figures had feasting scenes. To judge from the models, at least, ritual feasting was an activity conducted by all sectors of the society. The large village scenes with over sixty figures verify a milieu of entrenched social inequality in ways that are often quite explicit: in the case of the model in The Art Institute of Chicago, for example (see Townsend, fig. 2), the large, central male wears a fanciful feather headdress, whereas the majority of those who join him on the tiered platform are small and without any distinguishing social labels. In another notable sculpture (fig. 11), the principal figure, accompanied by a woman and a dog, is prominently adorned with necklace, nosering, earrings, and a fan, while the six naked figures or servants who bear the litter lack distinguishing societal group markings.

We have seen pairs of male and female figures bearing emblems of rank and status and modeled scenes with figures showing the rank of social groups. I will now look at the imagery of leaders, both individual and in pairs, in poses of ritual feasting. This category includes certain figures sitting on stools. Stools are associated with authority, for it is widely established that in ancient Amerindian art only leaders are depicted sitting on thrones, or stools, of power. In the Coahuayana style of Colima, impressive male and female couples—large earthenware figures sitting on stools—hold individual vessels (see fig. 12, and Townsend, fig. 31). These figures are intriguing for they support the pre-

Fig. 11 Couple carried on a litter; Ameca-Etzatlán style; Jalisco; earthenware. Private collection. Cat. no. 120.

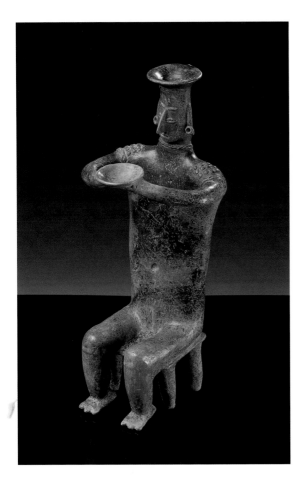

mise that socially equal males and females held authority and practiced ritual feasting together. It is probable that these imposing pairs portray leaders at mortuary or competitive feasts.

The art of West Mexico suggests that leaders engaged in small-scale warfare or ritualized battles to affirm their authority over subjects and rivals. The competitive and self-promoting aspects of war may have even been staged at feasting events and ballgames.[23] In many societies, both the battlefield and competitive, potlatch-like feasts are avenues for personal advancement and power. Striking Comala-style figures illustrate the relationship between warfare and ritual consumption, such as one wearing trophy heads and holding a bowl (see Townsend, fig. 10). A funerary scene portrays a seated leader drinking with standing warriors holding round shields, together with a seated beverage-keeper. The deceased lying in state before them may have met his end in a ritual military competition (see Townsend, fig. 38).

In summary, then, artisans of ancient West Mexico used adornments and dress to signal social identity and group member-

ship, as did many pre-Hispanic peoples.[24] They distinguished members of their society through several elements, including markers of gender, costume, accessories, and body paint, just as they could through the absence of these items. The recent discoveries of shell bracelets, greenstone pendants, and other treasures that embellish a small percentage of human remains in shaft tombs offer conclusive support for the argument that the adornments worn by the figurines expressed social meanings that were extant in ancient West Mexican society (see the essays by López and Ramos, and Patricia Anawalt in this volume).[25] Thus, data from art and archaeology complement each other and confirm that embedded social inequality, hereditary leadership, and hierarchical social structures prevailed in West Mexican societies during the period from 300 B.C. to A.D. 200 (the Late Formative period).

The Setting

The mortuary context of all West Mexican art, including the art of consumption, is the clearest message we have as to how the living thought of the dead. Ancient potters apparently created every large figure and small scene as an offering to the dead, whom they believed lived underground. They even depicted the underworld home

sierras holds that the soul first leaves the corpse as a bird or firefly prior to its journey to the ancestors.[27] Thus, it is likely the two-story models with birds, dogs, and scenes of consumption depict mortuary feasts. They send a message that the dead needed food and drink in the afterlife, as a pair of feasting skeletons reaffirms (see Furst, fig. 11).

The sculptures of figures with cups and the models of feasts that have been discussed thus far have frequently—and, in my opinion, mistakenly—been called "anecdotal" depictions of everyday life.[28] I propose, instead, that these genres of earthenware figures and models symbolize ritual feasts, rather than everyday meals. The large figures and model scenes, for example, display a small range of food types that are carefully laid out and never mixed. Many large hollow figures from different regions hold cups, drinking gourds, or large beverage vats; they often have quiet expressions suggestive of ritual contemplation or death itself (see figs. 15 and 28). Large vats that undoubtedly held ritual beverages are symbolically ornamented (see figs. 16 and 17). In the models, many platters and jars are very large, with food servings piled high. The adult figures who invariably hold vessels or gather around this food and drink emphasize orderly presentation. Platters and jars placed centrally in a room, or outside on a porch, indicate the

of the ancestors, using the device of a two-story ceramic model (fig. 8). The basement or lower chamber of these models is believed by some investigators to represent the physical place of the dead, which in West Mexico was the shaft tomb or sacred underground cave.[26] To test this interpretation, I examined the differences between the main floors and lower chambers on forty-five architectural models with two levels. In sharp contrast to the main floor, which is invariably filled with figurines and feasting elements, approximately half of the lower chambers were empty or had only dogs. These canine figurines may symbolize an ancient West Mexican rendition of Xolotl, the Aztec dog who guided souls of the dead across the underworld river. Some of the human figurines who also occupy the lower chambers of these models are slumped over, seemingly dead—as seen in the model in the Denver Art Museum collection (fig. 14). Their "companions" attend to them, with dishes of food nearby.

Birds, perched on roof tops, are the only other animal besides dogs that are represented on the models—as evident on both the Minneapolis Institute of Arts and Art Institute of Chicago examples (see fig. 6, and Townsend, fig. 2). The birds may represent the spirits of the newly dead, who have not yet descended to the underworld. Mythology from modern groups in the West Mexican

Fig. 16 Incised vessel on a four-legged animal support; Comala style; Colima; earthenware. Hudson Museum, University of Maine, Orono, William P. Palmer III Collection. Cat. no. 69.

Fig. 17 Seated male figure holding a vat and drinking cup; Comala style; Colima; earthenware. Private Collection. Cat. no. 40.

significance of public display. Scenes of eating and drinking in adult social groups represent not an everyday meal of beans and maize, but a momentous event, deemed worthy of meticulous and repeated dramatization. All of these ceramic forms were a means for West Mexican artists to portray ritual consumption. This art form is analogous to depictions in Mixtec codices (see fig. 18), Maya polychrome vases, and Central Mexican murals (see fig. 19).[29]

Fig. 18 *Pulque* scene from *Codex Nuttall*, Mixtec; c. 14th century. British Museum, London. A Mixtec couple celebrates over a vessel of frothing *pulque*.

West Mexican Mortuary Feasts

These West Mexican figures and models portray a tradition of feasting dating back to at least 100 B.C. Although some scholars have considered the archaeological evidence for ritual feasting to be ambiguous, because the preparation of a feast requires the same equipment used to prepare the daily meal, the practice of mortuary feasts can clearly be identified from the vessels and containers of food found in the shaft tombs. Members of social groups hosted funerary feasts for the dead and for the recognition of their own genealogy and lineage.[30] Hosting a feast for the dead, at which both the living and the dead eat and drink, would require diverse kinds of containers. Most ceramic vessels interred with the dead in ancient West Mexican shaft tombs are individual serving vessels such as cups, dishes, and jars—intended, presumably, for use by the dead.[31]

Fig. 19 Watercolor reproductions (c. 1971) of a *pulque*-drinking scene; Cholula; 200/300. Above, a male figure brings *pulque* to the feast. Below, men and women are shown drinking.

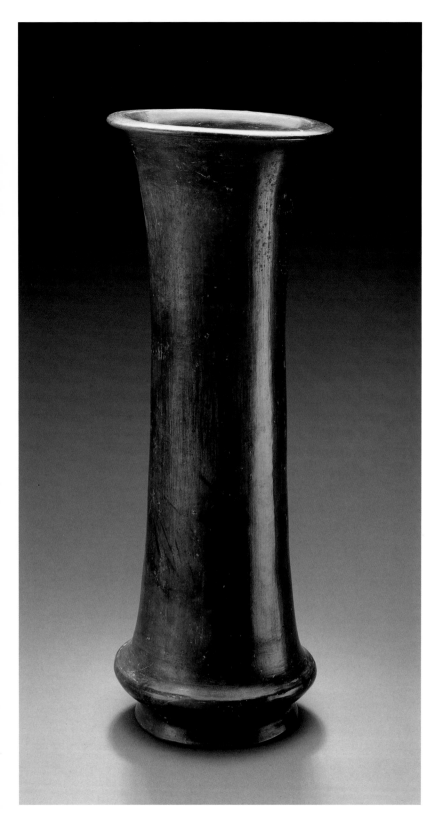

Fig. 20 Cylindrical
vessel; Chupícuaro;
Michoacán/Guanajuato;
earthenware. Fowler
Museum of Cultural
History, University of
California, Los Angeles.

In some cases, as in the shaft tombs of the Atemajac valley (near Guadalajara), rough cooking wares were also placed alongside the fine, painted pieces. Archaeologist Meredith Aronson has surmised "that the olla or bowl serves the same purpose in life as it does in the journey after death."[32] Although food and drink offered to the dead over a millennium ago generally do not survive in the archaeological record, at the recently excavated site of Huitzilapa, the shaft-tomb environment protected organic offerings that had been placed in the ceramic vessels. As presented in their essay in this volume, Lorenza López and Jorge Ramos recovered samples of organic material, presumably food, from a majority of the vessels.[33] The analysis of the organic remains and residues obtained from these vessels will provide intriguing insights into the practice of mortuary feasting in ancient West Mexican society.

Feasts for the dead have been a tradition in Central and West Mexico since the Formative period, as is especially seen in the range of elegant Chupícuaro wares (see figs. 20–24). Sixteenth-century ethnographic and historical documents indicate that ritual feasts for the ancestors endured into the Spanish colonial period. The *Chronicles of Michoacán,* for example, describes Tarascan customs at the time of the Spanish conquest, making it clear that in addition to an annual flagpole ceremony honoring the ancestors, the Tarascans placed great emphasis on mortuary rites.[34] They displayed their dead in public spectacles, accompanied by food and alcohol. As recounted in the *Chronicles,* following a gruesome battle, family members of the dead made "many offerings of bread and wine" at the temple along with the "wrapped heads of lords killed in war." The "wine" referred to was *octli,* the fermented agave sap that the cultures of ancient West Mexico produced. An illustration of this Tarascan custom, taken from the *Chronicles,* shows mounds of round maize tamales overflowing from large serving bowls that were placed in front of the wrapped heads of the deceased. In another account, Tarascans performed elaborate mortuary rituals to honor the death of a king. His death brought lords from throughout the province to their capital city of Tzintzuntzan. For the funerary procession, the lords prepared a litter with the body wrapped in blankets. They placed the king's

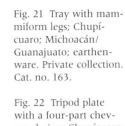

Fig. 21 Tray with mammiform legs; Chupícuaro; Michoacán/Guanajuato; earthenware. Private collection. Cat. no. 163.

Fig. 23 Cylindrical tripod vessel; Chupícuaro; Michoacán/Guanajuato; earthenware. Private collection. Cat. no. 162.

Fig. 22 Tripod plate with a four-part chevron design; Chupícuaro; Michoacán/Guanajuato; earthenware. Private collection. Cat. no. 166.

Fig. 24 Oval-shaped vessel with geometric designs; Chupícuaro; Michoacán/Guanajuato; earthenware. Private collection. Cat. no. 164.

head, also wrapped, on top of the grand burial litter. Those permitted to march in the royal funeral parade included extended family members and seven lords and forty attendants who, after drinking large amounts, were put to death so that they might serve the king in the afterworld. Accompanying the body into the grave were "many large earthen jars, smaller jars, wine, and food." Lords and commoners gathered for the mortuary feast held at the royal patio, where they feasted on "huge quantities of food that had belonged to the dead ruler." These Tarascan practices paralleled those of their contemporaries and long-term enemies, the Aztecs. Such pre-Hispanic traditions are also analogous to annual feasts for the dead and mortuary rites conducted by contemporary West Mexican peoples.

At the turn of the twentieth century, pioneering ethnographers such as Carl Lumholtz and Konrad Preuss recorded feasting customs among the indigenous Huichol and Tarahumara peoples of the western Sierra Madre. The Huichol observed the yearly cycle of ritual feasts, including those commemorating their ancestors. For the Feast of San Andrés, the ancestors were said to sit under the family hearth with their eating bowls raised, waiting for food. Women served the ancestors specially prepared corn cakes and oval rolls.[35] With eyes closed and holding forth their empty cups, some ceramic figures from ancient West Mexico seem a pre-Hispanic variant of the Feast of San Andrés. Other annual feasts, held in June and October, have parallels with the Aztec pole ceremony of *Huey Miccaylhuitl.* The Huichol feasts, the "toasting of corn" and the "ritual of *elotes*" (tender ears of new corn), took place in ceremonial plazas marked by a tall pole that reached "to the sky."[36] The pole, decorated with "beautifully patterned woven sashes," symbolized the celestial path. Each June, religious leaders danced around the pole, while families contributed mounds of tamales, toasted corn, and deity images made of amaranth and maize breads. In October, just prior to harvest, religious leaders impersonated the Huichol solar deities. They dressed as feathered eagles and offered new foods at the sacred pole.[37] The meaning of these Huichol events may apply to an interpretation of the ceramic models of feasting at pole ceremonies that are found in West Mexican shaft tombs (see Witmore, fig. 10).

In addition to the annual feasts for the ancestors, the Huichol also conduct mortuary rites. In the grave, the recently dead receive "a gift of water in a hollow reed and five tortillas."[38] After five days, the family holds a feast presenting all the favorite foods of the deceased. The spirit eats, and then turns into a small bird and flies away. The purpose of the Huichol funerary rituals is to help the soul of the dead find its place with the ancestors.[39] According to their myths, one reason the Huichol give food to the dead is to pacify the hungry dog who guards the passage to the underworld. The little black dog "is from ancient times. It died and then it remained there, to stand watch on the road.

. . . The soul takes the tortillas out of the bag," and gives them to the dog. Then, while "the dog is busy eating, . . . that soul can pass and it keeps on walking."[40]

The Tarahumara also offered food to the living and the dead at mortuary feasts. Lumholtz described their ritual:

> The body is wrapped in a blanket almost before it is cold, to be buried later, but food is at once placed around it . . . the dead keeps his buckskin pouch and three small gourds with beans. Three ears of corn are placed to the left of his head, as well as a small jar of *tesvino.* Another small jar of *tesvino* is placed near his feet.[41]

Tesvino (sometimes spelled *tegüino*) is fermented maize beer. The family of the deceased Tarahumaran hosted a series of three mortuary feasts (or four for deceased women) over the next three years. At each event, the family served special tortillas (sized according to the age of the deceased), as well as various meats from whatever livestock the deceased possessed and large quantities of intoxicating *tesvino.* Each mortuary feast lasted twenty-four hours, beginning "at the hour at which the dead breathed his last." They also offered sustenance to the dead, saying, "Here I leave this *tesvino* and food for you, the meat and tortillas, that you may eat and not come back."[42] The Tarahumara continue to host mortuary feasts at which large amounts of intoxicating *tesvino* are served: a ladle-full, "for each of the dead for whom the fiesta had been sponsored," believing perhaps that inebriation encourages grieving.[43]

To this day, Tarascans living around Lake Pátzcuaro near their ancient capital of Tzintzuntzan still celebrate the Day of the Dead in a fusion of Spanish Catholic and indigenous beliefs and customs. The feasts are family events that memorialize both the newly dead and the long-dead ancestors.[44] Liquor, music, marigold flowers, and food offerings provide a link between Christian family celebrations and ancient Amerindian ancestor rituals (see Townsend, fig. 1).

Ritual Drinking

Besides confirming the antiquity of feasting, the archaeological vessels, figures, and earthenware models, along with the ethnographic and historical accounts, also underscore the prevalence and importance of ritual consumption of intoxicating beverages in ancient West Mexico. *Octli* (also called *pulque,* the fermented sap of agave) and maize-beer *tesvino* were two of three native choices, the third being *mescal* (made from the fermented juice of baked agave hearts). All three have long traditions in West Mexico, although *octli* may have been the most preferred. The author of the *Chronicles of Michoacán* noted that "we have wine here that was made in the very stump of the maguey," and that "an official tavern keeper, called Atari, [receives] all the maguey wine that was made for the feasts."[45] Although the Tarahumara made *tesvino* from maize, they preferred it made from agave, because it was sweeter and tastier. The Tarahumara called the agave "the first plant created by God."[46] Spanish accounts tell us that indigenous peoples of Jalisco, Nayarit, Colima, and Michoacán fermented the most freshly drawn agave sap, called *aguamiel,* which was used as a fermented starter to make large amounts of *octli.*

Then, as now, the production of this beverage required two essential tools, one to scrape the hollowed-out inside of the agave and thus increase the flow of sap, and the second, a device used to suction the *aguamiel* out of the heart into portable containers. These two processing tools exist in the West Mexican archaeological and artistic records from the Late Formative period. The *ocaxtle* is a rounded obsidian blade used only for scraping the inside of agave hearts. Such tools have been found in abundance at archaeological sites such as Huitzilapa and Teuchitlán. *Acocotes,* the elongated gourds used as the suctioning device, do not survive in the archaeological record, yet they are still widely used in Mexico today and ceramic images of

these gourds in use do exist (see fig. 25). A Lagunillas-style figure from Nayarit holds an *acocote* in one hand and a cup in the other (fig. 15). Another figure carries the heart of the agave in a tumpline, portraying the return from harvest (see fig. 26). Finally, an Jalisco figure sits with a large pot, as well as a cup, enjoying the final stage of ritual drinking (fig. 17).

Women in Central and West Mexico may have had a particular social or economic function related to the production or control of agave or the consumption of alcohol. In contemporary communities of the Tarahumara, the cooking and monitoring of proper *tesvino* fermentation is the job of women.[47] That the Aztec deity for maguey is the female goddess, Mayahuel, hints at such a relationship (fig. 27). According to their legend, "here is how it happened: the maguey was scraped out, the bountiful maguey was discovered, from which *aguamiel* comes. The

Fig. 25 A farmer drawing maguey sap *(aguamiel).*

Fig. 26 Male figure carrying a maguey agave heart with a tumpline; Comala style; Colima; earthenware. Private collection. Cat. no. 28.

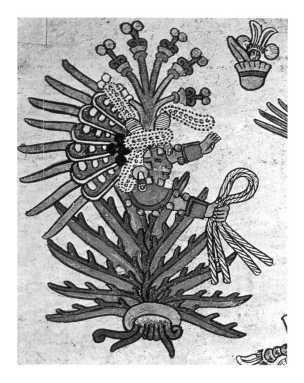

Fig. 27 Maguey god from *Codex Borbonicus*; Aztec; c. 1525. Bibliothèque de l'Assemblée Nationale, Paris.

first to discover the art of scraping it was a woman; her name, Mayahuel."[48] Perhaps Mayahuel came from the west, given the presence of *ocaxtles* and the early depictions of *pulque* feasts from West Mexico.

Models featuring ritualized drinking scenes at houses and patios show an assortment of tall vessels, large open vats, as well as serving vessels (see figs. 5, 6, 8, 10, and 13). The imagery of festival drinking in West Mexican ceramic art is accompanied by the rituals of dance and music. These contexts demonstrate that important social rites incorporated the drinking of *pulque*. West Mexican ceramic models of ballcourts suggest that they too were a venue for ritual drinking. In the ballcourt at the Yale University Art Gallery, the large jars held by two spectators on the ballcourt may signify the consumption of intoxicating *pulque* (see Day, fig. 21; alternatively, these large objects may be drums). In a preliminary study of ceramic sherds from a Huitzilapa ballcourt, I found that sherds from fine individual serving vessels were the overwhelming functional type, suggesting the consumption of ritual drink at regional competitions.[49] Feasting at West Mexican ballcourts was used "for the negotiation of power relations," as John G. Fox has interpreted evidence for ritual feasting at other Mesoamerican ballcourts.[50]

Conclusions

The large and small earthenware figures from ancient West Mexico discussed in this essay clearly demonstrate that ritual feasting was a way of life during the period from 300 B.C. to A.D. 200, when this art was interred in shaft-tomb chambers of the dead. Beyond this, the evidence is compelling that such feasting was much more than the equivalent of a modern holiday brunch or dinner: these events were an opportunity to negotiate social, political, and economic agendas.

For peoples who use feasts in this way, it is essential to control an environment capable of producing a surplus.[51] The countryside of West Mexico certainly has this capability. We may hypothesize that early leaders competing for followers attracted a growing population to the most favorable districts of West Mexico. For basic survival purposes, common folk aligned themselves with wealth—or, in other words, with the most generous leader occupying the richest lands. Leaders seeking to increase their power and control over territory gained great advantages by sponsoring major feasts. By receiving the loyalty and support of their own lineage and of increasingly larger populations, they correspondingly grew in political, religious, and economic power. The advantages that feasts and competitions provided to leaders fueled a social inequality based on wealth.

The distribution of Late Formative–period settlements across the West Mexican landscape points to the existence of a regional network. Settlements dating from 300 B.C. to A.D. 200 surround the West Mexican volcanoes (Colima, Tequila, and Ceboruco) and the vast highland lakes, and leaders of these communities probably exercised their authority by controlling the production and distribution of obsidian, salt, agave, and other restricted resources to exchange regionally.[52] The actions of these separate but interacting polities would also help explain the variability seen in the archaeological settlement pattern of ancient West Mexico. Scholars have suggested the competitive advantage that would have been held by leaders who were able to cultivate plants for the production of ritual beverages to serve at feasts.[53] Thus, the differential development of an increasingly complex society in the Teuchitlán tradition

around the Volcán de Tequila may reflect the wealth of lineages and their leaders who monopolized the precious agave resources—essential to the production of *octli* and required in all types of feasting.

West Mexican leaders utilized gift-giving at feasts as a political means to create and maintain personal loyalties and strategic alliances. The practice of such gift-giving is thus directly related to a tradition of local and regional exchange. The local exchange of ceramic art offers an explanation for the pervasive pattern of mixed figure styles found in the shaft tombs of elite members of society. It is quite probable that West Mexican leaders gave pottery as gifts to allies from other communities—near and far—to commemorate a specific feast, as did Maya hosts.[54] West Mexican shaft tombs also contain evidence for regional gift-giving in the form of imported objects. Perishable imports probably included rare foods, dyes, textiles, furs, and feathers.[55] In the archaeological record, the distribution and exclusivity of engraved and cloisonné conch-shell trumpets, slate mirror backs, shell bracelets, and worked pieces of obsidian, greenstone, and crystal define the extent of each leader's importance in a regional network. Virtually all of the precious objects known from ancient West Mexico have come exclusively from

shaft tombs. One can imagine the public displays of wealth that conferred status to the owner, in life and in death.

Thus, mortuary feasts served as occasions to bury the wealth of exotica and ceramic art that leaders manipulated for the cycle of ritual feasting. In addition, funerary rites exalted the living descendants. Surviving members of the lineage who feasted their ancestors in effect aggrandized and asserted their blood right to the privileges of the powerful dead. Using genealogy, these kin perpetuated social inequality by inheriting their status and positions of authority. Yet lineage groups were also surely obliged to keep up the process of recycling wealth by the festival system. In addition, these obligations involved the religious requirement to sponsor festivals and rites to maintain the balance of society and nature. During this period, the peoples of the core Teuchitlán area negotiated social status, political power, and resource privileges with feasts and drink. In their deep shaft tombs and through their rituals to the dead, they claimed the rights of their ancestors to the precious possession of agave and obsidian that flourished on the lands of the Volcán de Tequila.

RICHARD F. TOWNSEND

BEFORE GODS, BEFORE KINGS

Day of the Dead, Art of the Tombs

In the silence of the night, hundreds of candles burn by the graves and the rows of baskets that have been laid out with white cloths covering the offerings of holiday bread; everything about is sprinkled with orange marigold petals (see fig. 1). Small wooden altars also stand by the low mounds, each decked with bread, dried ears of maize, and the bright pungent flowers. The village women sit in vigil, wrapped in dark shawls and the red or black folds of their woolen skirts. Their only movements are to light a new taper or hush the fitful sleep of a child. In the stillness of this night an aged voice, a male elder, speaks out—calling to mind those who are departed, leading prayers, and inviting the souls to return and partake of the feast. The women respond in a hushed chorus of whispers and murmurs. Eventually, Allhallows night begins to pass as the stars disappear in the pale yellow light rising behind the indigo mountains. Peaked shapes of village tile roofs are silhouetted against the expanse of Lake Pátzcuaro, and the first wisps of smoke from charcoal kitchen fires eddy around the eaves of the houses. The red ball of the sun rises above the ancient shapes of volcanoes. Candlelight fades, children awake, and the great assembly of women slowly begins to arise and disperse. The grave mounds are left with their altars and carpets of marigold petals. Here on the island of Janitzío and all over Mexico on the Day of the Dead, from vast urban cemeteries to the small burial grounds of countryside towns, this is a time of communal reunion.

The participants are joined in asserting that death is not a final severance, for the dead have merely passed on to another existence. Their lives are recalled and forebears are solicited with prayer offerings, keeping alive shared memories and emotions.

Mexico is a land where time converges, where the sense of history and place unfold simultaneously. The Day of the Dead, embraced in the Christian calendar of Catholic ceremony, incorporates elements inherited and adapted from a centuries-old Mediterranean past. Yet the women of Janitzío sitting in all-night vigil, the strewing of marigolds *(tzempasúchitl),* the offering of maize (and, in many communities, the magenta tassels of amaranth grain), and the calling upon forebears also reflect patterns of ancient Amerindian belief and ritual. They remind us that in countless ways and in thousands of towns and villages, Spanish customs were adapted, absorbed, and transformed by aboriginal ways of thought and rhythms of life, governed by a profound sense of integration with the earth, the sky, and the changing seasons.

Before the Spanish arrived, the worship of ancestors and the offering of sacrifice were perhaps most fundamentally intended to invoke the spiritual powers of the deceased for the successful operation of the seasonal cycle. Among these ancient agricultural peoples, the lives of their ancestors were assimilated into the larger cosmic rhythms. The arrival of rain, the resurgence of the fertility of the soil after the long season of heat and dust, and the period of cultivation

Fig. 1 The night between All Saints' Day (November 1) and All Soul's Day (November 2) on the island of Janitzío, Lake Pátzcuaro. A fusion of Christian and indigenous customs is seen in this famous communal rite. The ancestors are called to an all-night vigil and invited to feast on offerings of bread and ears of maize.

and harvest that followed were special times for petitioning, or offering thanksgiving to, the ancestral spirits for their supernatural intervention with the deified forces of nature upon which existence depended. As we shall see in this essay, the sculptural art from tombs in ancient West Mexico is intimately bound with this fundamental meaning and purpose.

The art of ancient West Mexico has long seemed to belong to a world apart, to a culture and a geographical region far from the urban, statelike societies of central and southern Mesoamerica. Without colossal pyramids or monumental stone stelae proclaiming the deeds of powerful rulers, without sculptures and artifacts displaying the intricate symbols and paraphernalia of gods and reflecting the spectacular pageantry of public rituals, the artists of western Mexico instead portrayed their world by means of earthenware figures and vessels that were made to accompany the dead. Between 200 B.C. and A.D. 250 and continuing residually thereafter, in the mountains and basins between the deep canyon of the Río Santiago and the Pacific coast, powerful chieftains were building shaft tombs with burial chambers to commemorate their family lineages. Within these chambers the deceased were laid out in their regalia and surrounded with offerings of food and earthenware figures of warriors and ladies, models of festivals and models of buildings, and elegant vessels representing foodstuffs and many forms of animals and plants. There might also be figures of musicians and contortionists, carriers of gourds and large beverage jars, as well as shamans and dwarfs. Throughout the region, local styles vary the subjects, yet all show a predilection for figures in action, with animated gestures and lively expressions. Why were these diverse forms placed in the tombs? What were their functions for the living? What subjects were chosen for representation? In what way do these singular symbolic forms differ from those of other Mesoamerican centers of civilization? And what themes might these sculptures share with those of the other Mesoamerican traditions? In searching for answers we will explore the idea that West Mexican figures and vessels were made to function as a vital link in the network of religious connections leading outward from the living community to its ancestors, and through them to the greater,

all-powerful forces residing in the earth, in the rivers and lakes, in the sun and moon, and in the majestic and recurring phenomena of the dry and wet seasons. As our inquiry proceeds, we will begin to see that while this system of imagery and thought was profoundly rooted in the West Mexican region, it also belongs to one of the oldest, essential stratums of Amerindian belief and symbolism widely shared among many peoples of North and South America.

Tomb Models and Figures of Ancient Rites

Among all the types of West Mexican sculpture, the most detailed illustrations of ancient life were made in the vicinity of Ixtlán del Río, Nayarit. Tombs from this area have yielded a host of small-scale model houses, ceremonial centers, and ballcourts with scenes of communal feasting and other rituals (see fig. 2). Other models portray processions, dances, warfare, and elaborate funerals. Another tradition of modeling featuring scenes with many figures had also appeared in the art of Colima, but these examples are less complex and without architectural settings. The Ixtlán models are especially valuable not only for their sense of design and their highly expressive, often humorous, and always lively characterizations, but also because they form a visual text presenting an inventory of basic religious, social, and economic activities and the settings in which they took place.

When Hasso von Winning first described the Ixtlán and Colima models in his 1972 exhibition catalogue *Anecdotal Sculpture of Ancient West Mexico,* he noted that the apparent absence of temple architecture and representations of gods or rituals associated with such deities suggested that the models portrayed events of "secular ceremonialism." Indeed, the small figural scenes do not display the rectangular, tiered platform-pyramids surmounted by houselike temples, or the square platforms and plazas found in cities of central and southern Mesoamerica. Nor do any of the most familiar Mesoamerican masked or elaborately attired figures of gods appear in this tomb art; neither are there sculptural sun-disks nor other readily identifiable cosmological forms.

Since the late 1970s, however, the discovery and mapping by archaeologist Phil Weigand of dozens of circular ceremonial

sites concentrated in the lake-basin district of Jalisco and extending into neighboring districts of Colima and Nayarit have revealed that the models of village festival scenes correspond to the layout of these unique West Mexican circular ritual centers. The models represent thatched, houselike pavilions arranged symmetrically around an open patio with a circular, tiered pyramid rising in the center. An even more primary version of this type of ritual compound has recently been mapped in the field by Lorenza López and Jorge Ramos at the tomb site of Huitzilapa (see their essay in this volume). In more evolved form such sacred circles are seen at Santa Quiteria, Ahualulco, and related sites; the most elaborate formation, with interlock-

ing circles of multiple pavilions, is the great center of Teuchitlán (see also the essay by Weigand and Christopher Beekman). At Teuchitlán, the alignment of stairways on the two largest circular pyramids corresponds to the cardinal and intercardinal points, reflecting a well-known Mesoamerican cosmological format: the central pyramids become symbolic *axis mundis,* connecting the sky, the earth's surface, and the underworld, while the surrounding pavilions mark divisions around the circular rim of the horizon. Such mandala-like architectural settings describe basic principles of spatial organization and sacred geography and can be used for reckoning and using time. Elsewhere in Mesoamerica, this ordering system is commonly

Fig. 2 Model of a circular ceremonial center; Ixtlán del Río style; Nayarit; earthenware. The Art Institute of Chicago, gift of Ethel and Julian R. Goldsmith. Cat. no. 183. Standing atop a circular altar or pyramid, a chieftain brandishes a baton of office to the sound of conch-shell trumpets, a drum, and a chorus of singers.

Fig. 3 Schematic drawing of the cylindrical Tizoc stone; Aztec; c. 1470; Museo Nacional de Antropología, Mexico City. The sun diadem is carved on the top surface of the circular monument; the roll-out frieze of carved figures wraps around the cylindrical body. The composition represents the world, with the sun and a star-band above, and the earth-band below. Aztec warriors capture the gods of enemy towns in a repeated ritualistic litany of conquests. The Aztec state is shown as a cosmos.

expressed by the quadripartite, rectangular arrangements of great religious and political capitals such as Teotihuacan of A.D. 500 or the Aztec city Tenochtitlan of 1500. Even so, among such urban peoples there also persisted an old, universal religious practice of describing a ceremonial circuit by processing around a given area, object, or natural feature. Thus, an especially significant natural formation such as a mountain or lake, a man-made pyramid, or even a whole city would be enclosed by religious circumambulation. This was a widely established way of ordering or consecrating a discrete "home" area, beyond whose boundaries lay the unconsecrated, disordered domains of barbaric peoples and dangerous forces. Perhaps the most famous Mesoamerican sculptural monument expressing this concept in symbolic form is the Aztec circular stone of Tizoc, on which the emperor and his minions are shown capturing a succession of enemy towns by grasping their gods by the scalp lock; these ritualistic poses unfold around the monument, between the sun and the sky carved on the upper surface and register, and a band representing the earth on the register

below (see fig. 3). The historical Aztec conquests were shown as a ritual procession forming a cosmos, and the cosmos was seen as the Aztec state. Although the West Mexican ceremonial centers are unique in their circular architectural form, they reflect basic principles of spatial order manifested elsewhere in Mesoamerica.

The motif of the *axis mundi*—so clearly represented on the Nayarit models showing dancers and musicians beneath poles rising from the central circular pyramid—was also archaeologically found by Weigand at Teuchitlán: there, the second pyramid was found to have a small depression on the upper level corresponding to a pit where a pole would have been inserted. In the models a variant of this motif is also represented as a tree, around which celebrants are symmetrically seated; some models show the tree to have the spiky bark of the silk-cotton tree (ceiba or *pochotl*), regarded in Mesoamerica as a symbolic axis between the earth and the heavens. The white kapok of the *pochotl* floats away from open seed pods at the height of the dry season, suggesting clouds soon to usher in the period of rains. In some mythologies the ceiba tree is also identified as the birthplace of humankind, a variant of origin myths describing the birth of humans from the womb of the earth. Figuratively speaking, in the Nahuatl language of the Aztecs, rulers were likened to the *pochotl* tree, under whose protection the community prospered (see fig. 4).

The Ixtlán del Río models thus reflect ceremonial architecture and the organization of sacred and cosmological space, leading us to the subject of the division of time and the succession of festivals marking the important events of life. In the imagery of the central and southern Mesoamerican peoples, from the Olmec to the Classic Maya, Teotihuacan, and the Aztecs, the figures of gods provide an index to the cycle of calendrical festivals regulating the schedule of major communal activities according to the seasons of the year. The divination almanacs of central Mexico depict each "month" of the native calendar presided over by its assigned divinity, and the great monthly festivals of the Aztecs and their neighbors, described by Spanish friars in the early sixteenth century, were each devoted to these particular gods or to groups of related gods, personifying the deified forces of nature or ancestral heroes. The two great divisions of the year were the annual cycle of summer rains—the time for planting, cultivation, and the harvest that followed—alternating with the winter and spring dry season—the time for war and long-distance trade. But the general absence of masks and other emblems and paraphernalia of deities in West Mexico appears to leave us without one of the principal means for describing such a system in the ordering of ancient life. It was this absence that prompted von Winning's notion of a "secular ceremonialism." We must therefore look beyond symbols of standardized gods for an index to the events embodied by the Ixtlán models.

Rites of Passage

In any society the life of an individual is marked by a series of passages from one age to another and from one occupation to another. Transitions from one stage or status to the next are occasions for private and public ceremony and feasting—birth, social puberty, betrothal and marriage, advancement to a higher class or occupational specialization,

and death. In his classic study *Rites of Passage,* Arnold van Gennep argued that as the purpose of these highly structured events is to enable an individual to pass from one defined position to another equally defined, they also remind him or her that each higher or more advanced level also carries wider social and religious responsibilities within the family, the community, and the world. Rites of passage are also rites of initiation and renewal, corresponding to the need, in social as well as in biological activity, for exhausted energies to be periodically replenished or regenerated. Characteristically, rites of passage take place in three distinct phases, beginning with a separation from normal activities, followed by a time of transition and instruction in the group's mores and special activities and duties, and concluding with a phase of reincorporation or renewal as the participant rejoins the larger group. Among such peoples as those of Mesoamerica with strong leanings towards systematization, the most important human ceremonies tended to be keyed to major natural events: the rising and setting of the sun, the monthly phases of the moon, the equinoctial or solstitial markers of seasonal change, or the start of a new year. The phases of withdrawal, transition, and reincorporation occurring in the fundamental sets of ceremonies that accompany, facilitate, or affect the transitions from one stage to another in an individual's life, might also form part of the larger systems of ritual that benefited whole societies, such as rites of kingship or of the seasonal ceremonial cycle. In such grand systemic correlations, rites of passage, like other major social and seasonal rites of renewal, were also to various degrees modeled on remote mythic archetypes established by diverse nature-deities, heroes, or deified natural forces and phenomena *in illo tempore,* the time of creation. For in traditional and ancient societies, man's life resembled nature, from which neither the individual nor the society stood independent. The universe itself is governed by a periodicity that has repercussions on human life, with stages and transitions, movements forward, and periods of stasis or relative inactivity. It is indeed a cosmic conception that relates the stages of human existence to those of the seasons and plant and animal life, and, by a sort of pre-scientific divination, joins them to the great rhythms of the universe.

Fig. 4 Detail of the Aztec feast of *Huey Miccaylhuitl* from the *Codex Borbonicus;* Aztec; c. 1525. Bibliothèque de l'Assemblée Nationale, Paris. In the annual Aztec feast of *Huey Miccaylhuitl,* dancers circle the tall Xocotlhuetzi pole, ornamented with paper banners and royal quetzal feathers.

Although West Mexican tomb sculptures appear not to feature representations of gods as do other Mesoamerican symbolic systems, there is evidence that they represent a series of important rites of passage widely observed by the diverse peoples of the region. Indeed, it was Hasso von Winning who noted funerals and a possible marriage ceremony represented by models from Ixtlán del Río. As one who is familiar with Aztec rituals, I have noticed a series of West Mexican figures that point to the initiation rites of warriors and chieftains. In pursuing these clues it has become apparent that the models and large hollow tomb figures share an extensive imagery of rites of passage, and that such rites are linked to a well-developed custom of feasting and form part of the larger network of religious, political, and economic connections linking human society and its activities to the embracing order of nature.

Fig. 5 Standing warrior holding a dart; Ameca-Etzatlán style; Jalisco; earthenware. The Kistermann Collection, Aachen, Germany. Cat. no. 132.

The Hero: The Initiation of Warriors and Chiefs

To explore the themes of rites of passage, I will begin with a sculptural model from Ixtlán del Río, now in the collection of The Art Institute of Chicago (fig. 2). A lively festival is taking place, with groups of musicians, dancers, and pairs of men and women, as well as children and animals. The setting displays four thatched houses or pavilions with parrots on the roofs, and a circular, layered pyramid rising from the patio in the middle. While these individual features and groupings attract the eye with all their humorous and vivacious poses, the focus of the entire scene is clearly a tall male figure on top of the pyramid. Standing on the vertical axis, he occupies the place of tall poles or masts seen on similar models (see Witmore, fig. 10). This commanding figure holds a baton like those held by large, hollow earthenware sculptures representing warriors and chiefs. The large size of this figure in relation to others, the display of the baton, the special headdress he wears, and his heroic stance and axial position, all suggest that this is an important festival surrounding a leader whose power is being celebrated. Could this scene commemorate a ceremony such as the ruler's taking of office? Is there other evidence to be found in West Mexican tomb sculpture for the existence of this theme as a major rite of passage?

In Nayarit, Jalisco, and Colima, the figures of warriors are ubiquitous. Often they are modeled with protective basketry and leather armor, holding batons across their chests or wielding spears or slings in the "ready" position (see fig. 5). The most remarkable and largest figure of this type is the famous standing chieftain from Jalisco, now in the Los Angeles County Museum of Art (fig. 6). Clad in battle dress complete with hip pads and protectors, the effigy assumes a challenging pose; his face, streaked with war paint, belongs to a broad-cheeked, wide-jawed type associated with the Arenal style of the Magdalena basin; yet the face also displays a degree of naturalism suggesting an intention of portraiture. Although warrior imagery appeared in distinct local styles in West Mexico, its standardization speaks of the importance of raiding and small-scale warfare, the rise of powerful chieftains, and the importance of tomb sculptures in commemorating military ritual.

When we look elsewhere in Mesoamerica, it is apparent that warrior-rulers and high-ranking commanders were required to have personally demonstrated courage, skill, and leadership in battle. Advancement in rank was dependent on one's bravery and achievement in the field, and the taking of heads and the capturing of prisoners to be brought home for sacrifice were physical tokens of triumph and the acquisition of power (see fig. 7). As in other parts of the world where head-hunting cultures have flourished, warfare in Mesoamerica was only partly waged to obtain tribute. It was certainly in many cases a primary ritual activity. The Aztecs and their neighbors, for example, carried on a type of mock warfare that, though waged with gamelike rules, was nonetheless highly dangerous. This institutionalized conflict, known as "flower war," was designed for enemies to meet in a form of collective duel to wrest victims from each other to be taken for blood sacrifice upon pyramids of the home ceremonial center. The offerings were seen to build power and prestige by magically fertilizing the land of the victors. At the same time the captors confirmed their own power by taking an arm or a leg of the sacrificed enemy to be prepared at home for a ritualistic cannibal feast; a scalp lock and other tokens were placed in a box in the rafters of the captor's home and would not be removed until the victorious warrior's own death. In the public ceremonial place, the head of the victim was strung up along with many others on the fearsome skull-rack, *tzompantli.*

In addition to the figures of warriors, there are other sculptures that testify to military sacrificial practices in West Mexico. In Colima, figures of prisoners are shown bent and tied in attitudes of dejection and humiliation, stripped of all emblems of rank, sitting as trophies of battlefield triumphs (see figs. 8 and 9). Yet another type of Colima figure represents warriors drinking and wearing trophy heads, doubtless engaged in a victory display for boasting feasts (see fig. 10). Related to these figures are Colima vessels modeled with rings of human trophy heads (see fig. 11). All this imagery of warriors in action, poses of triumph, headhunting, prisoners, and victory feasts are signs of well-developed warrior ceremonialism. It is also important to note that in Mesoamerica, war was ordinarily practiced only on a seasonal basis. It

Fig. 6 Standing warrior; Arenal style; Jalisco; earthenware. Los Angeles County Museum of Art, The Proctor Stafford Collection, museum purchase with funds provided by Mr. and Mrs. Allan C. Balch. Cat. no. 151.

Fig. 7 Detail of Aztec capture scenes from the *Codex Mendoza;* Aztec; c. 1525; *Amate* paper. Bodleian Library, Oxford University. The standardized "capture" gesture is repeated by the warriors, for whom promotion required the personal taking of a battlefield prisoner for sacrifice. In monumental form, the same gesture is repeated by Aztec warriors on the stone of Tizoc (see fig. 3 above). The Spanish text describes the meaning of the imagery.

was customary only after the harvest, at the onset of the dry season, that ceremonies were performed to initiate the period for military expeditions. Towards the conclusion of this season young men proven on the field of battle would be initiated as warriors in a sacrificial rite of passage that would be part of a larger set of fertility rites designed to make blood offerings to the earth in preparation for the planting season to follow. Such rites of initiation and renewal were performed by the Aztecs in a festival corresponding to the month of March.

On a more ambitious scale, the rites of passage by which chieftains and rulers were initiated into office were also celebrated according to the religious almanacs at the appropriate time of year. In imperial societies such as those of the Aztecs, this ceremonial process took the form of coronation rites. Encompassing vast resources, mobilizing hundreds of thousands of people, and unfolding over a period of several months with spectacular public pageantry and lavish displays and feasts, such rites remained basically structured according to distinct stages of withdrawal, transition, and incorporation. The ruler-to-be first withdrew from society into a kind of ritual death. Then, at his investiture, the new ruler emerged to be publicly dressed in the regalia of office by allied kings, and to stand as the focus of a circular dance. Before a new ruler could be considered fully in command, however, he was required to lead the warriors into enemy lands to prove

his leadership in battle and capture prisoners as trophies for the final confirmation rites. The final stage of the sequence was the royal confirmation: this culmination began with proclamations and calls for provisioning the coming celebrations with foodstuffs and luxury goods, while the ceremonial center was repaved and cleaned, and a new layer of masonry laid over the principal pyramid. In metropolitan centers such as Tenochtitlan, the immense quantity of incoming goods was presented as tribute to the new ruler, who controlled the wealth and who would personally redistribute it, just as he would also hand out the titles and privileges accruing to all subordinates. The new ruler appeared in full regalia to present all badges and emblems of rank and status to the high military and priestly officials, as well as provincial governors and local chiefs. The long process of social reintegration was concluded with the sacrifice of the prisoners taken in the coronation war. The coronation war and sacrifice essentially repeated a mythic archetype established by the deified Aztec ancestor-warrior Huitzilopochtli, when he destroyed his enemies "in the beginning" on the mountain Coatepetl. By sacrificing victims on the symbolic pyramid mountain, the rulers fulfilled their obligation to return food and energy from the human sphere to their ancestors and the deified powers of nature. They also fulfilled a religious duty to renew the cycle of life. Among the Aztecs the conclusion of this kingship rite took place in June, bringing in the new time of rain and rebirth after the season of drought and war.

Thus, the reintegration and renewal of society was aligned with the cyclic renewal of nature. Considered in this perspective, the figure of the warrior posing triumphantly on the circular pyramid in the Ixtlán model stands as an assertion of rulership. The same may be said of the monumental standing Jalisco chieftain. Other figures of warriors and prisoners confirm rites of passage by which young warriors were initiated and high rulers attained new status and office.

The Great Goddess: Woman, the Earth, and Agricultural Fertility

From the earliest agricultural villages and Olmec capitals of the first millennium B.C., to Teotihuacan and Classic Maya cities between the first and eighth centuries, down to the Aztecs of 1500, the peoples of Meso-america featured female figures in their arts. In the most varied historical and cultural contexts, female forms appear as abstractions or generalized types, as likenesses of once-living women, or as mannequins displaying the prescribed poses, masks, and symbolic attire of earth, water, and maize deities. Their forms may range from clay figurines a few inches high to colossal stone monoliths of architectonic proportions, or they may be rendered as finely drawn images on the pages of painted screen-fold manuscripts. Nowhere in this array are there any works resembling the sensuous or voluptuous human figures of Hindu, Greco-Roman, or Renaissance art. Nevertheless, it is apparent that the female sphere of life was of funda-mental importance in the Mesoamerican worldview, for its imagery was everywhere invested with deep-seated meanings and expressive possibilities. In villages, towns, and city-state capitals, the female domain was acknowledged and revered as an essen-tial part of social and cosmological order. On one level this sphere embraced the idea of the earth as progenitor of all living forms, an inexhaustible source of new life, the mythic womb whence humankind originally emerged, and the place where the dead are laid to rest and from which, reborn, they will return to the living. On another level, women were closely identified with family continuity, descent and kinship, and lineage legitimacy. These themes were intertwined in the imagery of monuments, murals, and

manuscripts, and are also evident in the ethnohistorical accounts of the sixteenth-century Spanish friars. Yet, as is often the case in these texts—as well as in the ethno-logical reports of modern and contemporary male writers—detailed descriptions of young women's initiations, availability for courtship and marriage, and family responsibilities are much abbreviated (or lacking) in comparison to the literature on male rites and rituals. Although less precise documentary evidence is available from which to approach the strik-ing sculptural imagery of women in West

Fig. 8 Prisoner; Comala style; Colima; earthen-ware. Collection of Mr. and Mrs. Joseph Golden-berg, Los Angeles. Cat. no. 64.

Fig. 9 Prisoner; Comala style; Colima; earthen-ware. Private collection. Cat. no. 35.

Fig. 10 Drinking warrior with trophy heads; Comala style; Colima; earthenware. Staatliche Museen zu Berlin–Preussischer Kulturbesitz/Museum für Volkerkunde. Cat. no. 82. The display of trophy heads, the drinking of *pulque,* and the imagery of warriors in West Mexico indicate a well-developed pattern of competition between rival communities.

of Central Mexico such as Tlatilco and Chupícuaro, dating from the middle and late first millennium B.C. An El Opeño female figurine shows a flattened, attenuated torso and limbs, subtly articulated in profile and coated with a white post-fired clay slip (see Mountjoy, fig. 1). The Tlatilco-style "pretty lady" figurines emphasize enlarged hips and thighs on young women elaborately attired with cocoon rattles at the ankles and detailed hairdos. These finely modeled forms contrast with larger Tlatilco figures that tend to a somewhat rustic, tactile finish; yet the latter also call attention to hips and thighs as well as to items of ritual dress (fig. 14). The earthy modeling of these large examples contrast with the highly burnished style of Chupícuaro figures recovered from sites along the Río Lerma. Typifying this important late-first-millennium style is an especially imposing figure, standing in frontal pose with arms held close to the sides and hands resting on the midriff (fig. 15). The torso, oddly flattened and with a subtly modeled concave profile, abruptly swells outward in the convex bulbous belly, loins, and upper legs. Limbs, hands, and feet are tubular and much abbreviated, with slight indentations for fingers and toes. By contrast the head is detailed with a high elongated backward curving forehead: the wide, staring eyes and open mouth assume an especially intense expression. The effigy is dramatized with a highly burnished, deep red slip and a bold stepped-diamond pattern covering the face and the front of the torso. Other fine-line designs adorn the lower abdomen, buttocks, and thighs. This painted area does not represent a textile or clothing, for the genitals are clearly modeled. Instead, the intricate pattern seems to correspond to body paint applied by Chupícuaro women on ceremonial occasions.

The Chupícuaro archaeological sites were first explored in 1927, but it was not until 1946–47 that salvage operations were rapidly carried out before flooding by a major dam on the Lerma river. Although an archaeological report mentions a circular building, no monumental constructions were excavated. Attention focused primarily on the burial ground upon a small hill on an island in the river. Related sites were also found slightly west of there around Lake Cuitzeo. At Chupícuaro the burial of important persons included not only a preponderance of female figures, but also a great array of food

Mexico, enough may be brought to bear to illustrate the widespread idea of the earth as a female entity and its likely connections to young women's rites of passage as a field of symbolic expression in the tomb figures.

The large hollow figures from different styles show imposing women in standing and seated positions, most often elaborately painted or ornamented around the lower torso, hips, and thighs (see figs. 12 and 13). Such forms stem from old traditions, first evident in West Mexico in the El Opeño tombs of about 1500 B.C. and in later sites

Fig. 11 Vessel with trophy heads; Comala style; Colima; earthenware. Denver Art Museum. Cat. no. 79. Trophy-head vessels from Colima suggest the existence of a highly ritualized practice of eating some part of a sacrificial enemy as a means of assimilating his power.

vessels of specialized types. Immense quantities of small flat figurines were also recovered; these have simplified flat bodies and faces, with elaborate hairdressings and jewelry added with pellets, rolls, and striated or dotted pieces of clay. The great majority of these figurines are female. Such burial ensembles clearly connect the living and the dead, feasting and food, and indicate that they, like the earth itself, are strongly associated with female imagery. Chupícuaro sites were no simple village settlements: they were centers of a sophisticated long-lasting ceramic industry with important trade links along the Río Lerma eastwards to the great Late Formative urban communities of the Valley of Mexico, such as Cuicuilco and early Teotihuacan, and westwards towards Jalisco and the basins and ranges of the plateaus beyond.

Similarly, at Tlatilco, burial offerings yielded vessels in a great range of shapes, as well as a variety of animal and human figurines and large hollow figures. Although stylistically distinct from Chupícuaro, there can be little doubt that these communities shared related systems of belief and symbolism in the Middle and Late Formative periods. Yet

centuries earlier, by 900 B.C., on the Gulf Coast of Tabasco and southern Veracruz, a more complex society had already evolved with monumental ritual and political centers made of earthen pyramids and equipped with colossal stone sculptures. The imposing monuments of the Olmec portray rulers commanding statelike societies with great economic, religious, and political power and networks of trade connections with distant regions, reaching even the remote central highlands of Mexico. Best known for their huge stone portrait-heads, exquisite jades and greenstone masks, and finely carved figurines and ritual implements, Olmec artisans also fashioned ceramics of lasting significance. Among the latter is a vessel from the site of Santa Cruz, in the state of Morelos, on the Olmec frontier in the central highlands (see fig. 17). The vessel is in the form of an aged woman whose upturned face and protruding lip form the mouth of the container. Kneeling in the parturition pose, pregnant yet with flaccid breasts and a skeletal ribcage, the effigy suggests the concept of the earth as "grandmother," the eternal progenitor. This vessel is almost certainly an early visual expression of the female earth as ancient and

Fig. 12   Standing female figure; San Sebastián style; Jalisco; earthenware. The Art Institute of Chicago, gift of Mr. and Mrs. Joseph Antonow. Cat. no. 140.

Fig. 13   Seated female figure; Lagunillas "C" style; Nayarit; earthenware. Private collection. Cat. no. 206.

Fig. 14   Female figure; Tlatilco style; Central Mexico; 500/400 B.C.; earthenware. The Art Institute of Chicago, gift of Daniel Michel. Cat. no. 2

Fig. 15 Monumental standing female figure with geometric designs; Chupícuaro; Michoacán/Guanajuato; earthenware. Barbier Mueller Museum, Barcelona. Cat. no. 171. Shape, posture, and body decoration call attention to female attributes and powers in a range of Late Formative–period effigy styles.

Fig. 16 Seated rotund figure with hands on hips; Michoacán; earthenware. Private collection, New York. Cat. no. 158.

enduring; as "starved" in the long dry season, yet always carrying water within and always with the potential of regeneration. This theme is also expressed by a globular vessel in the form of a woman, from an unknown Formative site, probably in western Michoacán (fig. 16). Such archetypal notions were transmitted and preserved in the titles of various Aztec earth deities such as *toci*, "our grandmother," *tonan*, "mother," *teteo innan*, "mother of gods," *tlalli yiollo*, "heart of the earth."

Formative traditions thus speak of ancient associations and perceptions in which the earth and its properties were conceived in essentially female terms. That such concepts were also shared by the West Mexican peoples is indicated by a theme of fertility expressed in the art of Colima, where the figure of a seated woman is covered with eighty-seven tiny children (fig. 18). Similarly, the theme of sustenance is clearly indicated by the figure of a Nayarit Lagunillas-style woman, upon whose skirt a ceremonial meal is modeled complete with miniature participants (fig. 19). But the most prevalent type of female figures—closely resembling Tlatilco

and Chupícuaro forms and also recalling the Olmec vessel—are from tombs in the lake-basin area of Jalisco and nearby mountains of Nayarit. Typifying this genre is a San Sebastián–style effigy (fig. 12). Standing in frontal pose with arms held parallel to the sides and hands resting on the stomach, the stocky swelling body is supported by thick short legs and enormous arching feet that seem to grasp the earth with which the figure is symbolically connected. The face is generalized, but all details of the hairdo, jewelry, and body paint are rendered with meticulous care. Like the large Chupícuaro example, San Sebastián female figures are notable for having their abdomen, loins, and thighs elaborately decorated, calling attention to the genital area. The impression of such effigies is one of sturdy, enduring strength and energy. Nearby in the Ameca basin of Jalisco similar effigies often hold small jars or bowls in one hand, and in this style the breasts are especially ornamented with a dynamic pattern of spiraling lines. In the mountains of southern Nayarit where variants of the Lagunillas style were produced, female figures were sometimes rendered with considerable abstraction (see figs. 13 and 20). Heads and faces are enlarged and flattened and the figures sit directly on the ground with their legs splayed outward. Special designs and jewelry again underline the importance of the hips and loins, and accentuate the genital area. Yet other Lagunillas females are highly naturalistic and almost monumental in scale (see figs. 21 and 22). With smiling expressions they kneel in a frontal pose, arms close to the sides and hands upon the abdomen, their legs held open and their genitals clearly represented.

That there is an affinity between these seated poses and those of the Olmec vessel of the old woman, the unknown Michoacán figure, and poses represented centuries later on female Aztec earth-deities is, I believe, undeniable. These similar forms establish a base for informed conjecture about the existence of very old complexes of beliefs and religious practices concerning the earth and its properties. For example, the Aztec deity Tlaltecuhtli, "earth lord" or "earth lady," is usually represented squatting in the parturition position, with her head flung backward and her fearsome mouth of flint blades open. Her hair is covered with centipedes and serpents, associated with the

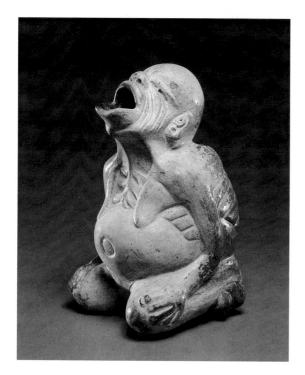

Fig. 17 Vessel in the form of a kneeling skeletonized woman; Santa Cruz, Morelos; Olmec; 1200/900 B.C.; earthenware. Raymond and Laura Wielgus Collection.

Fig. 18 Seated mother with eighty-seven children; Colima; Late Comala phase; earthenware. Private collection. Cat. no. 105.

Fig. 19 Female figure with an apron "table"; Lagunillas "C" style; Nayarit; earthenware. The Metropolitan Museum of Art, the Michael C. Rockefeller Memorial Collection, bequest of Nelson A. Rockefeller. Cat. no. 205.

earth's orifices, and also with spiders—the earth's great spinners and weavers. The open mouth and the skull symbols worn on her skirt, and the claws she wears on hands and feet, allude to the earth's role as the eventual devourer of all that walks or grows on its surface. Yet she was also a patroness of midwives; and in the creation legend recorded in the sixteenth-century *Histoyre du Mechique,* she is the earth itself. In the heterogeneous pantheon of the Aztecs, where deities from the traditions of many conquered peoples were being adapted and incorporated in the process of creating an embracing ritual system, related female earth deities were assuming interchangeable attributes. Such a one is represented on a famous page from the *Codex Borbonicus,* squatting in parturition (fig. 23). Her emblematic skirt-panel and the mat she squats on are both covered with symbols of the moon, indicating the periodicity of fertility. Here also we see the emblematic centipede, serpent, and spider. Other depictions in the fourteenth-century ritual almanac *Codex Borgia* show the female earth deity in elemental form (see fig. 24). Sitting at the center of four cultivated fields in each intercardinal quadrant, and again on a field at the bottom of the central panel, the female figures look upwards towards four rain deities in the sky and the fifth one under a band of clouds in the middle. The page is meant to signify rain

in all directions and the fertility of the fields with the coming of the planting season.

The widespread notion of the earth as the great progenitress provides a context for considering the standing and sitting female sculptures of West Mexico as commemorating rites of initiation, rites that were undoubtedly expressive of the connection between the fertility of the soil and the creativity of

Fig. 20 Seated female figure; Lagunillas "C" style; Nayarit; earthenware. Private collection. Cat. no. 210.

Fig. 21 Kneeling female figure; Lagunillas "A" style; vicinity of Compostela, Nayarit; earthenware. Stokes Family Collection, Upper Nyack, New York. Cat. no. 202.

Fig. 22 Kneeling female figure; Lagunillas "A" style; vicinity of Compostela, Nayarit; earthenware. Los Angeles County Museum of Art, The Proctor Stafford Collection, museum purchase with funds provided by Mr. and Mrs. Allan C. Balch. Cat. no. 201.

women. This basic concept is still held by the Pueblo of the Rio Grande, for whom farming is associated with the summer or "female" time of growth and fertility, and the fields immediately surrounding the villages are associated primarily with women's activities.

The religious customs of many peoples speak of female initiation rites involving ritual nudity, with the subject presented in proximity to or even upon the prepared or planted fields. In some societies women appeared nude in the fields to carry out the first planting. There are also a host of related ritual actions, such as signaling the descent of humankind from the earth by lying on the ground as soon as the pains of childbirth

begin, so that the mother will be on the ground when the child is born. In ancient Egypt, "to sit on the ground" was used in demotic writings to mean "giving birth." This extremely widespread behavior undoubtedly refers to the maternity of the earth. Certainly in ancient Mesoamerica the earth was seen as the origin-womb, a concept represented on the well-known Chicomoztoc "Seven Caves" page from the *Historia Tolteca-Chichimeca*, which shows seven Aztec tribes about to be summoned from the interior of the mountain Culhuacan by a priest who strikes his staff in the birth canal.

All of this is to call attention to a body of Mesoamerican beliefs of great antiquity, and to point to similar concepts held by peoples elsewhere. With reasonable certainty we may say that certain standing and sitting female figures from the tombs of West Mexico were placed there in testimony of the deceased having come of age through female rites of initiation. In such ritual processes young women also pass through the three stages of withdrawal, transition, and reincorporation, marking the passage from an asexual world of childhood into the world where court-ship and marriage are welcomed. In the first stage, the subjects may undergo ritual nudity, followed by the time of teaching by elder women in the customs and mores of the community. The concluding actions feature the public presentation of the young woman, often richly ornamented or symbolically painted and made the recipient of gifts, food, and acclamations. It is this pivotal public exhibition that is most likely represented by the West Mexican sculptures, showing them decorated yet with the lower body and geni-tals exposed as they stand or sit in contact with the soil. The young woman is thus pre-sented as an adult, ready for a creative role proper to women. In this action she becomes part of a hierophany, manifesting archetypal principles that reach back to the immemorial, universal idea of the earth as a goddess.

Primordial Pair: Marriage

The founding of a family follows the admit-tance of young men and women into adult-hood, and marriage is certainly the most important of all the transitions from one so-cial category to another. Marriage rites are fundamental because they represent and sanction biological continuity. As a rite of passage, marriage ceremonies may be as complex as those of a ruler's inauguration or a state funeral. In traditional societies the linked series of stages that make up the whole ritual sequence usually involve at least one of the spouses in a change of fam-ily, clan, village, or tribe. Each stage may be marked by formal speeches of instruction and counsel presented by parents and elders; rites of protection and fertility may be per-formed; and there also may be rites of sepa-ration from the old familiar environment of the bride or groom and incorporation into a new dwelling. Feasts are offered according to each particular occasion. But among these events the most critical rites are those of in-dividual union between bride and groom.

Fig. 23 Detail of the Aztec earth goddess Tlazolteotl from the *Codex Borbonicus*; Aztec; c. 1525. Bibliothèque de l'Assemblée Nationale, Paris.

Fig. 24 Detail from the *Codex Borgia*; Mixteca-Puebla region; 1300/1400; animal hide. The Vatican Library, Vatican City. Five versions of the female earth-deity crouch on cultivated fields in each corner panel and again in the center. Male rain-deities stand above, with water streaming from their hands. The fertility of the earth is depicted at the onset of the planting season.

Our point of departure for this theme is a model house, in this case not from Ixtlán del Río but from somewhere between Tala in the Ameca valley and Tonalá in the Atemajac valley (fig. 25). Finds of such fine red-slipped and white-painted figures have been made in the vicinity of Lake Cajititlan and Ixtlahuacan de los Membrillos, and, according to some verbal reports, along the northern borders of Lake Chapala and the estuary of the

Río Lerma (see map, p. 12). Sometimes called "sheep-faced" because of their long, tapering faces with widespread salient eyes and pointed ears, these figures emerge as a well-defined group in the West Mexican local traditions (see fig. 26).

The house model is finely detailed, with such architectural features as posts and rafters, and tie-knots represented inside and outside. Designs on the outside roof surface differ from those on the underside of the base, suggesting a symbolic division corresponding to sky and earth. Within the single chamber the central post separates a smiling couple seated with food placed before them. Another couple appear as witnesses to the scene, probably representing the family into which one of the young pair is to be incorporated.

A variation of the paired figure motif is seen on an especially complex Ixtlán del Río model, originally published by von Winning (figs. 27 and 28a–c). The setting is a circular plaza with its customary central pyramid, in this (rare) case surrounded on only three sides by houses or pavilions. A vast crowd swirls about, with musicians playing on top of the pyramid, men carrying others upon their shoulders, and still others holding fans, batons, and ceremonial objects. Children too are present, and men and women sit within the houselike pavilions, attired in festive regalia. The two subjects of this lively scene sit solemnly on opposite sides of the central pyramid. Each represents a couple wrapped with a blanket to indicate they have just been married. By calling attention to this feature, von Winning noted the frequent Mesoamerican custom of representing marriage ceremonies with couples enveloped in a blanket, as depicted, for example, in fourteenth-century Mixtec codices and fifteenth-century Aztec manuscripts. Even today among the Huichol of the Nayarit and Jalisco sierras, the conclusion of a marriage ceremony is signaled when the mother of one of the couple covers them with a blanket.

These modeled examples also cast light on one of the most frequently occurring and widely distributed types of figures throughout West Mexico: pairs of men and women who are most often seated but also sometimes standing and occasionally even modeled as a unit. There is always an air of festivity and high humor surrounding these images, whether they are in the relatively naturalistic or more abstract styles. This atmosphere of celebration and the occurrence of such pairs across the region indicate their importance as markers of an especially critical rite such as the commemoration of marriage. The pair of Tala-Tonalá–style figures mentioned above (see fig. 26) are arrayed in bright finery for the occasion: she with her braided headband, shell necklace, earspools, and stars-and-stripes skirt, and her hand holding the marriage-cup vessel; he with his shell-ornamented headband, earspools, necklace, and dotted shoulder-mantle, his hand holding a chieftain's baton. Remarkably, he wears no loincloth. As one of the finest pairs in this style, this bride and groom display an elegant, spare simplicity. In the vicinity of Ixtlán del Río, large-scale hollow figures sit typically wide-eyed with grinning expressions, torsos and limbs simply modeled yet holding an

Fig. 25 Model of a house; Tala-Tonalá style; Jalisco; earthenware. The Miller Family Collection, Chicago. Cat. no. 145.

Fig. 26 Standing couple; Tala-Tonalá style; Jalisco; earthenware. Galerie Mermoz, Paris. Cat. no. 146.

Fig. 27 Model of a ceremonial center; Nayarit; earthenware. Collection of Mr. and Mrs. Joseph Goldenberg, Los Angeles. The two pairs of married figures seated on opposite sides of the pyramid are barely visible in this view. Their placement is plotted on the plan (fig. 28a).

energetic tension, with all items of clothing elaborately detailed (see fig. 29). A vivid contrast is presented by Lagunillas-style couples who display a minimum of personal adornment (see figs. 30a and 30b). San Sebastián–

style couples present a more reductive, formal statement, with an especially elegant sense of modeling: their elongated faces with wide, staring eyes swell upwards in rounded, trapezoidal heads, repeating the monumental

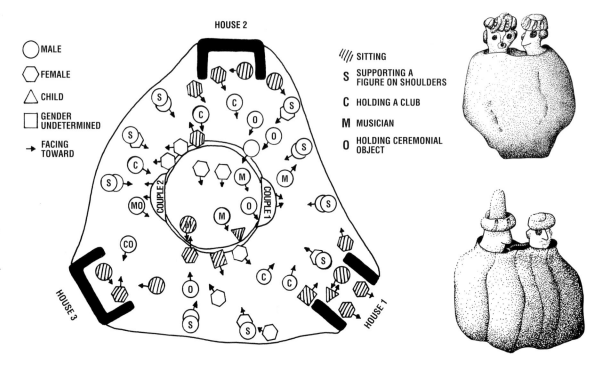

Fig. 28a Plan of the ceremonial center model, showing the variety of figures and their interactions with one another.

Figs. 28b, c. Detail of two marriage couples seated on opposite sides of the circular altar or pyramid.

shape of their torsos (see Braun, fig. 9). Nearby, in the Ameca valley, figures are often more naturalistic in the representation of emotions: in one remarkable example the man leans forward to embrace the woman, offering a cup in a sign of affection as she places her hand on his knee (fig. 32). Curiously, in the Colima sites along the Río Armería, no paired figures seem to appear in the classic red-burnished figural tradition. Yet farther south along the Coahuayana river between Colima and Michoacán, pairs of figures are modeled with full, rounded limbs and bodies, seated on four-legged stools (fig. 31). Their eyes seemingly closed and their faces composed with a sense of concen-

tration, these seated effigies seem suspended in a reverie of ritual introspection. Another Coahuayana valley substyle features more stiffly formal figures, sitting and monumentalized with an almost boardlike abstraction, their torsos covered with intricate patterns in negative resist (see fig. 33). But the most abstract of all the paired figures come from a burial ground on Cerro Encantado, a prominent hill not far from Teocaltiche on the eastern upland plains of Jalisco (see fig. 34). In this so-called "Zacatecas" style (so named after the neighboring state where related sites have been found), the male and female pairs are modeled with strong geometric simplicity. Torsos are reduced to flattened

Fig. 29 Marriage pair; Ixtlán del Río style; Nayarit; earthenware. Private collection. Cat. no. 193.

Fig. 30a Standing male figure; Lagunillas "E" style; Nayarit; earthenware. Collection of Mr. and Mrs. Morris A. Long, Castle Rock, Colorado. Cat. no. 218.

Fig. 30b Standing female figure; Lagunillas "E" style; Nayarit; earth-

enware. Denver Art Museum. Cat. no. 217.

Fig. 31 Marriage pair seated on stools and holding bowls; Coahuayana style; Colima/Michoacán; earthenware. Private collection. Cat. no. 112.

Fig. 32 Seated marriage pair; Ameca-Etzatlán style; Jalisco; earthenware. Private collection. Cat. no. 129.

tubular forms, tubelike arms loop around to create a circular pattern, and planar faces are sharply divided by angular intersecting eyebrows and noses. Eyes and mouths are circular holes, giving the figures an oddly quizzical expression. Male figures are portrayed with their hair tied in twin stems with spool-like knots on the ends. Both sexes are brilliantly painted with stripes and dots in reds, oranges, and yellow ochres as well as negative-resist black and white. There are also in some areas of West Mexico variants of the marriage-pair theme, as in the Ameca valley where couples may be represented proudly displaying an infant, the male holding a festival jar in sign of joyful celebration (see fig. 35).

Of all the Mesoamerican sources, the texts and pictorial manuscripts of the Aztecs portray marriage events in the fullest detail. An illustration from the *Codex Mendoza* (1525) depicts the bride carried by one of her kinswomen to the groom's house, after having said good-bye to her childhood home, in an evening procession by torchlight (fig. 36). Once inside the house, the bride and groom are seated upon a mat. A fire is lit in the hearth, incense is laid out, and gifts of fine clothing and speeches are presented. Texts by Bernardino de Sahagún record lengthy moral and practical admonishments, instructions, and counseling. Food is offered and the bride and groom are tied by their mantles and ceremonially fed by their mothers before leaving for the bedchamber. Four days of feasting typically follow the marriage, with more lengthy formal speeches. The older women of the groom's family speak to the bride on the importance of diligence, humility, and trust, while the bride's mother addresses the groom about his duties, exhorting him to hard work, conscientiousness, and self-sacrifice. We cannot say that such events were repeated in this particular format in ancient West Mexico 1,500 years before the Aztecs; yet the archetypal situation is surely embodied by the couples modeled for the tombs, as testimony that the deceased had accomplished the life-stage rites of marriage. For every marriage essentially repeated the time of genesis—the primordial union of male and female creative forces, who set time into motion by separating night and day before bringing the levels of the sky, the water, and the earth into being. In Aztec origin myths this first pair are personified

Fig. 33 Seated female;
Coahuayana style;
Colima/Michoacán;
earthenware. Private
collection. Cat. no. 109.

Fig. 34 Marriage pair;
Zacatecas style; Jalisco;
earthenware. Herbert
and Paula Molner, Chi-
cago. Cat. no. 149.

as Ometecuhtli (two lord) and Omecihuatl
(two lady), shown in the *Codex Borbonicus*
seated within a sacred enclosure at the beginning of time (fig. 37). In like manner, the
marriage pairs in the tombs of West Mexico
surely carried with them the solemnity and
joy with which traditional peoples imitated
everything that was done *in illo tempore,* the
beginning of time.

Passing to the Ancestors: Burial Rites

In *Rites of Passage,* van Gennep remarked that
of all the stages of funeral ceremonies (separation, transition, and incorporation), the last
phase, which brings the deceased into the
world of the dead, is often the most extensively elaborated and is assigned the greatest
importance. We have seen in the tomb of
Huitzilapa evidence of elaborate preparations
and all the material objects, such as clothing,
jewelry, amulets, utensils, sculptures, and
vessels of food and drink, that were meant to
assure the deceased a safe journey and a favorable reception—just as if they were living
travelers. The story told by the bones themselves speak of family lineage and of members who, having previously died, awaited
final burial with the chief. Yet, as we shall
see in a series of Ixtlán models, other stages
of the funeral process were also choreo-
graphed with high drama and purpose.

The first of these pieces represents the
wake of a chieftain (fig. 38). Seated within
a tall pavilion, a high-ranking man holds a
drinking vessel and looks upon the patio
where the wrapped corpse of another important figure, his face still exposed, lies in state.
Standing immediately below are two guards
with shields and spears, flanking another
seated man holding a large vessel containing
the beverage being drunk by the chieftain.
Three musicians stand opposite the pavilion,
two vigorously shaking rattles, while the
middle one holds a drum. Two dogs are also
included—one sits by the side of the presid-
ing chief, the other lies faithfully by the feet
of the deceased. There is a sense of formality

to this arrangement, with the chieftain ceremonially drinking as the guards stand in honor, and songs retell the brave deeds and high achievements of the departed or perhaps give him verses and passwords to take on his journey to the afterlife. This scene represents an early stage in the funeral process: the subject is separated, yet still recognizably present, entering the time of transition to the world of the ancestors.

Another, more elaborate model represents a later phase of a funeral ceremony (fig. 39). Described in detail by von Winning, this model shows a crowded procession crossing between two houses on opposite sides of a circular platform. The fully shrouded and bound body is borne by six identically clad pallbearers, and a line of conch-shell trumpeters accompanies the body. The cortege is led by a man holding a fan aloft in his right hand; another man holding a large beverage vessel stands to the left, and immediately before him a woman faces the oncoming procession. Ahead, a herald holding a rattle points to his mouth, probably signifying speech or song. Within the house, other figures are formally seated to receive the procession. A group of six female participants brings up the rear by the house from which the procession has issued. Around the periphery, at points corresponding to the cardinal or intercardinal positions, four bloodletting sacrifices are taking place. These take the form of a cheek-piercing rite, a peculiarity of funerary events in West Mexico.

It may be that the victims portrayed in this Ixtlán sacrificial scene were retainers of the high-ranking deceased, yet there is a very real possibility that they may represent

immediate family members. The nobility of the Olmec, Maya, and Aztecs regularly practiced forms of auto-sacrifice on diverse occasions, using implements such as perforators, stingray spines, obsidian blades, or sharpened jaguar bones to offer their own royal blood to the earth, the ancestors, and other deities. These sacrifices epitomize the recycling of food and energy between the living and the dead, between society and nature. In West Mexico, cheek-piercing involved both men and women, and the bloodletting implements were long poles or long obsidian blades. On the model in question, the first

Fig. 35 Family group; Ameca-Etzatlán style; Jalisco; earthenware. Private collection. Cat. no. 137.

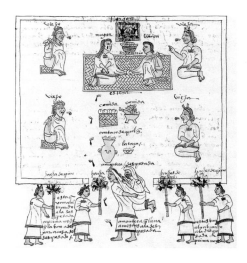

Fig. 36 Aztec marriage scene from the *Codex Mendoza*; Aztec; c. 1525; *Amate* paper. Bodleian Library, Oxford University.

Fig. 37 Detail of the primordial male and female creative forces, personified as Ometecuhtli-Omecihuatl from the *Codex Borbonicus*; Aztec; c. 1525. Bibliothèque de l'Assemblée Nationale, Paris.

scene shows a woman holding the head of the victim, while a man pierces his cheek with a blade. A bowl to receive blood sits on the ground below. In the second instance a man inserts a pointed rod through the cheeks of two standing males. Three figures, now missing, originally stood behind the victims and probably held them. In the third scene a woman holds the victim's head, while two men hold a pointed blade or pole to his cheek in preparation for piercing; again, a bowl is placed below to receive the blood offering. The fourth scene similarly shows a woman holding the head of the victim, while

another holds his shoulders so that a third figure can perform the piercing. Close by a man holds his hand to his cheek and a bowl stands immediately below, showing that he has already suffered the sacrificial operation.

Other sculptures represent these cheek-piercing rites as subjects in their own right. Set in front of a diminutive hut, one group shows three men strung together by a pole through their cheeks, while a man and woman preside (see fig. 40). The man holds a ladle in a large beverage vat, and another male stands beside, bearing a jar on his shoulder. Three other figures sit in attendance, while to the sides two others are shown in painful poses, holding their hands to perforated cheeks.

The instruments used for cheek-piercing appear in some instances to be sharpened poles—perhaps bamboo (see fig. 41)—while in other models a different implement is employed: long, tapered obsidian blades (see fig. 42). Measuring some 45 cm long, and with animal-like forms flaked out as the handles, these imposing and elegant instruments would have certainly been too brittle to have served a practical purpose in battle. Nor could they have been effectively used as sacrificial knives; those used by the Aztecs, for example, for performing human heart-sacrifice were shorter, with stubby blades fixed into durable wooden handles. The long

Fig. 38 Model of a funerary scene; Ixtlán del Río style; Nayarit; earthenware. Private collection. Cat. no. 185.

knives of West Mexico on the other hand were admirably suited for the cheek-piercing rite. The blood offerings received in the vessels may then have been included in the tomb offerings, or perhaps were offered at other shrines in the ceremonial center or in mountain caves, by springs or lakes, or in special groves and agricultural fields in the sacred geography of the district.

Cheek-piercing must be seen not only as an offering but also as an expression of mourning. For many traditional societies, mourning is a complex phenomenon—a transitional period for the survivors, who enter it through rites of separation and emerge from it through rites of reintegration into a society in which the period of mourning is lifted. During mourning the living and the deceased constitute a special group temporarily suspended between the worlds of the living and the dead. In some cases, this phase invokes the ritual cutting of hair, inflicting of wounds, and the use of professional mourners. Mourning requirements are usually based on degrees of kinship. Often the mourning period of the living is a counterpart to the transitional period of the deceased, and the termination of the first sometimes coincides with the termination of the second—that is, with the incorporation of the deceased into the world of the dead.

These matters are illustrated by models showing the aftermath of the cheek-piercing rite. In one example, a woman in a high pavilion, her cheeks still pierced by a rod, sits as an icon of family mourning. Another large house model shows four figures seated in the central pavilion with a large beverage vessel between them (see Butterwick, fig. 5). Two of these figures hold their hands to their cheeks, as does another seated man on the porch to the right, with a woman comforting him from behind. Yet another figure sits on the level below, also making the cheek-holding gesture. These groups indicate that the purpose of the models was to testify that the mourning of household members extended for a time after the performance of the sacrificial rite. The intense pain of the cutting, the closing of the mouth, and the endurance of food deprivation, carried the stresses of loss and mourning to extreme emotional intensity. That many endured and survived these fearsome trials is testified to by figurines and large hollow figures represented with mutilated, hanging cheeks, as in

Fig. 39 Model of a funeral procession and cheek-piercing ceremony; Ixtlán del Río style; Nayarit; earthenware. Present location unknown. The funerary bundle of the chieftain is borne by six pallbearers. A line of shell trumpeters stand to the left, as a group of notables leads the procession and women bring up the rear. Four cheek-piercing scenes take place at the intercardinal points.

Fig. 40 Funerary cheek-piercing rite; Ixtlán del Río style; Nayarit; earthenware. The Art Institute of Chicago, gift of Ethel and Julian R. Goldsmith. Cat. no. 187. Three men strung together by a pole through their cheeks stand before figures with an open vat of *pulque* and one with a jar on his shoulder. Two figures lean over the edge, left and right, holding their cheeks in pain.

Tenochtitlan were cremated on the main pyramid—a symbolic mountain—and their ashes were buried there on the upper platform before the temple of the tribal ancestor-hero Huitzilopochtli. Across Lake Tetzcoco in the Valley of Mexico, at the ritual hill of Tetzcotzingo, king Netzahualcoyotl was memorialized by a monumental sculptural relief recounting his life and achievements. A royal effigy standing beside this sculpture became the focus of a posthumous cult, for the spirit of the king within the mountain continued to act as a ritual intermediary between his people and the deified forces of nature. Far to the south among the Classic Maya, the royal ancestors in the underworld regions also continued to fulfill similar functions. Thus, a Maya noblewoman of the eighth century A.D., depicted on a stela from Yaxchilán, offers her blood and summons the spirit of a royal ancestor from the watery underworld. Even today among the Maya of Zinacantan, Chiapas, the ancestral gods are said to reside in the sacred mountains and hills above waterholes, where they speak to the earth lord and control the movement of rain clouds. And far to the north among the Pueblos of New Mexico and Arizona, the great tribal ancestral spirits and spirits of the departed are identified with the Kachinas,

Fig. 41 Funerary cheek-piercing rite; Ixtlán del Río style; Nayarit; earthenware. Los Angeles County Museum of Art, The Proctor Stafford Collection, museum purchase with funds provided by Mr. and Mrs. Allan C. Balch. Cat. no. 188.

Fig. 42 Two ceremonial blades; Colima; obsidian. The Art Institute of Chicago, through prior acquisitions of Mr. and Mrs. Dave Chapman, Mr. and Mrs. Richard Reed Armstrong, and the Robert A. Waller Fund. Cat. no. 18.

examples of an aged figure from Ixtlán (see Furst, fig. 11), and a seated Lagunillas male with vertical scarifications (see fig. 43).

Another known model of a funerary scene (illustrated in von Winning's book, fig. 89) shows a procession in which the deceased is borne in a large tubular catafalque, accompanied by a procession of individuals bearing folded textiles and platters of food. This model appears to represent the next-to-last phase of the funerary process, leading to the final deposition of the corpse in the tomb-chamber and the beginning of the journey of the soul towards the home of ancestral spirits and possible eventual reincarnation.

It is not yet known how the ancient peoples of West Mexico imagined the land of the ancestors, yet it cannot be dissimilar to that recorded in the traditions of other Mesoamerican peoples. The Aztec kings of

venerated supernatural beings who fulfill many roles. Thus, from the Rio Grande valley down the great chains of mountains and plateaus of Mexico and south to the Ulúa valley in Honduras, a deep current of thought was shared by diverse peoples, in which families, lineages, and entire communities were joined with their forebears as participants in a vital exchange with the remote and mysterious forces contained in the landscape. In the West Mexican villages, towns, and larger seats of power, the great lineage chieftains and leaders both male and female were obliged to maintain this essential colloquy during their time of service in life, and to prepare their tombs to continue the process upon their passage to the ancestral afterlife. The tomb furnishings were more than a form of conspicuous consumption by a vainglorious social elite: they were essential components of a deep-seated religious, intellectual, and artistic domain by which human society was kept as an integral part of the structure and rhythms of nature.

Conclusion: Purposes of the Tomb Sculpture

Among many Amerindian peoples, communion with ancestors is not only a matter of keeping a sense of family integration and continuity; it is also an essential activity for maintaining the well-being of the entire community and ensuring the orderly and productive renewal of the seasons. Thus, the shaft tombs of West Mexico functioned as sites where high-ranking people of dominant lineages buried their dead and kept up a dialogue among themselves, their people, and the spirits of the departed. But what, precisely, was the essential function of the sculptures, vessels, and offerings of food placed with the dead in the tombs? Certainly, it was important to express the continuing affection of the living for the dead and to memorialize their high standing in the community. It was also important to equip the departed for their safe and comfortable passage into the realm of the spirits. Most important of all, however, was the need to show that the dead were "mature, fully made people" who had achieved the appropriate rank and status to hold important ritual functions in life, and that they were therefore entitled to exercise these functions in the afterlife. This crucial task was assigned to the sculptures representing rites of passage. Warriors, prisoners, and

trophy-head vessels; figures of young women ceremonially adorned and in poses symbolizing reproduction and fertility; pairs of festive men and women certifying marriage; presentations of children; and models of funerary events and sacrifices—all were certificates offering testimony of initiations and changes that marked critical stages of life. Through these forms, the older tribal and ancestral spirits would recognize the status of those who were newly joining their host. The comparisons that have been drawn between these West Mexican forms and similar rites and religious customs among the Aztecs and others whose empires or states flourished elsewhere, centuries before or centuries later, are by way of recognizing the deeper, enduring structure of symbolism and meaning carried by rites of passage. Behind all these rites lie mythic archetypes: the hero, the great goddess, the primordial pair, and the ancestors' spirits arrayed on a cosmic arena.

Tomb sculptures of West Mexico offer a view of an old, basic stratum of Mesoamerican religious thought and symbolic expression that was there long before the proliferation of gods, long before the advent of kings. Beyond all their starkly archetypal imagery, our first visual impressions of the ancient West Mexican tomb figures remain lasting. There is a warm, lively humanity to them, an eye for detail, for expressive gesture, for a range of recognizable emotions. Affection, aggression, contemplation and laughter, pain and the sorrow of mourning, the exaltation of shared dance and song—these are matters of artistic intention, manifesting strong currents of sentiment that continued to join the pulse of the living to their forebears and beyond, reaching into the heart of the earth and the heart of the heavens.

Fig. 43 Seated chieftain; Lagunillas "E" style; Nayarit; earthenware. Private collection, Belgium. Cat. no. 212.

CHRISTOPHER L. WITMORE

SACRED SUN CENTERS

☀ *There is a biting chill in the morning air which nips at his toes through the weave in his sandals. His stomach, however, is still warm from the drink of hot cacao and honey that he had heated over an open fire. During the night he had taken shelter in a grove of huamuchil trees that now seem to vibrate from a faint pulsating drumbeat originating in the west. In that direction, just over a low hill of terraced farming plots, the traveler can make out tall poles stretching toward the last of the few remaining stars. He makes his way up a worn footpath bracketed by terraces of maguey cactus, headed in their direction. When he has at last reached the top of the hill, he is confronted by a series of immense circular compounds, shrouded in smoke from pyres of burning mesquite. Within these compounds, simple rectangular houses with high thatched roofs are placed atop platforms of earth and stone, in a ring that surrounds a circular stepped pyramid. In each of the three largest complexes, crowds are assembling inside the wattle-and-daub structures, as well as on a low patio area that forms a concentric ring between the houses and the central pyramid. The traveler, a stranger in the area, joins a large group of observers on the slopes of a natural amphitheater just outside the compound. He watches as the elders of this community, wearing elaborately decorated garments, place front-shields of the sun god around the ancient shrine. They also offer pouches of magical potions, ceramic vessels, and figurines, as well as decorations of folded paper, at a shrine nearby a natural spring that flows beside the amphitheater. Reciting prayers, they call upon the ancestors and the creator deities. From an elaborate vessel carved of wood from the pochotl tree, they pour water from the sacred spring over a kneeling figure as a gesture of symbolic purification. This figure then rises, and, leading a group of eight elders, proceeds to the pyramid that stands at the center of the oldest circular enclosure. Once the lone figure has reached the top, pairs of elders ascend the pyramid along each of four stairways. The crowd's attention is soon focused solely on the single figure who moves to the center atop the pyramid. This individual's full attention is fixed on the eastern horizon, where the sun will soon appear.*

Fig. 1 Model of a circular ceremonial center; Ixtlán del Río style; Nayarit; earthenware. Collection of Alan and Marianne Schwartz, Bloomfield Hills, Mich. Cat. no. 184. Originally surmounted by a dance-pole, the central pyramid rises as the *axis mundi* with pavilions situated at the cardinal or intercardinal directions, linking community festivals to the order of the world and the rhythms of the seasons.

Ritual events very much like the one depicted above are readily suggested by an extraordinary group of earthenware models from ancient West Mexico, small architectural scenes that allow archaeologists, anthropologists, art historians, and others to view such events through the art of the past (see fig. 1). The cosmology of Mesoamerica—the ways in which the peoples of this land perceived the structure of the universe—was projected in their art and remains encapsulated in their cultural artifacts. This book and the exhibition that it accompanies provide a rare opportunity to view such monuments and artifacts from across West Mexico, in the context of other sites throughout Mesoamerica, and to understand how they embody the perceptions and ideals of ancient peoples.

Archaeological research over almost the last thirty years has discovered a unique style of monumental architecture that was produced by communities known to us as the Teuchitlán tradition, named after a town in the Mexican state of Jalisco where some of the larger and better-preserved complexes developed in the first centuries A.D. Unfortunately, written manuscripts recording the history, beliefs, and customs of these societies are non-existent. In addition, a great deal of the knowledge that could be gained through precise archaeological investigation has been erased forever by looters. We do know, however, that these societies were agriculturally based and involved in the procurement and trade of high-quality natural resources, abundant in the mineral-rich regions they occupied. These peoples belonged to a society that might be best described as a chiefdom, a hierarchically organized, non-egalitarian social system made up of a federation of different kin groups. Within such a sociopolitical structure, authority is often hereditary. Religious life is deeply bound to the worship of ancestors and other powers that exist beyond the human world. Leadership in the chiefdom is also closely tied to the control of trade and precious resources, as well as to ritual obligations designed to ensure the succession of the seasons and abundance of crops. Having acknowledged this much about their society, however, it must be said that these people remain as mysterious as their monuments. Nonetheless, especially in the highland lake basins of Jalisco, they have left astonishing expressions

of architecture that are unique within Mesoamerica.[1]

Only in recent decades have these monuments captured the attention of scholars; our knowledge of them remains in its infancy. Most of the architectural analysis and survey associated with these structures has been conducted by archaeologist Phil Weigand. His definition of the circular mound complex at Teuchitlán—described in the opening narrative of this essay—is based on five diagnostic architectural features: (1) a central, circular pyramid; (2) an elevated circular patio, which surrounds the central pyramid; (3) a circular banquette surrounding the patio; (4) between eight and twelve evenly spaced, rectangular, platforms atop the circular banquette; and (5) subterranean burial crypts beneath some of these platforms. (For an archaeological example of such a burial site, see the essay by Lorenza López and Jorge Ramos in this volume).[2] Rubble and packed earth were the main materials used in the construction of the mounds, while the circular patio areas have tamped floors of clay.[3] The more intricate and monumental complexes range in diameter from 28 meters at Portrero de las Chivas to well over 100 meters at Guachimontón, the largest cluster of circular complexes at the Teuchitlán ritual site. The evolution of these circular compounds may have unfolded over the course of a thousand years. The earliest examples, complexes with four to eight orbiting platforms, are generally believed to date from 300 B.C. to A.D. 200 (the Arenal phase of the Late Formative period), while those with twice as many are attributed to the period from A.D. 200 to 900 (i.e., the Classic period).[4] Sites often contain an agglomeration of circular complexes, which in some circumstances are so juxtaposed and interconnected that they share exterior platforms (see fig. 2, the linking of circles one and two).

Unfortunately, virtually every circular complex has been damaged by looting, agriculture, or natural erosion over the course of centuries. Some of the largest and most highly developed sites have been devastated, and except for the relatively obscure site of Huitzilapa—studied by López and Ramos—none has been scientifically excavated. Associated with these circular complexes are a myriad of cultural characteristics that have only been glimpsed. In light of this, how are we to understand this unique architectural

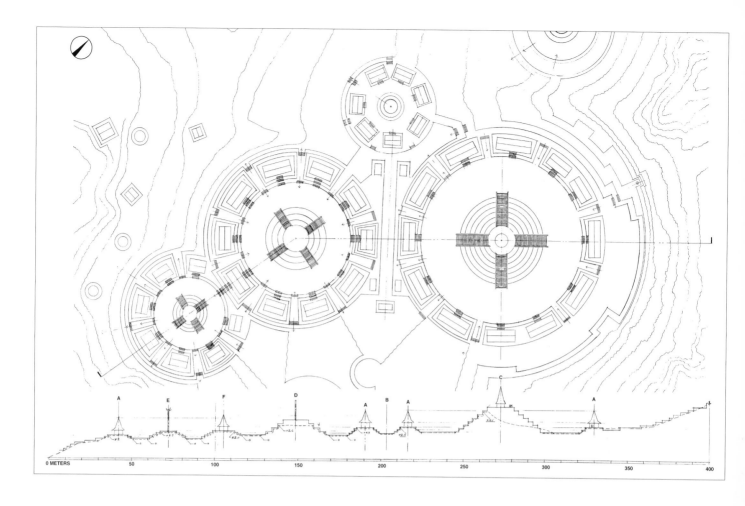

form? What significance did these societies attach to such ceremonial centers and to the structures that they once comprised? What functions did they fulfill?

Cosmology and Culture

First of all, we may be confident in believing that the themes that were animated in the architecture and activities at the circular mound complexes of ancient West Mexico were, at least in part, also understood by other cultures. One of the cornerstones of archaeological research is the recognition that a civilization's understanding of the world is intricately connected with the activities its people undertake. For Amerindians, this relationship was expressed in cosmological imagery, linking routine daily experiences, domestic architecture, and large ceremonial places. This is true regardless of whether we are considering the Maya civilization in the Yucatán in the twelfth century, or the world-view of the indigenous peoples of the Great Plains in the nineteenth century.

A fundamental example of this type of association between architecture and cosmology is seen in the circular earth lodges con-

structed by the Skidi band of Pawnee Indians of east central Nebraska. The domed roof of a Pawnee lodge was representative of the sky, while its floor stood for the earth. A circular hearth, symbolic of the sun, occupied the center of the lodge. Four main support posts, associated with the four stars that were believed to be the pillars of heaven, were placed in the intercardinal directions.[5] The interspaces between these posts were representative of the fourfold division of the universe. The movement of the constellation of the seven stars, Pleiades, could be observed through the smoke hole positioned over the central hearth of the lodge. During the course of the year, Pleiades passed directly above the smoke hole and thereby signaled the commencement of planting ceremonies.[6] In addition, the main axis of the lodge was oriented toward the east, thereby providing, through the eastern entranceway, a vantage point from which an observer could note certain celestial bodies at dusk, and, again, during another time of year, could see them upon the horizon at dawn.[7] At the equinoctial season, rays of sunlight would cast a shadow on a buffalo skull placed upon an altar at the

Fig. 2 Plan of the Guachimontón complex at Teuchitlán. Ceremonial architecture and programs of cyclic ritual became increasingly important in developing sociopolitical and economic cohesion. Ancestral temples belonging to leading family lineages surround circular pyramids marking the tomb of a great leader.

The elevation shown below this plan of the Guachimontón precinct is keyed to several particular features of the site: A) ring of pavilions; B) ballcourt; C) principal ceremonial center; D) secondary ceremonial center; E) third ceremonial center; F) interlocking pavilion.

Fig. 3 Ring of dancers with musicians; Colima/Jalisco; Late Comala phase; earthenware. The Saint Louis Art Museum. Cat. no. 95. Songs, dances, and music were central to the ancient system of festivals held to honor and praise the ancestors, propitiate the great natural forces, and celebrate victories, marriages, and similar events.

Fig. 4 Ring of dancers; Colima/Jalisco; Late Comala phase; earthenware. Private collection. Cat. no. 96.

western extremity of the lodge. This event allowed the Pawnee to denote the times for the renewal of life in the spring, while a different cluster of celestial observations marked the onset of the harvest season. Thus, the earth lodge was not only a cosmogram—the physical manifestation of Pawnee cosmology—but also a functional timepiece in which perceptions of time and space were fused and integrated into daily life. The Pawnee model demonstrates the significant link that exists between human affairs and an understanding of celestial structure, and between ritual events woven into the fabric of life and the form that architecture takes to serve those ritual expressions. This association has close affinities with patterns found elsewhere in the Amerindian world. Whether in domestic architecture or sophisticated ceremonial centers, the intimate bond between social and cosmological order is crucial to understanding the architectural form, significance, and function of the monuments of the Teuchitlán tradition.

In approaching the architecture of ancient West Mexican societies, we can draw upon fundamental symbolic expressions, what remains of the architecture itself, and the depiction of events preserved in the ceramic models. These models reveal to us images of a community with strong social customs: activities involving groups of individuals in celebrations or rituals, with some playing special roles as musicians, drummers, or entertainers while others join together in circular dance (see figs. 3 and 4). Insight into the function of the circular mound complexes may also be achieved through analogies with symbolic forms associated with the cosmological traditions of other Mesoamerican peoples. For the highly imaginative cultures of ancient Mesoamerica, cosmology took on a preeminent role in their lives and was manifested in ordered forms that were widely shared.

For example, a common Mesoamerican cosmogram is represented as a disk with a central circle or ring often surrounded by radiating concentric circles or rings. This motif is traditionally divided into four equal segments, as can be seen on the mosaic shield with cosmic designs originally placed as an offering in the pyramid known as the Temple of the Warriors in the Toltec-Maya capital of Chichén Itzá (from about A.D. 1100). The shield contains a central circle symbolic of the sun, with four plumed serpents or fire dragons placed within a concentric ring and spaced equidistantly around it (fig. 5). According to the *Codex Borgia*—a fourteenth-century Mixteca-Puebla screenfold manuscript containing hieroglyphic and pictorial systems and one of the best-known resources for the study of Mesoamerican cosmologies—similar serpents or fire dragons correspond to the four cardinal points: the four-quadrant division of the universe, which is a fundamental concept in the indigenous cosmology of the Americas.[8] The Maya commonly represented the vertical axis that originates from the center of the earth (the center of the universe) as a cosmic tree, the *axis mundi*. Certain traditions in Mesoamerica equated this axis with the ceiba tree (called *pochotl* in the language of the Aztecs), the towering and sublime tree associated with the primordial source of life.[9] This conception of the universe with the vertical and horizontal divisions in three-dimensional space is expressed in two dimensions on a ceremonial mosaic shield, now in the collection of the British Museum (figs. 6 and 7). At the center of the shield hovers a brilliant turquoise sun disk from which emanate rays pointing to the cardinal directions. Placed above the sun disk on the shield is the cosmic tree and a cartouche-enclosed anthropomorphic face that should be perceived as rising from the center of the universe and stretching toward the sun centered in the sky above.[10] Below the sun is an abbreviated *Tlaltecuhtli* mask, the symbolic entrance to the underworld. A great serpent rises, unifying the underworld, the earth's surface, and the sky above. The significance of the small human figure enclosed within the cartouche will be addressed at a later point in this discussion.

This metaphoric representation of universal structure is also incorporated in the Mesoamerican calendar. Two basic temporal cycles were recognized by ancient Meso-americans. First, there was a 260-day ritual cycle consisting of thirteen months with twenty days. A cosmological diagram in the *Codex Féjérváry-Mayer* incorporates this ritual calendar (see fig. 8). The *Féjérváry-Mayer* cosmogram also portrays a variation of the basic cosmological structure, with four great cosmic trees, the associated gods, totemic animals, and colors located in each quarter of the universe symbolized in the form of a Maltese cross. The sun disk rises above the

Fig. 5 Watercolor rendering of a mosaic shield with cosmic designs; Toltec-Maya, Chichén Itzá; turquoise, shell, and flint inlay. Plumed serpents or fire dragons mark the four celestial quarters arranged within a circle symbolizing the surrounding rim or boundary between the earth and sky.

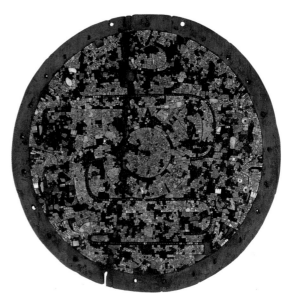

Fig. 6 Ceremonial shield with mosaic sun-disk design; Aztec; wood, turquoise, shell and gold. British Museum.

Fig. 7 Drawing of the ceremonial shield with mosaic sun-disk design. The composition portrays the sun with four directional rays at center; figures of sun sky-bearers at the sides; a serpent rising from the earth to the heavens; and a cosmic tree flowering above.

Fig. 8 Cosmological diagram from *Codex Fejérváry-Mayer;* Aztec/Mixtec; 1400/1521; animal hide. Liverpool Museum. Representations of space and time are conflated in this diagram. The Aztec God of Fire stands as the vertical axis in the central panel. The east is situated at the top where the sun rises; west lies below where the earth monster crouches. Trees rise at cardinal and intercardinal points, and are surrounded by a dotted band signifying a 260-day ceremonial calendar round.

creator god who stands at the center of the universe. Below are the jaws of the underworld that swallow the sun at the end of the day. Thirteen dots are contained within each of the linked trapezoidal and looped borders that correspond to the cardinal and intercardinal segments. Each dot about the periphery of the universe represents a day in the 260-day annual ritual cycle. Streams of sacrificial blood connecting the creator god with the beings at the corners of the universe express the necessary role of human beings in the continuation of the cycle. There was also a 360-day agricultural and solar cycle divided into eighteen twenty-day months with a five-day transition period added on. The 260-day ritual cycle and the 365-day solar cycle ran in tandem, falling back into synchrony with each other every fifty-two years. All aspects of life occurred in cycles: day and night, the movement of the sun along the horizon, seasons, cycles of creation and destruction, death and the renewal of life. Unlike the cosmogram, which is a manifestation of physical space, the Mesoamerican calendar expressed the unification with time, the fourth dimension.

The homogeneity of cosmological prin-

ciples in Mesoamerica is also expressed in the religious iconography of many Indian peoples today, such as the Huichol in the mountains of Nayarit. Just as with the distant Pawnee, cosmology is manifested in Huichol art and iconography, and it is evident in the way their communities were laid out. The Huichol divide the world into five sectors; the four cardinal directions and a fifth axis that is directed toward the highest point in the sky, the zenith—a concept very similar to the cosmic tree or *axis mundi* represented in the British Museum shield.

Front-shields heralding the Huichol god Father Sun were often represented in a similar way to sun motifs of other traditions in Mesoamerica and were intended as prayers for fertility and rain (see fig. 9a).[11] Grandfather Fire and Father Sun were very closely associated in Huichol mythology. According to Carl Lumholtz, who conducted an ethnographic study of the Huichol at the turn of the century, the sun was in reality a new impersonation of the god of fire who possesses similar powers and functions.[12] Because of their close association, the two gods share similarities in symbolic design as well. Disks of Grandfather Fire incorporate four exterior circles placed equidistant from one another about a central face of the sun, a design that, according to Lumholtz, represents a quartering of the horizontal plane of the universe with the cardinal directions like the four serpents or fire dragons in the mosaic shield.

The god of fire, in Huichol religion, is represented by two idols, one above ground and one underneath. The latter stands in a cavity, the opening to which is entirely covered by a disk, on which the upper idol stands.[13]

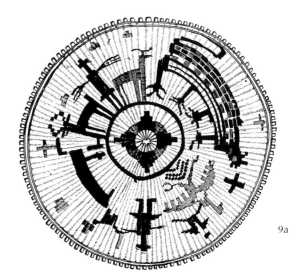

9a

9b

9c

9d

Disks of Grandfather Fire were not only representative of horizontal space with the sun at center, but also symbolic of the door that separates the upperworld from the underworld along a vertical axis. The edges of the disk are notched at regular intervals about both the upper and lower surface with a zigzag line ornamented about the rim (see figs. 9b–d). This design is symbolic of the hills and valleys projected upon the horizon, and therefore indicates that the central portion is a stylized representation of the earth. On the upper surface of the disk is an eagle, a totemic creature not only closely associated with the sun but with Grandfather Fire himself, who alone has the power of opening the door that separates the upperworld from the underworld (see fig. 9c). The eagle's body consists of a circle divided into eight radial sections of nearly equal size associated with the division of the universe. The undersurface of this disk consists of a sun circle from which rays emanate. This idol not only symbolizes the powers of Grandfather Fire who illuminates and warms the world, it is also, in itself, a cosmogram analogous to the Huichol division of the universe with the planes of the upper and lower worlds linked by the doorway that represents the earth.

The cosmological principles of various coastal peoples of West Mexico, contemporary with the societies of the Teuchitlán tradition, possessed many affinities with those of the Huichol. For example, in the Río Tomatlán area of Jalisco and the area around San Blas, Nayarit, major components of the indigenous cosmology were recorded in rock paintings and petroglyphic carvings (300 B.C. to A.D. 1600).[14] These paintings and carvings were arranged with a regard for spatial order in which the rock itself came to represent the upper sky, the horizon, and the earth. Often spirals were placed on the side of the rock, symbolic of the sun along the horizon, while lesser circles were carved near the apex of the rock, symbolic of zenith. Some carved motifs contain ladderlike glyphs that terminated in the sun motif, thereby signifying the path of the sun through the heavens. The principles followed in the design and organization of these glyphs reflect a clear understanding and acknowledgment of a cosmological structure. Like the front-shields of the Huichol, the individual rock-art motifs are physical representations of votive prayers. Frequently, these designs represented the eye or face of the powerful sun god, the provider of life-giving rain.[15] The pictographic and petroglyphic designs in the areas of Tomatlán and San Blas were a means of communicating with the sun god in hope that he would provide rainfall—a paramount concern for all people. Those who could intercede on behalf of society occupied a position of ritual and political authority. The fact that the entire highland lake basin area in and around the circular mound complexes is almost completely devoid of rock art may indicate that this necessary means of communication with the gods was fulfilled by some other means.[16]

Fig. 9 Illustrations of the Huichol Indians' Father Sun and Grandfather Fire from Carl Lumholtz' *Unknown Mexico* (1902): a) front-shield of Father Sun; b) Grandfather Fire standing on his disk; c and d) Grandfather Fire disk, front and reverse.

Fig. 10 Model of a pole-climbing ritual; Ixtlán del Río style; Nayarit; earthenware. Yale University Art Gallery, New Haven, Conn. Cat. no. 181. This formalized version of the tree-climbing rite (see fig. 13) took place in architectural settings.

✷ *The single figure, who has now seized the crowd's attention, wears only a yoke and a large conical headpiece. He holds an eagle feather in each hand. When the first rays of sunlight breach the horizon, he begins to make his way to the top of the central pole. Hand over hand, legs wrapped tightly about the pole, he pulls himself upwards toward the heavens.*

Cosmology and the Complexes of Teuchitlán

The monuments of the Teuchitlán tradition were clearly conceived as single entities: they were methodically planned and laid out to draw one's attention inwards, towards a particular focus, the central pyramid. It has been suggested that the circular complex served as an arena for the *volador* ceremony, a flying pole-dance in which a shaman—a person of importance within the community who maintains a special connection with the cosmos—balances himself atop a pole and transforms himself magically and momentarily into an eagle for passage between levels of the cosmos and the spiritual worlds (for a discussion of the shaman, see also the essay by Peter Furst in this volume). Several West Mexican ceramic models depict the *volador* ceremony taking place in the center of stylized circular structures (see fig. 10). In addition, archaeological evidence of a post hole that would have supported the pole required for the *volador* existed until recently as a small depression in the central pyramid of the middle circular complex in the Guachimontón series at Teuchitlán.[17]

The transformation by the shaman into an eagle is essential if he is to pass between levels of the cosmos to communicate with the gods and ancestors. Among the Aztecs, the sun god Tonatiuh, generally represented as a disk, was evoked by various names including "the eagle that soars." For the Huichol, as we have seen, the eagle is a cosmologically significant animal because it is associated not only with the sun but also with Grandfather Fire, who controls the cosmic doorway. The eagle possesses the powers of movement through the spiritual worlds and of communication with the gods, ancestors, and supernatural beings. Movement between these worlds occurs via a cosmic axis *(axis mundi)* that rises from the center of the earth. In order for the shaman to breach the levels of the cosmos he must ascend the cosmic axis.

Common themes and structures apparent throughout Mesoamerica were understood and drawn upon in different ways. In the Teuchitlán core this construct of ideas and values was not only understood in the abstract but was also expressed in the organization of ritual space. Like the Pawnee earth lodge, the mosaic shield, the Toltec-Maya shield in the British Museum, the diagram in the *Codex Fejérváry-Mayer,* and the idol of Grandfather Fire, each circular platform complex is a cosmogram, the manifestation of universal order as envisioned by the peoples of the Teuchitlán tradition. This order was worked into the architectural fabric of the circular complexes on a monumental scale. Early in their development the centers were designed with the four orbiting platforms, symbolic of a quartered universe. Again, ceramic models support the idea that these complexes embody this cosmological framework. A model now in the collection of the Hudson Museum portrays a group of figures gathered in pairs, as though engaged in some ceremony, beneath the outstretched limbs of a stylized *pochotl* tree, which is shown with its characteristically nubby trunk (see fig. 11). That this indigenous tree held significance for the people of West Mexico is perhaps suggested by the rather exotic-looking vessel in the shape of a section of *pochotl* trunk (fig. 12). It should be noted as well that the Hudson Museum model also depicts birds, quite possibly eagles, perched on top of the *pochotl.* While another model in the collection of The Art Institute of Chicago displays a figure with a baton—possibly a triumphant chieftain, or perhaps a shaman—standing atop the pyramid at the very center of ceremonial activity (see Townsend, fig. 2), the connection between the *volador* pole and the *pochotl* may be more convincingly demonstrated by yet another ceramic model of a tree-climbing ritual in the Art Institute (see fig. 13). Quite clearly, the *volador* pole is the metaphoric representation of the *axis mundi* emerging from the center of the universe and bound within the architectural structure of the circular platform complexes. The origins of the *volador* ceremony are not altogether clear, but models suggest that it may have been first performed atop a *pochotl* tree, only later atop a tree trunk erected as a pole on the central mound.

At Tenochtitlan, the capital city of the Aztecs, traders were called *pochteca* from the traders' ward, *Pochtlan,* "place of the ceiba tree."[18] The word *pochteca* was also closely

associated with the meaning "protector" or "ruler." Trees are frequently associated with rulership, for it is metaphorically in the shade of a ruler that the community is protected.[19] Here the significance of the small human face enclosed in the cartouche of the mosaic shield in the British Museum becomes understandable. He probably represents a powerful individual, one of the governing elite who maintains a special relationship with the cosmos and is himself a shaman or a ruler with shamanistic functions. In this respect the mediation between the cosmos and people of the Teuchitlán tradition takes on a sociopolitical connotation.

The very presence of a figure positioned atop the *axis mundi,* occupying a plane separate from this world, must have been a powerful sight. This personage alone possessed the esoteric knowledge necessary for communication with the gods, ancestors, and supernatural forces. The shamanistic responsibility to understand and communicate with the forces of the universe was openly displayed, reinforcing the exceptional power and knowledge with which these cosmic "specialists" were imbued in the eyes of the observers. The ruler-shaman thus held a position above and apart from society by virtue of his esoteric, sacred-and-secular knowledge.[20] The bird's-eye view or aerial perspective that would be reserved only for those who could achieve it—including the figure positioned atop the *volador* pole—also reinforced the sanctity of his position and the legitimacy of his power. The architectural pattern that depicted the cosmos on the ground would also have been seen by the sun god from above, and this would have gained these societies favor in the god's eye, an important West Mexican belief.[21]

The roots for the development of these circular complexes can be seen in the Late Formative–period circular burial platforms that were associated with the earlier shaft-and-chamber mortuary complexes of the highland lake district. These complexes began as sacred places, separating the burial crypt—the underworld—from the upperworld. In this sense they were symbolic doorways between levels of the universe. This concept was given greater articulation with the subsequent addition of four, and later eight, orbiting platforms arranged according to the cardinal directions. As the ceramic models portray them, these complexes were a focus

Fig. 11 Model of a *pochotl* tree surrounded by four feasting couples; Ixtlán del Río style; Nayarit; earthenware. Hudson Museum, William P. Palmer III Collection, University of Maine. Cat. no. 186. The *pochotl* (ceiba) tree releases silk-cotton wind-borne seeds from its pods, which were likened to floating rain clouds.

Fig. 12 Vessel in the form of a section of *pochotl* (ceiba) tree; Comala style; Colima; earthenware. Fowler Museum of Cultural History, University of California, Los Angeles. Cat. no. 75.

for communal activities, festivals, and other ceremonies. Within the structure of the general cosmic order, each individual reacted and viewed his relationship with the cosmos in different ways. The individual's presence within these complexes linked him or her to the grand scheme. It was through participation and performance that people understood and reaffirmed their place in the world. In the complexes their participation took the form of dance, making music or playing drums, simply observing events, or entering as athletes in the ballgame.

Throughout the Teuchitlán core, ballcourts adjoined the circular mound complexes and, in some cases such as Teuchitlán itself, were an integral part of the fabric of the entire architectural ensemble (see the essay by Jane Day in this volume). Ballcourts in Mesoamerican cosmology could assume symbolic functions, representing the path of the sun on its nightly underworld passage. In this respect the cosmology of the Meso-

american ballcourt and that of the circular complexes complement each other. The two teams were personifications of the forces of light and darkness, which meet in conflict at dawn or dusk. The game, on occasion, could be an expression of the individual's connection with the cosmic order, and time could continue only through human action. The Mesoamerican ballgame was ritually played to ensure that the cycle of the setting, death and the rising and rebirth of the sun continued. These games would be associated with the agricultural cycle based on the analogous renewal of both sun and maize.[22] Played at the vernal equinox, the games would form part of the ritual program directed towards the burning of the fields and other activities associated with the height of the dry season. At the summer solstice, they would usher in the season of rain; at the autumnal equinox the harvest would be in, and at the winter solstice the dry-season time for long-distance trade and warfare would begin.[23]

An archaeological site contemporaneous with the Teuchitlán tradition (A.D. 315–1050) in which such solar cosmology was manifested in architecture exists near the modern town of Chalchihuites, Zacatecas, just a few hundred kilometers north of the Teuchitlán core area. Here, the builders of Alta Vista, following the Mesoamerican calendar, incorporated the fourth dimension of time into the design of their ceremonial center. A main feature of this site, the hall of columns, was laid out cardinally, and it is thought to have been dedicated to the god of the four world quarters (see figs. 14–16).[24] It has been further suggested that the large circular columns

placed in the four corners of the hall are representative of the great world trees, making the hall itself a cosmogram, experienced through entry and counterclockwise processional movement.[25] Alta Vista is located near the Tropic of Cancer, the point at which the sun appears to stop and reverse its course. A long processional roadway led outward from the entryway passage of the hall of columns and across the wide valley toward a peak on the eastern mountain horizon where the equinox sun rises. On those days of the year, the first rays of sunlight penetrate the entryway into the hall of columns. Associated with Alta Vista are two pecked or carved circles that bear a resemblance to the circular complexes of the Teuchitlán tradition. These small circles are made up of 260 holes carved into rock. Both were divided into four quadrants and although their precise function remains a mystery, they are themselves ritual calendars. The location and structure of holes associated with the pecked cross circles indicate that they supported gnomons that were perhaps used in an elaborate shadow-casting system akin to a sundial. There are only a few examples of gnomons elsewhere in Mesoamerica, although the movement of shadow around ritual structures was a common means of following the movement of the sun.

The day the sun reached zenith was an important event in the agricultural year throughout Mesoamerica. For the Aztecs this solar event occurred on 4 *Toxcatl* in their ritual calendar (May 17 by the modern calendar), and Aztec religious celebrations were held on this date because it coincided with the beginning of the rainy season.[26] During the ninth century, at Xochicalco located approximately 70 kilometers southwest of Mexico City, a vertical shaft was constructed from the floor of a platform leading downward to a cavelike chamber. On the day of the zenith, sunlight streams directly into this shaft, illuminating the interior chamber.[27] The passage of zenith for the people of the Teuchitlán tradition would have been spectacular. Shadows normally cast by the *volador* poles would have disappeared at noon on the day of zenith. Demarcating the passage of the solar year would have been possible by utilizing the other features in these complexes as reference points for the shadow. Is it possible that these poles were intended to be used as gnomons?

At Teuchitlán and elsewhere in West Mexico, the majority of circular platform complexes are oriented along an east-west axis (see fig. 2). The deliberate orientation of these complexes toward the sun at a particular point along the horizon strongly suggests their calendrical function as solar observatories.

The ruins of the Guachimontón series at Teuchitlán evoke a sense of power, mystery, and awe. They demonstrate the complexity and precision of design achieved by this distinctive tradition and clearly embody specialized functions. The three main circular complexes alone cover an area of four thousand square meters. The middle complex is the earliest within the series and must later have become a pivotal focus bracketed by the two other complexes. The original complex

Fig. 13 Model of a tree-climbing ritual; Ixtlán del Río style; Nayarit; earthenware. The Art Institute of Chicago, gift of Ethel and Julian R. Goldsmith. Cat. no. 182. Events such as the tree-climbing ritual depicted here were probably held at hallowed places in natural settings, part of the sacred geography surrounding local communities. They may represent an older, original form of the rite shown in fig. 10.

lies along an axis formed by the east-west stairways of the central pyramid and the interspaces between the orbiting platforms oriented towards true east. This axis traces the path of the sun on the day of zenith. The same orientation is found at Teuchitlán, both complexes at Santa Quiteria, circles A and B at Arroyo de los Lobos, and in the vestigial remains of the large complexes at Ahualulco. But only the complexes at the Teuchitlán ritual site have been systematically investigated to provide a detailed plan of reconstruction (see Weigand, fig. 22).[28] The small circular complex to the south is oriented along the same axis as the old central complex, with their stairways aligned to the cardinal directions; in addition, the stairs of the largest pyramid correspond to the intercardinal points.

The repetitive and continued agglomeration of circular complexes at the Teuchitlán sites reflects a ritual emphasis on cyclical rebirth and renewal. It is a reassertion of the significance and history of the society and their natural setting and reflects the integration of a people and their place. This cosmological framework was maintained and elaborated over time to find its greatest expression in the large ritual complexes.

To directly classify every complex as a zenith observatory would be misleading, because other complexes have varying orientations. But the main axial orientation of the dominant complexes, as well as many others,

Fig. 14 Chalchihuites mountains over the hall of columns at Alta Vista in Zacatecas. The top of the peak in the center, Cerro Picacho, is the point of the first flash of sunrise at equinox. Traces of architecture and ceramic debris have been found at the summit. The coordination of ritual architecture, festival cycles, and prominent natural features is central in all Amerindian sacred geographies. In this way the human community was affirmed as an integral part of the order of nature.

Fig. 15 First flash of light a few days before equinox sunrise at Alta Vista.

Fig. 16 Equinox sunrise at Alta Vista showing long shadows cast by the crowd in attendance and the sunlight shaft part way up the zigzag entry corridor (see arrow). The corridor is aligned with the peak of Cerro Picacho, the equinox marker on the eastern horizon.

falls neatly between the solstitial extremes of the annual movement of the sun along the eastern horizon. These other complexes may have been associated with other important dates in the temporal cycles and may have been oriented towards the point on the horizon at which the sun would appear during those times. The orientation of each complex at La Providencia, for example, located a few kilometers northwest of the Teuchitlán ritual site, indicates that their alignment coincides with the point at which the equinoctial sunrise would have appeared.[29] The degree of accuracy associated with the axial orientation and the appearance of the sun along the horizon, however, can only be determined through the kind of detailed survey and excavation that have yet to be conducted at many West Mexican sites.

Conclusion

The acceptance of these monuments as cosmograms brings us a step closer to understanding the ideological order of the mysterious West Mexican tradition. These sacred sun centers embodied fundamental principles and beliefs on which their universe was founded. So powerful were the principles that they informed every aspect of what took place within the centers. In building and using these monuments, people renewed their concept of time and space, their relations with gods and with each other. Those individuals who controlled important rituals could work events to their advantage. But always there was a danger that the gods would not listen, that their calls for help would fall on deaf ears. When this happened, the delicate balance of society and nature could be interrupted; authority could be undermined; and a time of disruption might follow. Hence the obligation of the great chieftains and shamans to keep the rites that would ensure the continuity of the moral order through the continuity of the seasons.

☀ *Eventually, the lone figure, arms spread, feathers in hand, balances himself atop the pole. The steady pulsating beat of the drums sinks to a deep thunderous roar at an increasing pace. Suddenly he breaks into a shrill, yet rhythmic, chant, not unlike the call of an eagle. He swoops and turns, soaring majestically with a supreme sense of balance. The crowd has already noted the shadow that he and the pole cast between two of the rectangular houselike pavilions to the west. Meanwhile, the eight elders survey the whole event from the top of the central pyramid. Standing at the corners of the world, they face each other and the center pole, the axis of the universe. When the elders have seen that the shadow falls in the correct place, they release an eagle for each direction into the sky. Below in the low patio area, the crowd, joining hand in hand, circles the central pyramid counterclockwise: close kin, relative strangers, even those who seem only to appear when people gather to dance around the pole. Their energetic song and dance matches the pace of the roaring drums. Indeed, the traveler has come at the correct time. There will be festivities throughout the day. The morning ballgame will soon begin. The day of zenith has come.*

JANE STEVENSON DAY

THE WEST MEXICAN BALLGAME

To play alone is a primary move
of mind,
    but to learn the rules
for playing with another
is a partnership of mind and spirit,
    to bounce the ball
between you and me . . .
with a sense of team . . .
an arrangement between players,
an identifying of body and soul to win
    not as one
    but as a team . . .
a gathering of bodies to play
with the bouncing ball. . . .

            —Miguel Algarin

Introduction

Everyone who visits the grand archaeological sites of Mesoamerica will find, among the tiered pyramids, open plazas, royal residences, and processional ways, certain open courts, usually made in the shape of a capital I, with parallel stands along the sides, markers set at regular intervals, and defined zones at either end. These are ballcourts, where games were played between two teams using a latex rubber ball. Played for sport, to adjudicate quarrels, or for a range of ritual occasions, ballgames were the subject of imposing sculptures, paintings, and portable paraphernalia in all the diverse artistic traditions of this vast region. This is no less the case in West Mexico, where a set of clay ballplayer figurines from the site of El Opeño—dating from c. 1500 B.C.—are among the earliest in Mesoamerican history. The poses and gestures of these miniature male players and

their female companions convey a sense of the animation and conviviality that surrounded the game in early village festival life. These are the earliest of many clay figures and modeled scenes that, together with archaeological remains of ballcourts at ceremonial sites, testify to the role played by the ballgame in creating and sustaining ancient communities throughout the West Mexican region.

PUTTING THE GAME IN CONTEXT

Games have been part of human culture for thousands of years. The ancient Chinese, Egyptians, Greeks, and Europeans all competed on the field of sports. In these early civilizations, most sports, such as footracing, wrestling, and swimming, were tests of individual ability and strength; even the early Olympic tradition emphasized individual competence and skill. But in pre-Columbian Mesoamerica, there was not such a strong emphasis on personal prowess in sports. Long before the arrival of the first Spaniards in Mexico, there was, at both a religious and a secular level, an amazing enthusiasm for team sports. As in modern sports, professional players, stadiums, special equipment, rituals, and heroes all played roles in ancient Mesoamerican team games. The pitting of one team against another in games using a rubber ball has become a tradition in American culture and a phenomenon of twentieth-century life around the world.

THE PRE-COLUMBIAN BALLGAME

The pre-Columbian ballgame was probably born about thirty-five hundred years ago in

Fig. 1 Model of a ballcourt; Ixtlán del Río style; Nayarit; earthenware. Los Angeles County Museum of Art, The Proctor Stafford Collection, museum purchase with funds provided by Mr. and Mrs. Allan C. Balch. Cat. no. 180. Spectators watch as a player slides to return the oversized ball with his hip. Three zone markers divide the I-shaped court.

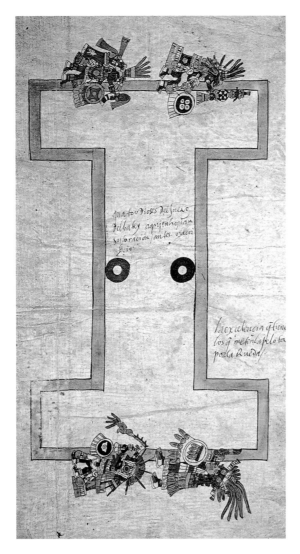

Fig. 2 Illustration of a ballcourt from the *Codex Borbonicus;* Aztec; c. 1525. Bibliothèque de l'Assemblée Nationale, Paris. Four deities play a ritual ballgame on an I-shaped court during the Aztec festival *Tecuilhuitontli,* dedicated to the goddess of salt and held in late June.

Fig. 3 Ballcourt at Xochicalco, Morelos; A.D. 900/1000. Maya-affiliated rulers commissioned this court.

the tropical rubber country of Gulf Coast Mexico. There, in the sweltering jungles of Veracruz and Tabasco, the sport was played by Olmec kings, the rulers of Mesoamerica's first great civilization. Eventually variations of this ritual game spread throughout all of Mesoamerica and even into the U.S. Southwest. Until the time of the Spanish conquest, in 1521, the game was an important part of the ancient cultures of Mesoamerica.

The massive investments of time and labor that were made in building ballcourts reflect the significance the game had to the people of Mesoamerica, as do the fine stone sculptures, ceramic figures, and colorful painted murals that depict ballgames and the accoutrements and ceremonies associated with them. Examination of the remains of the art and architecture associated with these ancient ballgames has yielded information about the variety of functions and meanings of the game in different social contexts and on ceremonial occasions.

Ballgame contests were held on the I-shaped stone courts, with parallel masonry walls forming a rectangular playing alley (see fig. 2). These courts measure 37 by 9 meters on average, though some were much smaller, and the largest, at Chichén Itzá in Yucatán, measures some 150 by 35 meters. More than twelve hundred of these ballcourts, most of which are of masonry and many of which have fine sculpted reliefs, have been found at sites ranging from Honduras to northern Mexico (see fig. 3).[1] The ball, made of solid latex rubber and weighing about six to eight pounds, was bounced back and forth between team members and against the walls of the courts. In one form of the game, known by its Aztec name, *ulama,* the ball could be hit only with the hips or buttocks. Ancient imagery shows us, however, that other styles of the game existed in which the ball was struck with sticks, bats, or the hands and feet.

Ballgames were often elaborate rituals, accompanied by music, dancing, and drama. Although the game had secular aspects and was sometimes used as a means of mediation or possibly even as a substitute for war, it also always had a religious significance, for participants and spectators alike. The ritualistic nature of the game evolved from the cosmic view and religious beliefs of the indigenous people. While its meanings clearly varied among the highly diverse Mesoameri-

can peoples, and scholars sometimes interpret its meanings in different ways, the most widely held interpretation is that the ball and its movement in the court represented the movement of heavenly bodies in the sky. The game may have been seen as representing the cyclic battle between the sun, and the life-giving qualities of light, against the moon and stars, which were associated with the underworld. The opposition of day and night, light and dark, and life and death were symbolically enacted on the ballcourt. Fertility symbolism, related to this celestial imagery, was also important in the ballgame. Like agricultural peoples everywhere, the peoples of ancient Mesoamerica were dependent upon the productivity of the earth, which relies in turn upon the sun and the rain and upon seasonal change. Ballcourt rituals were one means through which they sought to maintain the regularity of the seasons, whose changes are marked by the regular movements of celestial bodies, and to assure that the sun would re-emerge each morning from the underworld realms of night. A related, recurrent subject of the game's imagery is sacrifice of the losing team's captain by decapitation; the blood that spurted from the victim's neck was seen as symbolically nourishing the earth or offering sustenance to the sun in its battle against the forces of darkness.

THE WEST MEXICAN BALLGAME

In the farming villages and larger towns or urbanized areas of ancient West Mexico, the tradition of the ballgame and the ceramic art connected with it are as old if not older than in any other area of Mesoamerica.

In 1970 the El Opeño ballgame figurines (see fig. 4) were discovered in some ancient shaft tombs in association with a *yugito*,[2] a small curved stone object possibly used as knee or hand protection during a game. In 1991 similar material, including a number of decorated *yugitos*, was recovered in new excavations at the same site. These ballgame-related discoveries have been radiocarbon dated at around 1500 B.C.,[3] placing them securely in the Early Formative period (1500–900 B.C.). The El Opeño figurines were found together in a group of sixteen and appear to represent a scene from a ballgame. Of the eight figurines illustrated here, five males, all nude except for the leg or knee protectors they wear, are standing, three of them holding squared paddles or large, heavily padded gloves for hitting the ball, the other two apparently ready to receive or return a ball. Three females, also nude, sit or recline as if spectators at a game. The date connected with this grouping makes it roughly contemporaneous with and perhaps even earlier than other known Mesoamerican ballplayer

Fig. 4 Drawings of eight ballgame figurines; El Opeño, Michoacán; c. 1500 B.C.; earthenware. The sense of energy and emotion expressed by these early figurines remained a standard element of ballgame imagery in West Mexico for over fifteen hundred years.

figures of the Early Formative period, including ones from Olmec sites in Veracruz and Guerrero and from Las Bocas and Tlatilco in the Valley of Mexico.[4] The presence of these sculptures in West Mexico at such an early date firmly establishes the antiquity of the game in the region.

Many other ballgame-related ceramic figures, as well as several ceramic models of ballcourts, have been found buried in shaft tombs in Colima, Nayarit, and Jalisco. Most of them date from the Late Formative period (300 B.C.–A.D. 200), and a few from the Early Classic period (A.D. 200–400), all at least twelve hundred years later than those found at El Opeño. Archaeological surveys in Nayarit and in the fertile highland lake districts of Jalisco have uncovered as many as fifty-five actual ballcourts dating from about 600 B.C. to A.D. 700, although no ballcourts from these periods are known in the state of Colima. All but seven of these fifty-five courts appear to date from the Early Classic (A.D. 200–400) and Middle Classic (A.D. 400–700) periods and are connected with the circular ceremonial architecture of the Teuchitlán tradition (see the essay by Phil Weigand and Christopher Beekman in this volume).[5] The chronology that places some of the ballcourt architecture later than the florescence of the shaft-tomb burials containing ballgame-associated ceramics remains a problem that needs to be addressed archaeologically. It is possible that earlier ballcourts underlie some of the Early and Middle Classic ones; this remains to be seen, however, as little excavation has occurred at these sites. Also, most of the ballgame figures from shaft tombs in Colima, Nayarit, and Jalisco were removed by looters rather than through controlled excavation, leaving room for uncertainty about their associations with specific sites and with the ballcourts themselves. In spite of this, the presence of so many ballcourts, small ceramic replicas of them, and ceramic figures depicting ballplayers leaves little doubt that a version of the pan-Mesoamerican game was played over a long period in West Mexico.

Since the early 1900s, various scholars, including both archaeologists and art historians, have examined the shaft-tomb ceramic figures of West Mexico,[6] but little research has focused on their reflection of the ballgame as it was actually played there.[7] This essay presents an overview of some recent research on three groups of ceramic ballgame figures: large male figures, figurines, and ballcourt models. These sculptures will be considered in light of information from the recently discovered Late Formative tomb at the site of Huitzilapa in Jalisco (see the essays by Lorenza López and Jorge Ramos and by Robert Pickering and Teresa Cabrero in this volume) and in comparison with material from other regions of Mesoamerica. Although lack of context remains a problem, these ceramic images, when considered in relation to archaeological evidence of ballcourts, provide valuable information about the nature and significance of the ritual ballgame in ancient West Mexico.

Ballgame-Related Tomb Sculpture
LARGE MALE FIGURES

The best-known ancient West Mexican figures associated with the ballgame are a number of large, hollow ceramic depictions of male players holding rubber balls. Most of these are attributed to shaft tombs in Nayarit and Jalisco (see figs. 5 and 8); a smaller number, most with horns tied onto their foreheads, are known from shaft tombs in Colima (see fig. 6). The most obvious correlation between these figures and the game is that many of them hold playing balls. Also, many of these figures wear specialized garments with readily identifiable protective elements.

An imposing Ameca-Etzatlán-style ballplayer from Jalisco (fig. 5), his decorative shoulder scars and artfully arranged headdress emblematic of his rank or status, sits in an attentive pose, carefully holding a playing ball in his hands as if formally presenting it at the opening ceremony of a game. Short pants of protective leather such as the ones this figure wears are a common element of ballgame attire. A sculpture from Colima (fig. 6) depicts a less formally attired player in action, his arm drawn backwards, ready to throw a ball. This figure is shown wearing protective body armor, probably made of woven fibers or of leather. A heavily muscled Jalisco ballplayer attired in full game rig (fig. 8), his expression keenly alert, stands with arms close to his body and hands held open, as if ready to receive a ball or defend his team. His codpiece, heavy belt, and thick leather hip-pads would have offered essential protection during the game.

Ballgame accoutrements and attire clearly had emblematic as well as practical functions. A seated Nayarit couple (fig. 7), lavishly attired in jewelry, turbanlike headdresses, and decorated textiles, and with complex designs painted on their faces, is shown in what is probably a scene commemorating a high-status marriage or other rite of passage. The male figure holds a ball and wears protective leather short pants and a belt with a shell-like element, perhaps a genital protector, hanging from it. Here the ballgame accessories have no practical function, but are emblematic of his role as a ballplayer, serving to notify or remind fellow members of his community of his place in society. High-ranking people who were ballplayers undoubtedly wore or carried certain ballgame-related items as part of their customary dress on formal occasions, even those not directly related to the game, much as a modern military officer might wear his uniform at his wedding. Many West Mexican figures dressed as ballplayers are shown holding fans, musical instruments, cups, and other items. This suggests not only that ballplayers wore emblems of their connection to the game at non-game-related events, but that the game was itself a ceremonial event that formed part of or encompassed a large complex of rituals that included dance, music, and drama.

Protective leather pants such as those described above occur with practical functions in another context, that of battle. An armored, spear-wielding warrior figure (Townsend, fig. 5) also wears protective leather pants, suggesting that war and the ballgame were related, as we shall see again in this study. This idea is supported by evidence from the skeletons of individuals found in the tomb at the site of Huitzilapa, which have arm lesions consistent with throwing spears repeatedly and hip lesions attributable to hitting balls with and falling upon the hips—in this case, ballplayers and warriors may have been one and the same.

Recent discoveries at Huitzilapa have given us our first glimpse of an undisturbed high-status shaft tomb. Excavations at this site have revealed four rectangular ballcourts associated with nearby circular enclosures, each with four or more platforms arranged around an open plaza. These platforms were foundations for houselike structures; beneath

Fig. 5 Seated ballplayer; Ameca-Etzatlán style; Jalisco; earthenware. Private collection. Cat. no. 122. A high-ranking player, perhaps a chieftain, presents the ball with a sense of formality and disciplined concentration.

Fig. 6 Drawing of a ballplayer figurine holding a ball; Colima; earthenware. Private collection.

one of these structures, the rich, two-chambered shaft tomb was found to contain, among other things, a large, hollow ceramic ballplayer figure (López and Ramos, fig. 19). Radiocarbon dates derived from shell and bone from the tomb place it and its contents at around A.D. 100.[8] The tomb also contained several human skeletons; numerous fine, thin-walled polychrome vessels; jade objects; thousands of shell beads and ornaments; shell trumpets; and a number of Arenal-style ceramic figures. The ballplayer's shoulders are covered with decorative scars and he wears earrings, nose rings, painted armbands, trunks, and a headband with small decorative shells sewn to it in rows. On the front of the headband is a section without shell decoration where a geometric emblem is painted in white on the red-brown background. Three other ceramic male figures from the tomb, two standing and one seated, wear headbands of the same design,[9] which may indicate that the figures represent people of the same clan or lineage. At least two other Jalisco figures with shell headbands almost identical to those on the four Huitzilapa tomb pieces are known.[10] These two unprovenienced pieces may originally have been found in the Huitzilapa area or perhaps even at the site itself. They are of the same ceramic type as the four Huitzilapa tomb figures, wear the same type of clothing, and are generally very similar in appearance; they may even be from the hand of the same potter. That four ballcourts were found in the area of this fairly small site is also interesting.

Fig. 7 Marriage pair; Ixtlán del Río style; Nayarit; earthenware. Private collection. The male figure of this marriage pair holds a ball as an emblem of status and rank.

Fig. 8 Standing ballplayer; Ameca-Etzatlán style; Jalisco; earthenware. Private collection, Barcelona. Cat. no. 131. A powerful player with protective hip padding stands alert and at the ready.

from the shaft tombs to be certain of such clusterings. The grouped figurines from the early El Opeño tomb suggest this was the case, however, as do the many platform models depicting village life that have been found in tombs in Nayarit and Jalisco.

BALLCOURT MODELS

Most of the few known ancient West Mexican models of ballcourts depict games in action. Often complete with balls, players, and spectators, these small ceramic model courts give us clear evidence of the nature and importance of the game in ancient communal life. For the most part, they portray a game played by hitting the ball with the hips. This resembles the game traditionally played in Central Mexico during the Postclassic period (A.D. 900–1521) and witnessed by the Spaniards during the conquest of the Aztecs in 1521. Although the models generally are very similar, they exhibit some interesting thematic variations. While numbers of sherds or fragments from miniature ceramic models of ballcourts have been recovered,[18] only

perhaps seven complete models survive, all from shaft tombs in the vicinity of Ixtlán del Río, in Nayarit. The four models in this exhibition are from the Rijksmuseum voor Volkenkunde in Leiden, The Netherlands (fig. 20), the Los Angeles County Museum of Art (fig. 1), the Yale University Art Gallery (fig. 21), and the Worcester Art Museum in Massachusetts (fig. 22).

The Leiden Model

The ballcourt in the Leiden model (fig. 20) is I-shaped with parallel walls on either side of the court and internal benches along the foot of each wall. Small protrusions aligned along the center of the court serve as playing-field markers. Six figurines, all wearing red-and-white-striped twisted turbans on their heads, earspools (decorative flat discs inserted into enlarged holes in the earlobes), and trunks with loincloths, are competing on the court. Three players stand on either side of the court, each side facing the other. The game is in full swing: one of the players on the team at left, wearing a codpiece, has

Fig. 20 Model of a ballcourt; Ixtlán del Río style; Nayarit; earthenware. Rijksmuseum voor Volkenkunde, Leiden, The Netherlands. Cat. no. 177. A player extends his body to return the ball with his hip. This dramatic and standard motif suggests a meaning such as "victory" (see also fig. 1).

thrown himself to the ground near the center of the court to strike a large ball with his hip; the other players appear focused on this action. The size of the ball may be exaggerated. This model suggests that the ballplayers occupied fixed positions in opposing ends of the court, as in modern volleyball. An attentive gathering of spectators, attired in turbans of various styles, sits on the ground at the ends of the court and atop the side walls, each figurine sitting alone, engrossed in watching the competition.

The Los Angeles Model
Only part of the Los Angeles model ballcourt (fig. 1) survives; one end has been broken off, leaving about three quarters of the court. As in the Leiden model, the court is I-shaped, with parallel walls at the sides of the court and internal benches at their bases. Three raised markers are evenly spaced along the middle of the playing surface. Raised cylindrical pedestals at the ends of the walls provide special seating for two important figurines who wear visorlike, draped turbans. The court and figurines are decorated with red, white, and yellow paint.

Five figurines wearing turbans, earspools, necklaces, white loincloths or yokes, and painted leg bands and armbands are shown competing on the court; the figurines at the broken end are missing. Four players are positioned at the opposite end, two of them at the far marker, the other two at the center marker. One of the players at the center marker may be a referee. At the center of the court, a fifth player, wearing a genital protector, is portrayed in the recognized "action" pose, hitting the ball with his hip. This player and the player standing to the left of the farthest marker wear twisted red-and-white turbans; the other three wear turbans with red, white, and yellow stripes. A crowd of spectators, mainly men in loincloths and red-and-white-striped turbans or draped headdresses with red, white, and yellow stripes, is following the action on the court. Some of the figurines in the crowd have their arms around each other in a seemingly friendly fashion, while others turn and gesticulate, expressing appreciation for the ballplayer's elegant move.

It is interesting to note a number of textiles, probably belts or yokes, draped in piles at the end of one wall. A conch-shell trum-

pet, possibly representing a trumpet sounded as part of the ballgame event, sits on top of one of these. Perhaps the textiles were elaborate garments or even ritual costumes that were worn into the court by the players, then removed during the actual play of the game. But they also may represent awards or gifts of valued cotton textiles for the winners of the contest. From Fray Diego Durán,[19] a sixteenth-century ethnographer and chronicler of Aztec religion and history in Central Mexico, we know that among the Aztecs textiles were often part of the wealth wagered on the outcome of the ballgame and that textile cloaks and loincloths were frequently presented as rewards to the winners of the game.

The Yale Model
Like the Leiden and Los Angeles pieces, the Yale model (fig. 21) is I-shaped with parallel walls and internal benches running along their bases. In this model, five raised court markers are set irregularly along the central length of the court, unlike the three markers on the Los Angeles court, which are aligned along the center. These five markers may reflect the movement or bounce of the ball. This ballcourt is more elaborate, with steps leading up the exterior sides of both walls and three cylindrical pedestals, providing special seating perhaps for dignitaries or judges, rising from each wall. Remnants of white paint remain on the figurines and structures of the model.

Two groups of three figurines each face each other on the court. Another figurine, perhaps a referee, stands at the midcourt marker. The players are all dressed in padded textile loincloths or yokes with genital protectors and wear red-and-white-striped, crescent-shaped cloth headbands. Spectators, including men, women, and children, sit on the walls or on the ground at either end of the court, many of them holding and touching each other, the women with arms around their children. Two men, seated on pedestals, hold what may be drums, instruments that may have been used as signals during games, much as whistles are used in modern sports. Almost all the figurines seem happily concentrated on the events of the game, though two figurines stand on the stairs outside the court and do not appear to be watching. The women wear skirts and crescent-shaped headbands; the men, loincloths and the same type of headband. This is the only model of the four in which all figurines are shown wearing the same type of headdress. All the spectators wear earspools and painted jewelry, suggesting a festival occasion attended by high-status personages.

The Worcester Model
In the Worcester ballcourt model (fig. 22), as in the other models, the court is I-shaped with interior benches running along the insides of each of the side walls, although there are no markers on the floor of the court and no ball is present. Steps on either end of each

Fig. 21 Model of a ballcourt; Ixtlán del Río style; Nayarit; earthenware. Yale University Art Gallery, New Haven, Conn. Cat. no. 178.

wall lead up to raised, square pedestals, perhaps representing special seating for honored
guests or judges.

The subject of the Worcester ballcourt
model differs dramatically from those of the
other three. On this court a different type of
action is taking place. Rather than depicting
players engaged in active competition, it
shows four men, dressed as ballplayers, participating in what appears to be a game with
ceremonial overtones. Two of the participants, one bareheaded and the other wearing
a pointed hat, stand locked together in a
fighting stance in the center of the playing
field; the other two, both wearing turbans,
stand at one end of the court, appearing to
be observers, though one looks over his
shoulder in the opposite direction. A lone
naked male figurine (not visible in this picture), perhaps a captive, is isolated behind
one end of a court wall, as if waiting to be
called onto the playing field. The crowd
seated along the walls of the I-shaped ballcourt includes skirted women with bare
heads and breasts, naked children, and men

in loincloths and hats, turbans, or feathered
headdresses. These figurines, all decorated
with white paint on red clay, are seated close
together; they converse, watch the activity
on the field, and gesticulate, as do crowds at
any sporting and social event.

It is difficult to interpret this curious
scene. Paired fighting figures are known
from tombs elsewhere in the region; in one
especially violent pair (fig. 23), the combat-
ants are actually dressed as ballplayers, with
the dominant figure shown pinning his
opponent to the ground and wrenching his
head backward, ready to strike with a round
weapon. But the possible relationship of such
scenes to the event depicted in the Worcester
model is unclear. In any event, the Worcester
scene tells us that activities other than ballgames occurred on the courts. Perhaps it was
desirable or necessary to use ballcourt structures, which involved large investments of
time and labor, for more than one purpose.
Also, it is highly likely that many diverse
events were associated with the ballgame,
and that those events together formed a

sequence of ceremonies and rituals. Rites of passage such as initiations or accessions to office might have been celebrated in part on the sacred space of the ballcourts. Or perhaps the courts provided space for public spectacles such as wrestling matches, dramatic performances, or executions. Whether the scene shown in the Worcester model is related to human sacrifice is uncertain, but we cannot rule out the possibility. An ominous atmosphere is created in the Worcester model by the interplay of the conflict on the field and the isolation of the naked male figurine behind an end wall.

☉   ☉   ☉

Evidence from the four models shows that the ballcourts of pre-Columbian West Mexico, at least those in Nayarit, resembled the larger masonry courts of other parts of Mesoamerica. Actual ballcourts of the Teuchitlán tradition have been identified in association with the circular ceremonial complexes of Nayarit and Jalisco. In the archaeological ballcourt classification system developed by Phil Weigand, these small models correspond to the type-III category: a midsized court with open-ended playing fields, parallel walls, interior benches, and no end-zone architecture.[20] In addition, the models have cylindrical pedestals or seats for dignitaries or judges rising from the ends of the side walls. These type-III courts are associated with the Late Formative and Early Classic periods, the periods most closely associated with the shaft-tomb ballgame figures of Nayarit, Jalisco, and Colima.

The ballcourt models also offer evidence that the game being played in West Mexico at least as early as 200 B.C./A.D. 400 was similar to a hip ballgame that is well known from other parts of Mesoamerica and that flourished in the Late Postclassic period (A.D. 1400–1521). Either the ball size in these models is exaggerated or a larger ball than is known from other Mesoamerican regions was used in the game. We cannot say how many players made up a team in the ancient West Mexican game since differing numbers of players appear on the models: six on the Leiden court, five on the remaining three quarters of the Los Angeles model, and seven on the Yale court. The only ballplayer figurines known from Nayarit are those represented in the miniature ballcourt models. In contrast to the large ballgame figures of the region, which are, on the whole, different from one another and elaborately dressed, the small ballplayers seen in these models are homogeneous—all dressed alike, with thick protective loincloths and textile headbands or turbans. The variant headdresses may indicate differences in rank, but there is no recognizable hierarchical pattern. Little differentiation is noticeable among the assembled spectators or players.

Conclusions

The ceramic ballcourt models suggest that the Colima ballgame differed from the one played in Jalisco and Nayarit. They confirm that, at least in Nayarit, ballgames were played on constructed courts such as those made of adobe, stone rubble, and plaster masonry in the major archaeological sites of the region. The absence of actual ballcourts and of ceramic replicas of them in Colima, however, indicates that masonry ballcourts may not have existed there and that the game—evidence of which is seen in the ballgame-related Colima tomb figurines— may have been played in open fields. Differences between the ballgame represented in the Nayarit ballcourt models and the Colima ballgame are also suggested by the fact that traditional Mesoamerican-style ballgame yokes of stone, leather, or textile such as those seen on the Colima figurines are not seen on the large, hollow Nayarit figures. In addition, the diversity of equipment and costume seen on the Colima figurines implies that more variety existed in that region in the form of the game itself. The presence of a few Colima female figurines wearing ballgame yokes indicates that women almost certainly played the game in that region. Finally, the presence of severed heads in certain Colima sculptures provides some indication that decapitation or the taking of trophy heads was practiced there, but such sculptures are not associated with ballgame attire or equipment, and it remains to be seen if this form of sacrifice was indeed a feature of the ballgame there.

Like the Colima figurines, some of the figures from Nayarit and Jalisco carry musical instruments, indicating that music and dance were a part of ballgame celebrations. Elsewhere in contemporary Mesoamerica, there are many examples of murals, ceramics, and stone sculptures showing the affiliation of music, dance, and drama with ballgames.

On the brightly painted walls of Tepantitla at Teotihuacan, the great Central Mexican metropolis of the Classic period, we find a colorful intermingling of dancers, singers, and ballplayers. These murals, which depict a variety of ballgames, give us concrete evidence that the sport was played in a number of different ways and that in at least one game, a bat was used to hit the ball.[21] The type of bat shown in these murals is similar to the type held by Colima warrior figurines; this reinforces the idea that the Colima bats were used in the ballgame rather than as weapons in warfare. In the Gulf Coast state of Veracruz, at the archaeological site of Tajín, one of the many ballcourts has a carved frieze showing musicians hovering near a reclining figure in ballgame attire.[22] In the center of the Aztec capital of Tenochtitlan, the ruins of which lie beneath modern Mexico City, buried caches near the location of an ancient ballcourt have been found containing miniature musical instruments in association with a statue of Xochipilli-Macuixochitl, the Aztec god of the ballgame.[23] When considered in relation to data from the West Mexican ceramic figures, such widespread evidence of the pageantry surrounding ritual ballgames supports the idea that the yokes and associated attire worn by West Mexican ballplayers were also sometimes worn by musicians, dancers, warriors, and elite members of the society, all of whom thus appear to have participated in various ballgame events.

It is clear that the West Mexican ballgame was related to the pan-Mesoamerican game played throughout a wide area for at least three thousand years. Yet differences suggest that each society in the region selected for itself, perhaps both consciously and unconsciously, specific rituals and activities that best served local needs. We have already seen evidence of such differences within the ancient West Mexican region itself, where the Colima game seems to have differed from the Nayarit game in that it was probably played in open fields. In the highland lake area of Jalisco and in nearby Nayarit where the Teuchitlán tradition flourished, growing populations and political and religious centralization may have correspondingly demanded a more standardized game with the formal masonry courts that we have seen incorporated into the unique circular ceremonial complexes.

The three sizes of ballcourts in a series of circular ceremonial complexes revealed by Weigand's surveys and research in the Teuchitlán region of Jalisco have led him to postulate that economic and political competitions at various hierarchical levels were played out on the ballcourts of villages, towns, and larger communities, and that games were a means for achieving greater social cohesion across a wide region.[24] In this same vein, Beatriz Braniff has proposed that in west and northwest Mesoamerica the sport was strongly linked to diplomacy, politics, war, and conquest. Drawing analogies from sixteenth-century Spanish ethnohistoric accounts from Central Mexico that describe the game as an elite sport, Braniff suggests that it was similarly used by high-ranking families and lineages in West Mexico as a political device to determine territorial acquisitions and resolve disputes.[25] In West Mexico the game may actually have become a substitute for war itself, an idea supported by the close relationship between warrior figures and ballgame attire.

Recently Rex Koontz suggested that warfare and the ballgame at Tajín in Veracruz were two components of a complex ritual sequence concerned with alliances. He finds that this included ballgames and sacrificial decapitations, enacted on the many ballcourts at Tajín and at smaller sites in the city's surrounding hinterlands. The game was apparently an essential integrating device for Tajín and its satellites during the Early Postclassic period (A.D. 900–1100) when, after the fall of Teotihuacan, Tajín rapidly developed growing populations and political, religious, and economic power.[26] This integrating device offers an analogy for the situation in the highland lake area of Jalisco and in nearby Nayarit at around A.D. 200, when there also was a growing population and a concentration of people, power, and wealth, in sites with concentric circular architecture and a system of hierarchical ballcourts.[27] In both areas the ballgame served as a device for encouraging cohesion among the expanding diverse communities. Certainly the tomb sculptures portray distinct ethnic types, even within the relatively contained lake-basin district. Perhaps the hierarchical ballcourts at sites of the Teuchitlán tradition, like the many courts at Tajín, reflect particularly volatile sociopolitical situations in which solutions to social and economic problems were sought on the ballcourts as well as on battlefields.

It is the circular architectural style of the Teuchitlán tradition that sets Nayarit and the highland lake region of Jalisco apart from the rest of Mesoamerica, yet it is interesting to note that its ballcourts maintain a form long affiliated with the traditional pan-Mesoamerican game. While the impressive public architecture of the Teuchitlán tradition is constructed in a unique round form, the attached rectangular ballcourts link the game to external traditions. This is one of many indications that the assumption that West Mexico was peripheral to much of Central Mesoamerica during the Late Formative and Early Classic periods is erroneous. The presence of sculpted ballgame yokes, jaguar-head hachas, shell trumpets, severed human trophy heads, and balls, as well as of the courts themselves, clearly reflects pan-Mesoamerican relationships and shared traditions.

On another level of meaning, the figurines, large hollow figures, and models of ballcourts showing games in progress reveal that the energy, emotion, and sense of bonding shared by spectators and teams in action were important in communal life. The figurines from El Opeño portray players not only with ballgame paraphernalia but with alert stances and gestures, with paddles held at the ready, charged with the tension that goes before placing the ball in motion. The players are accompanied by female figurines, modeled with engaging vivacity, who are lively spectators to the ballgame action. This interaction of players and onlookers reappears much later in the Ixtlán del Río model ballcourts, in which players cast themselves dramatically downward to return the ball as spectators turn and gesticulate in appreciation, conversing with excitement and spontaneity. Although the larger ballplayer figures from Jalisco and Colima were not made for groupings, they are nonetheless often invested with a feeling of physical tension and force. This is clear in the standing Jalisco ballplayer (fig. 8), whose rugged, compact torso, blunt hands held open in readiness, and intense staring expression suggest a formidable player. At the game's most extreme level, the passion induced in spectators and players at ballgames no doubt could have produced dangerous, even fatal, situations. The sculpture of the fighting ballplayers

(fig. 23) graphically reveals that ballplayers participated in ritualized violence, possibly associated with the taking of captives in war.

In great part the significance of the models and figures to the people of ancient West Mexico was bound up with their ability to remind the deceased with whom they were buried of the physical and emotional bonding produced by the collective action and shared excitement of ballgames. The team sport of ballplaying, like coordinated group ritual dancing and certainly like the muscular drill required of warriors for battlefield success, was surely a powerful agent in promoting collective solidarity and cohesion. As the historian William McNeill has suggested, shared movement—resulting in emotional and "muscular bonding"—has been essential in building a sense of community from Paleolithic times to the present.[28]

Fig. 23 Combat scene with two ballplayers; Colima; Comala phase; earthenware. Galerie Mermoz, Paris. Cat. no. 89. Pinning his opponent to the ground, a fighting player prepares to deliver a fatal blow.

SHAMANIC SYMBOLISM, TRANSFORMATION, AND DEITIES IN WEST MEXICAN FUNERARY ART

Introduction

Ancient West Mexican funerary art has long been famous for its ceramic representations of the natural and social world, but only recently have sacred, symbolic, supernatural, shamanic, and other phenomena outside everyday experience begun to be recognized as important subjects and functions of this art. If the "non-ordinary" is even now not always recognized for what it is, at least a dimension of the spiritual or magical is now acknowledged as a significant component of the ancient mortuary ceramics of Colima, Jalisco, and Nayarit.

This is a major step forward. Only forty years ago, none of this was even conceded, at least in the literature on pre-Columbian art. The figures accompanying the deceased in ancient West Mexican shaft tombs were taken as purely secular and "anecdotal," representing ordinary, everyday life and hence lacking symbolic significance. Sculptures that did not accord with the "naturalistic" model were thought not to signify and were ignored.

Even Miguel Covarrubias, ordinarily one of the most astute students of pre-Columbian art, fell into that trap, insisting, in 1957, that there were simply no sacred or "supernatural" themes in West Mexican mortuary art at all. In his classic work *Indian Art of Mexico and Central America,* these effigies and other ceramics were described as being purely "realistic and anecdotal, concentrated in minute and detailed representations of the fauna and flora, the family life, occupations, and ceremonies of their makers, without trace of religious or symbolic concepts."[1]

Covarrubias' opinion was widely shared at the time among art historians, museum curators, archaeologists, and those who, like the great twentieth-century Mexican artist Diego Rivera, collected West Mexican ceramics on a grand scale. The idea that the mortuary art of Colima, Jalisco, and Nayarit was purely "anecdotal," nonsacred, and nonsymbolic was to endure, almost to the point of dogma, for about another decade. Some writers carried it even further. I remember another arguing that West Mexican Art so "obviously" lacked any overt reference to the sacred and magical that its creators must have been free from the control and heavy hand of religion evident elsewhere in the pre-Hispanic world. Not surprisingly, that was at least in part what had attracted Rivera to it in the first place.[2] Free from domination by priests and the demands of complex rituals, according to another authority, the ancient West Mexicans had had time to concentrate on "the little things in life."

Apparently alone among their pre-Hispanic contemporaries, then, the people of ancient West Mexico, who went to so much trouble to inter many of their dead in shaft tombs and to fill the tombs with mortuary offerings were, it was conceived, a people virtually without gods, or at least without much thought given to their relationship to unseen powers, the sphere we call, for want of a term more accurately reflecting the indigenous worldview, "supernatural." Had this been true, it would have made them unique among all First Americans, from the Arctic to the Tierra del Fuego.

Fig. 1 Crouching male figure with a smoking tube and animal visor; Ixtlán del Río style; Nayarit; earthenware. Collection of Mr. and Mrs. Joseph Goldenberg, Los Angeles. Cat. no. 196. The smoking of narcotic plants and tobacco was, and still remains, one of the shaman's methods of entering a state of supernatural communication.

NON-ORDINARY REALITIES

Strange as it now seems, nothing was said in the literature of a whole range of figures and other ceramics that could by no stretch of the imagination be made to fit into a "non-symbolic" mold. What is "ordinary" or "non-symbolic" about a dog metamorphosing into a human, or vice versa (see fig. 2), or wearing a human mask (see fig. 26)? Did the ancient West Mexicans really encounter giant sharks with human arms and legs (see fig. 29)? Figure 3 shows what is obviously a curing scene. But why a badger as doctor and a bear as patient? In Hopi animal lore, the badger is, because of its fondness for roots, a doctor who cures with medicinal herbs. Did the people of Colima who made this sculpture share these ideas because they, too, thought by analogy and based their symbolism on observations of nature? And might the bear have been for them, as for the Hopis, one of the beast gods of the four world directions, his recovery from illness vital for the cosmic equilibrium? What about men riding drums (see figs. 24 and 25) as though they were horses—animals that had become extinct in North America eight thousand years before the shaft tombs were built? Why so many drummers and men shaking rattles? Are these just musicians? Not likely, because everywhere, from Siberia to indigenous North and South America, these instruments belonged preeminently, if not exclusively, to the shaman as healer and intermediary between this world and that of gods and spirits. And since when do trees sprout from a man's back (see fig. 4)? What

might be the significance of the little people that some small, unslipped male figures, such as one armed with a club and looking to his left in figure 5, carry on their backs? Who has ever seen a woman with scores of miniature infants attached to or crawling all over her body (see fig. 13, and Townsend, fig. 18)? With all that we know of the ritual and shamanic context of intoxicating substances such as snuffs, peyote, and fermented drinks, is it possible that ancient West Mexican artists would have depicted their use as nothing more than a secular, recreational pastime, without reference to the sacred or "supernatural" (see figs. 6 and 7)? What is the meaning of the chimeric head supports from Colima, part bird, part human, part mammal (see figs. 8 and 9)? Their popular name is *reclinatorios,* or recliners, because the local people who have been discovering tombs and emptying them of their salable contents for well over a century say they are always found beneath the head of the deceased. How does their composite symbolism figure into the widespread conception of the head—

shared by the Aztecs—as the seat of the soul or animating force, and into the idea of shamans and certain animals, particularly birds, as guides of the soul into the otherworld? What do the old men and women emaciated almost to the point of skeletonization in the funerary art of Nayarit represent (see fig. 11)? Are they really no more than evidence of hunger and malnutrition? Were snakes with heads at either end, such as those forming gateways for walking figures on some cylindrical Colima pots (see fig. 10), a common sight? And did men actually grow horns from their foreheads that looked like those that appear over and over again on the foreheads of figures in the mortuary art of Colima (see figs. 17–22 and 25, and Graham, figs. 1–3, 16, and 17)? And why so many whistles, hundreds upon hundreds of them, many in the form of birds and other animals, or embedded in the heads of small, unslipped male figures (and never of female ones)? Why can some of these whistles not be blown, at least in this world, because the mouthpiece is obstructed —by a tree (see fig. 4), for example, or a bird, or the little people some of these miniatures carry on their backs (as in fig. 5)? And how might these whistles fit in with the continued use in contemporary Mexico of archaeological whistles to call the spirits of the deceased, especially of dead shamans?[3]

The list could go on and on; suffice it to say that had the ancient West Mexicans really seen in their physical surroundings everything they reproduced in clay, their

world would have to have been a very different place indeed from our own. By now I trust most everyone is agreed that the dogma of a purely secular and nonsymbolic mortuary complex is, and always was, unreasonable. Clearly the sculptural subjects entioned here merit study aimed at uncovering their deeper significance. In this essay I will explore in some detail themes suggested in selected examples of ancient West Mexican funerary phenomena: the shaft-tomb architecture itself; a vessel depicting a two-headed snake; several categories of sculpture, including those of emaciated couples, mother goddesses, figures with single horns on their foreheads (or "One-Horns"), figures riding

Fig. 6 Male figure inhaling intoxicating snuff; Comala style; Colima; earthenware. Private collection.

Fig. 7 Hunchbacked dwarf gesturing with paired peyote buds; Comala style; Colima; earthenware. Private collection. Widely employed in different parts of Mexico as a ritual inebriant, peyote grows naturally only in the north-central Mexican desert and the lower Rio Grande valley, and must have been widely traded or obtained on pilgrimages similar to those of the present-day Huichol.

Fig. 8 *Reclinatorio* with a dog's head in rear; Comala style; Colima; earthenware. Collection of Barbara and Justin Kerr, New York. Cat. no. 86.

Fig. 9 *Reclinatorio;* Comala style; Colima; earthenware. The Miller Family Collection, Chicago. Cat. no. 85.

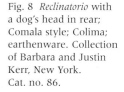

drums, and dogs with human faces; and a remarkable sculpture of a shark with human limbs.

THE USES OF ETHNOGRAPHIC ANALOGY

Before embarking on any such exploration, however, we must explore the means available to us. In trying to discover meanings, however hypothetical, we must remember an unfortunate fact: that, much as recent archaeology has contributed to a better understanding of West Mexican funerary practices, archaeology alone cannot tell us very much about what the ancient West Mexicans believed or about the nature of their relationship to the dead and to the unseen powers that, in the indigenous worldview, are integral to the natural environment. Even if it could, the problem would remain that there has been far too little controlled excavation: the percentage of tombs that have been discovered and excavated by trained professionals is so minuscule in comparison with those that have been looted as to be effectively invisible. This is not to take away from the considerable contributions that have been made possible by recent investigations such as those into the Huitzilapa tomb, a Jalisco shaft tomb whose discovery and excavation are described elsewhere in these pages (see the essay by Lorenza López and Jorge Ramos in this volume)—rather, to state the obvious: against the hundreds of shaft-tomb burials that have been discovered and the thousands of West Mexican figures that have come into private and public collections since the late 1800s, we have but two or three tombs that have had the benefit of controlled excavation and study from start to finish.

It goes without saying that, especially where a burial was not disturbed and disarranged by subsequent interments, it would be useful to know the original placement and orientation of sculptures in relation to the deceased, or what correlation, if any, there was between types of offerings and gender. That such knowledge is forever beyond recovery when a tomb has been looted does not mean, however, that the West Mexican works of art available for study are without intrinsic value to scholarship. But to unravel the deeper meanings that invariably underlie the immediately obvious, to go beyond aesthetics and impressionistic descriptions and understand something more about West

Mexican tomb sculpture, we need to draw on a whole range of resources. Ethnology, comparative religion, and mythology are at the top of the list, as they must be if we are to make sense out of some of the more enigmatic motifs in pre-Columbian art.

Death and Rebirth in Shaft-Tomb Architecture

The labor-intensive architecture of the shaft tombs, in which all of the objects discussed here were found, was no doubt itself fraught with symbolism, perhaps a reenactment in reverse of birth and a return to the Earth Mother's womb. This would account for the very narrow horizontal tunnel that typically connects the burial chamber with the vertical shaft and through which the corpse, after being lowered through the shaft from the surface, would have had to be pulled and pushed, recalling the infant's passage through the birth canal. It would also account on a broad level for the fact that the womblike burial chambers were filled with cooking vessels, foodstuffs (real or in ceramic effigy), tools, weapons, and, above all, representations of people, plants, animals, curing, feasting, architecture, and family or communal ceremonial activities such as the boys' initiation rite depicted in the crowded house and plaza group from Nayarit illustrated in these pages (Townsend, fig. 27), even if the significance of this or that ceramic sculpture is not always easily decipherable for us now. Why all this effort, unless the survivors were certain of a continued existence of the deceased on another plane, a mutual dependency between them and their ancestors, between the living and the dead (as is believed today among the Huichol Indians in the Sierra Madre Occidental of Nayarit and Jalisco)? Surely there was a desire both to protect the dead from harm by sorcerers and witches (still a widespread concern), sometimes—as symbolized by the sub-floor burial chambers of some Nayarit house models (see Butterwick, fig. 6)—to keep them close enough so that they would even have been able to hear the footsteps of the living above their heads, and to make them feel content with their new environment and therefore well disposed toward the survivors. For mixed with love and concern for the dead there is, and must always have been, a certain fear of them, of their displeasure at neglect and ill-treatment, or at slights or injury remembered from life. And why, if not to protect them, include among these ceramic companions of the dead not only representations of everyday life, religious ritual, magical transformation, or effigies of "technicians of the sacred" (to use Mircea Eliade's elegant definition of the shaman), but even some of what I have long been convinced are deities?[4]

The Two-Headed Snake

In some cases the search for analogies takes us some distance from West Mexico, while still remaining within the greater Native American culture area. Take the two-headed snake, a mythic creature that has a very wide distribution in pre-Columbian art and iconography and that is depicted on the cylindrical Colima pot in figure 10. Why a head at either end? Although occasionally a snake may be born with two heads side by side, there is no snake in nature with a head at both ends. So the explanation must be sought in symbolism. One answer may lie in what the Colombian anthropologist Gerardo Reichel-Dolmatoff learned in his work with the Kogi, who live on the northern slopes of the Sierra Nevada de Santa Marta in Colombia. Kogi shamans say that with a head and eyes at either end, the bicephalic

serpent can see at the same time into both the world of humans and animals and that of the gods, linking them with one another and serving for shamans as a bridge when they travel in their ecstatic trance states from the ordinary to the nonordinary realm. The Kogi are the inheritors of numerous pre-Hispanic traditions in the so-called Intermediate Area between Central America and South America, of which some may have been shared by the ancient West Mexicans. Theirs may be only one of several possible explanations for the two-headed snake in Mesoamerica, but one has to admit that it makes a good deal of sense.

Skeletonization: Death or Life?

The sculptures of aged, emaciated couples also raise some interesting questions that take us beyond West Mexico. These figures come mainly from tombs near Ixtlán del Río, in what is now the state of Nayarit. All have similar characteristics, whatever their place in the chronology of shaft-tomb burials. They are bent with age and have prominent rib cages and projecting spinal columns. Their lips may be pursed in song or chant. The female figure may be shown preparing food, and the male figure shown wearing a dog-skin headdress and playing a rasp or, as in the example illustrated here (fig. 11), blowing into a bowl through a tube, as some shamans still do to infuse their medicinal preparations with their breath, and with it their special powers (see also fig. 12).[5]

What have we here? Testaments to starvation or to a wasting disease? Probably not. Skeletonization, partial or total, is not uncommon in pre-Columbian art and often carries meanings we now know to be quite the opposite of death. Mesoamerican Indians shared, and still share, with many other indigenous peoples a belief in the bones as the seat of life and even in regeneration from skeletal parts. These beliefs explain why many people in Mexico and Guatemala today refer to the hard seeds of the avocado and other fruits not as *semilla*, the usual Spanish term for seed, but *hueso*, bone. Depictions of the skeletal, aged couple are not restricted to Nayarit, but are found also elsewhere in Mesoamerica, where they are represented not as ordinary folk but as deities. Hence there is a good chance that the Nayarit couples with prominent skeletal markers are not symbols of sickness, famine,

Fig. 10 Cylindrical vase with four reliefs; Colima; Comala phase; earthenware. Private collection. In each of the reliefs on this vase, a human figure walks through an archway formed by what may be the double-headed cosmic snake that figures in the chthonic architecture of some indigenous peoples in Mexico. This figure may symbolize the sun god on his nocturnal underworld passage.

Fig. 11 Elderly pair;
Ixtlán del Río style;
Nayarit; earthenware.
Private collection.
Cat. no. 189.

decay, or death, but that they are the opposite: creator deities, an earlier, West Mexican version of the primordial creator couple the Aztecs called Ometéotl and Omecihuatl, Bone Man and Bone Woman. Other possible analogues are the old gods and goddesses depicted with skeletal features in such beautiful pre-Hispanic pictorial manuscripts as the *Codex Vienna*. As J. L. Furst has demonstrated in her study of this manuscript, their skeletonized faces identify them not with death but, on the contrary, with creation and fertility.[6]

Like other Mesoamerican deities, the aged and emaciated Nayarit couple may also have had other guises and functions. This exhibition includes a sculpture of a seated

male who appears to be blowing tobacco smoke from a tubular pipe (fig. 1). Though he lacks the emphasis on the skeleton and his body decoration is different, the distinctive dog-skin headdress he shares as his special attribute with the male of the skeletal couple and some other details indicate that he may be a different aspect of the same god, perhaps one with rain as his principal domain. His connection to rain is suggested both by the tubular pipe and some of his body paint. Blowing clouds of tobacco smoke from a tube (a "cloud blower") to call the rain is not uncommon among Native Americans, including the Pueblos and the California Chumash. By analogy to Puebloan art, we can see that the parallel white lines painted on his legs very likely also symbol-ize rain.

We may find that other kinds of oft-repeated figures in ancient West Mexican shaft-tomb art represent deities, for, as the art historian Leonhard Adam pointed out in 1940,[7] when one encounters the same type of sculpture over and over in nonwestern or tribal art, it is more likely representative of a deity than of a real person or ancestor. Yet West Mexican tomb art has usually been thought to depict neither gods nor priests, probably in part because none could be rec-ognized from characteristics that identify them as such in the arts of the great Meso-american civilizations.

Mother Goddesses

Consider the class of Colima effigies depicting a seated woman covered with scores of tiny children such as those shown in figure 13 (see also Townsend, fig. 18). The distinctive iconography of this class of figures crosses local stylistic, geographic, and even chrono-logical boundaries. It is obvious that these figures represent something more than hu-man maternity. But, what?

We may have one rather satisfying ex-planation close by, in the sacred chants and rituals of the present-day Huichol, whose territory lies mainly within the states of Jalisco and Nayarit. I turn to the Huichol because, for a variety of reasons, their rich and varied traditions preserve, better than any other in Mesoamerica, some themes and

motifs once shared not only among speakers of Uto-Aztecan languages (these include both the Huichol and the Hopi, and, in the view of some linguists, possibly the West Mexican culture area of two millennia ago as well), but also across ethnic and linguistic bound-aries. The Huichol have a heterogeneous ancestry, and what we now know as "Huichol mythology" is, and always has been, an as-semblage or synthesis of different oral tradi-tions and histories including, possibly, those that express themselves in the mortuary ceramics of ancient West Mexico. By extend-ing into the archaeological past the analo-gies between contemporary Huichol and Puebloan symbolism that have been noted by some scholars, I have occasionally found Huichol mythology, ritual, and iconography to be useful for the interpretation of West Mexican tomb art.[8]

A particularly interesting example of such correspondences is a remarkable Colima figure of an armless young woman reclining on a metate, a stone used for grinding maize (fig. 14). This could almost serve as a literal illustration for a Huichol myth of the origin of maize, in which Blue Maize Girl, a young maize goddess, provides sustenance for the

Fig. 12 Male figure blowing through a tube into a bowl; Ameca-Etzatlán style; Jalisco; earthenware. Ron Mes-sick Fine Arts, Santa Fe. By analogy to a similar practice of contemporary Indian shamans per-formed in the prepara-tion of their potions, this figurine from Jalisco appears not to be drink-ing from the bowl, but using a tube to "charge" the medicinal prepara-tion with his breath, and hence his shamanic power.

Fig. 13 Mother goddess figure; Colima; late Comala phase; earthen-ware. Private collection. Numerous tiny figures of children cover this figure. Three horned male figures are seated on her lap and a fourth, wearing a rayed head-dress that may represent the sun, astride her shoulders.

people by lying on a metate and grinding herself, her limbs disappearing and becoming bloody *masa*, the dough that is used to make tortillas.[9] Inevitably one also has to wonder whether, and how, this tale, which is not limited to the Huichol, might relate to the burial on a string of three metates of a woman in the Huitzilapa tomb.

If we can accept that the Colima effigies covered with little children such as the one in figure 13 are not human but divine, akin, perhaps, to Xochiquetzal, the young mother goddess of the Aztecs, there is a remarkable analogy for them in what Carl Lumholtz, a turn-of-the-century explorer of West Mexico, called the "First Fruits" ceremony, and which the Huichol celebrate as *Tatéi Neirra*, Dance of Our Mother. Years before I had seen such a figure, the late Huichol artist and shaman

Ramón Medina Silva related to me a version of the chant associated with this rite, which usually takes place around October. In it, the officiating family shaman symbolically transforms the smallest children, who are identified with the first squashes, into a flock of little birds. Chanting and pounding his drum, the shaman—*mara'akáme* in Huichol—guides the children on a three-hundred-mile dream flight to Wirikúta, the Huichol name for the sacred peyote desert in San Luis Potosí, primordial birthplace of the Sun God. The celestial trail follows the same path as that taken by the divine ancestors on their peyote hunt and followed ever since by Huichol on their annual pilgrimages made to collect the divine psychoactive cactus.[10] When the children arrive, the shaman sings and they meet their Mother, the goddess whose home is in the peyote country and who, surrounded by beautiful flowers, awaits them. When they see her, they crawl over and touch her body to learn how she looks and feels and of the love and promise of life they may expect from her. But there is undoubtedly more to the goddess represented in Colima art than even the Huichol tradition suggests. The male seated astride her shoulders and wearing a rayed headdress may represent the Sun God (who in Aztec myth is the son of the young mother goddess Xochiquetzal), and the trio of male One-Horns found on her lap around a prone individual may be curing shamans, or gods functioning in that capacity. But the magical encounter of the little children with the mother goddess in the Huichol chant is uncannily reminiscent of what this effigy and others of its type may signify.

The Colima One-Horns

Figures with single forehead horns occur sporadically throughout Mesoamerica, beginning in the Early to Middle Formative periods (2000–300 B.C.), as well as in Central America and Andean South America (see figs. 15 and 16). But it is among the red-slipped male figures of Colima, and some of their smaller, solid, unslipped counterparts, that it is most common. Such a curious feature raises questions. In Colima, this type of figure, the "One-Horn," occurs again and again, over several centuries, in tombs scattered over a wide area, and in different poses and activities. The forehead horn is a phenomenon that, surely, no one could, or should, have taken as naturalistic, anecdotal, or in any sense representative of everyday, ordinary life. The horn itself, along with certain iconographic details commonly associated with it, taken together, clearly form a pattern or symbolic unity, each element of which may well be analogous to phenomena in the natural world that might be recoverable even at this distance in time and culture. Or are they part of a mental universe that will forever be beyond our reach? Probably not. For if the ancient West Mexicans were anything like indigenous peoples today, their thought operated "primarily by analogy," thus creating "a chain of associations," as Reichel-Dolmatoff wrote of the Kogi.[11]

I proposed in 1965 that a shamanic religion and shamanic practices similar to those documented in other parts of the Americas and Asia prevailed among the village societies of West Mexico, and that this is reflected in some of the imagery of shaft-tomb art.[12] My primary evidence was the Colima One-Horns, which can be better understood as shamans and shamanic tomb guardians than as warriors, which is what they had for so long been labeled. I am not sure now that this group of sculptures does not also include representations of a patron deity of shamans who shares such characteristics as the horn with his earthly representatives. But if, like some of the divine patrons of Pueblo societies, these deities have the same distinguishing traits as the shamans themselves, how can one determine which representation is supposed to be divine and which human, the more so in that what we call "impersonation" in indigenous ceremonies—in the masked *kachina* dances of the Hopi, for example—is, for both participants and audience, qualitative identity?

The 1950s and 1960s saw substantial advances in worldwide awareness and scientific as well as humanistic studies of shamanism in its different cultural contexts. One need not go so far as to call shamanism humanity's oldest religion, but there are good reasons to believe that it is a very ancient formulation of spirituality, even the most ancient, and that much of its underlying worldview was widely shared across a good part of the planet. Similarities that are sometimes startling can be found reaching across cultural, linguistic, geographical, and temporal boundaries among shamanic beliefs and practices. Such similarities exist not only

among techniques of curing, shamanic paraphernalia, and symbolism, but even more so among beliefs about life, the cosmos, and the relationship of people to the universal order. During the 1950s and 1960s, common assumptions about such matters as the relationships, and even qualitative equivalence, between all life forms were examined. Similar conceptions of cosmic architecture, including the idea of a stratified universe the different levels of which are accessible only to the specialist in the sacred, i.e., the shaman, and that replicates itself in sacred structures as well as domestic dwellings, were found to exist, as were corresponding ideas

Fig. 17 Seated male figure with a horned headdress; Comala style; Colima; earthenware. Private collection. Cat. no. 43.

about the nature and role of helping spirits. Among other ideas discovered to be widespread were a belief in the animate and sentient nature of even those phenomena that we in the West regard as "inanimate," and the idea of the shaman as a kind of spiritual warrior. All these and more were explored by scholars in various disciplines. During the 1960s and early 1970s, some anthropologists of religion were talking about a common archaic shamanic substratum undergirding all Native American religions, even those of the most complex indigenous civilizations, and linking them with Siberia.[13]

For an argument so critical of long-held preconceptions, the shamanic reinterpretation has fared surprisingly well. This may be due less to the way the argument was constructed in my 1965 paper, or to the rather far-flung cross-cultural evidence I cited in its support, than to the publication in 1964 of the first English edition of Mircea Eliade's pivotal study *Shamanism: Archaic Techniques of Ecstasy* and to a growing body of ethnographic literature on shamanism; the time proved propitious for broadening the scope of the comparative study of shamanism from ethnology and the history of religion to pre-Columbian art and iconography. If what sounded so revolutionary thirty years ago has not been long in being accepted into the literature on pre-Columbian art, this is not to say that there has not also been some resistance. Interpretation of ancient art by ethnographic analogy is not to every archaeologist's liking, particularly in the absence of a demonstrable genetic connection between the archaeological data and a contemporary social analogue, such as that we find in the Puebloan Southwest. But there has also been some prejudice against the very idea of shamanism and shamans in West Mexico. This has derived from a fundamental error: that shamanism is a phenomenon of pre-agricultural hunter-gatherers, especially those of the Asian and American Arctic, and thus can not possibly be attributed to such developed and socially and economically stratified village societies as those responsible for the shaft tombs and their art.

The idea that shamanism is limited to the hunter-gatherer way of life is old-fashioned and quite clearly wrong. In our own hemisphere, ethnologists such as Reichel-Dolmatoff have shown that shamanism is today very much alive—with some striking correspondences in belief and techniques within and outside the Americas—among Amazonian agricultural societies whose socioeconomic organization is no less complex than that assumed for West Mexico of two millennia ago.[14] This idea also contradicted the ethnohistoric evidence, including the works of the sixteenth-century chroniclers, above all those of Fray Bernadino de Sahagún, who had much to say about Aztec shamans and "doctors"—*ticitl* in Nahuatl—in the *Florentine Codex,* his great work on Aztec civilization. There is documentation as well for the persistence of shamanism throughout the colonial era, such as the testimony of Hernando Ruíz de Alarcón, a seventeenth-century parish priest and representative of the Holy Office in Guerrero, Mexico. In a treatise addressed to his bishop and his fellow clerics on the "heathen superstitions" of his parishioners, he described a whole series of beliefs and practices that, having survived the Spanish invasion, stubbornly persisted, against his most determined efforts to uncover and suppress them, even a century after the destruction of Aztec civilization.[15] Among these were the veneration and ecstatic-divinatory use of *ololiuhqui* (the Nahuatl [Aztec] term for the potent psychoactive seeds of the morning glory *Turbina corymbosa*), as well of peyote. Today we recognize the phenomena Ruíz de Alarcón describes, including the ecstatic plant inebriants, animal familiars and spirit helpers, transformation, prognostication of the future, magical incantations, and so on, as typical of shamanic practice.

The fact is that even among the Aztecs, who had one of the most complex and advanced urban civilizations in the ancient Americas, alongside a priesthood that was trained in special schools and that had charge of the temples and the great calendrical ceremonies, there was always a large class of urban and village shamans who divined the causes of illness, cured with both practical and magical means, prognosticated the future, conducted local rituals, and guarded the social, physical, and psychic equilibrium of their clients. When the Spanish smashed the state religion, its priests, and their schools and temples, it was the shamans and their beliefs and practices that survived, as they did in Ruíz de Alarcón's village and as they do to this day among indigenous Mesoamericans. Hence, the idea of shamans

Fig. 18 Seated dwarf with a bird necklace; Comala style; Colima; earthenware. The Cleveland Museum of Art, fiftieth anniversary gift of the Women's Council in honor of the museum's seventy-fifth anniversary. Cat. no. 39.

and shamanic beliefs, symbols, and practices among the village societies of ancient West Mexico, and their representation in objects made for and accompanying the deceased on their journeys to the otherworld, was and is perfectly plausible.

THE HORN AS INSIGNIA OF SUPER- NATURAL POWER

The argument in favor of a shamanic reinterpretation of the Colima "warriors" rests, in part, on such observations as these:

There is obviously a reason for the horn. Horns are one of the most widespread—indeed, universal—insignia of supernatural, priestly, and shamanic power, so much, from the Paleolithic to the ethnographic present, and in so many places, that one hardly needs to make a case that it had the same meaning in pre-Columbian art and symbolism. The morphology of the horn depends on which animals might have been the inspiration. Reindeer, sheep, bison, and wild and domesticated cattle have all served this purpose. The single horn in the center of the forehead is less easily accounted for, but then so is that of the unicorn. One possibility for Mexico is the native male turkey, which has a hornlike wattle above the beak that becomes especially prominent during the mating season. Another, less obvious, is the rhinoceros beetle, which some Mexican Indian peoples connect with the underworld. Or it may be none of these but, like the single horn of the Avanyu, the horned serpent of the Puebloan Southwest, and the single horn that occurs sporadically elsewhere in Mesoamerica, the Andes, and Asia, may have originated in myth and in observations and reformulations of natural history dating back to an ancient common shamanic substratum.

For North America, an interesting recent example is a late-nineteenth-century Sioux medicine man, appropriately named One-Horn, who tied his hair forward so as to resemble a horn. Edward Curtis photographed him like that in the early 1900s, and that is how he portrayed himself in a pictograph. For an Asian analogue to the Colima One-Horns, we have the venerable figure of Hermit Single-Horn of Indian, Chinese, and Japanese mythology, an ancient shaman and healer. There are numerous variants on the Hermit Single-Horn legend in art and literature; one of the earliest, in the *Mahabharata*, India's greatest epic, describes a holy man with a single horn on his head (but some other sources give him two). In the dramatic plays of Japan and Tibet, the masks of Hermit Single-Horn show him as a man with a single forked horn, a long curved horn extending from his brow, or a short, stubby horn.

Other iconographic details often associated with the single horn of the Colima figures also point to shamanism. One that may not be immediately apparent, but that is integral to the argument, is the headband. Some full-figure One-Horns and horned "head pots" lack the head strap. But where it occurs, as it does especially in the armed figures, it is looped in a more or less consistent manner: from the crown downward under the chin, describing a full circle around the upper part of the head, and looped around the base of the horn. It may be prominent, modeled three-dimensionally, or indicated only by incised lines and/or a different shade of slip. But it always exhibits a curious and no doubt meaningful feature: it is nowhere tied together but is continuous, without beginning or end (see figs. 17, 18, and 20, and Graham, figs. 1, 3, 16, and 17).

There is clearly a relationship between these headbands in West Mexican funerary art and the headdresses and headbands many shamans, in the Americas as well as Asia, wore or still wear—indeed, *must* wear—when shamanizing, lest their performances be ineffective. Here again there are some striking parallels between the Americas and North and East Asia. According to Eliade, among certain Siberian peoples, as, for example, the Yurak-Samoyed, the shamanic cap or helmet is considered the most important part of the shamanic costume, containing as it does a great, if not the greatest, portion of the shaman's power. As Eliade has pointed out, it is for this reason that Asian shamans frequently leave off their caps or headbands when asked to perform for strangers, since without it they have no real power and their ceremony is only a parody. Some Samoyed shamans wore headband-like iron rings around their heads to contain their powers, which they believed might otherwise burst the bounds of the skull. Might the strap around the horns and heads on Colima figures have served a similar purpose?

Be that as it may, even without resort to analogies, the headband appears to me to constitute almost a unified symbol complex with the horn and must itself have been invested with power. Like the different sizes and appearances of the horn itself, the presence or absence of the band must have had meaning that was shared by the sculptor with his or her contemporaries, even if two thousand years later we can only guess at it. If the shape and dimensions of the horn are indicative of the degree of power and vital substance—or, to borrow a term from the Aztecs, *tonalli*[16]—acquired by, or, if we are dealing with a deity, inherent in its owner, it would explain why some horns are little more than immature knobs and others are prominent and supple, sweeping upward to a sharp point. The extraordinary male figure illustrated here (fig. 19) is particularly interesting and instructive. Here we see both kinds of horns, the prominent horn on the brow of the adult and the small immature projection just emerging knoblike from the forehead of the boy. Suspended upside down, with his legs slung over the man's shoulders and his arms raised for additional support, the boy is positioned so that his head appears almost like that of a baby emerging from his mother's body. To add to the apparent mystery, the older man holds a knife-like weapon in one hand and a severed head identical to the boy's in the other. It is indeed an extraordinary scene, perhaps even unique among the mortuary figures of Colima.

But it is no great mystery, beyond our understanding. What it seems to represent is the initiation of a young shaman by his master, a life crisis that ideologically replicates birth itself. That this is no ordinary initiation but that of a young shaman who is about to be "born" is self-evident from the contrast between the horns. Rather than representing a trophy head, the severed head may symbolize the dismemberment of the candidate shaman and his reconstitution—a frequent, though not universal, aspect of shamanic initiation. Not infrequently, such rituals also replicate the birth process, and that is what this dramatic figure appears to represent with the placement of the young initiate's head. That the older man is carrying the boy presents no great puzzle, for in initiations there is typically a stage at which the novice cannot, in his liminal state, walk or even stand on his own, but must be carried like a newborn infant by an adult—an uncle, perhaps, or one from whom he has acquired the necessary practical and esoteric knowledge to take his rightful place in the adult world.

The closest analogy of which I am aware to men acting out the maternal role and symbolically giving birth to initiates happens to be in Papua New Guinea, where just such a ritual was filmed some years ago for the documentary feature *Mondo Cane*. If this sculpture is not completely idiosyncratic, it suggests some similar custom in ancient West Mexico, although the more usual practice, well known also from Pueblo initiation rituals, seems to have involved the young initiates being carried in the arms or on the shoulders of their adult sponsors. It is this that leaves little doubt that the purpose of the crowded ceremony represented in elsewhere in these pages (Townsend, fig. 27) is initiation.

As for the horn, if its size is one indication of the degree of a shaman's *tonalli*, his vital essence and sacred power, it would also explain why the horn on a head pot representing an aged man with sunken cheeks (fig. 21) leans backward, appearing weak and flaccid, as though with advancing age its owner's *tonalli* had spent itself and perhaps even departed.

Fig. 19 Shaman with a young initiate hanging down his front; Comala style; Colima; earthenware. Lowe Museum of Art, University of Miami, Fla.

THE SHAMAN AS WARRIOR

The armed Colima One-Horns that were for so long taken to be warriors were, without speculation as to why a warrior should have a horn growing from his head, regarded simply as evidence for endemic warfare. But another crucial detail that was ignored is that armed Colima One-Horns invariably face left (see fig. 20, and Graham, fig. 3), while those without weapons look straight ahead or up (see figs. 17 and 18). It is not difficult to guess the reason for the former. Many Native Americans share with much of the rest of humanity the association of the left side with misfortune, evil, and death, and, judging from the many examples in pre-Columbian iconography, so did their ancestors. The examples are too numerous and too well known to require documentation here; suffice it to say that over and over one encounters references to sorcery and witchcraft as emanating from the left direction. To mention but two examples from my own field-work in the Maya region: in the Guatemalan highlands sorcerers are said to perform their nefarious deeds with the left hand, and Maya children are warned to sow seeds only with the right hand, never the left, lest the crops wither in the fields or be devoured by worms and other pests. In archaeological representations of life-death duality, particularly in the art of Mexican Veracruz, the left side is that of death, the right of life. Clearly, then, these shaman figures facing left are armed to do battle with the forces of evil.

Thus the conflict between the old identification of certain figures as warriors and the new as shamans is more apparent than real. Shamans by definition are warriors, combat being integral to their vocation. Eliade gives numerous examples, as does much of the ethnographic literature on shamanism. The difference is that ordinary warriors (and there are surely those as well in West Mexican art) fight against human enemies, while shamans do battle with witches and sorcerers and the unseen agents of sickness and misfortune—specifically, those that threaten and afflict their clients, living or deceased. Shamans also fight with human enemies, however, sometimes with magical weapons shot from afar (the Huichol call these "arrows of sickness"), sometimes face-to-face, as documented in the literature and permanently enshrined in tomb art (see fig. 22). The military elements of figures formerly called warriors thus take on a new dimension.

COLIMA ONE-HORNS AND THE HOPI KWANITAKA

As it happens, both the horn and the sinistral orientation turn out to have analogues in the American Southwest. Almost two millennia and a thousand miles separate the Hopi of Arizona from the unknown people who interred at least the more prestigious of their dead in shaft tombs. That is a considerable distance in both time and space. But the ideological difference between them may not be quite so great.

That there is a certain correspondence between the Colima One-Horns of two thousand years ago and an esoteric Hopi society was first brought to my attention some three decades ago by Isaac Eastvold, a campaigner for the protection of Native American rock art who in his twenties was already a keen student of Hopi intellectual culture.[17] About a year after the publication of my 1965 essay on the Colima One-Horns as shamans and tomb guardians, Eastvold pointed out to me that the most convincing analogy of all, both for the horn and the sinistral orientation of these sculptures, was to be found among these Uto-Aztecan speakers, whose language is related to that of the Huichol and possibly even to that which was spoken by the people

Fig. 20 Male figure with a horned headdress; El Chanal, Colima; earthenware. Private collection. This one-horned figurine, armed with a sling and with a prominent band wrapped around the horn on his forehead, faces left, the side universally associated with sorcery, witchcraft, and misfortune.

Fig. 21 Vessel in the form of a human head; Comala style; Colima; earthenware. Private collection.

Fig. 22 Two shamans in combat; Comala style; Colima; earthenware. Denver Museum of Natural History.

of ancient West Mexico. Nothing appeared more similar to the Colima One-Horns and the functions I had proposed for them than the Hopi Kwanitaka, also known as One-Horns or Agaves (from the agave spikes they attach to their headdresses in imitation of a horn). Like the shamans I believe to be represented by the Colima One-Horns, the Kwanitaka relate to the underworld as conveyors of dead souls to the otherworld and as guardians of the deceased; those selected to accompany the souls of the dead to the beyond remain with them as protectors against supernatural harm.

The Kwanitaka also play a vital role as combative guardians of the village and of new initiates in the *Wuwutsim* (or *Wowoshim*) ceremony. In preparation for the *Wuwutsim*, they circle the village incessantly counterclockwise, i.e., to the left, making noises to frighten witches and striking with their spears and clubs at unseen hostile beings that threaten the spiritual integrity of the young initiates in their defenseless, liminal state, and of the community at large. Thus the Hopi One-Horns are indeed warriors. But their adversaries are supernatural rather than human—precisely the function I suggested for the One-Horns as warriors in Colima tomb art. (For a different interpretation of the horn, see the essay by Mark Graham in this volume.)

Once the idea of shamanism and shamans in ancient West Mexico, with analogues in the ethnographic present, ceased being such a novelty, interpretations of some "nonordinary" figures other than the One-Horns began to fall into place as well. There is not space here to consider them all, but three deserve special mention: figures riding on drums, dogs wearing human masks, and a shark with human arms and legs.

Riding the Shaman's Drum

Nowhere in the indigenous Americas, any more than in Asia, was the drum only a musical instrument, any more than were the rattles that either replaced the drum (in some areas) or accompanied its steady beat. Rather, as I have already noted, both drum and rattle were preeminently associated with shamanic practice. Rattles were particularly important in curing ceremonies; in many places the gourd, from which rattles are commonly made, continues to symbolize the universe and, where the handle is not just attached at the base but passes through its entire length (as is the case in South American shaman's rattles), it represents the *axis mundi*, while the stones that produce the sound embody the spirits of ancestors. It follows that, by analogy to other drumusing cultures from Siberia and the Asian and American Arctic to the very tip of South America, we can say with reasonable certainty that every drummer in West Mexican

art has to be, by definition, a shaman, and
that the rattle is likewise a percussion instrument associated with shamanic curing and
other kinds of rituals.

Further, in many places it is the drum
and its rhythmic beat (see fig. 23) that take
the shaman into otherworlds, just as in the
Huichol ceremony described above, in which
the drum and its sound waft the shaman and
the little children in his care into the sky for
their journey east to the land of peyote to
meet their divine Mother.

The drum as mount into the otherworld
comes to mind in trying to decipher West
Mexican figurines of men riding drums, especially that illustrated in figure 24 (see also
fig. 25). How would such a symbolism occur
to people who, before the European invasion, had never seen a horse or any beast of
burden other than the dog? In Asia the drum
as mount into the otherworld is well documented, even for reindeer herders or horse
breeders whose shamans believe themselves
to travel into the sky on a stag or horse, or
on a sled pulled, like that of Santa Claus, by
a team of reindeer. True, in Central Asia and
Siberia, riding is an ancient art that had no
parallel in the Americas before the European
invasion. But who is to say that the idea of
the shaman's drum as his spirit mount did
not exist among the Asiatic ancestors of the
First Americans long before the wild horse
was tamed?

The curious sculpture depicted in figure
24 is incomplete, but what is missing from

it is almost as important as what remains. There is little question that the two figures are embarked on a journey. The one in front, astride the drum and pounding it with both hands, has a traveling bag on his back, suspended, in typical Mesoamerican fashion, from a carrying strap across his forehead. The standing figure carried something on his back that has been broken off and lost. But through examination of what remains on this sculpture and of other small, unslipped miniatures of this type, such as the one in figure 5, we know that it was a little person.

As is common with unslipped male figures, both figures in figure 24 have whistles in their heads, but the rear figure's whistle could not have been blown—except by someone who had become incorporeal, i.e., a spirit—if the tiny figure that he was once carrying were still in place. It is the missing figure that seems to me the key: perhaps it was a representation of a soul on its way to the otherworld, and the men are shamans helping to guide it and protect it. Like funerary chants from any cultural tradition that recite the soul's path to the beyond, the

sculpture as a whole can almost be read like a page from an imaginary Mesoamerican "Book of the Dead."

The Dog with the Human Face

Let's now look at the dog (fig. 26), which, with some other examples of its type, differs from the well-known and very numerous naturalistic canine effigies from Colima in that it wears a human mask. Colima dogs with human masks on their faces are relatively rare, but there are enough of them in private collections and museums to recognize them as a special category. Yet even those that have nothing about them to suggest anything out of the ordinary (see Braun, figs. 6 and 19, and Schöndube, figs. 15 and 16)—and they number in the many hundreds—invite speculation. They all seem to represent one or more varieties of the breed known as the Mexican Hairless, which, without turning to useless speculations about trans-Pacific diffusion, should be noted to have very similar counterparts in both China and the Andes. But why so many sculptures of dogs?

Fig. 26 Dog wearing a mask with a human face; Comala style; Colima; earthenware. Los Angeles County Museum of Art, The Proctor Stafford Collection, museum purchase with funds provided by Mr. and Mrs. Allan C. Balch. Cat. no. 48.

Several possibilities come to mind. None is altogether satisfactory, because each can apply as well to other mortuary contexts in which dog effigies occur, though in far smaller numbers. There is, for example, the widely shared tradition, within and outside of the Americas, of the dog as guide of the soul on its journey to the underworld, and as guardian of way stations on the chthonic road, the road to the underworld, and of the land of the dead itself. In Central Mexican tradition, a man's or woman's dog, provided it was well treated in its former life, awaits the soul of its deceased keeper at a river that divides this world from the next, to help the soul get safely across. The Huichol also speak of a body of water on the trail taken by the soul of the deceased. But, in their tradition, the dog itself waits for its former owner earlier on, where, if it was not well treated by its owner in life, it threatens to bite but is quickly pacified with a meal of tortillas that the soul has brought along for that purpose.

If this does not really explain the Colima dogs, there is still another tradition, equally widely distributed, of the dog as ancestor. This class of origin myths, which extends all the way from Mesoamerica to the Northwest Coast and across the Bering Sea to Asia, includes the Mesoamerican tale in which a previous creation was destroyed by a great flood, from which only one man saved himself. In some versions, including those told by the Huichol, it was the old earth goddess herself who saved him and who gave him a little female dog as his companion. After the earth dried out, the dog transformed itself into the woman who, in the Huichol myth, became the mother of a human race. This story inevitably recalls the dog-to-human transformation illustrated in figure 2.[18]

Yet another theory, which I find less credible, is that because the Aztecs bred dogs as food, the Colima dogs, though predating the Aztecs by almost fifteen centuries, must have served a similar purpose, if only in ceramic effigy. Whatever its purpose—and there are no doubt still other possibilities in Mesoamerican mythology—it is clear that the dog played a major symbolic as well as practical role in the lives of the ancient Colimans.

The class of Colima dogs that is not easily accounted for by reference to myth or stomach is that of the canine with the human mask. For many years my own preferred

explanation was transformation: if a man or woman who puts on a mask thereby assumes the identity of, or transforms into, whatever animal or spirit is represented by the mask, as is believed in many cultures in the Americas and throughout the world, the reverse should apply to a dog that is given the face of a human being.

I have since come to a different, though not unrelated, conclusion, which is that although the human face worn by this class of Colima canines resembles ceramic funerary masks in the Colima style, it may not be meant as a means of magical transformation, or to preserve, as funerary masks are often intended to do, a semblance of the features of the deceased. Rather, as in some Inuit art, the human mask may represent the animal's *tonalli,* its inner essence, soul, or life force, which is here given a human guise.

This is only an impression, but it is reinforced by something superficially at much greater remove, culturally and spatially, from West Mexico. And that is the Inuit concept of the *inua,* the essential being, spirit, or soul that resides in and animates people and animals and even inner organs such as the bladder and other body parts, tools, harpoon points, fish lures—indeed, every artifact—and features in the physical environment, and that remains unchanged even if its physical manifestation takes on a different appearance or undergoes a whole series of transformations. In the "surrealist" composite animal masks from Alaska so admired by Max Ernst and other surrealist artists exiled in New York during the Nazi era, the *inua* is most often represented by a human face superimposed onto or peering out from the animal's likeness.

Like the Inuit *inua,* the vital force the Aztecs called *tonalli* can also mean appearance, or likeness. If the Colimans shared this idea, it might account for the human face atop the Colima effigy vessel in the form of a disembodied deer antler in figure 27—perhaps the face personifies the object and symbolizes its vital essence or life force. It is, of course, possible to carry analogies too far, but this elegant, two-millennia-old Colima pottery sculpture strikes me, notwithstanding the enormous chronological, cultural, and geographic distance between them, as conceptually remarkably similar to the Alaskan nineteenth-century Inuit shaman's fetish shown in figure 28. This is a naturally

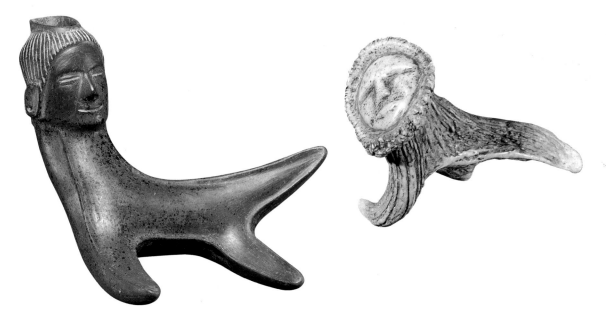

Fig. 27 Model antler with a human head; Comala style; Colima; earthenware. Private collection. Cat. no. 31.

Fig. 28 Antler fetish; Inuit; nineteenth century; bone. Private collection.

malformed antler that probably attracted attention precisely because of its anomalous appearance, and into whose base its owner carved the masklike face of its *inua*.

One has to look for it and not be afraid to speculate, but there is evidence in Colima art that the head was a metaphor for vital essence, life force, or soul. What else but "soul catcher" could be the purpose in one Colima funerary sculpture of a miniature ceramic sling surrounding a disembodied human head that is also a whistle? Enter the Huichol once again, this time with a mortuary tradition in which the shaman tracks the soul on its journey to the village of its ancestors in the underworld. They greet it joyously with a fiesta, and it joins in the drinking and dancing. The shaman finally warns that it is time to say good-bye and return once more, if only for a brief moment, in the form of a firefly or other flying insect, to its living relations, to allow them to bid it a final farewell and see that it does not return unbidden. But the soul is having too much fun and demurs, compelling the shaman to ensnare it with a sling so that they can return to the *rancho* where it had its home for the closing rite of the mortuary ceremony. Not coincidentally, in their art the Huichol often represent the soul as a disembodied head.

The Shark as Initiatory Demon

My final speculations—and that is what all these have been—concern the curiosity illustrated in figure 29: the shark with human extremities swallowing a human being. With its human arms and legs it cannot possibly be understood as just a man-eating shark, any more than can the anthropomorphic fish monsters depicted in combat with men or gods on the stirrup vessels of the Peruvian Moche culture be interpreted just as ordinary fish, or the ancient West Mexican figure wearing a shark as a helmet mask (fig. 30) be understood as just a participant in a Mardi Gras–like entertainment. But if not, what is it?

As it happens, in shamanic mythology up and down the west coast of North and South America, monstrously large sea animals—especially the orca, or killer whale, but also sharks, squid of giant size and power, and similarly fearsome creatures—devour candidate shamans, disgorge them as full-blown practitioners of the magical arts, able to understand and speak the language of birds, fish, and land and sea mammals, and thereafter serve as their allies or spirit helpers. On the Northwest Coast they may also be among the founders of clans and lineages, transferring to the ancestral shaman-heroes their spirit power and the right to depict them in masks and enact their stories in ceremonies.

Even in the interior, not only land animals but water monsters may act as shaman-initiator. Highland Guatemalan Indians, for example, tell of a man who came to a river on the opposite shore of which he saw deer and other animals and plants he could hear conversing but whose language he could not understand. Suddenly a huge fish appeared at his feet, opened its jaws wide and

Fig. 29 Shark swallowing a man; Comala style; Colima; earthenware. Private collection. Cat. no. 53.

Fig. 30 Male figure with a shark headdress; Comala style; Colima; earthenware. Private collection. Cat. no. 30.

from which they emerge, or are reborn, with esoteric knowledge, spirit power, and skills to which they could not previously have laid claim.

The giant shark, as the ancient Colima artist represented it here, with human extremities and in the act of swallowing a man or youth, is a rare example of its kind. Missing, though it may well exist in some collection somewhere, or even still secreted beneath the ground, is its inevitable corollary: a sculpture depicting the man's reemergence, head first, from the initiatory monster with newly acquired power and knowledge. Contrary to first impressions, then, this remarkable scene, like that of the shark impersonator in figure 30, suggests that some ancient Colimans, probably those who lived in close contact with the sea, viewed this creature not as a fearsome, man-eating predator, but as something that could be endowed with human characteristics and sensibilities; surely they respected it, as Northwest Coast and other Pacific coastal peoples did the killer whale as protector, initiator, and ally of shamans.

Of course there is no historic or genetic connection across two thousand years of time and thousands of miles of space, not to mention the considerable differences in ways of life and adaptations between West Mexico and the Arctic or the Northwest Coast, or, for that matter, Siberia. That leaves whatever analogies we might perceive between the one and the other to the nonmaterial realm of intellectual culture and ideology. And that leads us to the possibility of a very ancient and widely shared shamanic substratum of which remnants shine through with greater or lesser force in archaeological and contemporary indigenous religions, myths, rituals, and art. There is no way to prove it to everyone's satisfaction, but there are too many correspondences to dismiss it out of hand.

Postscript

Two crucial issues about the West Mexican shaft-tomb complex and its art remain yet to be considered. These are (a) what relationship, if any, there is between the two major foci of shaft tombs in the Americas, the one in West Mexico, the other in the Andes; and (b) given the shamanic symbolism of certain West Mexican figurines, what the ethnohistoric evidence for a functional relationship between shaft tombs and shamanism in Inca

invited him to enter. It was pitch-dark in the monster's body and the man feared that he would never see daylight again. The great fish did Jonah's whale one better, because after it deposited him safely on the other shore, the man found himself not only alive but in possession of faculties far beyond those he had had before his ordeal: he could now understand and speak the language of the deer, the birds, and even the trees and flowers he had seen and heard conversing from afar. The story has obviously become truncated, and the hero is not explicitly identified as a shaman. But he does not have to be. Who else but the shaman is able to converse with and understand animals and birds? So it is not difficult to recognize his adventure as the sort of initiatory ordeal candidate shamans commonly undergo, and

Peru might tell us about who was interred in the much earlier West Mexican counterparts of the Inca tombs and about the manner in which the distinctive shaft-tomb architecture —which famously includes, in both regions, vertical "soul ducts," or, in West Mexican parlance, *claraboyas* (skylights) and, among burial offerings, numerous conch-shell trumpets—might have facilitated continued contact between the deceased and the living. According to the Inca specialist Tom Zuidema, there is reason to believe that Inca shaft tombs were frequently intended as burial-places for shamans.[19]

That evidence of shamanism in ancient West Mexico was not limited to identification of shamanic motifs in West Mexican tomb art but that, as in Peru, the principal occupant of such a tomb might her- or himself have been a shaman had, frankly, not occurred to me until my colleague Clark Erickson at the University of Pennsylvania drew my attention to Zuidema's essay and the issue of the journal in which it appeared, which was entirely devoted to problems of Andean–West Mexican connections. In a case described firsthand by a sixteenth-century Spanish priest and cited at length by Zuidema, a shaft tomb was dug for a young woman who was sacrificed and at death became an agricultural deity and who, at the request of shaman relatives who made offerings to her, dispensed the life-giving rains on which the crops depended. Might the woman interred on three stone metates laid end to end in the Huitzilapa tomb, described elsewhere in these pages, have had a similar function after death? Might the connection between shamans and shaft tombs in the Inca period also exist, like other Inca beliefs and practices, for their pre-Inca antecedents and, by extension, for ancient West Mexico as well? And is the varying depth of the West Mexican tombs presumably not a function just of the prestige and wealth of the principal occupant, but, if she or he was a shaman (as we know as many as a third to half the adults were, and still are, in some traditional societies), of the fear that, along with respect, inevitably attaches to the dead, especially those who in life commanded the greatest respect for their spiritual power?

In the same issue in which Zuidema presented his shamanic hypothesis, Michael E. Smith, drawing on descriptions of Andean and West Mexican shaft tombs published by Zuidema and by me, proposed a model of how an alien mortuary complex—in view of its antiquity and wide dispersal in western South America, from Colombia and Ecuador to Peru, and its presence in Mesoamerica only along and inland from one section of the Pacific coast—might have come to be assimilated into the cultural milieu of agricultural village societies in Colima, Jalisco, and Nayarit. If it originated in the Andes, he writes, shaft-tomb architecture must have been introduced into Mexico as a function of a well-established two-way coastal trade in precious goods by a group of individuals who were "seen as having more prestige, status, or power than simple sea-going traders." He suggests that these were South American shamans

> who for some reason were thought to possess such superior power and prestige. If important ritual goods were already being obtained by sea trade (e.g. conch and other shells, including *Spondylus*), then the arrival of powerful shamans who knew the proper use of these goods would be an important event. These supernatural specialists would have advocated the use of shaft tombs, thus providing an effective inducement to the indigenous culture to assume the practice of shaft tomb burial.[20]

Zuidema's account of shaft-tomb architecture and contents in relation to shamanism and shamans, with the latter frequently the principal occupants, and Smith's model for diffusion seem to me to demonstrate a shamanic dimension that goes beyond individual mortuary figures and into the shared shamanic worldview that informed and inspired this art and its architectural context.

THE ICONOGRAPHY OF RULERSHIP IN ANCIENT WEST MEXICO

Pictures of West Mexico

Pre-Columbian studies have so far produced three different interpretive models or paradigms of the cultures that existed in ancient West Mexico before the rise of the Tarascan state in the Postclassic period. These models, which might be handily tagged "Daily Life in Marginal Villages," "Shamanism," and "Complex Society," were developed successively, although the latter two models were more shifts of emphasis in research than explicit efforts to progress from a critique of an earlier model.

The Daily Life model describes ancient West Mexico as a kind of developmental cul-de-sac or dead end, where the village ways of life of early agriculturalists remained unchanged until the rise of the Tarascan state in the Postclassic period after A.D. 1200. As the art historian and museum curator Michael Kan noted in his excellent survey of the history of scholarship on West Mexico, for Miguel Covarrubias and Hasso von Winning, the art of these villages was anecdotal, and for Geoffrey Bushnell it was folk art. For George Kubler it was the village art of isolated tribes, and for R. E. W. Adams, the village scenes offered "a rare look at daily life."[1] By the 1960s West Mexico seemed to be securely defined as a kind of frontier Eden, a place that had avoided the authoritarian states and empires of Mesoamerica proper. The romanticized rural way of life imagined for West Mexico may have appealed to urban intellectuals, especially leftists such as Diego Rivera (who amassed a great collection of ceramic figures from the "village cultures" of Mexico, and whose collection was the basis for the first exhibition of the art of ancient

West Mexico in 1946), because of the obvious contrast with the failed agrarian reforms of the Mexican Revolution (see the essay by Barbara Braun in this volume).

But in the mid-1960s, this tranquil image of ancient West Mexico was disturbed by events in Los Angeles, at the University of California, where anthropology faculty such as Clement Meighan and H. B. Nicholson and graduate students such as Peter Furst and Stanley Long were actually excavating West Mexican sites pertaining to the "shaft-tomb cultures" and their hoards of ceramic figures.[2] It was in the particularly fertile setting of the UCLA Department of Anthropology that the new model, Shamanism, erupted. Furst proposed, on the evidence of both general ethnographic analogy (to Siberia and South America) and local ethnographic analogy (to the modern Cora and Huichol groups of Jalisco, Nayarit, and Zacatecas), that much of the visual culture, including many types of the famous ceramic figures that had been appearing in the thousands from looted shaft tombs, could be explained by the practice and symbols of shamanism, a magico-religious worldview focused on the individual attainment of "ecstasy" on behalf of the group and distributed in particular around the land masses of the Pacific rim (see also the essay by Peter Furst in this volume).[3] Furst's vision of shamanic art in ancient America has remained stable in structure and in scope since his dissertation (1966). In a series of long articles beginning just before the completion of his dissertation and continuing into the 1970s, he addressed different dimensions of the shamanic worldview.[4]

Fig. 1 Seated male figure wearing a conch-shell headdress; Comala style; Colima; earthenware. Utah Museum of Fine Arts, University of Utah, Salt Lake City. Cat. no. 42. In addition to the headdress, the pierced nose septum and earlobes and the club or staff are emblems of status or rank.

Furst constructed a worldview for ancient West Mexico that emphasized the intellectual and imaginative faculties of ancient minds, and his work placed a high value on the ceramic sculpture of the region, quite in advance of pre-Columbian studies generally and of art history in particular. In survey treatments of Mesoamerican art and archaeology, the Shamanism model has been effectively merged with the Daily Life model: what is not accounted for by shamanism becomes a part of daily life in farming villages. In both models, the culture of pre-Tarascan West Mexico is set apart from that of the rest of Mesoamerica, particularly in relation to religion.

In 1985 Phil Weigand published the first synthetic statement based on his previous decade of survey and excavation in Jalisco, leading to the identification of the Classic-period (A.D. 200–900) Teuchitlán regional tradition (see also his essay in this volume).[5] The Teuchitlán tradition defined by Weigand provided the first clear signs of the settlement patterns, site plans, and architectural forms associated with the latest phases of the great regional ceramic traditions of West Mexico. In Weigand's "Evidence for Complex Societies during the Western Mesoamerican Classic Period," he trenchantly criticized what he called the "simplicity complex" in the study of West Mexico, the tendency to reduce West Mexico to an imperfect echo of Central Mexico; this article marked a watershed in studies of ancient West Mexico. In settlements that were not simple farming villages but central places in a regional settlement hierarchy, Weigand found and recorded architectural remains that incorporated the famed shaft tombs and that appeared both to replicate and to explain the distinctive ceramic architectural models.[6] For the first time, scholars had the outlines of a temporal and spatial model of pre-Tarascan West Mexico based on controlled archaeology and settlement studies.[7] Whereas Furst's model had emerged from his analysis of individual ceramic figures, from the identification of iconographic categories, and from postulates of links to modern Indian behavior, Weigand began at the macro-level of sites and settlement patterns and aimed explicitly to reconstruct the ancient West Mexican landscape. Until now the two models have seemed to be exclusive, not to say antagonistic, with no apparent bridge concept that would allow

Weigand's Complex Society model to be articulated with Furst's Shamanism-based approach and its Daily Life addendum. Other scholars have, for the most part, seemed more interested in taking sides than in exploring the possible articulation of the two models. For his part, Furst insisted that the ceramic sculptures from the shaft tombs did not represent the actual arrangements of power in society, but spiritual power in Furst's "otherworld-view," the world of the dead.[8] As I will suggest below, part of the problem seems to stem from conceptions of shamanism that are too strongly based in ethnography and too concerned with shamanism's therapeutic dimensions. Both Mircea Eliade and Furst derive the majority of their data on actual shamanic practices from small-scale societies, and they repeatedly stress the role of the shaman as healer, as master of sickness and disease—hence, their concern with the use of drugs and narcotics and with such imagery as that of flight and transformation. It will be my contention here that such a view of shamanism has little relevance to the problem of interpreting the technically demanding and iconographically complex art traditions of ancient West Mexico. Whatever visionary qualities one may see in this art were the work of sober minds.

In Mesoamerican chronology, the periods of the "shaft-tomb tradition" of West Mexico are the Late Formative (400–100 B.C.) and the Protoclassic (100 B.C.–A.D. 200), and the Teuchitlán regional tradition as defined by Weigand belongs to the Early Classic (A.D. 200–600) and the first century or so of the Late Classic (A.D. 600–900). Within Mesoamerica and along its southern margins, the Late Formative and Protoclassic periods are characterized by the emergence of polities uniting several or more villages, with the villages themselves typically ranked in a hierarchy below the paramount village or chiefly center. Apparently, an important means of giving artistic and ideological form to such emergent inequalities (in access to basic resources such as good land, for example, or in work or products owed the center) was the center's ability to convert surpluses of labor and materials into craft products of distinction. So-called sumptuary rules both conveyed and legitimized rank through the control of special garments and ornaments, while the production and distribution of deluxe versions of such things as serving vessels and figurines for domestic and burial rituals further reflected the increasing importance of craft specialization and, probably, the consequent loss of local autonomy over such activities. In these conditions of emergent social complexity, the expression of both solidarity and inequality through the manipulation of such artistic dimensions as style, material, and subject amounted to a coded expression of new political realities.[9]

Pre-Columbian studies have responded slowly and somewhat indifferently to the mountain of evidence that a paradigm shift is under way in studies of ancient West Mexico.[10] For example, a proper art-historical critique of Furst's work has simply never happened, even though his arguments proceeded from contested interpretations of imagery and even though his proposed iconographic identifications seemed to many observers to answer questions that art historians' focus on style had avoided. What is to happen to the postulated imagery of shamanism in the new Complex Society model? A more critical approach to interpretation may help to bridge these seemingly incompatible paradigms.

The Visual Evidence for Rulership in Colima

The so-called horned figures of Colima are the one category of ceramic sculpture from ancient West Mexico for which a shamanic reading has been most widely accepted (see figs. 1–3, 16, and 17, and Furst, figs. 17–22 and 25).[11] Collectively, the figures are identified as shamans with supernatural horns of power, supposedly often oriented to the left in a hypothesized "shamanic fighting stance," with clubs or other weapons for spirit combat (see fig. 3, and Furst, fig. 20). No one, though, seems to have questioned the basic semantic assertion embodied in this chain of identifications and assumptions, that the frequent appearance of a conical protuberance on or above the forehead of a human figure is a horn in a normative biological sense. In archaeologists' chronological classification of ceramics from West Mexico, the large hollow Colima figures with such features are burnished redware belonging to the Ortices (100 B.C.–A.D. 300) and Comala (A.D. 300–600) phases defined by Isabel Kelly.[12] Most of these figures have one conical element in the front of the head or on the

Fig. 2 Seated chieftain with a conch shell and headdress; Comala style; Colima; earthenware. Private collection. Cat. no. 36.

forehead, and all, or virtually all, are male. Because the identification of this conical element was the initial focus of Furst's dramatic reinterpretation of the art of West Mexico in the 1960s, it is the logical subject for a reassessment of that model. But first, a brief examination of the concept of iconography, which must figure in any reassessment.

The art-historical concept of iconography has been widely misunderstood in pre-Columbian studies. Iconography is frequently equated *tout court* with symbolism, and the symbols are typically explained or decoded from a universalist or Jungian perspective, very often without reference to other image traditions, or even to any other contempora-

Fig. 3 Seated warrior; Comala style; Colima; earthenware. Los Angeles County Museum of Art, The Proctor Stafford Collection, museum purchase with funds provided by Mr. and Mrs. Allan Balch.

described (and prescribed) the analysis of iconography in three stages:

1) The identification of subject matter.

2) The interpretation of the subject through reference to textual or other sources, and the placing of the image within image traditions.

3) The relation of the image and the subject to the ideas and the values of the culture, this ultimate stage sometimes termed iconology.

More than any other pre-Columbianist art historian, George Kubler was explicit about his efforts to apply Panofsky's method to pre-Columbian art, but he also felt that interpretation of subject matter would generally require textual sources, which are absent from many archaeological cultures.[16] In practice, there are no archaeological cultures of pre-Columbian America, including those of West Mexico, that could not be indirectly approached through texts, in a manner akin to a navigator's triangulation. Moreover, the close analysis of particular images and configurations across time, space, and culture can sometimes permit the identification of subject matter once an image has been placed within a larger tradition of representations. The famous "horned" figures of Colima may be such a case.

neous evidence. But in art history, iconography is both a theory and a method, an approach to culture and a technique for its analysis.[13]

The central figure in the modern understanding of iconography is Erwin Panofsky (1892–1968), a German art historian who emigrated to the United States in the 1930s.[14] For Panofsky, iconography was not a thing, like a symbol, but sets of relationships, between an image and others of a tradition and between an image and the culture that produced it.[15] Panofsky's notion of iconography has much in common with semiotics, which conventionally distinguishes between a sign (word, picture, gesture) and its referent, between a signifier and a signified. A symbol, in semiotic terms, is a special kind of sign, one in which the relation between the signifier and its signified is essentially arbitrary, and not a property of the signifier. Panofsky's approach to iconography is also strongly dependent on the use of texts to elucidate images. In several celebrated essays, Panofsky

Furst has characterized this conical element as a literal representation of a supernatural horn, "a natural bony growth emerging from the head in the manner of horned animals."[17] According to Furst, all such cranial cones are horns, an interpretation I wish to dispute. Although the single conical element appears to spring directly from the head of some of the figures, in the majority of figures with a single conical element, the cone is clearly held in place by an arrangement of straps that cross over the head and run under the chin; a "natural bony growth" could not, by definition, be part of a strapped-on assemblage. In these cases, the conical element is clearly separate from the leather or cotton straps, and the ensemble forms a headdress; the conical elements appear to be detachable and individual. A Colima figure in the Utah Museum of Fine Arts in Salt Lake City, seated with a staff or club, has a single front conical element attached by a strap, which is fairly common, but here the arrangement is complemented by a crown or diadem of four more conical elements crossing the head from ear to ear and held in place by a decorated chin strap (fig. 1).[18] The four-part crown of this figure is clearly represented as a separate feature, apart from the single conical element over the forehead; the two sets of conical elements are connected through the strap assemblage. However natural it may seem to label these features horns, to do so without any evidence is to prejudice the work of identification which, for Panofsky, was the first step of iconographic analysis.[19]

The arrangement of four graduated cones behind the frontal forehead cone in the Utah figure resembles nothing so much as the conical spires of a conch shell and suggests that the most likely natural source for all of these conical elements is a conch shell with its pattern of radiating and graduated spires or cones (see fig. 5), especially the large *Strombus* species of the Caribbean such as *S. gigas* (see fig. 4).[20] The Utah figure, as is clear, is an exceptionally complex example of the Colima "horned" figure, but not, probably, unique.[21] It has in common with most of the "One-Horn" figures the clear delineation of the head and chin straps that secure the conical element over the forehead. The Utah figure differs from those simpler figures, of course, in the addition of the corona of cones as a kind of sagittal crest, but, I think importantly, the added elements are secured by the same kind of strap assembly as in the "One-Horns." As sometimes happens in iconographic analysis, the correct identification of a complex version of a subject allows the recognition of epitomized or abbreviated versions, and this is what I think the Colima figures with one or two conical elements represent. Thus, a preliminary identification of at least part of the subject matter of this category of Colima figures has opened up a new direction for iconographic investigation, the representation of conch shells in headdresses and elsewhere.

One of the earliest appearances of a figure wearing a conch shell in a headdress is on Stela 11 from Kaminaljuyú, Guatemala, a Late Formative (perhaps 200–100 B.C.) monument of the Southern Highland Maya Miraflores–Arenal subtradition (fig. 6).[22] KJ (as Kaminaljuyú is commonly abbreviated) Stela 11 is one of the first representations of a ruler in Maya art in a configuration that was to become standard for the repre-

sentation of rulers in succeeding periods. The figure stands on a cosmic mouth, flanked by incense burners marked with the glyphs for *copal* incense, with the handle of a chipped stone ax in his left hand and a staff tied with long cloths in his right hand. He wears a nose bead, visible through his cutaway mask, and in the headdress above, resting on another cosmic mouth, there is a cut-down conch shell the spires of which are represented by the depiction of three incised or inlaid disks; three leaves grow from the end of the shell. The same type of head-dress can be found on the back of a Middle Formative Olmec jade at Dumbarton Oaks, a winged pectoral that as an heirloom was incised on the reverse with

Fig. 4 Model of a *Strombus* conch shell; Comala style; Colima; earthenware. Collection of Barbara and Justin Kerr, New York. Cat. no. 32.

Fig. 5 *Turbinella* conch shell; Colima. Private collection. Cat. no. 14.

6

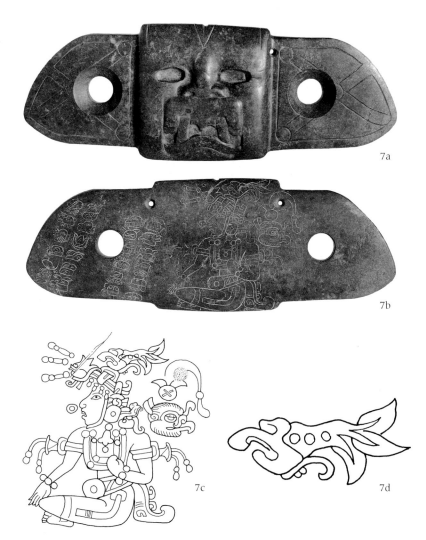

7a

7b

7c

7d

a Maya image and text of Late Formative or Protoclassic date (see figs. 7a–d). Here in an accession scene a seated Maya ruler or *ahau* wears a flowering conch-shell headdress marked by three disks as in the KJ Stela 11 headdress.[23] On the Dumbarton Oaks image the shell has been more smoothly merged with other parts of the headdress, but still the three disks remain as its markers. These disks denote the inlaid or painted decoration of the spires that have been found on actual shells, and they are represented on conch shells at Teotihuacan, the great Central Mexican metropolis of the Classic period, in wall paintings in the Temple of Agriculture (see fig. 8), and in painted relief sculpture in the Palace of the Plumed Conch Shells (see fig. 9). Conch shells are also represented in the complex symbolic façade reliefs of the Pyramid of the Plumed Serpent at Teotihuacan, probably the seat of rulership (see fig. 10).

The Colima figure's headdress is different from the Maya conch-shell headdresses, where much of the body of the shell is depicted, but they are semantically equivalent.

How much of the difference in the representations of the conch-shell headdresses is due to the preference for frontal points of view in the Colima figures, as against the three-quarter views of the Maya portrayals, remains undetermined. Both the KJ Stela 11 and the Dumbarton Oaks pectoral conch-shell headdresses emphasize the ruler figure as the context and font of natural growth: in each, the conch spires metamorphose into leaves of vegetation, apparent metaphors of growth from the head of the ruler, conveying in a direct visual fashion rulers' claims to be bringers and guardians of fertility. The Late Formative and Protoclassic periods in the various Maya regions marked the simultaneous emergence of distinctive visual traditions for the representation of rulership, and such visual configurations were an integral part of the ideology of emergent institutions of central authority.[24] Both of these Maya monuments are associated with rulership: the stela is the art form *par excellence* of Late Formative and Classic Maya rulers, and the pectoral—an heirloom, perhaps from an Olmec ruler, the back of which is inscribed with the image and text of a ruler's accession —is a standard item of Maya regalia.[25]

Maya groups continued to portray rulers' headdresses with conch shells through the Classic period. At Yaxchilán, Chiapas, a ruler's son named Bird Jaguar II, who was attempting to gain the office of ruler for himself after his father's death, was portrayed (on Stela 11, dated A.D. 755) wearing in his headdress a conch shell decorated with a sky band and quetzal feathers.[26] He was attired in imitation of the god Chac-Xib-Chac, who was especially associated with sacrifice, and shown standing over noble prisoners to be sacrificed as part of his accession (see fig. 12).[27] In Classic Maya iconography, the god Chac-Xib-Chac is identified by his conch-shell diadem and usually by an ax for sacrificing. In another Maya iconographic context, the cosmos was personified by a great two-headed dragon known as the Bicephalic Monster (see figs. 11a and 11b). In one of his aspects, his rear head is marked by a conch shell, along with a stingray spine (an implement for and symbol of bloodletting) and an offering bowl in reference to royal sacrifices and offerings (see fig. 11b).[28] Another version shows the body of the monster as a sky band with planetary signs extending between the front and rear heads (see fig. 11a). As noted

by Miller and Taube, the Bicephalic Monster often occurs as a frame for scenes of rulership and accession to office.[29] Here again, the conch shell is associated with the imagery of rulership and its cosmic dimensions.

The association of conch shells with sacrifice and blood offerings did not originate with the Maya. The oldest graphic signs for sacrifice and blood offering in Middle America are marked by a scalloped profile. The Olmec graphic sign called the "knuckle-duster" is often represented with a scalloped and pointed profile, and this sign long antedates a Maya written verbal sign for blood sacrifice that has a scalloped profile, as in the inscription on the Hauberg Stela, dated A.D. 199 (see fig. 13). "Knuckledusters" are thought to be depictions of sectioned conch shells, and the conch shell and a staff have been identified as badges of office both among the Formative Olmec (see fig. 14) and at Teotihuacan (see fig. 15).[30]

Throughout tropical ancient America, conch-shell trumpets announced important events and convocations. Maya lords and priests apparently imagined that properly embellished conch-shell trumpets were intermediaries between their blood offerings and the gods. The text on the Classic Maya Pearlman Trumpet, in the Chrysler Museum in Norfolk, suggests that the conch-shell trumpet was itself even imagined as an animate being or spirit.[31] At Teotihuacan conch shells functioned as cosmic locatives or place markers, as in the façade of the Temple of the Feathered Serpent; the paintings in the Temple of Agriculture (see fig. 8); the reliefs on the walls of the Palace of the Plumed Conch Shells, where all of the two-dimensional conch shells are marked with the three disks (see fig. 9); and the reliefs on the tiers of the Pyramid of the Plumed Serpent (see fig. 10). The presence of shells in so many of the burials at Teotihuacan and their particular patterns of association begin to suggest the importance of shells as indices of wealth and status.[32] At Teotihuacan, as elsewhere, conch shells marked some temples as sacred places of creation. Centuries after the fall of Teotihuacan, the rulers of Tula, Hidalgo, partially enclosed their principal temple platform, Pyramid B, with a *coatepantli* or serpent wall topped by a stone mosaic frieze of sectioned conch shells.[33] The locative function of shells—their use as cosmic markers—is also abundantly documented

Fig. 6 Drawing of Stela 11; Kaminaljuyú, Guatemala; Maya; 200/100 B.C.?; stone. Museo Nacional de Arqueología y Etnología, Guatemala City. The flat relief and dense encoding make this figure more difficult to read than the Colima figures with their clean contours, but there is no doubt that the figure's topmost headdress element, where the vegetation sprouts, is a conch shell, perhaps *Turbinella* sp., that has been cut down fore and aft to resemble a vessel.

Figs. 7a–d Pectoral; Olmec; 1000/600 B.C.; quartzite. Maya inscription (on reverse); 100 B.C./A.D. 100; quartzite. Dumbarton Oaks Research Library and Collections, Washington, D.C. The front of this pectoral (fig. 7a) is incised with an Olmec image of a supernatural mask flanked by crossed-band "sky" wings. On the reverse (fig. 7b) is a later, Maya image of a seated figure (see fig. 7c) with an accompanying hieroglyphic text. This pectoral was incised to record the accession to office, or "seating," of the depicted lord, who wears a headdress with a conch shell marked by three disks (see enlarged detail of conch shell in fig. 7d).

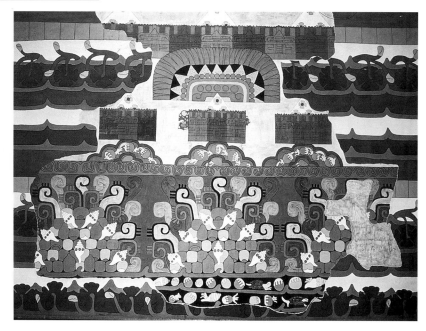

Fig. 8 Detail from a mural in the Temple of Agriculture; Teotihuacan; A.D. 150/750. The mural depicts conch shells (probably *Turbinella* sp.) set upon smoking mountains. The white shells emit scrolls of smoke or clouds and are consistently marked with three circles each, originally green (now faded) to imitate inlaid jade.

Fig. 9 Detail from the façade of the Palace of the Plumed Conch Shells; Teotihuacan; A.D. 250/450. This façade is decorated with pilaster-like bands composed of large low-relief depictions of conch-shell trumpets fitted with mouthpieces and festooned with quetzal feathers.

Fig. 10 Detail from the façade of the Pyramid of the Plumed Serpent; Teotihuacan; A.D. 300/400.

at the Aztec capital of Tenochtitlan, where, for example, conchs (especially *Turbinella* and *Strombus*) and other shells formed the lower layers of foundation deposits and caches at the site of the Aztecs' Great Temple or Templo Mayor, and monumental carved stone shells apparently served the same locative functions in more visible parts of the great ceremonial enclosure that marked the center of the Aztec cosmos.[34]

The documentation of the uses and meanings of shells by the Aztecs is more detailed than that for any other ancient Mexican civilization, and the textual sources of the conquest period are especially rich. The Franciscan Brother Bernardino de Sahagún, the great encyclopedist of the Aztecs of Central Mexico, wrote his *General History of the Things of New Spain* (the *Florentine Codex*) near Tenochtitlan in the 1560s, in which he provides very specific associations and contexts: the association of the

god Quetzalcóatl with a sectioned conch-shell emblem called the wind jewel; the association of this same wind-jewel emblem with the dress of rulers and nobles; conch-shell friezes on temple entablatures; and the blowing of conch-shell trumpets particularly during war and bloodletting.[35] There is even a conquest-period reference to the wearing of conch shells in headdresses. The Dominican Fray Diego Durán, writing at about the same time as Sahagún, reported in his *Book of the Gods and Rites* that priests of Topiltzin Quetzalcóatl, a famous ruler of Tula who may have been thought to be an avatar of the god Quetzalcóatl, wore conch-shell headdresses.[36]

The New Meaning of the Colima Figures

The iconography of shells in ancient Mexico reveals three semantic dimensions of possible relevance to Colima figures wearing headdresses with conical elements, or what other scholars have called horned figures: rulership, sacrifice, and a cluster combining references to cosmic geography and fertility or vegetal growth. The symbolic notions of cosmic growth and vegetation recall Furst's initial description of the Colima figures' conical elements as representing a "natural growth," but in the iconographic contexts that we have seen here, from the Olmec, Maya, Teotihuacan, Toltec, and Aztec cultures, such growth would more properly belong to the ruler's ritualized ideological claims to be the

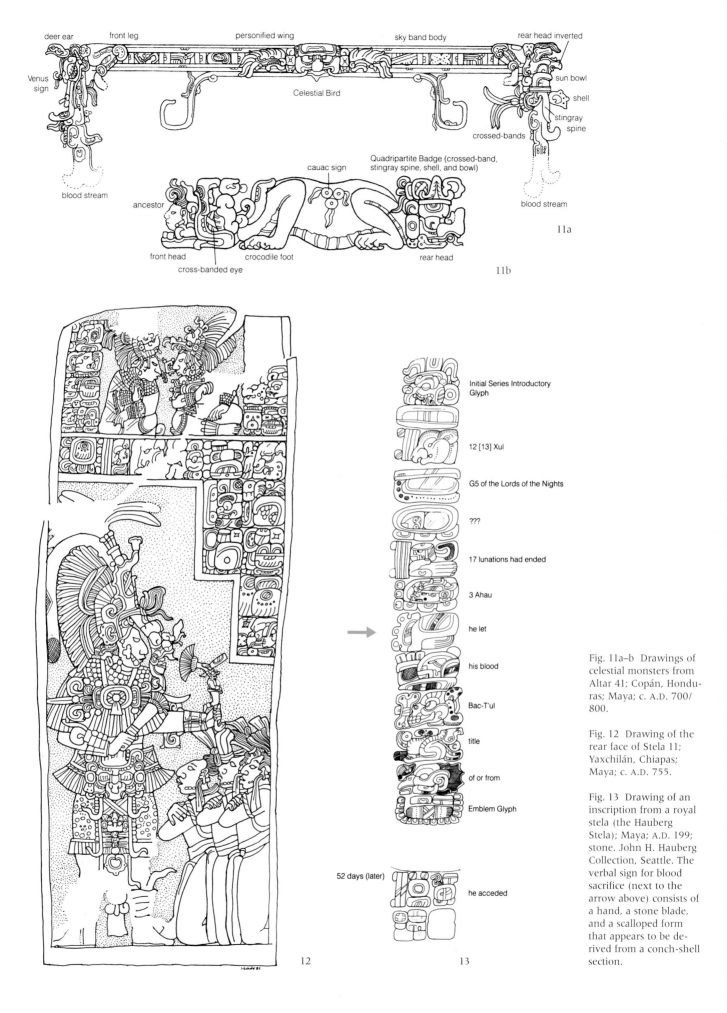

deer ear   front leg   personified wing   sky band body   rear head inverted

Venus sign

Celestial Bird

sun bowl

shell

stingray spine

crossed-bands

blood stream

blood stream

11a

Quadripartite Badge (crossed-band, stingray spine, shell, and bowl)

cauac sign

ancestor

front head   cross-banded eye   crocodile foot   rear head

11b

Initial Series Introductory Glyph

12 [13] Xul

G5 of the Lords of the Nights

???

17 lunations had ended

3 Ahau

he let

his blood

Bac-T'ul

title

of or from

Emblem Glyph

52 days (later)

he acceded

12

13

Fig. 11a–b Drawings of celestial monsters from Altar 41; Copán, Honduras; Maya; c. A.D. 700/800.

Fig. 12 Drawing of the rear face of Stela 11; Yaxchilán, Chiapas; Maya; c. A.D. 755.

Fig. 13 Drawing of an inscription from a royal stela (the Hauberg Stela); Maya; A.D. 199; stone. John H. Hauberg Collection, Seattle. The verbal sign for blood sacrifice (next to the arrow above) consists of a hand, a stone blade, and a scalloped form that appears to be derived from a conch-shell section.

font of fertility, rather than to such mystical concepts as magical growths.

In Mesoamerica another widespread cluster of shell imagery and of things with scalloped profiles is associated with sacrifice and blood offering. This cluster includes, for example, axes that were used for captive execution and verbal glyphs for blood sacrifice. Sacrifice is a traditional burden and prerogative of rulers, whether it is the offering of their own blood or the blood of others. Sacrifice as a ruler's burden and prerogative also may help to account for much of the supposedly martial iconography of West Mexico. The numerous figures wielding axes, clubs, and other weaponry might more appropriately be examined as the evidence and product of a new social and political need to represent the emergent superordinate ranks of nobles and their retainers, whose ceramic portrayals are visually marked by the emblems of their new ritual and political obligations.

This is certainly not to suggest that all of the Colima figures with conical elements represent rulers. Rather, it is more likely that the variety of conical configurations reflects a relatively fluid emergent hierarchy in which even the symbols and insignia of power were in a state of flux and adjustment. But some of these Colima figures, typically those that

are very finely modeled, bear additional iconographic traces of traditional Mesoamerican rulership. Many of the Colima figures with conical elements are seated. Seating is the most common verbal and visual metaphor for rulership in Mesoamerica, and the seated pose itself frequently characterizes portrayals of rulers.[37] The contexts of the seated pose in Colima figures deserve further investigation, given the political symbolism of seating in Mesoamerica.

Nose beads are common on Mesoamerican ruler portraits of the Late Formative, Protoclassic, and Early Classic periods, as on KJ Stela 11 and the Dumbarton Oaks pectoral. All of the Colima figures with nose beads also are seated and have conical headdress elements, which places them within the broad Late Formative-to-Early Classic iconographic type represented by the Maya figure on the reverse of the Dumbarton Oaks pectoral (see fig. 16).[38]

The iconographic evidence presented here is little more than the beginning of a larger endeavor, but it projects the outline of another dimension of meaning for the so-called horned figures of the Ortices and Comala phases in Colima, that of rulership or, more broadly, superordinate political rank. The proposed identification of the conical elements on Colima figures as the representations of pieces and sections of conch shells, some of them from Caribbean and Gulf Coast waters, immediately expands the frame of reference of this investigation. And, the redundant coding for rulership (i.e., the presence of several iconographic features, each conveying the notion of super-ordinate rank) would seem to reinforce the initial association of the conch-shell elements with Mesoamerican traditions of rulership iconography.

Iconographic analysis should never be limited by the borders of archaeological culture areas (not least because of the frequent arbitrariness of such borders), and in this case, the search for a tradition of images of conch shells employed in headdresses led straightaway to the Late Formative and Protoclassic Maya. Iconographic features have their own histories, which do not have to correlate with ceramic or architectural histories, and the conch-shell headdress may first appear in the Late Formative art of the southern Maya and their neighbors, in the stone monuments associated with such chiefly centers as Kaminaljuyú in Guatemala and Izapa in Chiapas, Mexico. In this context, the conch-shell headdress is part of a developing artistic tradition for the visual display of the ideology of rulership, in which the ruler, or rather his depicted body, is redundantly marked with signs of cosmic power and authority: the ruler of KJ Stela 11 is the cosmic world axis, literally the world tree, and his stack of masks includes one in which a decorated conch shell produces vegetation. Neither the name of the KJ Stela 11 ruler nor the occasion is known, but the nearly contemporary Maya ruler portrayed on the reverse of the Dumbarton Oaks pectoral wears the same headdress (marked by three disks) in an image that was incised on the back of an Olmec heirloom to mark his accession. The convention of marking the shell with three circles to represent inlaid disks of jade (or the painted imitation of greenstone inlays) is pervasive at Teotihuacan during the Early Classic period in mural painting in the Temple of Agriculture and in relief sculpture in the Temple of the Plumed Conch Shells. The mark of three disks on the shells is a cross-cultural fact, occurring in depicted shells of Teotihuacan and Maya provenience, and is perhaps related to the idea that the site of all cosmic creation was a planetary hearth made of three stones in the constellation Orion.[39]

Ultimately, the high-status arts of ancient West Mexico are an enlarged figurine complex. There is no public stone sculpture, no monumental imagery of aggrandizement and conquest, and there are no stelae or altars;

this absence of the more developed symbols of hierarchy that mark other Late Formative archaeological cultures in Mesoamerica might reflect the direct emergence in West Mexico of a structure of superordinate authority out of the hierarchies of gender, family, lineage, and village that characterize egalitarian societies. But such connections between art and society are often misleading. Teotihuacan, too, has little if any stone sculpture that has been persuasively construed as individual or dynastic, and the government of this enormous city apparently was able to convey significant political and ideological information through the production of ceramic figures and vessels.

The dating of the comparative material considered here accords perfectly with the known chronologies in West Mexico. There are no gaps in time, and we do not have to argue backwards from later evidence. These iconographic data suggest that the entire corpus of ceramic art from West Mexico should be systematically reexamined within

Fig. 16 Figure presenting a drinking vessel; Comala style; Colima; earthenware. Los Angeles County Museum of Art, The Proctor Stafford Collection, museum purchase with funds provided by Mr. and Mrs. Allan C. Balch. Prominent nose beads such as the one seen on this figure are common signs of rulership throughout Mesoamerica. The association of signs of rulership and drinking suggests the importance of ruler-sponsored feasting and drinking, the latter often involving fermented beverages.

a broader Mesoamerican comparative framework.

But beyond the need for better control of comparative material within Mesoamerica, there is an obvious need to consider other interpretative approaches involving shamanism and art, wherever they occur. A recent study of the famous and widespread bronze drums of the Southeast Asian Dongson tradition, which scholars had earlier identified as shamans' drums, reinterprets them as signs of political authority, the acquisition of the ornate drums marking religious recognition of political legitimacy.[40] The interpretative problems of Dongson archaeology intersect in numerous ways with West Mexican studies, not least of which are the numerous representations of drums in the ceramic figures and models of West Mexico (see Furst, figs. 23–25) and their specific shamanic interpretations. We might thus contemplate an approach to the depictions of drums in West Mexico that goes beyond their reflexive interpretation as either vehicles for magical shamanic flight or as the secular pictorial residue of daily life. Kwang-chih Chang, in a compelling study of the iconography of political imagery in Shang China (1700–1100 B.C.), constructs a persuasive model that links shamanism to emergent political authority and to the political value of aesthetics and of refined, complex art.[41] In contrast to the Jungian universals floating through Mircea Eliade's imaginative reconstruction of shamanism as an "archaic technique of ecstasy," the approach essentially adopted by Furst, Chang anchors his model of shamanism to its applications in politics and statecraft and shows how advanced, costly, and labor-intensive art, often using exotic materials, has a vital function in providing a compelling visual form to convey the hierarchical structure of the cosmos, the worldview of those with power. In Chang's view, shamanism was hardly an end in itself. And it would follow from this view that one factor limiting the archaeological relevance of many ethnographically based reconstructions of shamanism in the Americas is that such shamanic practices reflect largely the surviving therapeutic folk substrate of ideas and concepts that were more fully realized in the now-disappeared elite intellectual culture. If shamanism is to retain any relevance in this new era in the study of ancient West Mexico, it will have to emulate the sensitivity to the iconography of political practices of Chang's model of shamanism in ancient China, where shamanism is less an individualized, navel-gazing quest for "ecstasy" and more a sophisticated technique of political manipulation through the control of the form and content of high art production.[42]

Pre-Columbianist art historians have so far concerned themselves primarily with the stylistic and formal dimensions of the art of ancient West Mexico. Subject matter, largely by default, has become the almost exclusive preserve of archaeologists working in a limited art-historical mode. For pre-Columbian studies, the still-current notion of ancient West Mexico is largely a product of the belief that Mesoamerica is simply an aggregate of archaeological culture areas, a notion that comes freighted with some very reductive conceptual pairs, such as center versus periphery, mainstream versus marginal, civilized versus barbarian, complex versus simple, innovative versus derivative, a pantheon versus no recognizable deities, and so on in a virtually endless chain of subordination. Scholars often seem to have approached West Mexico with the expectation that they would be exploring the outer edges of a Mesoamerica that was most authentically defined by the supposed complexity of its centers, so it is hardly surprising that West Mexico was invariably cast as the inferior term in each pair. The culture area concept as operationalized with Mesoamerica produces marginal societies as, and at, its peripheries. If, from Central Mexico, West Mexico is made to appear as the periphery of a high civilization, from West Mexico such peripheral status is not so obvious. Marginality is by definition an artifact of perspective. Although many of the scholars currently contributing to the new picture of ancient West Mexico lament the tendency of Mesoamericanists to exclude West Mexico until the Postclassic Tarascan state, from the standpoint of iconographic studies, the same results would obtain whether or not West Mexico is considered a part of Mesoamerica. The new data from West Mexico give us an unexpected opportunity to examine, free from the influence of the reductive models of the past, the emergence of a complex society and its hierarchies. This cannot help but enrich our understanding of the ancient cultures of Mexico.

Fig. 17 Seated chieftain wearing a headdress with a horn and dog's head; Comala style; Colima; earthenware. The Art Institute of Chicago, through prior acquisitions of the Primitive Art Purchase Fund. Cat. no. 37. The unusual dog's head attached to this figure's headdress has affinities with animal-visored Nayarit figures; the necklace represents shells.

OTTO SCHÖNDUBE

NATURAL RESOURCES AND HUMAN SETTLEMENTS IN ANCIENT WEST MEXICO

For those of us who have a certain curiosity about human life, it is interesting to try to understand how different peoples lived in times past. Although the past can never be recaptured entirely, we are left with many types of evidence that allow us to imagine, with varying degrees of accuracy, how things may once have been. In this essay we will look at evidence that speaks of the interrelationship between humankind and the environment in the shaft-tomb area of Jalisco, Colima, and Nayarit in ancient West Mexico.

There are four sources that we must consider in approaching an understanding of this interaction. First is the landscape itself, such as we see it today, its components of climate, topography, geology, hydrography, and various forms of life. Second are written descriptions from the sixteenth century, the time of first contact between Spanish and indigenous cultures, as well as later ethnohistoric documents, many from the colonial period. Third are the archaeological remains left by ancient societies; many of these are beautiful objects that have been widely appreciated for their aesthetic value, but that also present a wider range of cultural meanings. Finally, there is information about the way people in the area live and use their environment today; much can be inferred from what has been handed down through tradition or has otherwise survived from the past.

The landscape of ancient West Mexico, with all its mountains, lake basins, river valleys, coastal estuaries, lagoons, and variations in altitude, has been described in other essays in this volume. Although I am not an advocate of geographical determinism, it cannot be denied that geography, with its gifts and challenges, is an element that influences human behavior. It is also true that many centuries of human occupation have modified the landscape, especially its immediate surface. But the mountains, gorges, and most climatic conditions are much as they have been for thousands of years, as are the native species of animals and plants known and used by the early indigenous peoples.

We can recreate the original landscape, that is, the landscape of the early indigenous inhabitants, by first erasing from that immense palimpsest all the plants and animals brought by the Spanish: oranges, limes, pears, peaches, and apples, in addition to those plants brought from other, more exotic places, such as coffee trees, sugarcane, mangoes, and tamarinds (see fig. 2). Let us keep only the original things named in the written sources as *de la tierra*: *jícamas, camotes* (yams), *aguacates* (avocados), *zapotes* and *chicozapotes* (sapodillas), *guanábanas* (soursops), *chirimoyas, xocotes* (Mexican plums), spiny *chayotes*, tomatoes, *chiles*, beans, and the many varieties of squash, as well as the unparalleled maize and the amaranth so widely used today in our breakfast granolas. There are also *chía* (sage seeds), which were added to some beverages; papayas; the maguey agave cactus; the humble spiny paddles and tuna fruit of the nopal cactus (see figs. 3 and 4); and the juicy *pitaya* fruit of the organ cactus (see figs. 22 and 23). The list could become incalculably long; I mention here only some of the cultivated or seasonally gathered plants of the region. We also must not forget the magnificent cacao, which was used in

Fig. 1 Bottle with three crayfish supports; Comala style; Colima; earthenware. Private collection. Cat. no. 66. The representation of edible fruits and animals on vessels is a hallmark of Comala-style pottery.

Fig. 2 Mercado Libertad, Guadalajara, Mexico. Amid abundant fruits, vegetables, and other foods of European, Asian, and South American origin, local produce of the original West Mexican diet appear.

Fig. 3 Nopal cacti were cultivated in groves for their edible tender paddles and juicy tuna fruits.

Fig. 4 Preparing the harvested tuna fruits for market involves brushing away their fine needles.

bartering as currency and as the primary ingredient of *chocolatl,* the beverage given to high-ranking persons and used in festivals.

In order to enter this early landscape, we must also forget horses, mules, burros, pigs, and chickens, as well as cows, goats, and lambs. We must eliminate the milk, wool, and meat provided by these animals, and, above all, the service they render as pack animals and the energy they furnish for the pulling of plows. The principal domestic animals the early indigenous peoples had were the dog and the turkey, and, in certain places, a tiny stingless native bee and the Muscovy duck (see figs. 5 and 9), which can still sometimes be seen on small, isolated family farmsteads. Before the introduction by the Spanish of large domesticated beasts, the only way to travel over land was on foot, and mere paths and trails were the routes of communication. Goods were carried on the backs of people. *Tamemes* (porters) placed their loads in nets or on carrying frames partly supported on their backs, but most of the weight was transferred to the head by a tumpline called a *mecapal* (see fig. 6). On water routes, people and goods could be transported by canoes. Although there is archaeological and documentary proof of commerce with people from far-off lands, most of the goods traded were luxury items of little physical weight, such as shell, turquoise, and other semiprecious stones. Obsidian and salt, of course, would have made for larger, heavier loads. This trade probably did not involve massive movement of populations, but, rather, only of those merchants dedicated to long-distance commerce. It is still to be determined whether this commerce was carried out directly from source areas by merchants or was a type of trade in which goods moved in stages from one group to another, each one serving as a step on the conveyor.

To understand the relationships of man and land, it is also necessary to become as familiar as possible with the prevailing technologies of different periods. In antiquity the principal farming instruments were the *coa* (a planting stick) and the primitive hoe. Rather than farming in furrows, the early peoples sowed seeds in individual holes in the ground. We know that this was carried out using a Neolithic technology, since metals did not come into use before the beginnings of the eighth century A.D. and even then

were rarely used to make farming implements. Cultivation was, for the most part, done during the wet season; the dry season was the time for hunting, fishing, and food gathering.

While most environmental studies focus on the food resources of the region, it must not be forgotten that there are also other resources, such as many varieties of stone, clay, and minerals, which were used in the fabrication of instruments and tools. There are also many plants, which were used to make the handles and shafts of axes and arrows; the fibers for cordage,

clothing, baskets, and other containers; dyes; tanning materials; and medicines. Plants were also used for firewood, as construction materials, and for ritual and ornamental purposes.

Today, in our predominantly urban culture, with its rapid and efficient transportation systems and processed, packaged foods, it is not easy to imagine direct contact with and dependence upon the world of nature. But in the ancient world of West Mexico, everyone had to be able to continuously exploit the surrounding natural environment. Although subsistence was primarily based on agriculture, people also relied to a large degree on wild, seasonally available plants and animals. It is important to understand that the natural environment of Jalisco, Colima, and Nayarit not only is climatically structured by several different elevations above sea level, but also holds a diversity of rather small, closely spaced local ecological niches and microenvironments that correspond to the topography of specific mountain and basin formations. Without having to walk great distances, ancient people would have been able to obtain a variety of products from warm and temperate zones as well as from cold environments. These benign conditions favored human settlement and helped in a certain way to shape the somewhat conservative character of ancient West Mexican society. The fact that local ecological settings tended to be small and differentiated also gave West Mexico another one of its characteristics: great wealth in the variety of its natural products, but only small quantities of each. Each territory had a limited capacity and could not tolerate extensive exploitation.

I believe that the technology and environmental conditions discussed here indicate that the settlement pattern over most of West Mexico was scattered and that its communities were limited in size because of the need for easily accessible, wide, open areas in which resources could be freely gathered without the need to travel very far. These could be called communal areas—shared spaces, the property not of individuals but of social groups that could defend their domains from neighboring groups. In the agricultural towns of ancient Mesoamerica, hunting, fishing, and, above all, the gathering of foods always played a very important role in the daily routine of the inhabitants, if not, strictly speaking, in their economy,

Fig. 5 Duck; Comala style; Colima; earthenware. Private collection. Cat. no. 52.

Fig. 6 Male figure carrying a vessel with a tumpline; Comala style; Colima; earthenware. Private collection, New York. Cat. no. 29.

the basis of which was agriculture. In my view this was particularly the case in ancient West Mexico.

Let us now turn to the historical texts that speak of the diverse resources of West Mexico. In the mid-sixteenth century, the Spanish crown, hoping to gain knowledge of the histories, societies, peoples, landscape, and natural resources of the newly conquered territories, compiled a list of fifty basic questions that were to be asked of the indigenous inhabitants. The famous *Relaciones geográficas* are compendia containing these fifty questions and their answers. Several questions concern native plants and animals, both wild and domesticated, as well as those that were brought by the Spaniards. Other questions were designed to locate the lands that were richest in stones, minerals, and salts. Most of the answers are quite brief, but they have given us a general idea of what was used or available in each region.

Two other West Mexican documents that are especially interesting and informative are the *Cuadro general estadístico de la Municipalidad de Sayula,* printed in 1880, and the *Relación de Ixtlahuacán (Colima),* written in 1778. The first gives the names of 409 plants, 75 of which have indigenous names. Although it does not describe the uses of these plants, we have been able to infer from other readings and investigations that 148 of the plants are certainly wild; of these, at least 124 have uses according to the following classifications: foodstuffs, 48; medicines, 39; woods, 11; fibers, 8; ornamental plants, 5; seasonings, 5; disinfectants, 4; dyes, 3; narcotics, 3; receptacles and tubes for drawing liquids, 3; tanning agents, 2; ritual substances or offerings, 2; soaps, 2; walking canes, 1; poison, 1; waterproofing agents, 1. Multiple uses of some plants result in a total of 138. Unfortunately, this source mentions few animals and does not tell us of their uses; nor does this document describe the abundance of the natural resources.

The second document, the *Relación de Ixtlahuacán (Colima),* is one of the most important sources of information about the original West Mexican biosphere, for it not only gives the names of plants but also their relative abundance, their uses, and, in the case of those plants that produced fruits, the time of harvest. The text describes almost 200 wild plants, 93 of which have indigenous names. The uses given to them are as follows: medicines, 82; food, 48; construction materials, 56; fibers, 8; poisons, 6; dyes, 5; tanning agents, 4; soaps, 3; disinfectants, 3; and diverse artifacts and implements such as the handles for instruments, canoes, etc., 25; again, multiple uses result in a total larger than the number of plants: 240.

In a study of illness and native medicine in West Mexico, I also found that the colonial texts mention approximately 90 afflictions that could be cured with the use of some 200 plants. In fact, the Spanish colonists did not consider it necessary that medical doctors be sent to them from Europe, for they considered the indigenous healers and native remedies superior.

Although it is conceivable that colonial and more recent sources fail to show the state of things many centuries beforehand, it seems more than likely that they offer meaningful clues into that more distant past. The questions presented in the *Relaciones geográficas* were directed toward the indigenous populations, and the two later texts, the *Cuadro general estadístico de la Municipalidad de Sayula* and the *Relación de Ixtlahuacán (Colima),* are from areas where the Indian mode of living persisted long into the colonial era and beyond, in some cases even into this century. Especially in rural areas, there are many cultural practices that persist and remain virtually unchanged—including those related to traditional medicine and to food. It is important to note that in West Mexico maize, beans, *chiles,* and squash have been part of the basic diet for thousands of years.

The names of towns, districts, and places are another way to learn about what once existed and was used in times past. For example, Mazatlán means "the place of deer"; Michoacán, "the place of fish"; Zapotlán, "the place of *zapotes*"; Tuxpan, "the place of rabbits"; Ocotlán, "the place of pines"; and so on.

In our survey of archaeological evidence, we may begin with the original indigenous diet. Minute food remains in ancient village trash deposits include abundant animal bones from deer, peccaries, hares, rabbits, armadillos, coatimundis, possums, prairie dogs, ducks, geese, doves, quail, turtles, fish, crabs, and crayfish, among others. Analysis of the contents of large shell mounds found by coastal lagoons and river estuaries reveals a great diversity of mollusks that were eaten and whose shells were used for ornamental

Fig. 7 Coatimundi; Comala style; Colima; earthenware. The Miller Family Collection, Chicago. Cat. no. 50.

Fig. 8 Prairie dog; Comala style; Colima; earthenware. Denver Museum of Natural History. Cat. no. 61.

Fig. 9 Joined ducks; Comala style; Colima; earthenware. Private collection. Cat. no. 63.

Fig. 10 Crab; Comala style; Colima; earthenware. Private collection. Cat. no. 51.

Fig. 11 Turtle; Comala style; Colima; earthenware. Private collection. Cat. no. 58.

purposes. Unfortunately, it is difficult to obtain evidence of vegetal remains, for very few specimens are left. Nevertheless, highly sophisticated methods designed to retrieve this kind of information are being used more and more frequently in archaeological investigations. Occasionally, and fortuitously, other types of dietary evidence are found, as in the case of a series of ovens associated with early settlements around the Sayula basin in Jalisco (see the essay by Francisco Valdez in this volume). Although the ovens contained only ash and calcinated stones, their shape and dimensions were comparable to those of ovens found in other places and described in ethnographic information, making it possible to deduce that they were used to make *mescal*, the sweet roasted large hearts and succulent leaves of the maguey agave cactus (see figs. 12–14). These roasted plants may still be bought in countryside towns. We should note that in Mexico today, the word *mescal* is also associated with the distilled alcoholic drink by that name; indeed, tequila is a variety of *mescal,* and its widely known name derives from the fact that it is produced in the vicinity of the town of Tequila, Jalisco.

Fig. 12 A *tlachiquero* trims the leaves of the maguey agave to obtain their succulent bases for roasting as *mescal* or to extract *aguamiel*.

Fig. 13 Sugary *mescal* for sale in the market.

Fig. 14 Vessel with roasted maguey leaves *(mescal);* Comala style; Colima; earthenware. Los Angeles County Museum of Art, gift of Mrs. Constance McCormick Fearing. Cat. no. 80.

The intimate contact between humankind and nature in West Mexico is manifested in physical form in the art of the shaft-tomb cultures of the states of Nayarit, Jalisco, and, especially, Colima. Indeed, a most extraordinary source of information on ancient foods is provided by the ceramic sculptures and vessels and related offerings recovered from the shaft tombs themselves. There is no doubt that the early populations believed in the existence of life after death and that the afterlife presented the same challenges that existed in life on earth. For this reason, the dead were buried with their utensils, implements, and insignia of rank and with amulets and images to protect them on the dangerous passage to the hereafter; but, above all, they were very generously provided with food and drink. Offerings of real foods, and sometimes of objects representing foods, and, in many cases, both, were placed in tombs.

The Huitzilapa tomb held a great abundance of vessels, many of which had covers and many of which contained organic remains that are now being scientifically analyzed (see the essay by Lorenza López and Jorge Ramos in this volume). There can be little doubt that these are the remains of foods, confirming that the dead were provided with real food. Many pieces from Colima illustrate offerings in sculptural form. A rich variety of fauna is depicted, including dogs (see figs. 15 and 16), coatimundis (see fig. 7), prairie dogs (see fig. 8), serpents, parrots (see fig. 17), ducks (see figs. 5 and 9), armadillos, peccaries, fish, crabs (see fig. 10), shrimp, crayfish (see figs. 1 and 28), turtles (see fig. 11), and the like. Some are easily identifiable but others can be classified only in a very general sense. Some can be tentatively identified because of their similarities to coatimundis, raccoons, and other small mammals that live in the warm lowlands. Undoubtedly many of the animals represented were eaten; yet others probably were not, though the Spanish said that the Indians were capable of eating anything, including serpents. There are Mesoamerican beliefs that dogs could be guides to help the deceased on the way to the underworld. However, the road to the hereafter was considered to be full of difficulties, and the Colima dogs, which are mostly represented as fattened and tranquil, were probably intended as provisions to be eaten en route.

As far as I know, no shaft tomb has thus far yielded figures that can be clearly identified as religious images or, more specifically, as representations of gods. Yet it seems that many of the animals represented, because of their appearance, behavior, and habitat, must have been associated with certain supernatural forces of the sky, water, earth, and weather. In this respect they also would have been featured in myths and beliefs, perhaps accounting for the frequent representation of animals that have a dual aspect or that represent hybrid beings such as humans with animal-like features or animals with certain human elements.

It is interesting to see how the forms of most of the ollas, jars, bowls of various shapes, plates, and saucers found in the tombs are inspired by the curving shapes of gourds, which were used to make containers long before the development of ceramics. Many varieties and shapes of gourds continue to be used as containers today. Almost all ancient West Mexican vessels have curved walls and bottoms, in contrast with the vessels seen in the ceramic traditions of the Olmec, Teotihuacan, Maya, and Zapotec peoples, which have straight walls and flat bottoms. In the period of the shaft tombs in West Mexico, ceramic containers were thus

largely inspired by vegetal forms and even by basketry.

Finally, we arrive at what I consider the finest examples of food representation in the ceramic art of West Mexico. These are a series of jars or ollas (called *cántaros* in local terminology) with narrow necks that make them appropriate for holding liquids. Whatever they once contained, they were clearly made as three-dimensional models of bowls full of foods. The lower part of the vessels always corresponds to the food container, the upper rim of which is always apparent

Fig. 15 Dancing dogs; Comala style; Colima; earthenware. Private collection. Cat. no. 47.

Fig. 16 Old pregnant snarling dog; Comala style; Colima; earthenware. Stokes Family Collection, Upper Nyack, N.Y. Cat. no. 54.

Fig. 17 Parrot; Comala style; Colima; earthenware. Private collection. Cat. no. 62.

Fig. 18 Vessel with *zapotes;* Comala style; Colima; earthenware. Fowler Museum of Cultural History, University of California, Los Angeles. Cat. no. 84.

Fig. 19 Vessel with squashes; Comala style; Colima; earthenware. Private collection. Cat. no. 83.

Fig. 20 Heaps of squash in a Guadalajara market.

(see figs. 18 and 19). Most of these bowls are smoothly burnished, but in some cases they are ornamented with incised decorations in the style of the Ortices-Tuxcacuesco area or with motifs made in the technique of negative-resist painting associated with Comala-phase receptacles from Colima. The representations are in general naturalistic, which makes them easy to identify. But in some cases, the forms are simplified and even to a degree abstracted, which makes their identification more problematic.

The most commonly represented forms correspond to squash, or at least to a fruit divided into gores (see figs. 19, 20, and 21). There also are *zapotes* (see fig. 18), probably of the black variety, although the white was also eaten, as well as *xocotes, pitayas* (the fruits of the *pitayo* cactus) (see figs. 22 and 23), and others. Figure 14 shows a vessel with roasted maguey leaves, or *mescal.* A very common representation is the *cuahuayote,* characterized by longitudinal crests that the Spanish called "Abbot's caps" (see fig. 25). Other, less clearly distinguishable fruits have elongated or globular forms suggesting *mamey, xocohuiztles, chicozapotes,* or *chirimoyas.* It is important to note that many of the plants represented are gathered in the wild while others are domesticated or semidomesticated species. This suggests the existence of orchards in ancient times and tends to explain the fact that certain plants or communities of plants are frequently found as relicts in association with archaeological sites. This is certainly the case for the *pitayo* cactus, *bonetes,* and the *capomo* (known in Maya lands as the *ramón* fruit).

The representation of animals sitting in bowls or laid out on trays is also common. Many shrimp (see fig. 26), freshwater crayfish (see figs. 1 and 28), and even lobsters (in complete form or without heads), appear, as do crabs (see fig. 27), fish, armadillos, and prairie dogs (see fig. 8). Only one ceramic piece that I know of represents a dog semiquartered and placed upon a rectangular tray (see fig. 29). All the animals, with the exception of the dog, were wild and had to be hunted or fished for. Although there is a great diversity in the flora and fauna represented, certain species predominate, indicating that these played a special role as food of the dead. Another representation of these

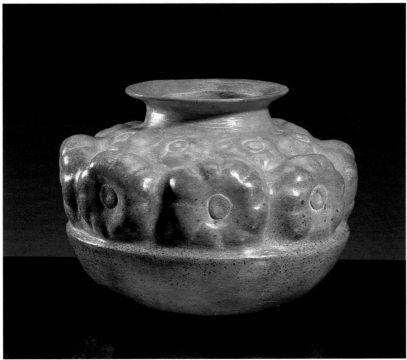

vessels, one that cannot be considered food, is that of human heads. This is a common theme in Colima ceramics, and it is possible that this type of vessel is linked to the idea of trophy heads (see the essay by Richard Townsend in this volume and his fig. 11).

Before closing I must mention a type of figure found in the tombs of Jalisco and Nayarit. These depict men or women presenting a small bowl in one of their hands while holding an elongated form in the other. Although these forms have been interpreted as scepters or clubs, because of their association with the bowl and because they are hollow, I believe they are a type of calabash or gourd called *acocote*, which is

Fig. 21 Squash vessel with parrot supports; Comala style; Colima; earthenware. Private collection. Cat. no. 72.

Fig. 22 Vessel in the form of a bowl of *pitayas;* Comala style; Colima; earthenware. Private collection.

Fig. 23 Bowl of *pitayas*.

Fig. 24 Vessel in the form of an organ cactus; Comala style; Colima; earthenware. Los Angeles County Museum of Art, The Proctor Stafford Collection, museum purchase with funds provided by Mr. and Mrs. Allan C. Balch. Cat. no. 71. Tall stems of the organ cactus *(pitayo)* grow in the fields, producing the sweet and succulent *pitaya* fruit. Organ cacti were and still are planted to form natural barriers.

used as a tube to suck liquid (see the essay by Kristi Butterwick in this volume and her fig. 1). The people being represented are therefore associated with the extraction of *aguamiel,* the sap of the maguey agave cactus, which could be left to ferment into *pulque.* Some of these sculptures almost certainly represent *tlachiqueros,* who extract the sap and who would have served this beverage to the soul of the dead. *Tlachiqueros* are also quite probably represented in the form of figures carrying large vessels (see fig. 6); this interpretation is confirmed by the fact that such figures appear only in the styles of the interior upland areas where the maguey agave prospers.

In this brief essay, I have called attention to a network of relationships that connected the ancient human populations of West Mexico to the environments in which they lived and its food resources. Without entering into further detail, I will conclude by emphasizing that although a great variety of resources can be documented, local ecological niches and microenvironments were small, limiting the quantity of resources they could provide. People had to live close to the natural products they needed and in a pattern that ensured these products would not become exhausted. These conditions, which prevail over much of the region, speak of a widespread pattern of human settlement in which the establishment of large communities was not possible. They suggest that, with

very few exceptions, settlement patterns were basically of the scattered village type and in many cases consisted of small hamlets or isolated clusters of family dwellings. In postulating this type of scattered settlement, I do not suggest that the populations of West Mexico were smaller than those of the other Mesoamerican cultural areas—rather, that in this region life did not thrive in large urban concentrations. To be sure, there were local areas where the political and administrative power must have become centralized and where rituals were performed to contribute to their cohesion. Yet the diversity of ar-

chaeological materials, seen in relation to the many local styles of ceramics and especially in relation to foods and their representations, reveals that during the period of the shaft tombs there existed in this region not what we could call extensive political and social areas under a single rule, but, rather, multiple units of a chieftainship type, each covering a territory of modest dimensions.

Fig. 28 Vessel with crayfish; Comala style; Colima; earthenware. Private collection. Cat. no. 67.

Fig. 29 Roasted dog on a platter; Comala style; Colima; earthenware. Private collection. Cat. no. 56. This life-sized representation is the only known example of its kind. Other works depicting roasted dogs were arranged in compositions on vessels similar to that shown in figure 28.

FRANCISCO VALDEZ

THE SAYULA BASIN
ANCIENT SETTLEMENTS AND RESOURCES

The art of ancient West Mexico has traditionally been treated in terms of a group of beautiful but enigmatic objects. Because of insufficient knowledge, however, the various regional styles have generally been classified according to their geographical location.[1] In spite of the unquestionable aesthetic quality inherent in these works, few specialists have attempted to trace the origins of their social, cultural, and symbolic functions, or of the societies that created this art. The lack of archaeological information on cultural contexts has made it difficult to distinguish regional boundaries or to determine the eras during which different groups flourished. While enormous progress has been made in Mesoamerican archaeology as a whole, relatively little attention has been paid to West Mexico, which is frequently seen as a region marginal to the cultural processes that took place elsewhere in central and southern Mexico. Fortunately, this situation has been gradually changing. For the past thirty years, regional studies have established a basis for defining the archaeological characteristics of West Mexican societies at different historical periods.

It has been many years since Isabel Kelly, the grande dame of West Mexican archaeology, proposed the existence of fourteen ceramic provinces extending from Sinaloa into Jalisco, Colima, Nayarit, and Michoacán.[2] Among these provinces, she identified one of particular interest where interactions apparently took place among the peoples of the interior of Nayarit, the uplands of Jalisco, and adjacent areas of Colima. She defined this intermediate area as the marshy lake basin between Sayula and Zacoalco, located in southern Jalisco. Despite Kelly's efforts, however, archaeological examinations of the surface of this intermediate zone did not produce the evidence necessary to identify interregional contacts during the early periods. Kelly herself pointed out the apparent absence of surface evidence of early dwellings, and, therefore, affirmed that the Sayula region was the weakest link in the assumed cultural chain that joined the neighboring provinces of Ameca in Jalisco in the north with Colima to the south.[3] Now, fifty years after Kelly placed the Sayula basin on the archaeological map, the Sayula Basin Archaeological Project has been able to identify and excavate residential areas that date to what we believe is the early horizon of civilization in this region, by which we mean that period of time during which the archaeological cultures across a broad region appeared to share certain defining characteristics, ranging from architecture and other material remains to identifiable economic, religious, and political concerns.

In the following pages, I will outline new data regarding the type of society that inhabited the Sayula region. Recent archaeological findings enable us to trace certain phases in the lives of these people, leading towards a more developed understanding of certain aspects of the social and economic organization of settlements in this area. The Sayula basin begins to emerge as a distinct area, differing in several important respects from the core Teuchitlán tradition area in the Ameca-Magdalena basins to the north.

Fig. 1 The Sayula basin. Agricultural fields bordered by mesquite and acacias lead into the shallow lake bed at the height of the December–June dry season. Volcán de Colima rises in the distance.

217

Fig. 2 By the end of
July, rains have covered
the lake bed with a thin
sheet of water and the
fields in the southern
part of the basin have
dramatically turned
green.

The Natural Environment

The Sayula basin is located approximately 70 kilometers (42 miles) south of the city of Guadalajara, between latitudes 19°8' and 20°11' north and longitudes 103°20' and 103°40' west (see the maps on pp. 12–13). It is indeed part of a natural corridor that joins the southern coast of Colima with the central highlands of Jalisco, and it has played a strategic role in the interaction between these two regions. The archaeological records of this basin offer abundant evidence of long, continuous settlements. The earliest sedentary occupations found to date can be traced back more than 2,000 years (see the essay by Joseph Mountjoy in this volume). The latest settlements thus far examined reveal the presence of the Tarascan state, which had its seat further south around Lake Pátzcuaro in Michoacán, dating from the end of the fifteenth century. Native history, of course, ends in the year 1528 with the arrival of the Spaniards. Yet, between these two chronological poles, there was a long sequence of interactions between the area and the neighboring regions. This is the evidence that Kelly had been looking for when she sought to identify the Sayula basin as a zone of interaction.[4]

The particular character of Sayula is revealed by three complementary factors: 1) a richness of natural resources found in its different ecological strata; 2) the seasonal presence of a mineral element, salt, which is scarce, valuable, and strategic for the development of any society; and 3) a stable population that completely occupied the territory, sharing the same sociocultural identity. The ability to function as a coherent, articulated social system is characteristic of groups that have developed a broad political organization such as that of a chiefdom. Perhaps at first, regional authority among scattered groups was carried out in an almost inconspicuous manner, promoting an exchange and reciprocity of locally available products and resources. A varied and abundant natural environment brought about the development of a village life in which small, autonomous groups gradually began interacting until they became organized into a broader society sharing the same cultural traits—though never submitting fully to a centralized power until roughly A.D. 200–400, the beginning of the Classic period.

Throughout West Mexico, vegetation changes drastically according to the amount of available moisture and the differences in elevation. These variations give rise to a diversity of complementary environments, each of which offers a wide range of resources. The distribution of human settlements over a given territory reflects the organization of the productive skills of a group and, eventually, the success with which they are able to adapt to a hostile environment.

In the Sayula basin, such differences are apparent as soon as one leaves the low-lying marshlands and gains elevation in the surrounding hillsides. Fertile lands are found on the first natural terraces on both sides of the lake. Around the southern half of the basin, a high water table provides constant moisture to the subsoil and allows for stable agriculture throughout almost the entire year (see fig. 2). During the rainy season, the lake bed overflows and many of the first terraces become completely flooded or turn into seasonal marshes (see fig. 3). The early inhabitants knew how to take advantage of this situation, however, and they transformed their environment accordingly. In certain places one can still find traces of ancient drainage systems that were built in order to send excess amounts of water out into the lake. Even during the dry season, these areas maintain enough moisture to be cultivated. At higher elevations, the mountainsides have permanent or seasonal streams at different elevations, allowing scattered settlements of small populations. Given these environmental conditions, it is not surprising to find that

the region has been continuously populated for more than 2,000 years.

A cross-section of the basin reveals three zones (see fig. 4), each characterized by a distinctive soil type and vegetation—differences that produced a corresponding variety of activities in ancient times.[5] In the highest zone, between approximately 2,700 and 1,700 meters above sea level (8,900 and 5,600 feet), the ground is very steep, frequently forming rugged slopes. Mountain forests of pine (*Pinus* sp.) and oak (*Quercus* sp.) predominate. The variety of fauna includes deer, wild boar, coyotes, and a large diversity of rodents. There is an abundance of rocks and minerals that were used for making tools and ornaments. In spite of the few traces of human settlements found in this area, the types of vegetation indicate that agriculture was once practiced on the less steep hillsides, probably in a very marginal manner. This area may very well have been designated for hunting and gathering, and obtaining raw materials and minerals.

The middle area, located between 1,700 and 1,450 meters, has natural terraces, covered with low mountainous forest with various types of trees such as the *iguamuchili* (*Phitecebollium dulce*), guavas (*Psidium guajaba*), plums (*Spondias* and *Prunus* sp.),

Fig. 3 Seasonal rains bring out smaller organisms, shellfish, and small fish, attracting flocks of birds to the shallow basin. Cultivated fields are seen on alluvial slopes in the distance.

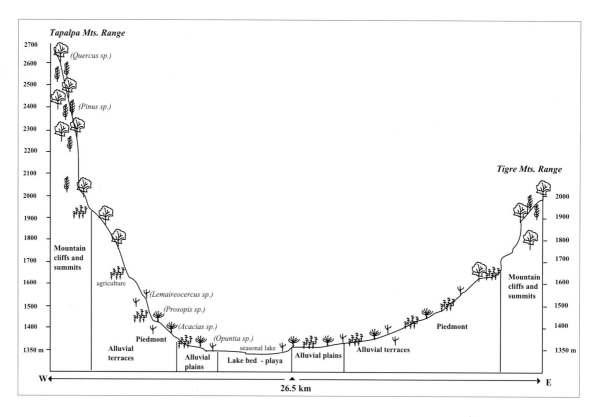

Fig. 4 From the surrounding hillsides to the lake bed, three distinct ecological zones are seen in the Sayula basin.

Tapalpa Mts. Range

2700
2600
2500
2400
2300
2200
2100
2000
1900
1800
1700
1600
1500
1400
1350 m

(Quercus sp.)
(Pinus sp.)

Mountain cliffs and summits

agriculture
(Lemaireocercus sp.)
(Prosopis sp.)
(Acacias sp.)
Piedmont
(Opuntia sp.)
Alluvial terraces
seasonal lake
Alluvial plains
Lake bed - playa

Tigre Mts. Range

2000
1900
1800
1700
1600
1500
1400
1350 m

Mountain cliffs and summits
Piedmont
Alluvial plains
Alluvial terraces

W ←——————————— 26.5 km ———————————→ E

icamichinesî, and figs (*Ficus* sp.), and obviously cacti, mesquites (*Prosopis* sp.), and *ihuizachesî* (*Acacias* sp.). The fauna include armadillos (see fig. 5), badgers, opossums, rabbits, and game fowl such as quails and *ichachalacasî* (a crowlike bird). This area is especially suitable for human settlements. Here, agricultural soil combines with undulating terrain, traditionally providing seasonal food for the great majority of the populations. Abundant clay deposits were used for manufacturing

pottery. Some cliffs have copper and tin deposits, but it is archaeologically unclear whether these were exploited during the periods in question. Brooks and springs from the mountainsides were used for partial irrigation of the land on this middle level.

The third area, from 1,450 down to 1,340 meters, is also covered with a low mountainous forest, with many of the same species of flora and fauna found in the previous area. The terraces next to the lake have abundant cacti, mesquites, *ihuizachesî,* and a variety of thorn bushes. Cattails and grassy plants grow on the moist banks of the lake, attracting multiple species of local birds. These sites also shelter various migrant bird species, such as geese, ducks, and pelicans. The first marshy terraces comprise the most fertile sector of the basin, with humus rich in organic components.

The lake basin receives water from mountainside drainage, increasing and diminishing according to the seasons. The rainy season begins during the first summer months (June–July) and the giant shallow basin is gradually filled, reaching an average water level of 50 to 70 cm. Vegetation becomes lush and the lake fills with fish and shellfish, becoming a noisy home for a great number of birds (see figs. 6–8). Towards the end of October, the rain diminishes and a

Fig. 5 Vessel with armadillos; Comala style; Colima; earthenware. The Saint Louis Art Museum, gift of Morton D. May. Cat. no. 68.

gradual transformation of the landscape begins. The basin loses its green color, until the brown and barren soil shows through the dry vegetation (see fig. 1). Little by little, the sides of the mountains lose their foliage and xerophytic vegetation prevails. The change is not as drastic in the far southern part of the basin or around some of the central sectors on the east side, which receive perennial spring water. The contrast with the barrenness of the exposed lake bed is striking. What was formerly an expanse of water becomes a harsh, dry plain, where reverberating heat produces local whirlwinds and dust storms. Years of this cycle have

formed sand dunes in various places around the lakeshore.

From a cultural point of view, this seasonal change in the environment had a great impact on the development of the early societies that settled on the basin. As

Fig. 6 Flocks appearing during the height of the rainy season suggest the teeming wildlife that once populated the entire Jalisco lake-basin region.

Fig. 7 Duck; Comala style; Colima; earthenware. Fowler Museum of Cultural History, University of California, Los Angeles. Cat. no. 60.

Fig. 8 Heron; Comala style; Colima; earthenware. Los Angeles County Museum of Art, the Proctor Stafford Collection, museum purchase with funds provided by Mr. and Mrs. Allan C. Balch. Cat. no. 59.

water evaporates and the lake bed becomes exposed, nitrous mineral sediments *(tequesquite)* that can be transformed into salt begin to rise to the surface by capillary action. This phenomenon was understood in early times. Along the swampy banks of the lake, traces can be found of ancient exploitation of this strategic resource. Today, as the lake seasonally dries up, hundreds of ancient salt-extraction sites appear (see fig. 9). The extraordinary number of these sites, made in the long course of perfecting the techniques of salt extraction, reveal the importance of salt in the local and regional economy.

For several miles along the shore, workshops, platforms, small dikes, and causeways—all built to connect the various production sites—can be archaeologically uncovered. The exploitation of salt reached its peak in the seventh century A.D., at which time the society was probably ruled by an elite class controlling its production and monopolizing its distribution at a regional level. It seems that the most important site during this period was a saltworks with a civic and ceremonial center, located at the far northern end of the basin. This site, presently known as Cerritos Colorados (Red Mounds), is composed of various platforms covered with heaped fragments of broken ceramic vessels.[6] Several sectors have been identified at this site: some appear to have ceremonial architecture; others are more clearly associated with the practical activity of salt extraction.[7] Although the main constructions for the salt deposits belong to the Classic period, evidence of earlier occupations, also related to salt extraction, have been found as well.[8]

Fig. 9 At Cerritos Colorados, foundations of ancient buildings appear amid heaps of broken pottery remaining from the dry-season saltworks.

Settlement Patterns in the Sayula Basin

Archaeological exploration has revealed a very clear pattern in which residential sites alternate with activity areas throughout the basin. The earliest residential sites are rather small and are scattered over the lower terraces of the mountains, close to well-irrigated fertile lands. It is only toward the end of the Postclassic period that we see evidence of dense, nuclear settlements on the lakeshore. We can, in fact, recognize three basic types of inhabited or utilized spaces: 1) residential areas; 2) areas for specific activities; and 3) places for gatherings and social interaction. As part of the first category we have identified isolated residential units as well as villages with large numbers of residences scattered in the fields over a broad area. Areas for specific activities include quarries or workshops where raw materials were transformed. Most sites within this category are located in marshlands used for extracting salt. The civic and ceremonial centers are characterized by the presence of mounds, platforms, or terraces that served as foundations for minor constructions, or that delimited interior boundaries and plazas. These structures are not monumental, but it is obvious that they required a type of collective work reflecting a shared communal life. These sites are generally associated with the residential areas.

Within these three types of sites it is possible to identify diverse functions that took place in certain spaces. First, there are sites used for gatherings or social interaction, such as the civic and ceremonial center of Cerritos Colorados, which displays a distinctive archi-

tectural complexity and a well-planned structure within the larger saltworks complex. Next, there are smaller sites that seem to have had a more local function. The great majority of sites, however, are residential areas, indicative of a type of village life with the primary seasonal activities that alternated between agriculture and salt production. These patterns appear to have been established from the earliest periods of occupation and were apparently maintained until the Spanish conquest.

Chronology

The accompanying chronological chart, based on seven years of excavation, indicates the main cultural transformations that took place within the Sayula basin, part of the larger archaeological picture of the Jalisco-Colima region (see fig. 10). With information obtained from research published on the southern part of Jalisco and adjacent areas of Colima, this chronology is built upon the ceramic sequence first presented by Isabel Kelly during the 1940s. Kelly based her own pioneering study on surface materials she collected during her initial survey of the Sayula area, strengthened with proven stratigraphic evidence from the neighboring Autlán-Tuxcuesco region.[9] Kelly identified three ceramic groups that demonstrate the qualities of work from the Sayula basin; unfortunately, having described these ceramics, Kelly never published her study.[10]

Nevertheless, research carried out during the 1990s has confirmed the validity of Kelly's sequence, and has also refined certain subdivisions she made within each archaeological phase. The main contribution of our present project has been to explain the chronology of these ceramic groups, especially the earliest one, originally named Verdía, and now renamed Usmajac, which Kelly's study of surface material had only partially identified.[11] Stratigraphic excavations carried out at five different sites within the basin have allowed us to obtain a series of twenty-seven radiocarbon dates that clearly show how long each defined ceramic phase lasted and how these phases reflect a pattern of cultural change. To establish these phases, we took into account not only the presence or absence of a predominant ceramic unit, but also the shifts revealed in settlement patterns, the use of space, and, above all, the possible changes in social organization inferred from all the

PHASES OF CERAMIC PROVINCES			
DATE—PERIOD	TEUCHITLAN TRADITION (WEIGAND 1985)	SAYULA BASIN (KELLY 1948 REVISED 1996)	COLIMA/JALISCO (KELLY 1949, MEIGHAN 1972, MOUNTJOY 1996)
1500–800—Early Formative	El Opeño		Capacha
800	San Felipe		
300—Late Formative	Arenal	Usmajac	
200			Morett
100			
0			Tuxcacuesco (Jal./Col.)
100		Verdía	Ortices
200—Early Classic	Ahualulco		
300			Comala
400—Middle Classic	Teuchitlán I	Early Sayula	
500			
600			
700—Late Classic	Teuchitlán II		
800			
900—Early Postclassic		Late Sayula	
1000			
1100	Santa Cruz de Barcenas	Early Amacueca	
1200—Late Postclassic			
1300	Etzatlán	Late Amacueca	
1400			
1528–32	Spanish Conquest		

evidence present in the archaeological record. Thus, the three phases not only concern ceramics, they also reflect a sociocultural dimension. The chronology is based on the stratigraphic sequence of well-defined archaeological assemblages in their contexts, and it has all been confirmed by radiocarbon dates.

Evidence reveals that the region has been continuously occupied for 2,300 years. To date, no trace of an occupation prior to the Late Formative period (300 B.C.–A.D. 200) has been detected, but, given the environmental conditions of the basin, the area was most likely settled before this time, and evidence for this will doubtless appear someday under a deep layer not yet disturbed by modern agricultural activity. Until then, we will have to be satisfied with the clear evidence of village life of an incipient complex society.

The first defined cultural phase is called Usmajac, after the name of the location where we clearly identified it for the first time (see fig. 10). The radiocarbon dates

Fig. 10 Chronology of the Sayula basin in relation to the Teuchitlán area and the Colima/southern Jalisco sequences.

place this phase between 1,990 (+/-60) and 2,060 (+/-70) years ago (or approximately 180 B.C.–A.D. 20), although it probably began around the year 400 B.C. Changes are detected in the archaeological record around the beginning of the first millennium A.D., revealing certain transformations in this society. Among other new things, ceramic forms and attributes defined by Isabel Kelly for the Verdía ceramic group appear. These are still found in contexts dated approximately A.D. 180–320. The refinement that our project has brought to this sequence has demonstrated that the Verdía is in reality only the last part of the earlier Usmajac phase. During the Verdía era, the construction of shaft tombs as a major form of mortuary practice began to lose popularity in the region. This generally corresponds to the slow decline of shaft-tomb burials charted in the Ahualulco phase of the Teuchitlán tradition north of the Sayula basin (A.D. 200–400).

The first centuries A.D. may be considered as an era of transition into the Sayula phase that followed, beginning around A.D. 380–480. The chronology of the transition between both phases roughly coincides with the beginning of the Classic period, and, in fact, the changes noted in the new phase are symptomatic of deep transformations within the nucleus of the society. Probably, influences from the north brought about the new social order that characterizes the region. The Sayula phase lasted approximately seven centuries, with two possible subphases: the Early Sayula (A.D. 500–800) and the Late Sayula (A.D. 900–1100). The researcher Jean Guffroy has proposed a division of the subphases based on the differences perceived in the ceramic body of the Cerritos Colorados site.[12]

The last phase of the pre-Hispanic period, labeled the Amacueca, is fully contained in the Postclassic period. The dates obtained for sites associated with this stage place its beginnings close to the eleventh century A.D. Cultural materials characteristic of this phase prevail until the end of the sixteenth century, in spite of the Spanish presence in the region. As in the previous stages, a division can be made between an early (1150–1350) and a late subphase (1450–1625). During the last part of the Amacueca phase, various Tarascan garrisons from Michoacán were established in the region. Evidence of their presence usually appears in late archaeological contexts, close to the towns of Teocuitatlán, Atoyac, Sayula, and Techaluta. These traces usually consist of body ornaments denoting rank, or of fine ceramic vessels, probably imported by the elite of the area.[13] The material culture of the indigenous people of the region maintains its recognizable characteristics during a couple of centuries after the conquest. It could therefore be said that the Amacueca phase lasted almost until the year 1600.

Having described the natural environment, the settlement patterns, and the chronology of the Sayula Basin, we may now outline salient aspects of the cultural, political, and economic history of the area.

Early evidence

The history of human occupation of the Sayula region probably began in the Paleo-Indian period (i.e., by approximately 7000 B.C.), when groups of hunters and gatherers crossed through the marshland in search of game and seasonal foods. In the neighboring lake of San Marcos, the discovery of two grooved projectiles offers unquestionable proof of the presence of early hunters.[14] Not surprisingly, however, the earliest reliable evidence of sedentary settlements consistently appears much later, toward the end of the Formative period. Well-established archaeological remains in the region of Sayula can be placed between 300 B.C. and A.D. 400—the era identified above as the Usmajac phase, which belongs to the same broadly based manifestation of culture that joined, at that moment, the populations of Colima, Jalisco, Nayarit, Michoacán, and possibly Zacatecas.

Isabel Kelly was the first to identify this cultural horizon, close to the Armería River, over a wide area located between the Tuxcacuesco region in Jalisco, and central Colima, as well as the valley of the Coahuayana River, on the Michoacán border. In Colima, the sites were associated with the Ortices–Comala phase, and in Jalisco with the Tuxcacuesco phase.[15] Clement Meighan also identified this horizon in the deepest deposits of the Morett site on the coast of Jalisco and Colima.[16] Recently, Joseph Mountjoy has been able to isolate at least two components of this same archaeological status in various locations on the coast of Jalisco.[17] Similarly, in the central part of the Jalisco highlands, the Tabachines, Colorines, and Arroyo Seco complexes also belong to it, as do the San Felipe, Arenal, and Ahualulco phases of the Teuchitlán tradition.[18]

All the ceramics of this period share formal, stylistic, and technological traits. These traits, along with a variety of mortuary paraphernalia including shells, greenstones, and obsidian, form part of the funerary ensembles and serve as a common denominator to the so-called shaft-tomb cultures. Local variations in the aesthetic decoration of ceramics have allowed us to identify the different regional styles.[19] These variations are especially noted in the anthropomorphic hollow tomb sculptures that are the universal hallmarks of West Mexican cultures.[20]

Similarities in the material culture of this horizon almost certainly reflect a sphere of interaction linking the majority of the West Mexican peoples.[21] Very little has been done, however, to understand the specific character of this close regional interaction. The fieldwork carried out by Phil Weigand constitutes the only serious effort to widen the limited interpretations that have been presented by ceramic typologies, offering instead an inclusive outlook on the dynamic process of cultural exchange in West Mexico.[22] Indeed, Weigand rejects the notion of an archaeological horizon for this phase, preferring instead the concept of "tradition." He employs this concept in characterizing the pre-Hispanic society of the Etzatlán-Ahualulco-Magdalena lake basin, embracing it with the generic name of the Teuchitlán tradition. He has proposed the existence of a ruling group, established in the nuclear area of Teuchitlán, that politically controlled the rest of the neighboring populations and established spheres of interaction over a broad territory. Although we may find the general scheme of Weigand's hypothesis seductive, the idea of including *all* the cultural manifestations of West Mexico within the same sociopolitical system still requires archaeological verification with evidence found in the areas presumably involved. The support or rejection of an all-encompassing hypothesis must be based on detailed study of the complete archaeological evidence from each specific region.

The following synthesis of our archaeological findings from the early horizon in the Sayula basin presents concrete evidence, allowing us to question the validity of Weigand's hypothesis within a local context. The evidence has been collected by systematically prospecting the region, and by excavating at numerous sites located in various sectors of the basin over a seven-year period. The territory covered in this archaeological examination extends over approximately 700 square kilometers, within which more than seventy sites that show signs of early occupation have been detected. The present description gives priority to the first stage of the established sequence, since it corresponds to a time in the cultural history of western Mexico about which we still know much too little. This era, lasting approximately 700 years, has generically been called the shaft-tomb period.[23] Our research in the Sayula region now offers a perspective on the dominant settlement pattern.

The regional survey undertaken by the Sayula Basin Archaeological Project has thus far located more than seventy sites from the Usmajac phase, the majority corresponding to small residential areas, exhibiting no remaining architectural evidence, but with traces of how residential spaces were used and transformed. The extent and density of the traces found on the surface indicate scattered domestic units or hamlets of no more than ten or twelve families. In three sites, various types of funerary structures were also found, including a type of shaft tomb that had never been reported in the archaeological literature.

Residential sites are mainly located on the first marshy terraces found in the southern half of the basin (see fig. 11). The hillsides of both mountain ranges exhibit a pattern of scattered settlements, at an altitude between 1,350 and 1,650 meters. The majority of the sites identified are no larger than 300 square meters—a space possibly occupied by a few domestic units. The surrounding area frequently displays evidence of land leveling, and the sites usually occupy positions close to seasonal mountain streams that flow from higher elevations. Concentrations of scattered sites are most often separated by distances of not more than a few kilometers. The areas in between could reflect the existence of zones used for domestic orchards, or forest areas kept as reserves for wood and for hunting small game. Partial excavations of two village sites now give us a view of daily life during the Usmajac phase.

A detailed study of one of these residential areas has revealed distinct features characteristic of villages during this time. The site

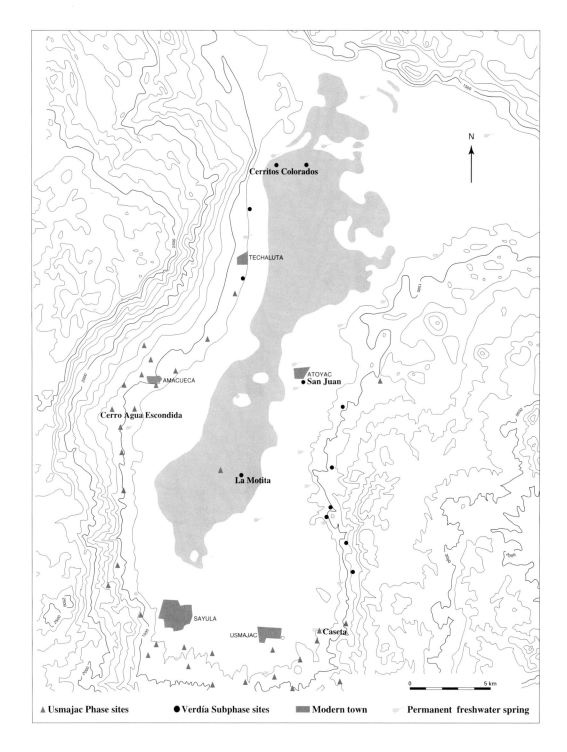

Fig. 11 Map of the Sayula basin showing Usmajac phase and Verdía subphase site locations.

TECHALUTA

Cerritos Colorados

ATOYAC
San Juan

AMACUECA

Cerro Agua Escondida

La Motita

SAYULA

USMAJAC

Caseta

0   5 km

▲ Usmajac Phase sites   ● Verdía Subphase sites   ■ Modern town   Permanent freshwater spring

known as Cerro del Agua Escondida (Hill of the Hidden Water), located on the first group of terraces a short distance from the lake bed, displays evidence of occupation over an expanse larger than one square kilometer (see fig. 13). The density of such vestiges, however, is not homogeneous, though they tend to be concentrated in at least four well-defined sectors. Each sector displays artificial rearrangements of the natural topography: steep terraces have been graded and small headlands have been leveled. On the hill-sides, flat spaces can be seen where partially buried stone alignments suggesting ancient structures are frequently found.

Shaft tombs have been found in three sectors of the site, and they all follow a similar architectural plan (fig. 12). To prepare the tomb, a deep pit was first excavated. At its bottom, a chamber was built with stone walls held together by a mortar of soil, plant matter, and fragments of ceramics to plug the gaps. A roof was then erected over the chamber by means of an ingenious system of stone

slabs placed as a type of self-supporting corbeled dome. At the entrance to the chamber,
a rectangular foundation was made with
small stones, so that the walls of the shaft
could be built up to the surface level. Once
the construction was finished, the space between the corbeled dome and the ground
above was filled, leaving the burial chamber
at a depth between 2.5 and 3 meters. Corpses
would be lowered through the shaft and the
entrance sealed with small stones and large
slabs. The dimensions of these chambers fluc-
tuate between 2 and 3 meters long, and 1.8
to 2.5 meters wide. The height of the dome
could reach 1.3 meters.

This type of funerary construction is a
variation on the type of tomb usually reported in West Mexico (see the essays by
Phil Weigand and Christopher Beekman and
by López and Ramos in this volume). Its
distinctiveness is interpreted as an adaptation required by the characteristics of the
local soil, where a loose conglomerate of
volcanic tuff and gravel is not sufficiently
solid to support the larger cavities that may
be found elsewhere, especially in the core of
the Teuchitlán area. The three tombs studied
in the Sayula basin reveal the mastery of
construction techniques that the early vil-
lagers possessed. This knowledge is also
expressed on the ground. Although the
dwellings themselves no longer survive, the
foundations can sometimes be seen, coinciding with areas that have a high density of
cultural remains.

Our archaeological excavation was concentrated on one part of sector 3 of the site,
because it showed signs of residences and
contained a partially looted funerary structure (see fig. 13). Sector 3 is located on a
hillside with a very irregular topography.
The ground drops sharply and then gradually
flattens to form a rolling plateau. Three terraces have been graded, gradually descending toward the lake bed. A small, seasonal
stream, now diverted to irrigate adjacent
lands, descends on the far southern part of
the site. To the north, the hillside is more
abrupt with a rugged surface reaching down
to the edge of the marshland. No surface
cultural material was found on this side.

We began excavating in the central part
of the highest terrace, situated at 1,430
meters above sea level. The area excavated,
covering a surface of 160 square meters, revealed part of the occupational contexts of an

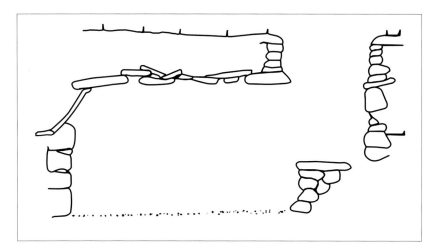

Fig. 12 Typical Usmajac-
phase shaft tomb of the
type found at the Cerro
del Agua Escondida site.

early village. The work centered on a small
patio, delimited by a semi-oval-shaped wall.
Areas for specific activities were exposed on
the periphery. Vestiges of domestic architecture were marked with stones and small
fragments of a mud wall. These constructions
became more striking as we surveyed and
explored the surrounding terrain. Underneath the occupation level of the excavated
area, clear evidence of the rearrangement of
natural topography was found. We discovered that, to grade the terraces, retaining
walls had been built at intervals and various
layers of fill had been used.

The organization of the habitational
space is evident in the patio that lies at the
center of the terrace. This patio distinctly
marks the separation of three complexes:

1. a residential area distributed over both
flat and steep parts of the ground;

2. a zone for communal activity toward
the northern end of the patio; and

3. an apparently sacred space, located
in the middle of the patio, where the
entrance to the shaft tomb was found.

The patio itself is marked by a line of
carefully chosen stones with regular shapes
that served as a foundation. At one time,
these stones, placed on top of one another,
were part of a small wall at least four rows
high, delimiting a surface of compacted soil.
In its present state, the foundation has an
ovoid shape, running eight meters from
east to west, before curving north to south,
finally extending eleven meters on this
north-south axis. A buried ceramic vessel
was found under one of the curves where
the wall turns, fifty-six centimeters below

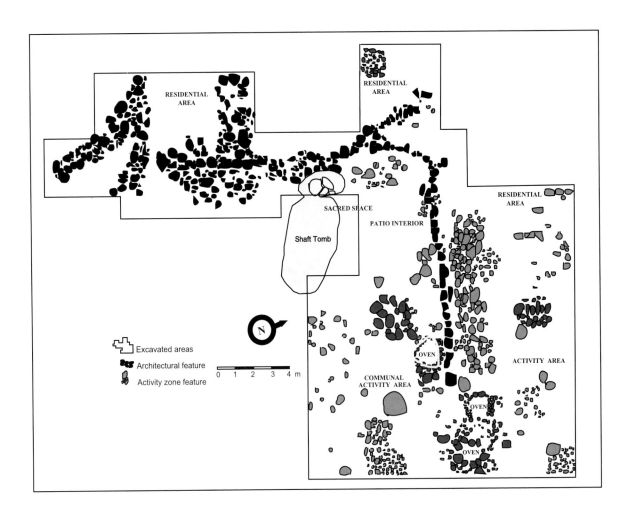

Fig. 13 Plan of sector 3
of the Cerro del Agua
Escondida site.

the present surface. As in the case of the offerings from the funerary chamber, the small earthenware bowl must have contained some type of organic material protected with an inverted plate placed as a cover. The floor of the interior patio showed no archaeological remains, in contrast to the exterior of the wall where the floors were covered with debris. The absence of material could be an indication of the restricted character of this space, or it could perhaps denote a concern in keeping the area clean in order to carry out a particular activity. The possible sacred nature of this sector is suggested by the presence of the tomb, the offering beneath the corner, and the contrast between the absence and presence of debris in the interior patio and exterior floors, respectively.

Lying beneath the patio, the tomb is oriented on the same east-west axis. The entrance to the shaft is fixed to the base of a wall in the central part of the patio, and was sealed by four large stone slabs. The diameter of the shaft measures one meter and it descends slightly more than two meters to the door of the burial chamber. Two stone slabs blocked the entrance to the interior where the bodies were placed.

Although the tomb had been partially looted several years before, excavation of the remaining debris allowed us to recover valuable first-hand information. One sector of the chamber had not been touched by the looters, and therefore, a general plan of how the bodies were laid out could be sketched and part of the offerings rescued. At least five people (four adults and one child) were laid out on the major axis of the chamber, their heads towards the entrance. The offerings surrounded the skulls in the space between the wall and the door of the tomb. These objects, found in situ, were decorated earthenware bowls and jars, some of which still had covers made from plates or inverted small wide bowls. Among the bones were various ornaments such as nose rings, necklaces, and bracelets made from worked seashells. Some pendants and beads for necklaces were made from polished, cut greenstones, and others from obsidian. The raw material for all these objects came from places far from the Sayula basin: they serve as testimony to the importance of commercial contacts maintained among the inhabitants of the various regions in West Mexico.

On the exterior, an activity area found on the other side of the wall that delimits the patio is notable for the manner in which its large space is organized. It contains three ovens placed around a rectangular walkway made from flat stones. Between the ovens, various concentrations of small stones that could have served as bases or supports were cleared. The ground displayed an important density of debris, including ceramic sherds, stone fragments, and bones.

The ovens are cone-shaped structures, excavated in the subsoil, to a depth of one meter. The diameter of the opening of the oven varies between 90 and 150 cm. Inside, a thick stone filling mixed with abundant ashes and charcoal was found. The form and size of the structures remind one of the ovens currently used in this region to roast the heart of the maguey or mescal cactus. The nutritional importance of this plant among societies in northwestern Mexico has recently been emphasized by Ben Nelson. Its presence in an area for communal activity is, therefore, fully understandable.[24] Various fragments of a broken ceramic vessel, probably from some domestic activity, were recovered from one of the ovens in an adjacent area. These fragments support the idea that different areas of the site were in use at the same time. Carbon samples for dating the time of occupation of this site were also taken from the ovens.

A similar spatial organization was found at another excavated village, located at the extreme southeastern end of the basin (see fig. 11). On the edge of a hillside at this site, known as Caseta, Usmajac-phase archaeological remains were also found. In addition, there is an early cemetery associated with the other evidence of ovens and the levels of domestic occupation.[25] Unfortunately, the stratigraphy of this site was greatly mixed with materials from later occupations, and it was not possible to obtain a clear idea of the original layout of the early levels. Nevertheless, a comparison between the structures and the materials recovered allowed us to mark the similarities and particularities of the different early sites.

From these sites, three basic types of diagnostic ceramic vessels have been identified, all of the Usmajac phase. The first is an ordinary monochromatic buff or red ware, with fairly thin walls, and a carefully burnished surface. The second type, characteristic of the early archaeological horizon, is a fine ware with a cream-colored slip, varying between buff and dark gray. The sides are always burnished and usually display some type of linear decoration painted red or a combination of red and white. The third type, which is less common, is also monochromatic, dark brown or black, with an incised or engraved zonal decoration, similar to certain decorative Capacha motifs.[26] As Mountjoy has argued in regard to his finds of such wares on the coast of Jalisco, these ceramics may be a continuation of the tradition in the Sayula region from the Middle Formative period.[27] The predominant forms in the three types of vessels are the shallow plate, the hemispheric earthenware bowl, the jar, and the medium-sized pot. Composite contours predominate among jars and bowls used as offerings, their shape resembling that of a gourd. In addition to these diagnostic vessels, we find solid anthropomorphic figurines, of the type defined by Isabel Kelly as the "Ortices-Tuxcacuesco" (see also the essay by Jane Day in this volume).[28] Fragments of these figurines abound in domestic contexts that characterize this early archaeological horizon in various states of West Mexico.

Usually, the distance between the residential sites and the lake bed is less than four kilometers. Easy access between both areas made it possible for various groups to keep permanent agricultural fields in the rich alluvial lands next to the water. This can explain the presence of ceramic fragments in flooded areas that seem little suitable for human settlements. Not far from these areas, on the swampy shore, we find salt-extraction stations that were exploited during the dry season. Ceramics from the Usmajac phase have been found in many of these stations, suggesting that salt was exploited as early as the first centuries B.C. In her work, Catherine Liot has identified various steps in the ancient method of salt extraction.[29] Several pertain to the early phase; these appear most often in the southern half of the basin.

At the La Motita site in the center of the basin, Liot studied various circular structures, buried at the bottom of the dry lake, that were used for concentrating and decanting the brine. She also identified the vessels used for inducing evaporation of nitrate liquid at

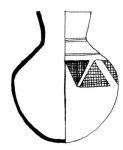

low heat to produce salt crystals. During the Usmajac phase, such vessels have a characteristic form, distinguishing them from those used in later phases. One group of vessels containing various forms related to salt production includes the following: 1) semispherical bowls, with a diameter between 35 and 50 cm, often decorated—inside or outside the bowl—with one or more red bands close to the edge or in the upper middle part of the vessel; 2) thick, well-fired cylindrical vessels; and 3) ordinary pots (see fig. 14).[30] Usually, this type of specialized, utilitarian ware is the only one found at the stations, although some finer well-decorated fragments, as well as pieces of solid anthropomorphic figurines, have also been found. Utilitarian material related to salt production rarely appears in domestic contexts. Some fragments of decorated vessels with red bands, however, have been recorded in a few early sites located on the alluvial terraces along the western border of the basin.

Toward the beginnings of the first millennium A.D., a new type of fine ceramic material—Kelly's Verdía—made its appearance, associated with certain stations on the northern part of the Sayula basin. Compared to the utilitarian material used for salt production, this finer example is relatively rare, its distribution throughout the area much more fragmented. The distinctiveness of this type lies in its having been found also accompanying surface burials from the Verdía subphase at sites on the shore.[31] These human burials, accompanied by ceramic non-utilitarian offerings at sites considered as specialized saltworks, may indicate the presence of a distinct group of people who began to control production and distribution of salt within the basin. The new group apparently no longer made use of shaft tombs and preferred to have their burials next to their sources of wealth, without any need for a complex funerary architecture. Another, alternative interpretation of this evidence is that those who were buried in the saltworks might have been sacrificed for propitiatory purposes and that their elegant offerings may simply represent implements used for the ritual. Whatever the case may be, from this phase on, the stations at the northern end of the basin increased significantly and became the hallmark of a new cultural phase—the Sayula phase—that appeared in the basin in the sixth century A.D.

Conclusions

The perspective presented by new regional information allows us to distinguish certain aspects of daily life during the Late Formative period in southern Jalisco. Within the Sayula basin, the settlement pattern recorded during the Usmajac phase suggests a social organization of clans, who may have been related and were spread around the lake. Each group, led by a cacique, was dedicated to exploiting its local environment in a relatively autonomous manner. Their livelihood was based on growing corn, beans, squash, and probably maguey from the hillside (wild or cultivated), but the population dedicated part of its time to activities related to salt extraction. The technology they employed and the organization of their work—as suggested by the evidence of this first phase—do not support the hypothesis of a centralized control of production, but rather suggest artisan-type activities possibly carried out by various members of a domestic unit. Specialization of labor and control of processes for extraction seem to have emerged toward the end of the phase, when shaft tombs were abandoned in the basin. The transition to the Verdía subphase clearly marks this new arrangement in the region.

The evidence obtained from the residential contexts of the Cerro del Agua Escondida site suggest a village life, centered around communal activity areas, which included rituals in an internal sacred space. The materials found at the site, above all the funerary paraphernalia, suggest the existence of various spheres of regional interaction. The presence of seashells, obsidian, and exotic greenstones reveals connections to groups established in the central regions with others farther south and east of Jalisco and Colima. Traces have not yet been found, however, of any extra-regional sociopolitical organization. In the Sayula region, there is no evidence found to date of the circular architecture that characterizes the Teuchitlán tradition in the neighboring Ameca and Magdalena basins. There is also no evidence of a decrease in the local population that would suggest a demographic implosion towards the nuclear Teuchitlán area as Weigand has posited for this period.[32] Whatever ideological inclinations may have existed are probably manifested in the organization of space and in the symbolic representations present in the cultural material. Furthermore, nothing of what

Fig. 14 Representative selection of Usmajac-phase pottery.

has been discovered in the iconographic sphere reveals any particular influence upon or from the Teuchitlán tradition. The problem may lie in the lack of information concerning the sphere of interaction between these areas. In Weigand's outlook, it is generally supposed that there should be centers with circular architecture that represent a macroregional sociopolitical order in all areas surrounding the nuclear zone of Teuchitlán. But this has not been demonstrated in the Sayula basin, and it may not actually be a necessary requirement even if we are to maintain the notion of a network of regional interaction. As a strategic resource, salt was undoubtedly important in the global economy of West Mexico. Nevertheless, we should bear in mind that we are dealing with a seasonal resource that is present during the dry season and is literally washed away with the first rain. At present, we do not know much about the ways in which salt was stored during the Usmajac phase, but we can assume from the lack of evidence that they were not very significant. We must remember that the Teuchitlán core area had no local salt sources. If salt seasonally appears and disappears in Sayula as "a gift from the gods," then we could infer that Teuchitlán's interaction in the basin fluctuated correspondingly. If this were the case, permanent administrative centers were not needed. During periods of production, the interested communities renewed their contacts and exchanged salt in the usual manner. On the other hand, we have not yet found any indication showing that during this period salt distribution was specifically directed toward the Teuchitlán region. Hypothetically, we might postulate that during the first centuries A.D. (in the Verdía subphase) a change occurred and, with it, a significant increase in production. Perhaps, from then on, a new collective system for storing the product was established. This change might thus have permitted a stable circulation throughout the year. Following our hypothetical reasoning, we might assume that there was an external influence that produced this change, and that it may have issued from Teuchitlán. What we do know is that by the sixth century A.D., when massive salt production began in the basin, during the Sayula phase, the height of the nuclear area in Teuchitlán seems to have begun its decline. The new architectural and ceramic styles that characterize this new stage

seem to be closer to those of the northern highlands of Jalisco and the neighboring Bajío.[33]

For several years, various authors have questioned the apparent lack of social complexity in western Mesoamerica and have proposed to change the "rural image" of the early populations of this region. In this regard, the work carried out by Weigand has established a solid basis in northwest-central Jalisco and in Nayarit. Nonetheless, the information recently obtained in Sayula does not always correspond with the guidelines of his proposed model. Social complexity has various faces and not all correspond, at a given moment, to the exact notion of a center and periphery at a macroregional level. Sociopolitical systems operate in ways that adjust themselves to the particular conditions of each group. Often, interaction does not lead to dominance, but rather to complementarity among entities that are considered equal. In spite of the fact that evidence of settlements during the Usmajac phase does not reveal a centralized social structure of a Teuchitlán type, there is nothing to keep us from assuming that the chieftainships in Sayula might have participated in an independent manner within the network of regional interaction prevailing during this period. A similar distribution of wealth among the different groups may be seen in the distribution of sites with equivalent shaft tombs in the central and southern part of the basin. Although this information may be incomplete, it suggests a society based on relations of equity among the different groups of the region. The absence of major architectural vestiges in the series of sites also tends to underscore this point.

The strategic importance of Sayula during the Late Formative period is documented by the number of sites found in the survey, although it is obvious that there should be many more. Although much remains to be discerned regarding this phase, detailed studies of residential contexts are beginning to bear their first fruit. Only from the evidence obtained from the various regions may we be able to confirm any hypotheses regarding the social development of the cultures of West Mexico.

PATRICIA RIEFF ANAWALT

THEY CAME TO TRADE EXQUISITE THINGS ANCIENT WEST MEXICAN–ECUADORIAN CONTACTS

The conquest of Mexico by Hernán Cortés took place between 1519 and 1521. In the years immediately following, the newly arrived Spanish overlords methodically searched for riches in the rugged terrain and diverse ethnic pockets of their recently acquired domains. Of particular interest to those conquerors were gold, silver, and other exploitable sources of quick wealth and lofty position. Thanks to the Spaniards' propensity for recordkeeping—the indigenous inhabitants of Mexico were the best documented of any of the newly discovered peoples in the Age of Exploration—the archives of Spain and Mexico are replete with accounts from New Spain of the ever-expanding Spanish presence. One of these early reports is particularly intriguing because of its reference to the existence of highly desirable trade goods hailing from faraway, unidentified lands.

In a letter to King Charles V dated December 15, 1525, the Spanish royal accountant Rodrigo de Albornoz, writing to His Majesty concerning the latest events in New Spain, reported the periodic appearance of distant traders who came to trade "exquisite things" for local goods in the port of Zacatula, located at the mouth of the Río Balsas in West Mexico (see fig. 2).[1] These merchants were said to have remained in the area for five or six months at a time, until good weather and calm seas permitted safe return to their homeland, located somewhere to the south. Who were these distant traders, what were the vaunted goods they brought, and what did they want in return? I think the visitors came from Manabí Province on the Ecuadorian coast, some 2,400 miles to

the south, and that they represent a long-standing tradition of seagoing coastal trade that reached far back into the history of West Mexico.

There is no question that at the time of the first Spanish contact there were short-range exchanges of goods throughout Mesoamerica.[2] Aztec imperial tribute tallies compiled in the indigenous pictographic script depict a variety of commodities, such as cacao beans, cotton, textiles, feathers, warrior costumes, gold, jade, and jaguar pelts, being traded throughout the area. Whether there was long-distance trade in West Mexico, however, is more difficult to determine because of the absence of a pre-Hispanic written record in that region and because little archaeological exploration has taken place along Mesoamerica's Pacific coast.

There is no geographic sphere in all of Mesoamerica whose archaeology is so distinct from that of its neighbors as the western sector of central Mexico. Several generations of scholars have reported on the distinct nature of much of West Mexico's material culture, including its shaft tombs,[3] mortuary offerings,[4] ceremonial architecture,[5] ceramic vessel forms,[6] and design motifs,[7] and on West Mexico's preeminence as the gateway for ancient Mexican metallurgy.[8] There has long been an interest in the idea that cultural interaction occurred between this area and Middle and South America in pre-Columbian times.[9] Parallels between cultural artifacts such as those mentioned here as well as in the distribution of two closely related species of jays and of the Mexican hairless dog suggest that economic ties existed between

Fig. 1 Marriage pair; Ixtlán del Río style; Nayarit; earthenware. Galerie Mermoz, Paris. Cat. no. 192. Splendidly attired in finery and holding emblems of rank, this marriage pair wears garments whose cut and geometric patterns suggest contact with peoples from northwestern South America.

233

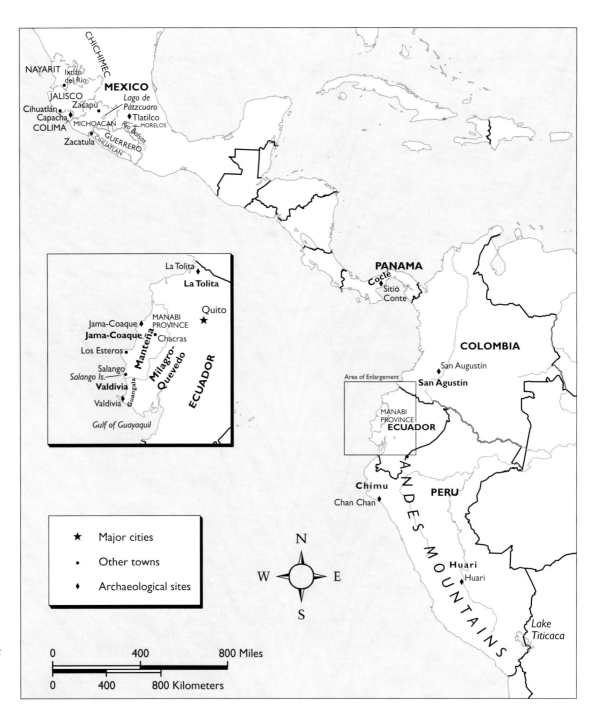

Fig. 2 Map of the Pacific Coast from West Mexico to Peru.

Ecuador and West Mexico for hundreds of years before Spanish contact.

I now can add similarities in clothing styles as further evidence for contact between ancient West Mexico and Ecuador. This new approach to the question of West Mexico's historical antecedents is based initially upon the study of an early colonial codex, the *Relación de Michoacán.* The illustrations in the manuscript demonstrate that at Spanish contact the apparel of the region was unlike that of any of the rest of Mesoamerica. By following the leads provided by these garments that deviate from the pre-

dominant Mesoamerican types, it is possible to gain further understanding of the West Mexican enigma.

Clothing Evidence
The best sources of information on Mesoamerica's conquest-period indigenous apparel are its codices. Using these pictorial documents, which contain the multiplicity of garment depictions necessary for comparative analysis, I have, over the course of several decades of research, accounted for almost all clothing styles worn by the various Mesoamerican peoples at the time of Spanish

contact.[10] At least by the Classic period (A.D. 250–900) and continuing until the Spanish conquest, the same simple, untailored garments were worn by virtually all levels of Mesoamerican society. A person's class and acquired status were displayed through the fiber or weave and degree of elaboration of his or her clothes. The fundamental costume for men included a loincloth, knotted in such a manner that the ends of the material hung down well below the groin, and a cape, a rectangular cloak tied over the shoulders (see fig. 3). The female equivalent of the obligatory loincloth was the wraparound skirt. Although in the tropical lowlands the skirt was sometimes worn topless, this was not the case in the highlands of Central Mexico, where women wore either a *huipil*, a blouse of varying length (see fig. 3), or a short cape and/or *quechquemitl*, a triangular shoulder shawl. In accordance with the culture area concept, which holds that a contiguous distribution of certain cultural traits exists throughout a defined geographic area, these basic clothing types might be assumed to have been worn throughout virtually all of pre-Hispanic Mesoamerica. But a completely different style of dress existed in the Tarascan kingdom of West Mexico, a region positioned well within the Mesoamerican culture area.

The Tarascans

Traditionally, the culture of the Tarascan Indians—more properly known as the Purépeche—is said to have come about in Early Postclassic times (A.D. 900–1250) from the amalgamation by force of the inhabitants of the Lake Pátzcuaro area of Michoacán with invading nomads from the north, Chichimecs who had founded Zacapu. The Tarascans of the Late Postclassic period (A.D. 1250–1519) were a remarkable people who built, from an obscure original settlement in Zacapu, a powerful empire that not even the formidable Aztecs could conquer. The Tarascans established successive capitals on the shores of Lake Pátzcuaro and spread out from there, eventually conquering much of the surrounding area in the modern state of Michoacán and beyond (see fig. 2). By the sixteenth century, the Tarascan kingdom had become a completely independent realm that controlled what can best be described as a rural empire, and its people were accomplished artisans, famous for their painted pottery, feather mosaics, and metalwork.[11]

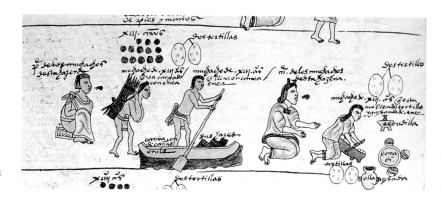

Because there are no pre-Hispanic pictorial records of any type for Michoacán, the primary source for indigenous Tarascan cultural history is the *Relación de Michoacán*. This colonial document, compiled by the Spanish historian and missionary Fray Gerónimo de Acalá between 1539 and 1541, describes the rites, ceremonies, government, laws, social and religious institutions, and imperialism that existed in the area before the arrival of the Spaniards. The *Relación de Michoacán* was probably written from the perspective of one particular lineage's claim to hold the chief power in the land;[12] despite this ruling-class emphasis, the document appears to provide an accurate picture of indigenous Tarascan life, as is confirmed by contemporary accounts that comment on the various cultural peculiarities of the region.[13]

Fig. 3 Detail from the *Codex Mendoza* illustrating typical Mesoamerican clothing; Aztec; c. 1525; *amate* paper. Bodleian Library, Oxford University.

Fig. 4 Detail from the *Relación de Michoacán* showing the unique male breeches worn by Tarascan males and a tunic-clad chieftain seated on a stool; Spanish colonial; 1539–41. Real Biblioteca de El Escorial, Madrid. Sitting on stools, a privilege restricted to the nobility, was a custom atypical of Mesoamerica but common to the Andean region.

Fig. 5 Detail from the *Relación de Michoacán* showing Tarascan males seated on stools and wearing checkered, tuniclike shirts; Spanish colonial; 1539–41. Real Biblioteca de El Escorial, Madrid.

Fig. 6 Detail from the *Relación de Michoacán* showing a high-status wedding; Spanish colonial; 1539–41. Real Biblioteca de El Escorial, Madrid. The female wears a short, tight skirt and a small *quechquemitl* around her neck.

Fig. 7 Detail from the *Relación de Michoacán* portraying the goddess Xaratanga wearing typical Tarascan female attire; Spanish colonial; 1539–41. Real Biblioteca de El Escorial, Madrid.

Tarascan Clothing Traits

One of the most notable aspects of Tarascan dress[14]—and one about which their enemies never tired of commenting—was the lack of a loincloth. Males covered their lower torsos with garments resembling short breeches and, rather than wearing capes, they wore sleeveless, tuniclike shirts, viewed by the scoffing Aztecs as women's *huipils.* These Tarascan shirts, many marked in squares that created checkered effects (see figs. 4 and 5), were such an oddity in Mesoamerica that they were repeatedly noted by both the sixteenth-century Aztecs[15] and Tlaxcalans[16] as well as by an eighteenth-century Spanish cleric, Fray Pablo Beaumont.[17] The clothing of Tarascan women, much of it striped or checked, was also atypical in relation to other Mesoamerican regions. The highlands of Michoacán are at elevations of seven to nine thousand feet, true *tierra fria,* where frosts are common from November to March. Despite the seasonal cold, females of the region not only wore unusually short, tight skirts, but often went about topless, either completely bare above the waist or wearing small *quechquemitls* that covered little more than the neck and one shoulder (see figs. 6 and 7). Beaumont illustrated two eighteenth-century Tarascan women wearing enveloping European-style blouses, each with an indigenous-style *quechquemitl* arranged over one shoulder—a testament to the tenaciousness of this pre-Hispanic dress mode. Tarascan attire was clearly not like that of other regions in pre-Hispanic Mesoamerica. From what source could this unusual clothing have derived?

Nearest Neighbor Search

Since the Tarascans of the *Relación de Michoacán* prided themselves on their Chichimec heritage, the apparel of those nomads of the northern Mexican deserts must be considered as a possible prototype for contact-period Tarascan clothing. Drawings in sixteenth-century pictorial manuscripts, however, show these particular forebears of the Late Postclassic Tarascans wearing loincloths and animal-skin capes, both tied in the Aztec manner.[18] This evidence favors the conclusion that Tarascan dress predated Chichimec arrival. Could these ancient Tarascan costume traits have diffused much earlier from the Chichimecs' more northerly neighbors?

To the north of the Chichimec deserts are the cultures of the American Southwest: Patayan, Hohokam, Mogollon, and Anasazi-Pueblo.[19] Before contact with the Spaniards, the descendants of the Anasazi-Pueblo tradition—the Hopi, Zuni, Keres, Tewa and Tanoan-speaking Indians—wore the kinds of cotton and deerskin clothing that are still worn today in their ancient dance dramas. Historically the men wore loincloths, belts, and simple shirts. These shirts, however, were unfitted tunics with partially sewn long sleeves, quite different from the shirts of ancient West Mexico. Women wore "dresses" made of a rectangle of cloth wrapped around the torso, fastened over the right shoulder, and sewn up the right side—attire that bears no resemblance to that of the tight-skirted, semitopless Tarascan women of Late Postclassic Michoacán.

Since no clothing prototypes can be found among the Mesoamerican, Chichimec, or Pueblan peoples, let us return to West Mexico to search its more distant past for analogues to the Tarascans' unique attire.

West Mexican Archaeological Evidence

Archaeologically, West Mexico—and the Tarascan area particularly—has been seen as lacking evidence of any longstanding, unifying cultural tradition.[20] Its costume record,

however, documents the same unique cultural elements appearing at least twice in a span of a millennium and a half. The garments worn by the Tarascans of the *Relación de Michoacán* are of the same style as those depicted on some ancient ceramic figurines found in the chambers of the remarkable shaft tombs of West Mexico, located to the northwest of Michoacán in an arc that extends through Colima, Jalisco, and Nayarit. The ceramics vary in style according to their region of origin; the pieces key to this study come from Ixtlán del Río, a highland site in the state of Nayarit.

The Ixtlán del Río figures, dated from associated shell material to 400 B.C.–A.D. 400,[21] range in height from thirty to ninety-four centimeters. These effigies, the facial features of which are greatly exaggerated, are unique among the entire complex of West Mexican shaft-tomb ceramics in two respects: they wear multiple rings around their earlobes[22] and distinctive clothing decorated with geometric polychrome motifs (see figs. 1 and 8).

The Ixtlán del Río females, created over a thousand years before the Tarascan empire developed in the mountains of nearby

Fig. 8 Couple with a child; Ixtlán del Río style; Nayarit; earthenware. Private collection. Cat. no. 194. The topless female wears a short, geometrically patterned skirt and displays elaborate body paint. The male wears a tuniclike shirt with chequered designs and breeches with an overhanging waist tab, possibly a real or symbolic genital protector.

Fig. 9 Female figure; Chacras, Manabí Province, Ecuador; Chorrera phase; earthenware. Collection of Mr. and Mrs. Presley Norton, Guayaquil. This figure wears a short, tight skirt and matching mini-mantle.

Fig. 10 Male figure; Chacras, Manabí Province, Ecuador; Chorrera phase; earthenware. Private collection. This figure wears a short shirt and breeches or body paint representing breeches.

Fig. 11 Figure wearing a short shirt and breeches; Chacras, Manabí Province, Ecuador; Chorrera phase; earthenware. Collection of Mr. and Mrs. Presley Norton, Guayaquil. The gender of this figure is ambiguous, although it is shown wearing "male" attire.

Fig. 12 Female figure; Chacras, Manabí Province, Ecuador; Chorrera phase; earthenware. Museo del Banco Central, Quito. Although this figurine is undoubtedly female, she is portrayed wearing "male"-style short breeches.

Michoacán, are all clad in similar tight, short, geometrically patterned skirts. Many of these garments have contiguous, decorated squares that collectively produce checkered effects. Some of the figurines also have matching cloth bands worn either under or over one shoulder. The Ixtlán del Río males wear, in place of the pan-Mesoamerican loincloth, Tarascan-style short breeches. In many of these sculptures, an oblong tab that may have served as a genital protector is seen hanging from the waist of these breeches. A large number of the male figurines are also depicted in short, tuniclike shirts, many of which have patterns of geometrically decorated squares.

Ecuadorian Archaeological Evidence

There is nothing in all of Mesoamerica similar to the West Mexican shaft tombs. Archaeological prototypes for this burial architecture do occur extensively, however, in Colombia and Ecuador, as well as in Peru, western Venezuela, and Pacific Panama. Although most of the South American tombs remain undated, a shaft tomb at San Agustín, Colombia, has a radiocarbon date of 545 B.C. (+/– 50 years), making it the oldest securely dated shaft tomb in the New World. In certain areas of Colombia and Ecuador, the use of shaft tombs for burials even in the present century has been reported.[23] In West Mexico, by contrast, shaft tombs were used during a single, discrete period from approximately 400 B.C. to A.D. 400. Obviously, this type of burial practice did not take hold in West

Mexico as early as it did in South America, suggesting that the trait originated in the south.

Ceramic Evidence

Aside from the Late Postclassic Tarascan apparel depicted in the *Relación de Michoacán,* there is nothing similar to the Ixtlán del Río attire in all of ancient Mesoamerica. It is only in the Ecuadorian coastal province of Manabí (see fig. 2) that there is evidence for this particular set of garments. At the Chorrera-phase site of Chacras (Early and Middle Formative periods, 1500–300 B.C.), hollow figurines have been found depicting females wearing tiny short skirts and mini-mantles (see fig. 9). Male figures from this site wear short shirts and breeches, although in the example depicted here (fig. 10), the "breeches" may also be interpreted as representing body paint. Another Chorrera-phase figure (fig. 11) from Chacras wears what appears to be male attire, although the figure itself has a feminine aspect. A fourth example (fig. 12) displays similar "male" attire, with tunic and breeches, yet the figure is clearly female. Thus, although the figures present some gender ambiguities, the types of garments depicted certainly show correspondences with those of Ixtlán del Río. The clothing of these figures is depicted by means of zone-punctation patterning— closely spaced indentations made in the wet clay before its firing—a ceramic technique also found in Colima at the cemetery site of Capacha, where Isabel Kelly found ceramics

with similar designs dating from 1450 B.C. According to Donald Lathrap,[24] the zone-punctation technique was developed in Ecuador during the Early Formative period (1500–900 B.C.); pottery sherds bearing this type of patterning have also been found dating from Ecuador's Valdivia 4–5 cultural phase (2000–1900 B.C.).

Capacha, which Kelly excavated in 1970–71, is an Early Formative site of simple burials clustered in small cemeteries, with no indication of shaft tombs, village sites, or trash heaps. The site did contain, however, a ceramic form that is a hallmark of pre-Hispanic South America: a stirrup-spout vessel, dating from 1450 B.C. (see fig. 14). In Mesoamerica, the distribution of stirrup spouts is both sparse and spotty—they have been found in the Valley of Mexico, at Tlatilco (see fig. 15) and in related sites in the state of Morelos, as well as at Chupícuaro, between Michoacán and Guanajuato—yet the Capacha stirrup vessels from Colima are clearly older than any others in Mexico.[25] In Ecuador, however, this distinctive type of vessel first appeared in the Machalilla phase (1500–1000 B.C.).[26]

Because Kelly's fieldwork in Capacha spanned almost forty years (1934–73), she was uniquely equipped to recognize an anomaly when she came upon one. The anomaly she found at Capacha was a class of objects apparently foreign to the familiar complex of cultural materials in that area— an indicator of connections with people from another part of the world. In a summary of

the Capacha phase (1870–1720 B.C.), Kelly said that it was neither typically Mesoamerican nor quite South American, although it did have perceptible ingredients—the stirrup-spout vessels and zone-punctation ceramic decoration, as well as certain artificial cranial deformities known as *tabla erecta*—that linked it to northwest South America. She had little doubt that there had been contact between Capacha and northwest South America during the Formative period, as early as 1500 B.C. Because no continuous distribution of ceramic elements similar to those found at Capacha extends through Central America, Kelly concluded that there had been sea trade along the Pacific Coast.[27]

Striking examples of West Mexican-Ecuadorian clothing similarities also come from Ecuador's Bahía-phase (500 B.C.– A.D. 100) coastal site of Los Esteros, in Manabí Province (see fig. 2). Large, hollow ceramic figures were found there that resemble those of Ixtlán del Río in their size, grotesque features, and clothing styles (see fig. 13). The haphazard excavation of these figures was as dramatic as the unusual figures themselves. On March 7, 1966, at the fishing village of Los Esteros, near the present-day town of Manta, there had been an unusually heavy surf that clawed great chunks out of the sandy shore. That evening, a little boy went down to the beach to survey the damage and was startled to notice several strange faces staring out at him from the dunes. Within hours of that first discovery, thousands of fishermen and their families began feverishly excavating the beach. Slowly a large ceremonial center was uncovered, although no human burials were

Fig. 13 Joined male-female pair; Los Esteros, Manabí Province, Ecuador; Bahía phase; earthenware. Denver Art Museum. The male wears a short shirt and curved pendant; the female, a geometrically patterned skirt.

Fig. 14 Drawing of a stirrup-spout vessel; Capacha, Colima; c. 1450 B.C.; earthenware.

Fig. 15 Drawing of a stirrup-spout vessel; Tlatilco; 1150/550 B.C.; earthenware. Museum of the American Indian, Heye Foundation, New York.

with large curved pendants worn over them (see fig. 13).[29] There is a well-developed tradition for such pendants in the neighboring archaeological area of Jama Coaque–La Tolita (A.D. 200–400), as seen in a figure of a seated chieftain (fig. 16). Such pendants also turn up in Panama at Sitio Conte and Coclé (A.D. 600–800). They may be made of boar tusks, whale teeth, whale ivory, or even greenstone, and are in many cases held in cast-gold settings (see fig. 17). There can be no doubt that they are emblems of high rank and status. Remarkably, a necklace featuring two similar curved, emblematic ornaments is worn by a hunchbacked figure from a Colima shaft tomb (fig. 18).

An Ecuadorian female figurine (fig. 19) from a later Manabí period, the Guangala-Manteña phase (A.D. 700–800), wears a mini-mantle and tight, short decorated skirt with geometric motifs nearly identical to those found on the West Mexican Ixtlán del Río female figures. Also, a fragment of cloth (fig. 20) from the subsequent Milagro-Quevedo culture (A.D. 400–Spanish conquest) is patterned with contiguous, decorated squares similar to the pattern on the skirt of the Guangala-Manteña-phase Ecuadorian female figurine. Thus it appears that a preference for clothing marked into such geometrically patterned grids continued on in Ecuador up to the time of European contact.

Ecuadorian–West Mexican Clothing Similarities

Garments decorated with squares are common in the long history of Andean weaving. Thanks to the ancient Peruvian practice of burying mummies in dry coastal sands, examples of checkered shirts have been found that date back from the contact-period Inca to the ancient Paracas culture (800–100 B.C.). The geometric motifs most analogous to the West Mexican ones discussed here are found on some Huari men's tunics (see fig. 21) from the south coast of Peru dating from around A.D. 500. But in none of the Andean high cultures was the male tunic or shirt found in association with short breeches; nor were female short skirts worn with mini-mantles. Depictions of these particular combinations of garments occur only on ceramics from coastal Ecuador, where the tropical climate rarely permitted survival of the textiles themselves.

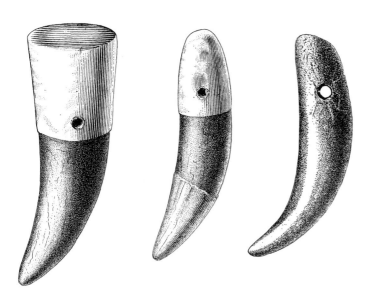

found. Within the span of a few weeks, the frenzied excavators had completely destroyed the site and most of its archaeological and artistic treasures. Although perhaps seventy-five of the large figures were discovered, very few survived the mass destruction.[28]

Some of the Los Esteros figures are adorned with multiple earrings, as are their slightly later West Mexican counterparts. The Los Esteros female figures are attired only in decorated skirts and necklaces; the male figures are attired in short shirts, in some cases

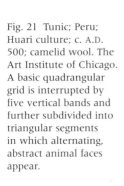

Within Mesoamerica the tradition of Ecuadorian-style clothing marked into geometric squares is known only in West Mexico, both at Ixtlán del Río (400 B.C.– A.D. 400) and, over a thousand years later, among the sixteenth-century Tarascans. Similar garment types do not occur in any other Mesoamerican culture of any period. That these distinctive styles occurred earlier in South America and were dominant in the Andean cultures suggests that the attire originated there and was subsequently introduced into West Mexico. Either the same attire, once introduced, persisted in West Mexico throughout this period, or repeated Ecuadorian contacts served to periodically reintroduce this same type of apparel. While archaeological evidence for the continuity of these clothing styles in ancient West Mexico has yet to be discovered, a number of other striking parallels confirm the idea that repeated contacts occurred.

Metallurgical Evidence

Dorothy Hosler, who has documented similarities between West Mexican and northern

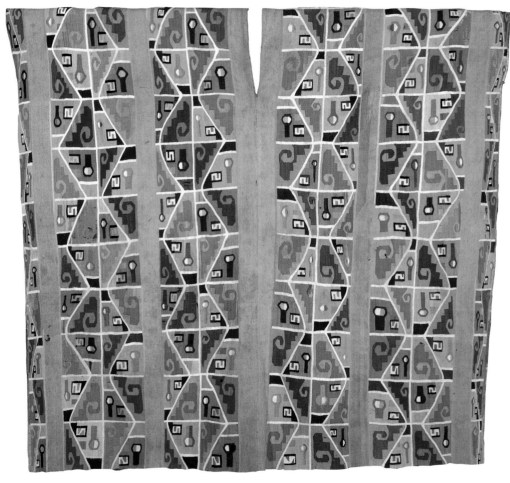

South American metallurgical techniques, including formulas for alloying copper and arsenic, fabrication methods, and artifact types, believes that metallurgical technologies were introduced into West Mexico from Ecuador.[30] She notes:

> Metalworkers who recognized the ore minerals of silver, arsenic, and probably tin, and who knew how to process these ores, must have been physically present in [West Mexico]. The smelting technologies are sufficiently complex that personal contact [would have been] essential to communicate information about extractive metallurgy as well as about processing and manufacturing techniques.[31]

Hosler does not believe raw materials were traded; examination of the isotopic signatures of metal artifacts from the two countries indicates that they were made from different ores.

The metallurgy introduced into West Mexico had been developed over a long period in Ecuador. The earliest evidence for Ecuadorian metalworking has been found at the Chorrera-phase coastal site of Salango (1500–500 B.C.) in Manabí Province. The first objects fashioned by these metalsmiths were status markers—rings, nose rings, and bells—of copper, silver, and gold. By the subsequent Regional Development period (500 B.C.–A.D. 800), the distinctive metallurgy of southern Ecuador had developed further, and Ecuadorian metalsmiths had added tools to their repertoire: crafting tweezers, needles, fishhooks, and awls, made of copper. They also began to experiment with the two alloys, copper-arsenic and copper-silver, that became fundamental to the metallurgy of the region.

The Ecuadorians also crafted axe monies, items that served as standards of value and mediums of exchange (see fig. 22). Technical study of Ecuadorian axe monies has shown that they were consistently made from a low-arsenic copper-arsenic. These axe monies had an intrinsic social and symbolic worth deriving from their axelike shape, and may have served as repositories for copper-arsenic metal, from which the large majority of Ecuadorian copper-based metal objects were made. The lack of iconographic features on the axe monies, bells, and rings suggests that they were fashioned for exchange.

Although the West Mexican metalwork-

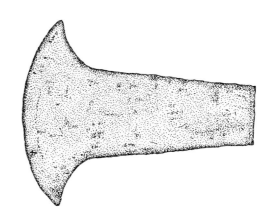

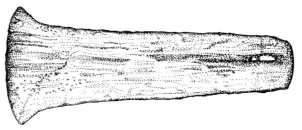

Fig. 22 Axe-monies; Ecuador (a) and Guerrero (b); copper-arsenic alloys. Axe-shaped monies were common in southern Ecuador and appeared in West Mexico after A.D. 1200. They may have been crafted for exchange.

ing zone varied topographically and culturally, the element that distinguishes it as a whole is its copper-based metallurgy. The West Mexican metalsmiths did not replicate the full array of Ecuadorian objects and techniques, incorporating only selected elements. But for a variety of object classes, West Mexican and Ecuadorian artifact types, fabrication methods, and materials are nearly identical. Among these are small portable pieces fashioned by cold-hammered work: bells, sewing needles, fishhooks, awls, depilatory tweezers, and open rings. The similarities between these artifacts suggest contact between West Mexico and Ecuador around A.D. 600/700 and again around A.D. 1200/1300.

Of particular note among the artifact styles that Hosler believes were introduced from Ecuador are the large, open metal rings she suggests may have been used as hairbands, a further indication that the West Mexicans were adopting foreign items of apparel. The *Relación de Michoacán* depicts another Ecuador-related artifact, a Tarascan priest's large, imposing pectoral fashioned in the shape of ornamental, emblematic golden tweezers (see fig. 23). The prototype for this unmistakable Tarascan design originated in northwestern South America (see also fig. 24).

In reviewing the Ecuadorian metallurgic similarities, Hosler concluded that, given the difficulties that the mountainous jungle separating West Mexico and South America

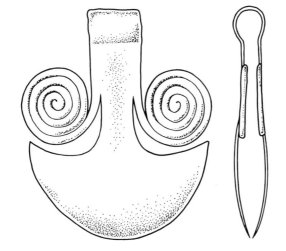

Fig. 23 Detail from the *Relación de Michoacán* depicting a Tarascan priest clad in a checkered, tuniclike shirt and wearing a large pair of golden tweezers around his neck; Spanish colonial; 1539–41. Real Biblioteca de El Escorial, Madrid.

Fig. 24 Drawings of a Tarascan tweezers (front and side views); Michoacán; A.D. 1200/1300; metal alloy. In Tarascan West Mexico, tweezers were items of priestly regalia. This design has Colombian and coastal Ecuadorian and Peruvian prototypes.

would have posed for traders and travelers, all of the cultural exchanges must have been by sea.

Faunal Evidence

There is further evidence for long-distance maritime contact in the widely separated distribution of two faunal examples: a bird and a dog. The painted jay *(Cyanocorax dickeyi)* is a brightly hued blue bird (see fig. 25) inhabiting a tiny range (193 by 32 km) in a mountainous region that covers parts of the states of Nayarit, Sinaloa, and Durango. The painted jay appears nowhere else in North or Central America, but its taxonomically closest relative, the white-tailed jay *(Cyanocorax mysticalis)* is known only in the coastal regions of Ecuador and northern Peru.[32] These two bird populations are separated by a distance of four thousand kilometers, one of the most unusual bird distributions in the Western Hemisphere. A feasible explanation for this anomaly is that the bird was imported via sea trade. Indeed, the biologist Paul D. Haemig has suggested that the painted jay was directly introduced into West Mexico from the Andean region by "ancient man."[33]

Noting that the Mesoamericans used the hairless dogs for food, Alana Cordy-Collins has speculated that the Ecuadorians took these exotic creatures along home with them to vary their diet en route and also, subsequently, to enjoy as pets.[34] The earliest evidence of the hairless dog in Peru is from the north coast, in a depiction on a Moche pot dating from about A.D. 750. In Peru the hairless dogs were, and still are, confined to the coast.

Donald Lathrap, however, interprets the diffusion of the Mexican hairless dog differently. Drawing on evidence from the Ecuadorian Formative period (3000–300 B.C.), he maintains that this dog originally was intentionally bred in Ecuador as a food-producing animal, "its low, massive body having the same relationship to the contours of a normal dog as our own Angus steer had to the configuration of wild cattle."[35] Lathrap pointed to depictions of these dogs on Chorrera-phase pottery dating from before 500 B.C. (see fig. 26), suggesting a long history of attention to the food potential of this oldest of domesticated animals. (The Chorrera-phase ceramic dog depicted here is not hairless, yet it is of the same breed. Both hairless and "normal" puppies may be born

in the same litter, the hairless strain inheriting the determining gene from one parent.) Lathrap argued that the breed first appeared in Ecuador and from there spread to northern Peru and West Mexico. If so, it would be the Ecuadorian canine who was ancestor to dogs represented by the whole range of dog effigies found in the shaft tombs of Colima. Inasmuch as no continuous distribution of hairless dogs extends through Central America, contacts by sea are indicated.

Navigational Evidence

That the Indian traders of the Ecuadorian coast had the navigational skills and oceangoing crafts capable of long-distance trade extending as far north as West Mexico is well documented. More than fifty years ago, the Ecuadorian scholar Jacinto Jijón y Caamaño suggested that these navigators, whom he identified as the Manteña and Huancavilca, were organized into a "league of merchants" on the Manabí coast—specifically in the region of Calangone, where present-day Salango is located—that served as the cultural nucleus of the area. Jijón y Caamaño based his assessment of pre-Hispanic Ecuadorian maritime trade on descriptions of Ecuadorian coastal vessels by sixteenth-century writers.[36]

More recent work provides information on the construction of those seagoing crafts. Clinton R. Edwards has suggested that although prehistoric Ecuadorian coastal people used a variety of boats and rafts for fishing and trading voyages, the most advanced were centerboard sailing rafts, built in the coastal regions from balsa trees (*Ochroma* ssp.), which are native to the humid, tropical forests of Ecuador.[37] Balsa wood has notable benefits: it is lighter and more navigable than cork, has a diameter of up to seventy-five centimeters, and grows straight, with few branches, to heights of forty to fifty meters. Further, green balsa logs retain their buoyancy for more than two years.[38] The large Ecuadorian trading vessels (see fig. 28) had hulls that were twenty-five to thirty meters in length, were made up of as many as thirty balsa logs, and were steered with multiple centerboards in the bow and stern. The triangular sails could point high enough to allow tacking against adverse winds or currents. Study of the pattern of Pacific currents shows that these sailing rafts would have been capable of making the voyage north to Mexico, either nonstop across the open sea or in stages along the coast.

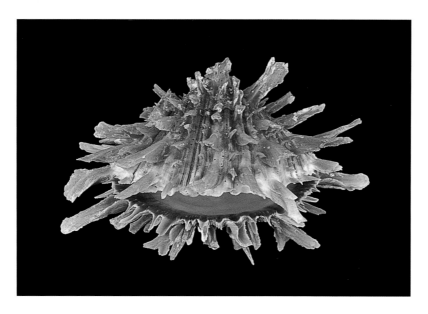

Fig. 27 The thorny oyster, *Spondylus princeps,* is a large, spiny, tropical bivalve, its exterior and lips scarlet, its interior cavity the color of white porcelain. These mollusks, found in warm waters clinging to reefs twenty to sixty feet below the ocean's surface, were very important in the Andean religious system and were the principal trading stock of Ecuadorian merchants with the ancient high cultures of Peru.

The Ecuadorian Merchants

The early colonial reports of maritime commerce that Jijón y Caamaño scrutinized were those collected by the sixteenth-century Spanish historian Gonzalo Fernandez de Oviedo y Valdes,[39] who recorded tales of New World exploration, and Juan de Samanos,[40] who was secretary to Charles V from 1516 to 1556. These two accounts describe the experience of Bartolomé Ruiz, navigator on Francisco Pizarro's initial 1525 voyage along the northwestern coast of South America. In the course of the exploration, the Spaniards encountered a large balsa sailing raft belonging to local merchants plying the Ecuadorian littoral to exchange worked luxury goods for raw shells. These shells were almost certainly the thorny oyster, *Spondylus princeps,* which was prized by the high cultures of the Andes (see fig. 27). The sixteenth-century Spanish described *Spondylus* shells as "reddish sea-

shells comparable in exchange value to gold, silver, fineware ceramics and fine textiles."[41] This mollusk was a principal item in the active Ecuadorian trade with the Andean high cultures. The resulting interaction apparently led to the transfer to the coastal merchants of certain Peruvian clothing styles, design motifs, and techniques of textile production.

The conquistadors with Pizarro visited the Ecuadorian traders' confederation of commercial villages and described the well-worked luxury goods they saw there, including in their descriptions details about the merchants' cloth and clothing. Fiber garments were reported to have been produced from llamas and alpacas. The Ecuadorians were said to have kept "sheep" (llamas and alpacas) that were sheared once a year, producing fiber that was dyed various colors, including red, blue, and yellow. These yarns were woven into textiles decorated with figures of trees, birds, fish, and animals. Among the garments mentioned were women's skirts and capes worn under the shoulder as well as men's breeches in diverse colors and embroidered wool shirts.

The *Spondylus* Trade

What would have prompted the prosperous Ecuadorian merchants to sail as far north as West Mexico to exchange their luxury goods? These traders may have needed to augment their most lucrative stock, *Spondylus* shells. There is evidence that from as early as the third millennium B.C. to the arrival of the Spanish in A.D. 1525, the people of the south coast of Ecuador were exporting *Spondylus* in

Fig. 28 Colonial-period illustration of a balsa raft sailing past a Spanish galleon near the mouth of the Bay of Guayaquil in Ecuador. Museo Naval, Madrid.

large quantities. From 2800 to 1100 B.C., these shells were traded only as far as the Ecuadorian sierra; from 1100 to 100 B.C., the trading area expanded south and *Spondylus* became entrenched in the high cultures of the Central Andes; and from 100 B.C. to A.D. 1532, the total trading system reached at least from Quito to Lake Titicaca, between Peru and Bolivia (see fig. 2). The trade routes between Ecuador and Peru ran along the Andean spine, with secondary pathways branching down the river valleys. In exchange for the massive amounts of *Spondylus* exported from the Manabí coast, the merchants received obsidian and also copper, which is not native to the Ecuadorian littoral.

The Andean cultures' increasingly insatiable obsession with the bright crimson *Spondylus* shells was particularly strong in the later, large expansionist states of the Central Andes. Among the Chimú of the kingdom of Chimor (A.D. 1000), *Spondylus* dust was regularly scattered in the pathway where the ruler was to walk, a literal rolling-out of the red carpet by a courtier who was known as the "Preparer of the Way".[42] At the Chimú capital of Chan Chan, all royal burials were accompanied by tremendous offerings of the shell: whole, cut into pieces, or pulverized into dust. The people of the subsequent Inca period (A.D. 1438–1534) regarded *Spondylus* as the favorite food of the gods and used it either whole, carved, ground up, or cut into pieces, offering it at springs to bring abundant rainfall to newly planted crops.

Clearly, the Ecuadorian traders' principal markets were the high Andean cultures where *Spondylus* served as a profoundly sacred and necessary religious commodity, an essential part of the sacramental system. But because *Spondylus* cannot survive in the cold, upwelling current off the Peruvian coast, it was acquired from the Ecuadorian traders, who regularly collected these valuable shells from their own warmer waters. There are depictions in Chimú art of diving platforms from which experienced Ecuadorian divers, cords about their waists, diving stones (weights) in hand, prepare to plunge some twenty to sixty feet below the ocean's surface to collect the valuable shells. The Andeans' ritual use of *Spondylus* apparently created a demand not always fully met from the Ecuadorian coast; as a result, the seagoing traders sailed north.

The Ecuadorians' Broad Reach: West Mexico

Spondylus grows in the warm waters of the Pacific Ocean in discontinuous pockets from the Gulf of Guayaquil, in Ecuador, to the Gulf of California. West Mexico provided a reliable supply of the mollusk, as depictions of these shells on a tribute tally from Cihuatlán, the Aztec empire's Pacific province, attest (see fig. 29). Spectacular *Spondylus*-shell jewelry carved with symbolic designs have been found in West Mexican shaft tombs, illustrating the extraordinarily high esteem in which this valued material was held (see figs. 30–34). As Hosler has pointed out, most of the West Mexican sites where metalworking is first in evidence lie along the coastal plain or have riverine access to it, precisely where *Spondylus* would have been gathered.[43] It is highly likely that, in exchange for these shells, the Mexicans received some of the visitors' colorful, exotic garments—"exquisite things" indeed.

Fig. 29 Tribute tally from the *Codex Mendoza*; Aztec; c. 1525; *amate* paper. Bodleian Library, Oxford University. This tally, which represents payment from the Pacific-coast imperial province of Cihuatlán to the Aztec empire, includes representations of the spiny scarlet-colored *Spondylus princeps*.

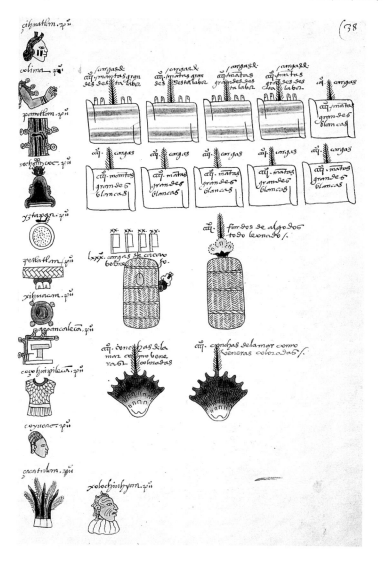

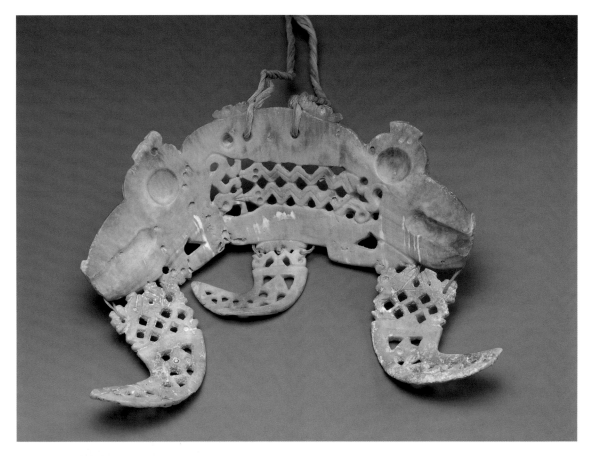

Fig. 30 Pendant in the form of a mythic double-headed creature with serpentine motifs; Colima; *Spondylus* shell. Collection of Anthony Patano, Oak Lawn, Ill. Cat. no. 8. This piece was reportedly found as a set with figures 31–35. The motif of a double-headed creature with serpentine attributes is found in South and Central Mexico and throughout Meso-america and is variously associated with rainbows, the sky, and the related forces of regeneration and fertility. As emblems of authority and status, these adornments would testify to the religious functions of a chieftain and identify him as such in the eyes of the ancestors.

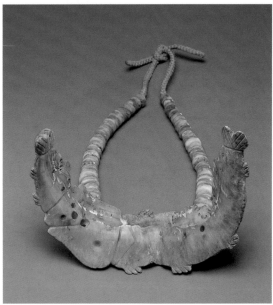

Fig. 31 Bead necklace and pendant in the form of a large fish eating a small fish; Colima; *Spondylus* shell. Collection of Anthony Patano, Oak Lawn, Ill. Cat. no. 7.

Because the ancient Mesoamericans lacked domesticated animals, all of their cloth had to be made from such bast-producing plants as yucca, palm, maguey, and, also, cotton. While yarns made from such plants can be finely spun and woven, dyes take better and last longer on wool. My guess is that the imported Ecuadorian textiles woven from llama and alpaca fibers were far more alluring than the locally woven fabrics made from plants and, hence, more apt to be copied. A cottage industry appears to have developed in which local textile fibers were used to create garments in imitation of the more desirable Ecuadorian ones, resulting in the clothing styles that endured until the time of Spanish contact.

Summer trade winds along the Pacific coast of northwest South America and Central America easily could carry a sailing vessel to the west coast of Mexico. As late as the 1930s, skilled Ecuadorian weavers of Panama hats would bundle up their merchandise, put together a balsa raft, sail north to Panama, sell the hats, sell the balsa logs, and hitch a ride back home on the next southbound steamer to start up the whole lucrative enterprise all over again. Given the seasonal variability of the trade winds, the ancient Ecuadorians would have needed to remain in West Mexico for long periods. These repeated, extended episodes of contact would have greatly increased the likelihood of the West Mexicans' adopting foreign ceramic and metalworking technologies, shaft tombs with attendant mortuary offerings, and Ecuadorian styles of dress.

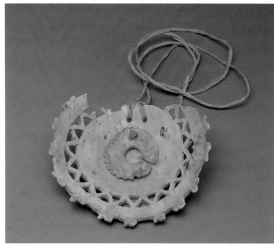

Fig. 32 Ceremonial earspools (above) and earspool attachments (below); Colima; *Spondylus* shell. Collection of Anthony Patano, Oak Lawn, Ill. Cat. nos. 4 and 5.

Fig. 33 Circular pendant with a serpentine motif (necklace); Colima; *Spondylus* shell. Collection of Anthony Patano, Oak Lawn, Ill. Cat. no. 9.

Fig. 34 Seated figure; Colima; *Spondylus* shell. Collection of Anthony Patano, Oak Lawn, Ill. Cat. no. 6.

Fig. 35 Necklace; Colima; greenstone. Collection of Anthony Patano, Oak Lawn, Ill. Cat. no. 3. Various kinds of greenstones as well as jade were considered precious in ancient West Mexico and were imported into the region from Michoacán, Guerrero, and areas further south. This necklace was probably part of a set of adornments that included several pieces of *Spondylus*-shell jewelry (see figs. 30–34).

Time and regular visits would have been needed for all of these influences to be transferred. I suspect that biological evidence in support of the idea of such ancient and prolonged contacts might result from a comparison of genetic codes between West Mexico's Tarascans and coastal Manabí's Ecuadorians based on that most indelible and lingering of life's fingerprints, DNA.

JOSEPH B. MOUNTJOY

THE EVOLUTION OF COMPLEX SOCIETIES IN WEST MEXICO: A COMPARATIVE PERSPECTIVE

Prologue

Even among archaeologists who work in the region, the definition of precisely what constitutes West Mexico remains unclear. Nevertheless, a combination of historical, geographical, and cultural features, none of which is entirely adequate on its own, can help us fix our focus on the indigenous cultures that developed in the area that today comprises the modern Mexican states of Colima, Jalisco, Nayarit, Michoacán, and Sinaloa, along with portions of Guanajuato, Zacatecas, and Durango. This region of West Mexico has been proposed as the place of origin of the Aztecs, as well as of their ancestors the Toltecs. Although West Mexico has sometimes been characterized by what it lacks—for example, stone sculpture such as the Olmec produced or cities comparable to those of the Maya—it is an area notable for the widespread expansion of certain cultures that have been identified through archaeological research and given various names such as the Capacha tradition, the shaft-and-chamber-tomb tradition, the Chalchihuites tradition, and the Teuchitlán tradition. These cultures have been defined most particularly by the distinctive types of mortuary vessels and figurines they produced and by their tomb and temple architecture.

The longest river system in Mexico, the Lerma-Santiago, originates just west of Mexico City and more or less bisects West Mexico into northern and southern halves. These two areas have some marked topographical and ecological distinctiveness. Much of northern West Mexico is composed of interior highland basins on its eastern side, rugged mountainous terrain in the central part, and piedmont and coastal plain on the west. The rivers that originate in the highland basins cut deep gorges through the mountains and deposit fertile alluvium in strips through the flat coastal plain and in deltas where the rivers empty into the Pacific Ocean. Southern West Mexico has generally less rugged mountains and intermontane valleys, and a narrower coastal plain.

The large size and great geographical diversity of West Mexico has had little or no positive correlation with archaeological research attention. More archaeological activity takes place during a single year at a single site in the Maya region—for example, at Copán in Honduras or Tikal in Guatemala—than sometimes occurs in all of West Mexico. Large areas of West Mexico have never been systematically studied for archaeological remains, and, in some of the areas that have been investigated, only a small percentage of the archaeological sites have been officially registered. If we compare it with an area of similar geographical size, such as the state of Arizona, which, like West Mexico, covers approximately 300,000 square kilometers, we will observe that while there are some 50,000 archaeological sites that have been officially documented in Arizona, only 2,880 sites have been comparably recorded with the National Institute of Anthropology and History for five of the states that comprise the heartland of West Mexico.[1]

By another measure of comparison, it has been noted that there are fewer than 400 radiocarbon dates available for excavated deposits in all of West Mexico, while over

Fig. 1 Female figure; El Opeño, Michoacán; earthenware. Stokes Family Collection, Upper Nyack, N.Y. Cat. no. 157. Among the earliest works found in West Mexico, figurines such as this one have been associated with the furthermost reaches of the Olmec world.

100 exist for archaeological deposits in the relatively small area that encompasses the Mexican states of Tlaxcala and Puebla, and around 50 are available for excavated deposits at the Central Mexican site of Teotihuacan alone.[2]

Nonetheless, as the preceding essays in this volume have made clear, there is much that can be said of the archaeological record of ancient West Mexico and the artifacts that have been uncovered there. In this essay, I want to describe the evolution of indigenous culture in West Mexico through five pre-Hispanic periods, the names of which are commonly applied to cultural developments in the rest of Mesoamerica: Paleo-Indian, Archaic, Early and Middle Formative, Late Formative, and Classic. This review will cover a broad expanse of years leading up to the archaeological period known as the Postclassic—an era dating from about A.D. 900 that is especially associated in the Central Mexican highlands with the Toltecs and their successors the Aztecs, and that ended with the Spanish conquest. To place these developments into a wider perspective, I will make some comparisons between what happened in West Mexico and similar cultural developments in other regions.

Paleo-Indian (prior to 7000 B.C.) and Archaic (7000–2000 B.C.) Periods

Archaeologists do not know for sure when humans first entered North and South America, although it is certain that people following a hunting-and-gathering way of life were spread throughout both continents by 7000 B.C., and they seem to have been present in many areas of the New World at least 2,000 to 3,000 years prior to that date. The West Mexican region, however, has produced extremely sparse and widely scattered remains that can be attributed to the Paleo-Indian period. In fact, much of the region appears to have been uninhabited. One exception is the complex of shallow lakes in the central highlands of Jalisco, the geographical and ecological conditions of which most closely resemble those of the highland basins of Central Mexico, where Paleo-Indians are known to have camped and hunted between 9000 and 7000 B.C., and may have done so as early as 20,000 B.C.[3]

During the Archaic period in North and South America, people gained an increasingly intimate knowledge of how to live off the land in an adaptive system that emphasized food gathering. In some areas this shift appears to have been prompted by the severe decline in the population—if not extinction—of large game animals that had been hunted in the Paleo-Indian period. In order to survive by gathering plant food, it was necessary for people to develop a systematic and reliable means of doing so. One tactic for achieving a more intensive and effective exploitation of plant and animal resources was to establish a system of base camps, from which seasonally abundant resources could be exploited, and to which bands of food collectors could return year after year.

Eventually, the cultivation of plants became a primary factor in the ability of people to settle permanently in one location. Because of the close relationship that exists between a settled village life based on plant cultivation and the development of pottery, the appearance of pottery is often taken to signify the end of the Archaic and the beginning of the Formative (or Preclassic) period. The great majority of available information regarding the Archaic period in Mesoamerica has come from the Central Mexican highlands, especially from the Tehuacán valley of southeastern Puebla.[4] In West Mexico by comparison, there is, again, a curious scarcity of Archaic remains, and those that have been found are often quite late in the period.[5] Some possibly Archaic tools have been found on the surface of settlement sites in the Magdalena basin area of central highland Jalisco, but their assignment to the Archaic is based either on the lack of pottery that can be associated with these finds or on formal similarities to Archaic tools found outside West Mexico. One intensive survey of archaeological sites in the Manatlán area of south-central highland Jalisco had the expressed goal of locating Archaic sites that might provide data on the domestication of corn that would be comparable to what has been found in the Tehuacán valley of Central Mexico: this survey, however, failed to find a single site that yielded securely identifiable Archaic remains.

The situation is about the same for the West Mexican coast, some areas of which—in Jalisco, Nayarit, and Sinaloa—have been subjected to intensive site survey and substantial excavation without a single site or artifact being discovered that is attributable to the Archaic period. This is the case, for example, with the southern half of the Banderas valley on the north coast of Jalisco, where in recent years I have recorded 107 sites and conducted 90 excavations without finding any Archaic material.[6] The same results held in the Tomatlán valley on the central coast of Jalisco, where 165 sites were recorded and 9 excavations were conducted.[7] Finally, in the area of San Blas, Nayarit, only one of 47 sites studied produced Archaic remains.[8] This general scarcity of Archaic remains in West Mexico is especially striking when compared to the abundance of such sites in other areas of the North American continent, as, for example, the southeastern U.S. where some 17% of sites have Archaic remains. A good part of the reason for the scarcity of Archaic remains in West Mexico may be ecological. In West Mexico there is a relative scarcity of such natural plant resources as the vast nut-producing woodlands of the southeastern U.S. that sustained large populations of deer and humans in the Archaic period, although in some areas of the West Mexican highlands the seed of the ramon tree would seem to have been a possible substitute. The rivers of the West Mexican highlands and coast were also without the abundant resources of fish and shellfish that were available to Archaic peoples in large areas of the southeastern U.S. Along the West Mexican coast itself there appear to have been few areas rich enough in shellfish to have supported human groups heavily dependent on them for their survival—this appears true even though some coastal Archaic sites in West Mexico may have disappeared due to coastal subsidence or erosion. In areas of the Central Mexican highlands like the Tehuacán valley where the Archaic adaptation was successful, a great deal may be owed not only to the kind of wild foods available and the seasonal scheduling of their utilization, but also to the incipient cultivation of some plants such as maize and squash.

Early (2000–1300 B.C.) and Middle (1300–300 B.C.) Formative Periods

It is doubtful whether the relatively egalitarian, small village, food-producing and pottery-using way of life that is characteristic of the pre-Olmec Early Formative period (2000–1300 B.C.) in southeastern Mexico extended into West Mexico. Instead, it appears much more likely that the expansion of village farmers into West Mexico was contemporary with the development of Olmec culture, beginning about 1300 B.C. on the southeastern border of West Mexico, and spreading at least as far as Nayarit by around 800 B.C.[9] This expansion of a food-producing way of life into West Mexico seems to have taken two routes. The more northerly one of these was along the Lerma-Santiago corridor to Jalisco and southern Nayarit; the other proceeded along the southern flank of the Central Mexican Volcanic Axis, westward through the Balsas river drainage and up the Tepacaltepec river drainage into the uplands of Colima and southern Jalisco, and ultimately up the coast into central Nayarit. The expansion along the northern route is evidenced by the archaeological culture called El Opeño, known primarily from a cemetery site in western Michoacán near the border of Jalisco.[10] The southern route has been connected with the archaeological culture called Capacha, identified with a cluster of cemetery sites in central Colima.[11]

The archaeological remains found at El Opeño consist of mortuary offerings deposited in tombs arranged in parallel rows running north-south along the flank of a volcanic hill. The tombs are found over four meters under the ground and are reached by a descending stairway. This form of tomb construction has been suggested as a possible antecedent to the shaft-and-chamber tombs that later became so abundant in some areas of West Mexico. No definite link between the two forms, however, has yet been established. Six radiocarbon dates from recently excavated tombs at El Opeño have central dates that range from 1214 B.C. to 891 B.C. and average 1049 B.C. (± 121 years).[12]

Offerings recovered from the El Opeño tombs include a number of items that appear related to the heartland of the Olmec archaeological culture situated far to the southeast. These include attenuated female figurines of fine white clay, displaying Olmec-like cranial deformation in a local expression that falls within the range of substyles found in the reaches of the Olmec world (see fig. 1). Also possibly Olmec-related are stone carvings of a turtle shell and a ritual scepter incised with the crossed-band motif, as well as a group of sixteen figurines that depict a ballgame with players and spectators (see Day, fig. 3), and one miniature ballgame yoke of stone.[13] Other items that point to ties with the Olmec are items of jade, presumably from the Motagua valley area of Guatemala, the only proven source of jade in Mesoamerica, and conch shells of Caribbean origin that probably entered Mesoamerica from the same area of Guatemala during the Formative period.

The mortuary pottery vessels from El Opeño are rather simple jars and bowls—some with incised motifs similar to those commonly found at Olmec sites—though other forms that might be expected are notably lacking in these mortuary finds. Phil C. Weigand has also found hints of the further expansion of El Opeño culture northwestward in some zone-decorated mortuary pottery unearthed in the central highlands of Jalisco near Etzatlán, and my own research has yielded an El Opeño–like style of solid pottery figurines in the area of Talpa in the central highlands of Jalisco, in the Banderas valley of coastal Jalisco, and in the central coastal area of Nayarit at San Blas. These solid figurines of humans are sometimes associated with other hollow sculptures of humans, as well as figurines of dogs and vivid polychrome pottery, all of which appear related to the shaft-and-chamber-tomb mortuary practices that were to develop later in Jalisco and Nayarit. But the spread of these Formative-period people must have progressed very slowly, for the El Opeño–like figurines of Jalisco and Nayarit are dated at around 300 B.C., about 700 years after those at El Opeño itself.

Although direct evidence of their subsistence is scanty, it is presumed that these people relied on farming small-scale gardens. The addition of cultivated plants such as corn, beans, and squash to their basic diet is also believed to have allowed a settled village way of life to spread into West Mexico. Some of the slowness of the expansion may have been due to the heavy labor involved in clearing areas of virgin vegetation before people could settle there and raise crops.

The southern route of expansion of part-time hunters and gatherers as well as garden farmers into West Mexico is known primarily from mortuary pottery deposited with human burials in subsoil pits in the central hilly interior of Colima, and northward into the uplands of southern Jalisco. From the four radiocarbon dates available for material related to the Capacha people of Colima, a range of 1200 B.C. to 800 B.C.—roughly con-temporary with El Opeño—seems most likely. About half of the Capacha mortuary pottery is of gourd form, often bilobed or trilobed designs resembling the *bules* that farmers in West Mexico still grow into artificially cinctured shapes that make them handy as portable water containers (see figs. 2 and 3). There are also Capacha jars and bowls, some of the neckless jars known as *tecomates*, but no bottles. There is one unusual form of mortuary pottery called a "trifid," which consists of two superimposed jar bodies connected with three tubes; perhaps such objects may symbolize the joining of the worlds of the living and the dead. Decoration is often with a sunburst motif that resembles the Olmec crossed band.

From Colima, Capacha-related people appear to have moved up the coast of Jalisco and into Nayarit, settling in the coastal river valleys where they could plant their crops and still be well situated to take maximum advantage of the local plant and animal resources. In the San Blas area of central coastal Nayarit, especially, seacoast resources were extremely important.[14] Like the more northerly El Opeño expansion, this coastal expansion also took a long while: Capacha-related deposits in the Banderas valley—midway between Jalisco and the Nayarit coast—have been dated in the range of about 570 B.C. to 300 B.C., and in the San Blas area from 890 B.C. to 335 B.C.

In comparative terms, it took the settled village agricultural way of life some 3,500 years (6000 B.C. to 2500 B.C.) to spread across the continent of Europe from east to west, a distance of about 2,400 kilometers, or about 1.4 km per year.[15] If the settled village farming way of life spread westward out of a Central Mexican highland area such as Morelos beginning about 1300 B.C. and progressed at the same rate, we would expect it to reach the central coast of Nayarit about 535 years later, or around 765 B.C. In fact, it appears to have taken about 400 years at least for Capacha influence to spread from the mouth of the Balsas river to the central coast of Nayarit, a distance of 600 km, or a rate of 1.5 km per year, a rate comparable to the spread of the Neolithic in Europe.

Late Formative Period (300 B.C. to A.D. 300)

In the heartland of Mesoamerica, the period from 300 B.C. to A.D. 300 witnessed the transition from a system of large villages and ceremonial centers, sometimes referred to as temple towns—such as is suggested by the great circular pyramid at Cuicuilco (see fig. 13)—to one of densely populated cities and city states, often accompanied by the development of systems of writing and complex calendrical calculations for ritual purposes as well. Prominent cities that developed during this period include Teotihuacan in the Central Mexican highlands, Monte Albán in Oaxaca, and El Mirador in Guatemala. Meanwhile, in West Mexico, as we have seen, some of the most prominent archaeological remains relate to a mortuary tradition called the shaft-and-chamber-tomb complex. The remains of this complex are found especially in a large arc extending at least from central Colima up through the central highlands of Jalisco and on into the mountain passes of southern Zacatecas and down through the southern highlands of Nayarit to the piedmont overlooking the Pacific coast.[16] While there is evidence to suggest that the distribution of such tombs extended to the Michoacán/Guerrero border on the south, and as far north as the piedmont of southern Sinaloa, not all areas of West Mexico had such tombs. For example, they seem to be lacking in a large area of south-central and coastal Jalisco where the Tuxcacuesco tradition flourished, as well as in the Guanajuato/Michoacán area where the Chupícuaro tradition was prevalent at this time (see figs. 4 and 5).

The several varieties of the form and construction of these shaft-and-chamber tombs have already been described by Robert Pickering and Teresa Cabrero and others in this volume. What is important to note here is that the remains of the deceased—whether single or multiple, cremated or not—are occasionally accompanied by dozens of clay pots that appear to have held offerings of food and drink, as well as hollow and/or solid pottery figurines. There may also be trumpets of conch shells from the Caribbean, mirrors of obsidian, or iron pyrites set in mosaic fashion, and an abundance of shell jewelry (see figs. 10 and 11). The earliest radiocarbon date for this type of tomb is in the range of 290 B.C. to A.D. 50. In some areas, however, such tombs may have been in use throughout the Classic period (A.D. 300 to A.D. 900) and possibly even into the early part of the Postclassic. Other forms of burial,

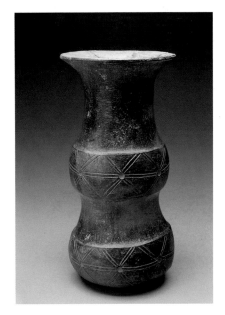 

such as interment in pottery urns or subsoil pits, were often used contemporaneously with the shaft-and-chamber-tomb burial.

Tombs of shaft-and-chamber form have also been found in Central America, mainly in Costa Rica, and in the Andean area, particularly Colombia. Some investigators have discussed the possibility that these tombs might somehow be historically related to those found in West Mexico.[17] The earliest South American shaft-and-chamber tombs seem to be those associated with the Primavera phase of the San Augustín culture in the Colombian highlands, dated within the first 300 years B.C., approximately contemporary with the earliest ones in West Mexico.[18]

The hollow figurines, human and animal, found in many of the shaft-and-chamber tombs, have been the primary defining archaeological trait of West Mexico since archaeology began there about a hundred years ago. These objects have been subjected to scholarly examinations from an art historical point of view and from an anthropological/ethnographical perspective, but, unfortunately, only rarely have they been looked at carefully from an archaeological perspective because most of them are without scientific context, having been removed from tombs by looters. Mortuary pots and figurines in the form of animals and humans are common grave offerings in many areas of North and South America, especially in the southeastern U.S. and the Andean area. Some of this mortuary art, especially that of coastal Peru, appears related to specific cultural

Fig. 2 Vessel in the form of gourds; Capacha, Colima; earthenware. Mint Museum of Art, Charlotte, N.C., gift of Dr. and Mrs. Francis Robicsek. Cat. no. 19. Ceramic vessels imitating the shapes of constricted gourds or superimposed gourd forms are among the oldest in Mesoamerica.

Fig. 3 Compound vessel; San Pablo, Morelos; 1200/500 B.C.; earthenware. The Saint Louis Art Museum. Cat. no. 1.

practices such as shamanistic curing rituals, and the enactment of ritual warfare.[19] Scholars have also long identified some West Mexican human figurines as shamans engaged in rituals such as guarding the tombs from evil spirits (see fig. 12; see also the essay by Peter Furst in this volume).[20] Ethnographically, some Huichol Indian shamans of present-day West Mexico are considered to be "singing shamans" whose rituals are designed to procure rainfall; other Huichols fulfill the role of "curing shamans." Both activities may be portrayed in the mortuary figurines, some of which are shown playing rasps, drums, and rattles. Other human figurines are shown whistling, blowing, or sucking—all common New World shamanistic practices. As a point of comparison, the Mochica of the north coast of Peru made pottery figurines of shamans who are shown carrying bundles that contained their curative medicines and other paraphernalia. Some of the plants and animals depicted in shaft-tomb pottery may likewise represent materials used by shamans for their presumed curative properties.

Among the other themes depicted in pottery is that of an "original couple," who were initiators of the human line or founders of a particular lineage.[21] Paired male and female mortuary figurines from West Mexican shaft-and-chamber tombs are quite common. It is also noteworthy that many of the West Mexican female figurines appear to represent different stages of pregnancy or maternity, a theme with strong antecedents in Olmec figurines of Morelos. Some other West Mexican figurines may have more directly to do with funerary rituals: these would include representations of bodies tied to litters, on which, perhaps, they were lowered down the shaft and into the tomb, and of females mourning for the deceased. A strong case has also been made for interpreting some mortuary pots as representing or symbolizing the baskets or similar containers stuffed with actual fruits and vegetables that were deposited with the deceased (see the essay by Otto Schöndube in this volume). Similarly, on the north coast of Peru, mortuary vessels representing stacked containers of peanuts and other foods offered in Mochica rituals have been found in graves.[22]

On the other hand, there was apparently a good deal of sub-regional variation in West Mexico in what local cultures chose to portray in their figurines and pots (see figs. 6–9). In addition, there may have been cultural variations in the utilization of the tombs themselves: for individual interments; for the interment during the dry season of the prepared remains of the community's or lineage's deceased; as family crypts; or for the burials of chieftains accompanied by sacrificed retainers.

In some areas of West Mexico, notably the Etzatlán-Magdalena lake basin area of central highland Jalisco and the adjacent foothills of the Volcán de Tequila, many ceremonial centers with cruciform and/or circular architecture have been found. At the Huitzilapa center, a shaft-and-chamber tomb that dates to the first century A.D. has been found associated with architecture of a cruciform pattern (see the essays by Lorenza López and Jorge Ramos and by Pickering and Cabrero in this volume). The circular architectural constructions of what has been called the Teuchitlán tradition, as has already been discussed by Weigand and others, have been radiocarbon-dated to the second century A.D., and may have developed from the cruciform pattern, lasting perhaps throughout the Classic period. The circular pattern com-

Fig. 4 Standing female figure with geometric designs; Chupícuaro, Michoacán/Guanajuato; earthenware. Fowler Museum of Cultural History, University of California, Los Angeles. Cat. no. 170. By Late Formative times, large hollow figures were being made in Chupícuaro and throughout West Mexico. Older customs and techniques in the manufacture of small solid figurines nevertheless persisted, often developing into coexisting but distinctive substyles.

Fig. 5 Standing female figure with geometric designs; Chupícuaro, Michoacán/Guanajuato; earthenware. Private collection. Cat. no. 169.

monly involves the construction of eight platforms around a central circular mound, with an intervening plaza between the platforms and the central mound (see Weigand and Beekman, fig. 17b). Ballcourts are also often found associated with these circular constructions (see the essay by Jane Day as well). This circular pattern is found in many of the same areas where shaft-and-chamber tombs are also located. In many other cases, however, one is found without the other. The significance of this variation is undoubtedly important, and, although a prevalent

view is that the circles evolved into more complex forms as the shaft-tombs diminished in importance after about A.D. 250, the matter has yet to be fully understood.

The Classic Period (A.D. 300 to 900)

The period from A.D. 300 to 900 witnessed some notable developments in West Mexico, several of which may have been related to the growing power and reach of the metropolitan center of Teotihuacan, at least until that state collapsed sometime around A.D. 600 (see fig. 14). Evidence of Teotihuacan-related penetration into West Mexico can be seen at at least five ceremonial centers in

Fig. 10 Conch shell; Colima. Fowler Museum of Cultural History, University of California, Los Angeles. Cat. no. 15.

Fig. 11 Mirror; Jalisco; obsidian. Natural History Museum of Los Angeles County. Cat. no. 115.

Michoacán, one of which is at Tingambato, about thirty-five kilometers west of the town of Pátzcuaro.[23] This center contains a six-tiered temple pyramid, adjacent to which is a large plaza with an altar in the center constructed in the *talud-tablero* style often associated with Teotihuacan, as well as a large ballcourt. Under the floor of a platform on the east side of the plaza was found a communal tomb of corbeled arch construction containing at least thirty-two human burials accompanied with funerary offerings: among these were pseudo-cloisonné-decorated pottery similar to Teotihuacan stuccoed and painted ceramics and pottery figurines—possibly warriors—with a strong Teotihuacan resemblance.[24]

The Classic-period ceremonial centers in Michoacán seem like little islands of

Teotihuacan-related materials that are surrounded by different, local traditions. It is not clear whether they represent interaction with Teotihuacan at its apogee, or with groups that migrated out of the basin of Mexico following the collapse of Teotihuacan after A.D. 600, taking refuge in an area geographically opposite that from which came the bellicose neighbors who were instrumental in the downfall of Teotihuacan.

Some 200 kilometers to the northwest of Tingambato there are two ceremonial centers on the northwestern fringe of Guadalajara, El Ixtepete and El Grillo, that also have *talud-tablero* construction, pseudo-cloisonné-decorated pottery, and pottery figurines resembling those of Teotihuacan. The excavator of the temple platform with the *talud-tablero* construction at El Ixtepete found it was painted white, and he suggested that this color symbolized its location on the western fringe of Teotihuacan expansion.[25] Teotihuacan-related materials have also been found at many sites in southeastern Michoacán and in the lower Balsas river drainage on the Michoacán-Guerrero border, and recently Teotihuacan-related *talud-tablero* architecture and pottery have been unearthed at the large La Campaña ceremonial center in central Colima.[26]

Another important development that may also be somehow ultimately related to Teotihuacan expansion was the appearance of a highly developed archaeological culture in Zacatecas, an area initially populated by village farmers during the latter part of the Late Formative period. The most prominent Zacatecas site of the Classic period was La Quemada. Located southwest of the city of Zacatecas, the La Quemada site includes ceremonial constructions, habitation terraces, and huge retention walls that literally cover a small mountain, giving it the appearance of a fortified center (see figs. 15–17). That the site may have some link to Teotihuacan is evident in pottery figurines similar to those made at Teotihuacan in the period A.D. 200–450, as well as some general technological decorative similarities between the La Quemada ritual pottery and Teotihuacan wares.[27]

Among the other more notable features at the La Quemada site is a large ballcourt with a stone-faced pyramid at one end, a huge hall of columns, numerous architectural complexes of plazas and altars, and ample evidence of human sacrifice along with the public display of the victims' bones. Another striking features of the site is the system of raised roads (similar to the raised Maya roads called *sacbes*) that extend from La Quemada to outlying villages.

Farther to the northwest in Zacatecas is a site that has been interpreted as a frontier outpost ceremonial center of an advanced local archaeological culture called the Chalchihuites. This site, called Alta Vista (see Witmore, figs. 14–16), besides yielding possibly Teotihuacan-related pottery, contains a ceremonial center with a number of features that seem precedents for the later Toltec culture in the Central Mexican highlands, including: (1) a hall of columns like that found at La Quemada, although much smaller, in which the number of columns appears to be related to a solar calendar, as well as a labyrinthine construction built for observing solstice and zenith sun positions; (2) a temple platform that at one time had large human statues of clay on the top, and the burial of a priest/ruler within the platform; (3) human remains indicating human sacrifice and the use of a rack to display skulls; and (4) a wall built around the center that resembles the serpent walls found at the Toltec capital of Tula and the Aztec capital of Tenochtitlan.[28]

Some of these Toltec-related features at Alta Vista have also been found at the site of Cerro del Huistle, Jalisco, roughly midway between Alta Vista and La Quemada.[29] There seems to be some link between the Chalchihuites culture and the Classic-period developments in the area of La Quemada, but the nature of the relationship and its extent have been hotly debated by archaeologists working in these respective areas.[30]

The Teuchitlán Tradition of Ancient West Mexico

Archaeologists and anthropologists have been arguing for a long time about what characteristics define cities, states, and civilizations, and how these characteristics may be evidenced in archaeological remains.[31] For example, the disagreement over whether the Olmec were a "civilization" and/or a society at the "state level" or at the "chiefdom level" has been debated by scholars for the past thirty years.[32] In a similar fashion, the Teuchitlán tradition —one of the focal points of this book and its accompanying exhibition—has long been recognized as one of the more advanced and complex of West Mexican developments. Phil Weigand has proposed that the Teuchitlán tradition developed to its fullest architectural complexity and geographical extension during the Classic period.[33] He has also proposed that by the time of the Middle Classic period the Teuchitlán tradition was evolving into a unique West Mexican civilization that clearly displayed certain aspects of urbanization and statehood. It is not clear if there existed some relation between the Teuchitlán tradition and the growth, expansion, and decline of Teotihuacan, but given the importance of the control of major sources of high-quality obsidian to expansionist Mesoamerican states, the desire to control the huge obsidian resources at the western end of the Lerma-Santiago corridor would logically seem to have been a strong incentive for some kind of intervention by the Teotihuacanos, or at least by intermediaries closely linked to them.

Fig. 12 Standing male figure with a patterned shirt and conical hat; Ixtlán del Río style; Nayarit; earthenware. Los Angeles County Museum of Art, The Proctor Stafford Collection, museum purchase with funds provided by Mr. and Mrs. Allan C. Balch. Cat. no. 190.

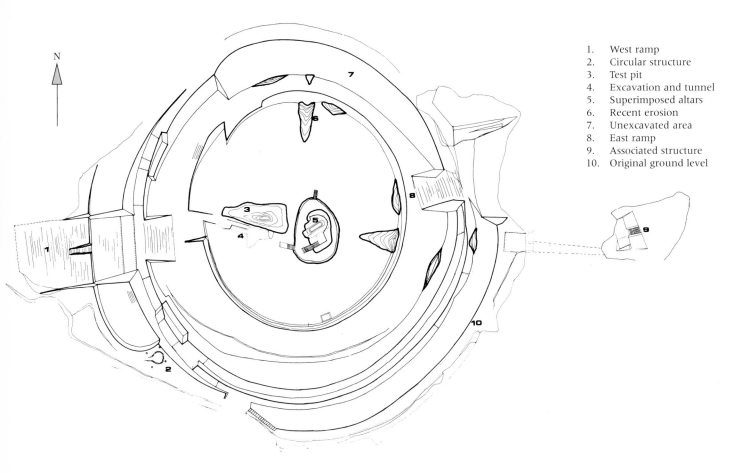

1. West ramp
2. Circular structure
3. Test pit
4. Excavation and tunnel
5. Superimposed altars
6. Recent erosion
7. Unexcavated area
8. East ramp
9. Associated structure
10. Original ground level

Fig. 13 Plan of the Cuicuilco pyramid. The largest structure of a community of 40,000 inhabitants, this circular monument was oriented on an east-west axis and was surmounted by a dual altar, one of which was dedicated to the Old Fire God. Similar characteristics appear in West Mexican ceremonial architecture between 100 B.C. and A.D. 700.

Weigand has also described the Teuchitlán tradition in terms of eight characteristics that he believes show its evolutionary advancement toward civilization. These hallmarks include: (1) architectural monumentality in both volume and complexity, including the development of a regional hierarchy of sites according to ceremonial construction and population density; (2) agricultural intensification with terraces, canals, and *chinampa* farming plots; (3) organization and alteration of the landscape on a grand scale, including border fortifications; (4) increased population density and nucleation marked by demographic implosion; (5) craft specialization, especially in pottery; (6) specialized resource exploitation, especially in salt and obsidian; (7) an expansionist economy with long-distance commerce; and (8) a codexlike glyphic system of ideographic writing present on some ceremonial pottery of pseudo-cloisonné type.[34]

Although I am not likely to resolve the debate over these issues in this essay, the matter of the relative degree of advancement of the Teuchitlán tradition merits some consideration from a comparative perspective. The discussion below treats Weigand's criteria point-by-point.

Fig. 14 Great Plaza at Teotihuacan. The vast space of Teotihuacan is organized on a regimented gridlike plan with strongly defined hierarchical scale, providing a setting for centralized rule.

(1) **Architectural monumentality** in volume and complexity is associated with many early civilizations, but it also seems to be characteristic of numerous advanced Neolithic societies that are considered to be complex chiefdoms, for example, the Anasazi of the southwestern U.S., some Late Formative–period societies of the Maya in Mesoamerica; and various Megalithic societies of Neolithic and Bronze Age Europe.

The Teuchitlán architectural tradition is also intriguingly similar in volume and complexity to the archaeological societies that developed in the southeastern U.S., for example, the Poverty Point tradition that

began about 2200 B.C. in the Late Archaic period and lasted into the Early Woodland period up to about 500 B.C. Both Teuchitlán and Poverty Point have very distinctive and unusual architectural patterns at their main ceremonial/habitation centers.

The main site at Poverty Point, Louisiana, covers about nine hectares and consists of six concentric habitation ridges arranged in an arc of five segments that is open-ended toward the rising sun, plus four ceremonial mounds (see figs. 18 and 19). The largest of the ceremonial mounds is an oval 207 meters on a side and 23 meters high, built of approximately 200,000 cubic meters of earth.[35] By comparison, the extended ceremonial/ habitation center of Teuchitlán covers approximately twenty-five hectares and the largest ceremonial mound there measures 18.5 meters on a side and rises 12.1 meters in height. The volume of this mound construction and associated plaza and mounds is 42,447 cubic meters, and the total volume for all the ceremonial constructions at the Teuchitlán center is just under 75,000 cubic meters of earth and rock.[36]

In both traditions there are a similar number of secondary centers that are many times smaller than the primary ones, and that repeat somewhat the basic architectural pattern of the main centers. The Poverty Point tradition extended throughout the lower Mississippi Valley, from New Orleans to the southern tip of Illinois, a distance of 800 kilometers. The north-south extension of the Teuchitlán tradition is approximately 375 km from central Colima to southwestern Zacatecas. The average east-west width of the Poverty Point tradition is about 235 km, about the same as that of Teuchitlán.

There are also some important dissimilarities between the two traditions, such as a more advanced pottery craft, more highly developed agricultural base, and well-defined social stratification in the Teuchitlán tradition. Recent evidence indicates that Poverty Point was constructed by a predominantly hunting-and-gathering people. Much of what the Poverty Point tradition lacks in comparison to Teuchitlán eventually develops in the southeastern U.S. at least by the time of the Mississippian tradition, at such regional centers as Moundville in Alabama and Etowah in Georgia, centers believed by southeastern archaeologists to have been organized and run as hereditary chiefdoms.[37]

In the case of Moundville, which flourished between A.D. 1200 and 1350, an argument has been made, based on excavated burials and ethnohistorical records, that the twenty-one mounds surrounding the plaza at that ceremonial center were associated with specific corporate subclans, ranked in status in descending order from north to south (see fig. 20). Furthermore, there is an alternation of small and large mounds along the sides of the plaza; the small ones contain high-status burials and the larger ones appear to have been residential substructures, indicating a pattern of noble residences each associated with an ancestral mortuary temple. Such mounds are paired with their mirror-image counterparts on the opposite side of the plaza and are oriented along the line of the winter solstice.[38] This situation is intriguingly similar to the alternating size of platforms in the Teuchitlán circles and to Kristi Butterwick's argument presented in this book that the mounds that ring the central mound in the Teuchitlán tradition were related to lineage-based ceremonial feasting. It also accords well with Christopher Witmore's analysis of the ways in which the circular architectural pattern of the Teuchitlán tradition may relate to solar observations and the use of this pattern as a diagrammatic calendrical structure.

Another important aspect of architectural monumentality and complexity at a great number of the ceremonial centers of the Teuchitlán tradition is the presence of one or more ballcourts—the size and number of which may be related to the rank of importance of individual centers in the regional hierarchy. As Jane Day has discussed in her essay in this volume, pre-Hispanic ballcourts were numerous and widespread, with a long history in Mesoamerica. They were also fairly common in many other areas of North, Middle, and South America. Over 200 ballcourts of the Hohokam tradition, for example, have been located in southern and central Arizona; on average they appear to have larger playing fields than those of the Teuchitlán tradition or La Quemada/ Chalchihuites tradition.[39]

One possible interpretation of the Hohokam ballcourts is that the games played there functioned to integrate the communities of the Hohokam regional system. But a different interpretation has been offered for Mesoamerican ballcourts: that is, that they were

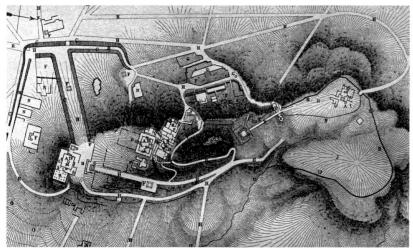

Fig. 15 Ballcourt at La Quemada, Zacatecas.

Fig. 16 Grand stairway at La Quemada, Zacatecas.

Fig. 17 Plan of La Quemada, Zacatecas. Approached via a wide processional way, this commanding acropolis contains ritual enclosures, residential compounds, and other religious and administrative monuments arranged upon a sacred mountain.

most common in regional systems that lacked strong, centralized political control; thus they functioned as stages on which rivalries could be played out in a ritualized manner in chiefdom-type societies where those in authority lacked the coercive power that characterizes more complex societies.[40]

Kristian Kristiansen has postulated that a major difference between complex chiefdoms and archaic states was the way they organized labor for large-scale public works projects—in this case, ceremonial mounds and ballcourts. The complex chiefdoms did so through social obligations and ritual feasting, while the archaic states accomplished the same end through land ownership that allowed them formalized control of constituent communities.[41] Kristiansen's description of the "complex chiefdom" model seems appropriate for the Teuchitlán tradition.

(2) **Agricultural intensification,** especially on a grand scale, is a general char-

acteristic of early civilizations, and in the areas under consideration in ancient West Mexico, there is extensive terracing of hill slopes associated with the Teuchitlán ceremonial centers and what appear to be house mounds, as well as canals and large tracts of *chinampa,* lake-bed agriculture in the Magdalena basin area. The key question that remains to be answered through field research is how much of this apparent agricultural intensification can be dated contemporary with the Classic-period florescence in the valley, as opposed to the later, Postclassic development.

(3) If the terraces, canals, and *chinampa*-like lake-bed farm plots all date to the Teuchitlán tradition, they, along with the great number of circular ceremonial complexes with ballcourts and the construction of sites at strategic points along natural routes of communication, would certainly indicate a rather large scale of **organization and alteration of the landscape.** However, more field data are needed to assess the idea that certain sites were border fortifications rather than, for example, terrestrial ports of trade.

(4) Nearly fifty years ago, V. Gordon Childe suggested a benchmark of at least 7,000 inhabitants for the first cities of the Old World.[42] **High population density and nucleation,** sometimes along with a demographic decline in the hinterland, can be shown to be associated with the development of some early New World urban centers such as Teotihuacan and Monte Albán in Central Mexico.

There seems little doubt that during the Classic period the highland Jalisco lake basins —the core area of the Teuchitlán tradition— supported a dense population in comparison with many other areas of West Mexico. It is virtually impossible, however, to determine the actual population figures from surface-surveyed archaeological remains in the absence of extensive excavations. This is because what is usually desired is knowledge of how many people were living in a given area at the same time. This requires precise enough archaeological data to be able to determine that a given number of mounds or domestic structures in the various archaeological sites were all occupied at the same time, and that they supported houses in which a specific number of people lived.

In this regard it is instructive that recent excavations in several areas of the city of

Teotihuacan conducted after the population estimates made by the large long-term Teotihuacan Mapping Project have shown how the surface-survey data of that Mapping Project have led to erroneous chronological placement of some ruins, casting doubt on the accuracy of the population estimates made for the various periods of that city's growth.[43] Clearly, accuracy in population estimates is considerably increased through the controls afforded by the kinds of extensive excavations presently lacking in Teuchitlán sites.

(5) **Extensive craft specialization** is sometimes found associated with advanced Neolithic societies, for example at Catal Huyuk in Turkey.[44] Craft specialization associated with early civilizations is generally characterized as large-scale and carried out by full-time artisans controlled by a state-level organization, as was clearly the case with Teotihuacan in Mexico, Pharaonic Egypt, and the Shang dynasty in China. The pottery specialization of the Teuchitlán tradition is impressive in artistic quality and diversity but it seems to resemble more in scale and effort certain advanced Neolithic societies such as the Anasazi or Mimbres of the southwestern U.S. And one thing that seems to be lacking is mass-produced mold-made pottery like that turned out by the Chimú civilization of the Peruvian north coast.

Craft specialization in other, non-perishable items, notably obsidian and shell, is well developed, but seems to be similar to the level of craftsmanship in stone and shell achieved by New World Neolithic-level societies such as the Hohokam of the southwestern U.S. and the Hopewell of the southeastern U.S.—aside from the Hopewell's excellent craftsmanship in copper and silver, which is without counterpart in the Teuchitlán tradition.

(6) **Specialized resource exploitation** by ancient societies, apart from edibles, dates back to the acquisition of special kinds of stone in the Old World Paleolithic, although it certainly increases in scale up into early civilizations. For the Teuchitlán tradition the focus is on salt and obsidian, principally the latter. There are many sources of high-quality obsidian in the Teuchitlán area, and some large obsidian workshops are near the Classic-period ceremonial centers. It seems logical that the exploitation of this resource might have been instrumental in the expan-

sion of the Teuchitlán tradition, but so far the analysis of obsidian artifacts from sites peripheral to the Teuchitlán core—both north and south—has not supported the idea that the Teuchitlán core was a major supplier of Classic-period obsidian.[45] In addition, as noted in the essay by Francisco Valdez in this volume, Teuchitlán circular ceremonial complexes have not as yet been found in extensive surveys of the nearby Sayula basin in south-central Jalisco, an area known to have had a huge salt-production industry during the Classic period.

(7) Evidence of specialized resource exploitation is also vital for understanding the extent of **long-distance commerce** and the possible expansionist nature of the economy, as contrasted to a model of expansionist religion or ideology. Some Teuchitlán burial offerings were acquired from far distant sources. The acquisition of rare resources like copper and mica from remote sites for ceremonial items or burial offerings is notable in other Neolithic-level, chiefdom-type New World societies like the Hopewell or Poverty Point. For example, the Teuchitlán tradition acquired conch shells and jade from the Guatemala-Caribbean area 1,700 kilometers distant, and Poverty Point in Louisiana acquired exotic cherts for spearpoints from Tennessee and Oklahoma, and red jasper for jewelry, the nearest source for which is 1,200 km distant in west Texas.

(8) A well-developed system of writing is a hallmark of many early Old World civilizations such as the Sumerian and Egyptian, although it is not a hallmark of some New World civilizations such as the Teotihuacan and Inca. The presence of a **codexlike glyphic system of ideographic writing** on ceremonial pottery associated with the Teuchitlán tradition is an intriguing argument put forth by Weigand.[46] But Weigand himself is not sure whether these codexlike motifs were introduced through contact with a more advanced and more literate society or were indigenous West Mexican developments. The relationship of this pottery to the Teotihuacan/central highland civilization has been mentioned above, and its iconography is most suggestive of ties with the Metepec phase (A.D. 600–750) at Teotihuacan. Yet, because the primary examples Weigand cites are from a large collection of pots looted in 1898, their exact relation to Teuchitlán remains unclear.

Fig. 18 Aerial view of Poverty Point, Louisiana.

Fig. 19 Plan of Poverty Point, Louisiana. Around 2000 B.C. Poverty Point was probably the largest civic and ceremonial center in the North American hemisphere. Six concentric semi-circular platforms face east across the Bayou river; a major pyramid and other platforms are located to the west.

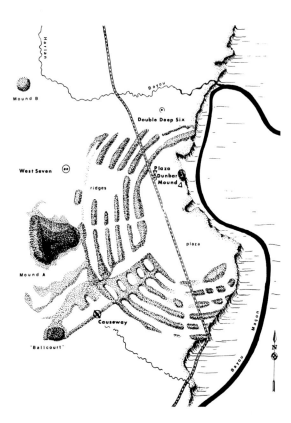

On the other hand, I think it is probable that designs placed on all West Mexican pre-Hispanic pottery had a symbolic content intended to convey meaning to the people and to their gods, just as the Huichol Indians encode symbolic meaning into the designs they weave and embroider into their textiles. In a way, these examples, as well as West Mexican pre-Hispanic petroglyph and pictograph designs, could all be considered rudimentary ideographs with mnemonic functions that approach those of writing.

Conclusion

Apart from the above discussion of the comparative degree of advancement of the Teuchitlán tradition in accordance with the characteristics proposed by Weigand, there are a few others often attributed to early civilizations that merit consideration here. For example, there is no monumental stone carving associated with the Teuchitlán tradition. Nor is there clear evidence of the indigenous development of a tradition of metal-working associated with Teuchitlán, although some early copper items, especially bells, appear to have been traded into West Mexico during the Classic period and occasionally ended up as offerings in shaft-tomb and other burials.[47]

The Teuchitlán tradition does appear to involve a group of relatively elite people with greatly disproportionate access to certain resources, though the mechanism through which they attained their status is not yet clear. Thus, it seems impossible to demonstrate with available data that the Teuchitlán tradition had a state level of sociopolitical organization in the sense of its having been an autonomous political unit with a centralized government consisting of a ruling class or a governing bureaucracy having the power to collect taxes, draft people for public works and warfare, and decree and enforce laws.[48] Nor can it be demonstrated that the people of the Teuchitlán tradition conducted organized warfare with standing or ad hoc drafted armies, although one function of border sites may have been for defense, and at least ritualized combat and the taking of captives on a small scale appear to be documented in some shaft-tomb figurines (see Townsend, figs. 8 and 9).

A recent analysis of the rise of Zapotec civilization in Oaxaca suggests that "states arise when one member of a group of chiefdoms begins to take over its neighbors, eventually turning them into subject provinces of a much larger polity."[49] Large-scale human sacrifice and public display of the victims' remains—such as are found in the La Quemada/Chalchihuites tradition—might be taken as evidence of such domination, but any such evidence is lacking in the Teuchitlán tradition. Ben Nelson has used the evidence of human sacrifice to make the case that La Quemada was the major center of a "coercive chiefdom," rather than a state, and he has contrasted that type of chiefdom to the "collaborative" type he believes characterizes the Anasazi society of Chaco Canyon in the Southwest U.S.[50] The Teuchitlán tradition might fit somewhere in between the two, especially if the ballgame played at the ceremonial centers was a force that worked for sociopolitical integration by ritualizing (and thereby defusing) conflicts.

Timothy Earle has defined a chiefdom as "a polity that organizes centrally a regional population in the thousands and is characterized by some degree of heritable social ranking and economic stratification."[51] Of the various kinds of chiefdoms discussed by Earle, the description that I think best fits the Teuchitlán tradition is: complex in scale, wealth-based in finance, and individualizing. Such a chiefdom is characterized as having polity sizes in the tens of thousands, two levels of political hierarchy above the local community, and an emergent stratification. Such chiefdoms procure items of symbolic value, often through long-distance exchange, which are used to define the elites' social position and economic prerogatives. And they emphasize the distinguishing of elites by status-defined adornment and special houses and burial monuments.[52]

There is certainly nothing bad about being a "complex chiefdom." And some "civilizations" are infamous for having done some pretty rotten things. The "complex chiefdom" designation would put the Teuchitlán tradition in with some rather good company, including the Olmec and Monte Albán until about 300 B.C., and Teotihuacan up to A.D. 1, as well as later cultures that left the richly endowed burials at Coclé and Sitio Conte in Panama; and a multitude of regional cultures that developed during the Bronze Age in Europe.[53]

Epilogue

Obviously, a great deal remains to be understood about how and why the cultures of West Mexico developed in the ways they did during the period from initial human occupation of this area to the rise of the Toltecs sometime around A.D. 900. Some of the developments presented in this essay seem uniquely West Mexican in origin; others were more than likely introduced from groups living outside the region. Throughout the five periods of cultural development discussed in this essay, there

was considerable variation in the complexity of the societies of people who lived contemporaneously in different areas of West Mexico. Three were undoubtedly much more advanced than some of their neighbors: the Teuchitlán tradition centered in the highlands of Jalisco; the Chalchihuites/La Quemada tradition in southwestern Zacatecas; and a Teotihuacan/central highlands tradition that was especially widespread in Michoacán. What should matter most, however, is our recognition of West Mexican cultures, whatever their level of complexity, for the value they have in contributing to our understanding of cultural evolution in the Americas and all of its fascinating and instructive diversities and similarities.

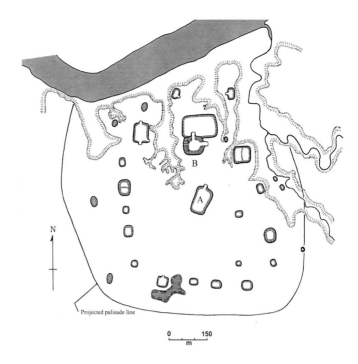

Fig. 20 Plan of Moundville, Alabama. Moundville was the site of a town and ceremonial center along the Black Warrior River. The great quadrangle is defined by large platforms that supported nobles' residences alternating with lesser ones for pavilions used for mortuary and other functions. Mound B, near the northern end of the plaza, rises fifty-eight feet high.

N

Projected palisade line

0   150
m

WEST MEXICAN ART AND MODERNIST ARTISTS

The idea that the so-called primitive art of Africa and Oceania has had considerable influence on a number of major twentieth-century artists is hardly novel. Such a relationship was demonstrated and solidified by, among other things, Robert Goldwater's pathbreaking study *Primitivism in Modern Art,*[1] a number of exhibitions in the past half-century in London and Paris, and a major show at the Museum of Modern Art in New York ten years ago. But the impact of the pre-Columbian art of Mexico, Central America, and the Northern Andes on some highly significant modernist artists—including Paul Gauguin, Henry Moore, Diego Rivera, Frank Lloyd Wright, Joaquin Torres-García, and other, more contemporary artists—has been much less explored.[2] The reasons pre-Columbian art had so strong an influence on certain artists are various, ranging from interest in the forms themselves to particular biographical and sociocultural factors. Gauguin was inspired by the extraordinary ceramics of ancient Peru; Moore, by the imposing monumental stone sculptures of Mesoamerica; Rivera, by ancient West Mexican clay and small-scale Aztec sculpture; Wright, by Mesoamerica's great architectonic forms and decoration; and Torres-García, by the impressive graphic and woven geometric designs and stonework of ancient Peru. This is a large subject, with many fascinating historical, national, and cultural ramifications, but here I intend to focus on a comparatively narrow aspect of it: the clearly discernible impact of the terra-cotta (earthenware) art of ancient West Mexico on a small but important group of modernist artists.

During the period 1930–50, when the shaft tombs of Jalisco, Colima, and Nayarit were first being explored archaeologically, a number of artists began looking at ancient West Mexican ceramic art intently and incorporating elements of it into their work. Most of these artists, including Frida Kahlo, Rufino Tamayo, and Miguel Covarrubias, were Mexicans following the lead of Diego Rivera. But some, including the British sculptor Henry Moore and perhaps a few North Americans associated with the unlikely figure of Walt Disney, were non-Mexicans. How they regarded and used these forms in their work—what appealed to them about West Mexican art, what they took from it, and why—is the subject of this essay.

These artists' assimilation of ancient West Mexican art was just one example of their remarkable receptivity to new currents and of their extraordinary powers of creative synthesis. Mexican artists such as Rivera, Kahlo, and Tamayo had a special and more immediate relationship to pre-Columbian culture than did artists from Europe or North America. This relationship was a result of their familiarity with pre-Hispanic remains and their awareness of and access to ongoing excavations. Perhaps a more significant influence was the nationalist revival movement, or Mexican Renaissance, which followed the Revolution of 1910–20 and appealed to Mexicans to rediscover and preserve indigenous arts and crafts and to develop a new autonomous national art that was based on the great native heritage.

West Mexican figural sculpture came to the fore through Hans-Dietrich Disselhoff's

Fig. 1 Diego Rivera; detail from *The Tarascan Civilization;* 1942; fresco. Palacio Nacional, México, D.F. Angled rooflines, circular temples, and the atmosphere of "daily life" reflect Rivera's incorporation of ancient West Mexican sculptural motifs. A noble couple, recognizable by their elaborate jewelry, body paint, headdresses, and the symbols of office associated with the chieftain—conch shell, fan, and club—recall figurines from Ixtlán del Río.

field reconnaissance of Colima shaft tombs, in 1932, which furnished detailed descriptions and drawings and mapped the locations of tombs; Eduardo Noguera's discovery of shaft tombs at El Opeño in northwestern Michoacán, in 1938; and a great deal of surreptitious digging in Nayarit, Jalisco, Colima, and Guerrero. By 1941 Rivera himself had already acquired enough West Mexican material to fill a book, which was published by Oxford University Press. *Art in Ancient Mexico* contained photographs of selected objects from his collection and helped establish a fashion in the United States and abroad for collecting the terra-cottas of Nayarit, Jalisco, and Colima.[3] Then, in 1946, the first major exhibition exclusively devoted to ancient West Mexican art, based on Rivera's collection, was held at the Palacio de Bellas Artes in Mexico City and accompanied by an authoritative catalogue.[4]

At the time, West Mexican art was generally thought to be secular in character, or at least free of many of the symbolic trappings of other pre-Columbian art, and to be the spontaneous expression of noncivilized, or at least nonurban, cultures. These ideas, which have since slowly been disproven, were ratified by archaeological surveys of the 1930s and 1940s and by the then-respected German art historian Paul Westheim's studies in Mexico in the 1940s, 1950s, and 1960s. The notion of West Mexican material as the product of relatively simple sociocultural entities (chiefdoms, tribes) probably intensified its appeal to modernist artists who saw it as analogous to the so-called primitive tribal art of Africa and Oceania, which was so attractive before and after the first World War to Parisian modernists, including Picasso, Matisse, and Appolinaire, and, later, the Surrealists under the influence of André Breton and Max Ernst. In contrast, the artifacts of urban civilizations of Mexico and the Maya area were probably less appealing, since they were often viewed as the products of a courtly and statist tradition—one developed in densely populated cities and characterized by great temples, palaces, writing, and calendrics—that showed it to belong to a higher rung of civilization.

For artists imbued with indigenist ideas —such as Rivera and his compatriots—an additional appeal of the nonhierarchical, supposedly symbol-free clay sculpture of West Mexico was the possibility of casting it as the equivalent of the humble clay craftwork of disenfranchised Indian peasants of Mexico in their mundane daily life. They saw in it an expression of nativist gaiety, humor, sexuality, regard for animals, and intimacy with nature. Rivera identified strongly with Mexican Indian peasants and their popular arts, which he believed to be derived from ancient indigenous forms.[5]

Diego Rivera

Diego Rivera cherished the formal inventiveness, exoticism, and frank expression of death and sex in the ancient objects of Tlatilco and West Mexico—the same traits that many modernist artists located in the primitive. He must have found their mortuary character, which indicated the importance of the cult of the dead in ancient West Mexico, as attractive as their extraordinary plastic and expressive power and the invaluable ethnographic information they provided. And he undoubtedly viewed their celebration of both the gaiety and terror of Mexican life as a manifestation of the dualism at the core of ancient Mexican religion and cosmology. It is therefore not surprising that quantities of objects from Colima, Nayarit, and Jalisco, as well as from the central Mexican site of Tlatilco, constitute the heart of Rivera's art collection and are among the primary pre-Columbian sources for his murals.

Rivera's ethnographic knowledge of pre-Columbian cultures was unsurpassed among Mexican and non-Mexican artists. Although he had repudiated modernist abstraction in favor of a realism that could be understood by the masses, he organized his mural compositions around abstract geometric structures of interlocking, cubically flattened volumetric forms and shallow, tightly controlled spaces deriving from Synthetic Cubism. His major pre-Columbian models fit in well with this design scheme; they are the tight, hard, plastic forms of Aztec and West Mexican sculptures, which Henry Moore admired and imitated for their geometric stylization and mixture of reality and abstraction. In a general sense, the caricatural aspects, anatomical distortions, schematic sharpness, and exaggerated postures and gestures of the terra-cotta figures of Jalisco, Colima, and Nayarit appealed to Rivera as expressive devices for his paintings. He also adopted the red-tinged earth color of many West Mexican figural sculptures

as the skin color for indigenous people in his murals.

Rivera produced his most important work—his Mexican murals at Chapingo, at the Ministry of Public Education, and at the Stairway of the National Palace, and his murals at the Detroit Institute of Arts in the United States (1932–33)—during the heyday of modernism in the 1920s and 1930s. For these nationalist murals he turned mainly to Aztec and colonial codices and Aztec sculptures as sources. Only later, in the 1940s and 1950s, in lesser works in the Hospital de la Raza and the Patio Corridor of the National Palace, did he use West Mexican forms conspicuously, after they had become well known and after he had amassed a huge collection of them. These late-period compositions are generally less inventive, their forms more descriptive, than those of earlier efforts. Sometimes there is in them a sense of nostalgic yearning for a primitive agrarian world, a regressive impulse that summons pre-Hispanic forms in an antiquarian spirit.

The artist's mural for the national Hospital de la Raza (1953) (fig. 2), a health facility for the working class population, commemorates ancient and modern Mexican technical

capabilities. Titled *The People's Demand for Better Health*, it explores ancient Mexican healing practices as precursors of modern scientific medicine and advocates public-health services for all Mexicans. With the aid of archaeological material from different regional cultures and periods, principally West Mexican and Maya, Rivera reconstructed the pre-Hispanic healing arts—surgical and herbal treatment of eye, intestinal, skin, orthopedic, and vascular diseases. He also prominently depicted childbirth as the special province of the Aztec fertility goddess Talzolteotl, whose huge image, quoted from the *Codex Borbonicus*, presides over the mural. Talzolteotl is also an avatar of Toci, the goddess worshipped by pre-Columbian physicians, curers, and midwives (see the essay by Richard Townsend in this volume).[6]

Rivera's Patio Corridor murals (1942–51) include nine dioramas that dramatize the achievements of ancient Mexican civilization. The largest and most compelling panel depicts the fifteenth- and early-sixteenth-century Aztec capital of Tenochtitlan and the vast market of its sister city, Tlatelolco (fig. 3). Here Rivera used the various pre-Columbian regional styles mainly to convey the ethnicity

Fig. 2 Diego Rivera; *The History of Medicine in Mexico: The People's Demand for Better Health;* 1953; fresco. Hospital de la Raza, México, D.F. Combining figures quoted from several Mesoamerican traditions, Rivera drew attention to Mexico's past as an integral part of its experience of modernity. Ancient and new approaches to healing are embraced by an Aztec mother goddess. A West Mexican diseased figure is seen at center right (see Pickering, fig. 18, for a similar figure).

Fig. 3 Diego Rivera; *The Great City of Tenochtitlan;* 1945; fresco. Palacio Nacional, México, D.F. This idealized depiction of the famous Aztec market includes burden-bearers with tumplines inspired by figures of similar carriers from Rivera's extensive collection of ancient West Mexican sculptures.

Fig. 4 Figure of a man bearing a burden of pottery; Comala style; Colima; earthenware. Private collection. Cat. no. 26.

Fig. 5 Diego Rivera; *The Flower Carrier;* 1935; oil and tempera on masonite. San Francisco Museum of Modern Art, Albert M. Bender Collection, gift of Albert M. Bender in memory of Caroline Walter.

and costumes of the inhabitants of these Mesoamerican regions who came to the market to sell their wares. Figures of porters carrying heavy loads of agricultural produce and manufactured goods (with the aid of forehead tumplines), for instance, imitate many Colima ceramic sculptures from the artist's collection (similar to the one shown in fig. 4), which also contained numerous Aztec stone representations of the same subject. For Rivera the hunched figure of the burden bearer, the humblest member of Aztec society, was the quintessential Indian peon. He used it in a number of panel paintings of the 1930s and 1940s, often associating it with the Mexican flower market at Xochimilco (see fig. 5), another of his favorite emblems of indigenous culture.

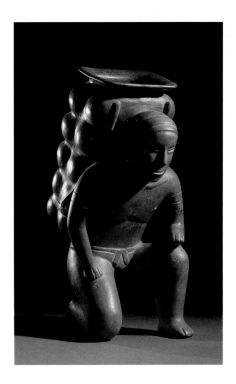

The Tarascan panel (see fig. 1), one of four portraying the arts and industries of regional cultures, features textile dyeing and contains many references to West Mexican figural sculptures. Art historians have faulted the fanciful antiquarianism of this construction of pre-Columbian culture, in which images from disparate times and places in the Mesoamerican universe are combined and conflated. For example, Rivera juxtaposes an Aztec codex, held by a priestly figure, with a mother and child and pitched-roof houses inspired by Nayarit terra-cottas (see Witmore, fig. 1), situating them within a typical Central Mexican landscape of snowcapped volcanoes.[7] But Rivera's method, like that of so many "primitivizing" modernists, was one of bricolage, culling and combining a variety of pre-Hispanic styles and motifs, piecing together fragments of forms and myths irrespective of cultural or ethnic boundaries and creatively adapting them to his own aesthetic. Intent on making something new out of borrowed designs, he was unconcerned with historical accuracy, even when leaning on archaeological data. A more serious, although related, criticism involves Rivera's idealization of the pre-Columbian world; in his zeal to make it attractive, he made it seem idyllic. There is no hint in the Tenochtitlan panel of the Aztec imperialism and exploitation that made the Tlatelolco market possible. A substantial percentage of the food staples and artisanal wares displayed in the market in such abundance were amassed as harsh tribute, not voluntary contributions; they were the products of subjugated districts and conquered territories.[8]

The Colima dog, which had a central position in Rivera's museum, is the most common animal effigy known from ancient West Mexico. Often it is represented as a vessel, with a spout skillfully incorporated into the overall design, and is usually of fine workmanship (see fig. 6). With a strong element of caricature in both features and movement, it is shown standing, seated, snarling, playing, sleeping, or wearing a turtle or armadillo shell on its back or a human mask. It had a special place in Rivera's collection and in his late work, functioning as an affirmation of indigenous people and values and sometimes as a signifier of anti-imperialism. These canines appear in the Patio Corridor murals several times: in a side panel celebrating native paper fabrication; in

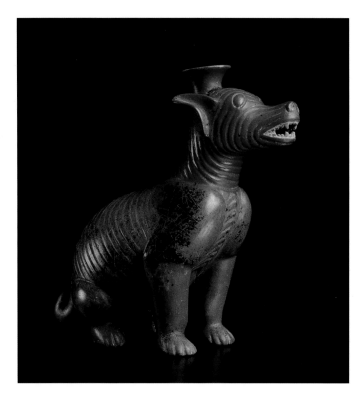

Fig. 6 Snarling dog; Comala style; Colima; earthenware. Stokes Family Collection, Upper Nyack, N.Y. Cat. no. 55. Hairless dogs are among the most well-known subjects of West Mexican tomb sculpture, and were often assimilated in the art of Diego Rivera and Rufino Tamayo as politically charged iconographic motifs.

Fig. 7 Diego Rivera; detail from *Colonial Domination*; 1951; fresco. Palacio Nacional, México, D.F.

the Tenochtitlan panel, where Colima-style figures proffer a fattened dog for sale; in the Totonac panel, as an object of Aztec mercantile activity in the Gulf Coast region; and in the *Colonial Domination* panel (see fig. 7), depicting Cortés in Mexico, where one snarls at a pen full of domestic animals imported from Spain. Another late work, painted in 1947–48 for the lobby of the Hotel del Prado and entitled *Dream of a Sunday Afternoon in the*

Fig. 8 Diego Rivera;
detail from *Dream of
a Sunday Afternoon in
the Alameda;* 1947–48;
fresco. Hotel del Prado,
México, D.F.

Alameda (see fig. 8), prominently features a Colima-style dog tearing at the hem of a fancily dressed lady promenading in the park. These dogs punctuate, often humorously, the artist's point of view within the spectacle of a scene and symbolize nativist resistance to imperialist oppression. Many Mexican artists followed Rivera's lead in depicting Colima dogs as allegorical indigenous icons, as we shall see.

Dog effigies have a number of connotations in Colima art, many relating to death. They represent a special hairless breed with short legs, upright ears, a short thick neck, and a long tail, which was fattened and eaten at feasts, possibly as a sacrifice. Its Nahua name is *xoloitzcuintli,* meaning "strangely formed." These dogs are believed to have guided the dead to the underworld in Aztec and Colima cosmology,[9] a belief strongly reinforced by their ubiquitous presence as companions to the dead in Colima shaft tombs beginning as early as about 400 B.C. Rivera must have embraced Colima dog effigies with this in mind, since for him the central metaphor of native culture was the positive connotation of death among the Aztecs and indigenous Mexican peasants— that is, the idea that death is not about the absence of life but about transformation and the creation of new life through the destruction of the old. He used this idea over and over again as the leitmotif of his murals celebrating Mexican history and prominently in the design of his museum, Anahuacalli,

which houses his vast Pre-Columbian collection and which he gave to the people of Mexico.

Henry Moore

From early in his career, Henry Moore was well informed about archaeological discoveries in the Americas. Moore was interested primarily in the ancient stone-carving tradition of the Mexican highlands, especially the severe, angular, rough-hewn volcanic stone monuments of the Aztec, Toltec, Teotihuacan, Mezcala, and Olmec cultures. He distilled from the arts of these disparate cultures certain shared basic formal traits that give them a broad stylistic unity: blocklike form, smooth unadorned planes, rhythmic equilibrium, and hard-stone materials. The sculptor's semiabstract carved animals, masks, and seated and reclining figures, which conventionalize naturalistic forms into a cubic geometric structure, are profoundly indebted to these sources, as are such signature traits of his sculpture as the twisted, upright head of each of his reclining figures that ultimately derives from the monolithic, recumbent Toltec-Maya figures known as "chacmool."

After completing his breakthrough sculptures of the 1920s and early 1930s, which were based on Aztec, Olmec, and Toltec-Maya images, and after a subsequent encounter with Surrealist ideas, Moore turned once again to pre-Columbian models when, as Britain's preeminent sculptor, he was called upon to create national monuments during and after the Second World War. These sculptures included a series of family groups (see fig. 10)—a theme he began exploring around the time of the birth of his daughter, Mary—consisting of two adult figures holding one or two children. It is clear that both ancient West Mexican ceramic sculptures (such as the one shown in fig. 9), which he was aware of through the publication of Rivera's West Mexican collection in 1941, and Renaissance images of the Holy Family provided solutions to this new formal problem.

Moore made numerous small clay and plaster maquettes for these mother-father-child groups of the mid-1940s before having them enlarged as bronzes. A comparison of one of these, *Family Group* (1947) (fig. 12), with a representative Jalisco joined couple (fig. 11) reveals striking similarities in their figural proportions and attitudes. They share the same kinds of exaggerated gestures and

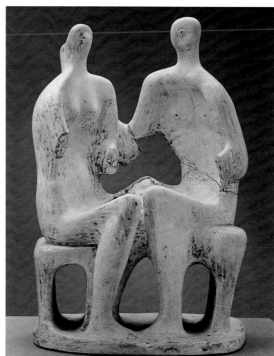

Fig. 9 Seated marriage pair; San Sebastián style; Jalisco; earthenware. The Miller Family Collection, Chicago. Cat. no. 142.

Fig. 10 Henry Moore; *Family Group;* 1948–49; bronze. The Museum of Modern Art, New York, A. Conger Goodyear Fund.

Fig. 11 Joined pair; Ameca-Etzatlán style; Jalisco; earthenware. Los Angeles County Museum of Art, The Proctor Stafford Collection, museum purchase with funds provided by Mr. and Mrs. Allan C. Balch. Cat. no. 118. Smooth burnished surfaces, abstract figural proportions, and rhythmic alternation of concave and convex masses and spaces are among the formal qualities shared by certain West Mexican sculptures and works by Henry Moore.

Fig. 12 Henry Moore; *Family Group;* 1947; plaster. Art Gallery of Ontario, Toronto, gift of Henry Moore, 1974. Cat. no. 226.

anatomical distortions, including broad, flat, concave upper torsos; long, tubular curving arms; truncated hands and feet; and blurred features. There are also correspondences between their smooth, burnished surfaces and their rhythmic alternation of masses and spaces. Even specific details of Moore's work at this time, such as the protruding vertebrae and slouching posture of his male figures, are directly traceable to West Mexican models from Colima and Jalisco. Unlike his Mexican colleagues, however, Moore was uninterested in the ethnographic meaning or nativist connotation of these ancient terra-cottas; he focused exclusively on their suggestion of new formal possibilities for his work.

Frida Kahlo

Frida Kahlo's work, unlike that of her husband, Diego Rivera, addresses the private rather than the public realm, the microcosm rather than the macrocosm. Her canvases employ masking devices, dreams, popular devotional imagery, and ancient West Mexican terra-cottas to explore personal concerns —issues of identity, gender, sexual preference and ambiguity, emotional pain, physical tragedy—not to make grand rhetorical state-

ments. Within this framework she used replicas of West Mexican figures as self-referential metaphors for her passionate nationalist and indigenist sympathies—her *Mexicanidad,* or Mexican cultural identity—and for aspects of her troubled personal history. Within her pictures she often juxtaposed these ancient clay figures and vessels with seemingly unrelated objects and gritty physiological imagery, furthering their associative meanings and deepening their mystery.

The earliest example of West Mexican material in Kahlo's work occurs in *Self-Portrait on the Border between Mexico and the United States* (1932) (fig. 13), painted when she and Rivera lived in the United States, while he was executing his murals in Detroit. The organization of the picture is dualistic, following the compositional formula of her husband's frescoes. The left side represents Mexico as a barren, rocky landscape littered with vestiges of the pre-Columbian past—a pyramid ruin, an Aztec stone carved skull, and two clay female "idols" (her term), one from Jalisco (Arenal-style; a similar sculpture is shown in fig. 15) in West Mexico and the other a pregnant figure from the Casas Grande (also known as Paquimé) culture of

Fig. 13 Frida Kahlo; *Self-Portrait on the Border between Mexico and the United States;* 1932; oil and collage on masonite. Private collection. A landscape evoking Mexico's agricultural economy and rich historical past is juxtaposed with a highly industrialized North American cityscape. Both settings are ultimately mythic, but the artist expresses her inclinations toward the strangely flowering world of broken yet powerful earthenware figures and stone monuments.

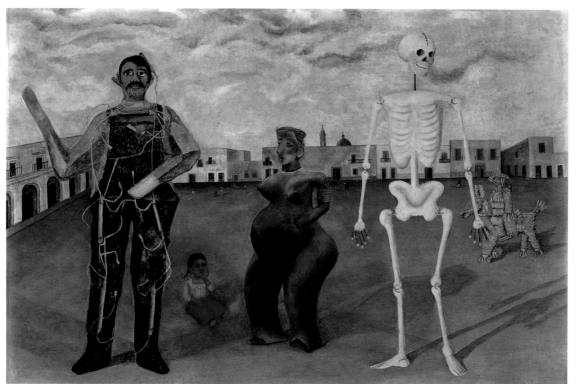

Fig. 14 Frida Kahlo; *Four Inhabitants of Mexico;* 1938; oil on wood panel. Private collection. Cat. no. 223. A papier-mâché Judas figure, a West Mexican tomb sculpture, a skeletal figure of death, and a straw man seated on a burro accompany the artist, depicted as a child, in a vast city square.

northern Mexico—but with fantastic, blossoming flowers also firmly rooted in the arid ground. On the right, a bleak industrial environment, devoid of history, represents the United States in the present: featureless skyscrapers, grim factories, sterile mechanical forms, and appliances attached to electrical cords stand in contrast to the archaeological and natural forms opposite them. In the sky celestial forces such as the sun and moon are aligned on the Mexican side, while on the right the American flag, emblem of North American imperialist power, rises out of smoke belching from factories. Standing in the center of the picture, traversing both sides, Kahlo is demurely posed in a pink dress, like a young Detroit society matron, yet defiantly she holds a cigarette and a Mexican flag: there can be no question that her allegiance is to her agrarian Indian cultural heritage. The painting dramatically conveys her alienation from the United States and longing to return home. While Rivera was idealizing the industrial might of Ford's River Rouge plant in his Detroit murals, she expressed profound skepticism about the value of factories and machines.[10]

Another painting that celebrates Mexican life and its vibrant culture of death is *Four Inhabitants of Mexico* (1938) (fig. 14). Lined up on an empty plaza recalling Giorgio de

Fig. 15 Standing female figure; Arenal style; Jalisco; earthenware. Hudson Museum, University of Maine, Orono, William P. Palmer III Collection. Cat. no. 150.

Chirico's early metaphysical paintings are a grinning *calavera* (a skeletal figure associated with the annual Indian celebration of the Day of the Dead); a giant papier-mâché Judas effigy of Spanish origin wrapped in firecrackers of the type that are set off in Catholic street festivals (as entertainment and a means of defusing class envy and rage); and, in the center, a replica of a very pregnant Jalisco-Nayarit clay effigy of the San Sebastián style (for a similar San

Fig. 16 Frida Kahlo; *My Nurse and I;* 1937; oil on metal. Fundación Dolores Olmedo Patiño, Mexico.

Fig. 17 Family group: a) seated female figure nursing a baby; b) gesturing seated chieftain with a young female figure; Ameca-Etzatlán style; Jalisco; earthenware. Private collection. Cat. no. 121. Kahlo's collection of ancient art contained a West Mexican figure like that of the mother and child seated to the left in this group; that sculpture was among the sources for the monumental earth mother in *My Nurse and I* (fig. 16).

Sebastián–style figure, see Townsend, fig. 12; see also the closely related Arenal-style figure shown in fig. 15)—all casting long shadows. In the distance is a fourth inhabitant of the square, a child's toy made of reeds woven into the form of a horseman and possibly representing Pancho Villa, one of the great leaders of the revolution of 1910–20. A solitary little girl seated on the plaza floor represents Kahlo as a child, contemplating these emblems of her cultural heritage. The Nayarit figure, a metaphor for the Mexican Indian, has been broken—its feet are missing and its decapitated head has been repaired—but it is still fecund. In an interview Kahlo explained that it represented her conception of the Indian—inert, but with something alive inside.[11] Here, the West Mexican figure also foreshadows the little Kahlo's future broken physical condition (she was later to contract polio and to become the victim of a crippling bus accident that rendered her unable to bear children).

Two of Kahlo's own favorite paintings also feature West Mexican terra-cottas. In *My Nurse and I* (1937) (fig. 16) she transformed a Jalisco clay figure of a nursing mother from her own collection (similar to the one shown in fig. 17) into a compelling testimony of her *Mexicanidad*. By depicting herself, as both infant and adult, being suckled by an Indian wet nurse (actually her own experience) wearing a Teotihuacan stone mask, she asserted that she had been nurtured by both her Indian and ancestral pre-Columbian cultural heritage, making clear that a Mexican identity encompasses several overlapping cultures.[12]

A late painting, *The Love Embrace of the Universe, the Earth (Mexico), Diego, Me and Mr. Xólotl* (1949) (fig. 18), is a mystical expression of her encompassing love for Rivera and of the ancient Mexican concept of the alternation of day and night, dry and rainy seasons, life and death—of creation through destruction. As in *My Nurse and I*, a monumental Indian earth mother, symbolizing Mexico past and present, holds a baby, this time with the adult face of Rivera, who is also held by Kahlo. Encompassing them are the great arms of the goddess of the cosmic duality, which also support Kahlo's familiar desert flowers, here rooted in the ether. On the dark side of the universe, nestled in the great goddess' arm, Kahlo incorporated a sleeping Colima dog (similar to the one

Fig. 18 Frida Kahlo; *The Love Embrace of the Universe, the Earth (Mexico), Diego, Me and Mr. Xólotl;* 1949; oil on canvas. Collection of Jacques and Natasha Gelman, México, D.F.

Fig. 19 Sleeping dog; Comala style; Colima; earthenware. Collection of Barbara and Justin Kerr, New York. Cat. no. 49.

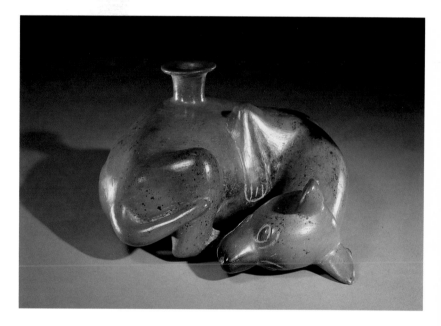

shown in fig. 19)—she called it an *escuincle* dog, referring to the hairless breed of West Mexico—modeled after the favorite one in her collection, which she named Xólotl,[13] perhaps in anticipation of her own death, as her health was worsening. Xólotl was identified by Salvador Toscano in 1946 as a god of death who conducted the dead on their journey to the underworld; also, according to some interpretations of Aztec mythology, he was identified with the planet Venus as the deified evening star and a twin brother of Quetzalcoatl, represented as having the head of a dog.

Rufino Tamayo

Rufino Tamayo's art is closer to Kahlo's than to Rivera's in its Surrealist affinity, humor, intimacy, and size (like Kahlo, Tamayo is primarily an easel painter), though he carried on Rivera's primitivizing well into the 1950s and 1960s. He came of age as a painter in the late 1920s, after the first great wave of the mural movement, and there is a sense now that he deliberately incorporated Mexican motifs into his paintings as a picturesque means of appealing to the purchasers of his art rather than as an expression of national identity—as Rivera may also have done in his easel paintings. Tamayo, a Zapotec Indian who identified strongly with the pre-Columbian tradition, amassed a large, choice collection of ancient Mesoamerican art, which he donated to his native state of Oaxaca. He used West Mexican terra-cottas extensively as sources for his paintings, combining them with Picasso's Synthetic Cubism; the vivid, saturated colors of Mexican tropical fruits and flowers; and the forms and colors of Indian popular art—ex votos, embroideries, weavings, lacquerware, brightly

painted papier mâché, carved wooden and baked clay figurines and masks, and toys and decorations of woven reed, palm, and maguey.

In many ways, Tamayo's appropriation of ancient West Mexican artifacts was most original. Unlike Rivera and Kahlo, he was not interested in the plastic power of these sculptures, though he too imitated their gestural eloquence and abbreviated natural forms. Also, he never replicated West Mexican sculptures in a literal fashion, distorting them instead to strengthen the decorative and emotional impact of his paintings. He was drawn mainly to their apparently playful (but in fact also religious and symbolic) representation of the everyday life of Indians: couples holding hands, making love, and delousing each other's hair; men making music, lounging, cavorting, juggling, holding implements or weapons, eating, and drinking; females who are pregnant, birthing and nursing babies, and supporting vessels; feast scenes; and natural forms such as fruits, vegetables, and animals.

In the mid- and late 1930s, Tamayo borrowed the distinctive expressionless faces (the odd, elongated heads, lozenge-shaped staring eyes, long sharp noses, thin lips,

Fig. 20 Rufino Tamayo; *Woman with a Birdcage;* 1941; oil on canvas. The Art Institute of Chicago, gift of the Joseph Winterbotham Collection. Cat. no. 224. The elongated face, nose, and pointed chin; the lozenge-shaped eyes and open mouth; and the thick, rubbery arms and stubby fingers of West Mexican figures appear as stylistic devices in Tamayo's paintings of idealized indigenous figures.

Fig. 21 Seated male "storyteller" figure; Ameca-Etzatlán style; Jalisco; earthenware. The Art Institute of Chicago, Estate of Ruth Falkenau. Cat. no. 119.

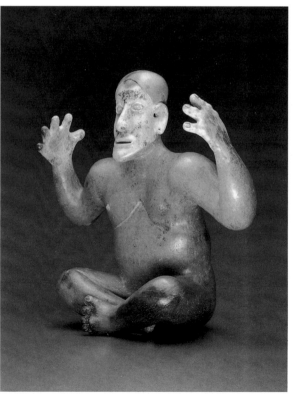

filleted headbands, and jutting ears) and distorted bodies (the thick necks, broad shoulders, tubular arms, and convex torsos) of the terra-cotta figures of Nayarit and, particularly, Jalisco (see fig. 21) for his vernacular scenes with Surrealist overtones and indigenous subjects; this tendency continued into the early 1940s with such works as *Woman with a Birdcage* (1941) (fig. 20). In *The Fruit Vendor* (1943) (fig. 22), Tamayo incorporated features similar to those seen on the elegant, abstract Colima mask shown in figure 23. He employed sharper stylizations of West Mexican objects to great effect in some works from the early 1940s such as *Animals* (1941) (fig. 24), where he transformed the characteristic strong curves, schematic features (even the frequently bared teeth), and burnished red-brown surfaces of Colima clay dogs (see fig. 6) into hard, clearly defined masses with a tough compositional structure to express ideas about human alienation and resistance to the horrors of war.

But Tamayo's art primarily concerns sensations of color, form, and touch, rather than ideas or ethnographic meaning. And his distinctive relation to West Mexican art has to do with his strengths as a painterly artist. He was far more attuned to the coloristic possibilities inherent in West Mexican objects than were most other painters, and found much in their techniques of surface patterning—positive and negative slip coloring, incising, polychromy, painted abstract designs, and manganese oxide staining—to use in enhancing the surfaces and textures of his paintings, especially after the late 1950s.

Miguel Covarrubias

West Mexican forms could be said to have corroborated Miguel Covarrubias' innate caricatural tendency; he was a highly successful caricaturist in 1920s New York, working for *Vanity Fair* and the *New Yorker*. By the 1930s, when his compatriots were looking closely at these West Mexican forms, his interest in caricature was waning while his interest in anthropology was increasing. He collected a great deal of West Mexican sculpture, just as other artists did, but the impact of West Mexican forms on his work is hard to pin down. If anything, it was tangential, and may perhaps be glimpsed in the stance, posture, and gestures of some of his caricatures, as well as in the unique volumetric sense of the subjects conveyed in his

Fig. 22 Rufino Tamayo; *The Fruit Vendor;* 1943; gouache over graphite on white wove paper. The Art Institute of Chicago, Elizabeth F. Chapman bequest. Cat. no. 225. The oval face, triangular nose, and stylized ears on the figure depicted here are derived from the abstract visages of Colima earthenware burial masks.

Fig. 23 Burial mask; Comala style; Colima; earthenware. Private collection. Cat. no. 87.

Fig. 24 Rufino Tamayo; *Animals;* 1941; oil on canvas. The Museum of Modern Art, New York, Inter-American Fund.

Fig. 25 Duck; Comala style; Colima; earthenware. Private collection. Cat. no. 57.

drawings. After abandoning caricature as a profession, he made many "scientific" studies of West Mexican figures as an anthropologist, some of which are reproduced in his ethnographic maps and books about pre-Columbian art and culture.

In 1937, for *Vogue,* Covarrubias painted a gouache caricature of the principal cartoon characters of Walt Disney—Mickey Mouse, Donald Duck, Pluto, Goofy, Peter Pig, Clara Cluck, Horace Horsecollar, and Clarabelle Cow—seeking shelter from a wild world in an ark (fig. 26).[14] Soon afterward, Disney released his first full-length animated film, *Snow White and the Seven Dwarfs.* This world-renowned caricaturist-cartoonist and his cohorts may also have profited from an awareness of West Mexican figural sculptures. The sharply rounded, forcefully stylized, dynamic, expressive animals—ducks, mice, dogs, birds, pigs—and human characters in Disney cartoons seem surely to have absorbed the morphology of ancient West Mexican art.

Walt Disney Studios: A Possible Link?
In view of the extensive economic, social, and cultural linkages between Mexico and Southern California in the period under review, it is tempting to think that Colima duck effigies, which occur frequently in the canon, might have inspired the form and spirit of Disney's Donald Duck, who was introduced to the world in 1934. The Colima ducks, which often appear to be

quacking, have a hyperreal visual consistency, with smooth surfaces, large heads, straight legs, and bulky, rounded, featureless bodies (see fig. 25). The playful, animated, comic cast of these effigies certainly presents suggestive correspondences to the lively, excitable cartoon character with his big bill, twistable neck, and substantial backside (see figs. 26 and 27). Although Disney was, like most modernists, a "very eclectic borrower,"[15] there is no evidence of any direct relationship between the two icons. But there is a great deal of information about the dense pattern of associations existing among Latin America, Mexican artists, and Disney during the 1930s and 1940s—many previously unexplored—that is suggestive in this context.

Immediately after the creation of *Snow White and the Seven Dwarfs,* Walt Disney embarked on a program of feature-length films, and felt a great need to improve the quality and techniques of art and animation in his studio. Intent on educating his animators and artists about world art and on getting design tips from wherever he could,[16] he arranged for a very extensive training program to take place in the studio in 1938–39, sparing no expense in his effort to bring him closer to his goal.[17] Disney was not to hold another such training program until many decades later, so the techniques and concepts these artists acquired in the late 1930s were perpetuated for a long time; in fact, many of those who were trained at this time continued to work at the studios until the 1970s.[18]

Many well-known artists came to Disney during this time of improvement. Rico Le Brun, an esteemed California muralist (who had worked in Mexico with Rivera) and expert on animal anatomy, was hired as an instructor in the program. Thornton Hee, an artist at the Disney Studios (signing himself T. Hee) who was an avowed admirer of Covarrubias and greatly influenced by his work, gave a series of twelve lectures on caricaturing. Among the many visiting lecturers asked to talk about techniques of art and animation was Frank Lloyd Wright, whose intense involvement with pre-Columbiana began in the early 1920s when he modeled his Los Angeles textile block houses after Maya and Mixtec architecture.[19] Another was Jean Charlot, a French painter transplanted to Mexico in 1921 who was an active member of the Mexican Renaissance and who worked alongside Rivera in the mural movement. Charlot was also a close friend of Jose Clemente Orozco, Tina Modotti, and Frida Kahlo, and a staff artist for a team of archaeologists from the Carnegie Institution of Washington that explored the Maya-Toltec site of Chichén Itzá in Yucatán from 1926 to 1929. From April to June of 1938, Charlot gave a series of eight illustrated lectures at Disney Studios about the principles of picture-making, in which he mentioned Maya and Mexican Indian arts and crafts.[20] Thus, certainly by the late 1930s, if not earlier, Disney Studio artists were cognizant of modern and ancient Mexican art.

They were soon presented with an opportunity to become a great deal more familiar with it when Disney, his wife, and a group of his artists and animators made several government-sponsored trips to Latin America in 1941–43, arranged by Nelson Rockefeller, director of the new Office of the Coordinator of Inter-American Affairs, and his close associate John Hay Whitney, head of its Motion Picture Section. They had a number of aims: to encourage South American cooperation with U.S. war efforts, to help secure markets for North American products at a time when Europe was inaccessible, and to conduct research for planned propaganda films promoting the Good Neighbor policy as a cover for increasing U.S. corporate and political domination of regions south of the border.[21] This entourage, billing itself "El Groupo," toured Argentina, Peru, Brazil, Chile, and Mexico. Their itinerary, which facilitated absorption of the "authentic exotic" material culture and customs of the host countries, included visits to picturesque sites, museums, and collections, as well as meetings with important local artists, dancers, and musicians.

On the basis of material collected on these cross-cultural junkets, Disney produced at least eighteen educational and commercial short subject and feature films. The educational short subjects about health care and sanitation targeted mainly poor, uneducated Latin American audiences in anticipation of their intended role as workers in expanding North American companies, including communications media companies—operating in the areas of telephone, film, and books—as well as such companies as United Fruit and Goodyear. The three commercial films intended mainly for U.S. consumption (but also shown in Latin America), *South of the Border with Disney* (1942), *Saludos Amigos* (1943), and *The Three Caballeros* (1945), combined live action and cartoon footage. The first two were actually packages of shorts that mixed travelogues of Disney's tours with animation. In *Saludos Amigos*, Donald Duck visits Lake Titicaca, Goofy is an Argentinean gaucho, and Joe Carioca, an umbrella-toting, samba-dancing parrot from Rio, is introduced. *The Three Caballeros,* the longest and most technically and artistically accomplished film, features three primary cartoon characters—Donald Duck, Joe Carioca, and Panchito, a boisterous Mexican cowboy rooster (see fig. 27)—interacting amorously with three live Latin female singer-dancers, including a famous sequence with Aurora Miranda (Carmen's sister) dancing with Donald Duck.

The core presentation of *The Three Caballeros* is the exotic and irrational spectacle of the Latin American landscape. The film's culminating sequence, "La Piñata," inter-

Fig. 26 Miguel Covarrubias; *Walt Disney and His Cartoon Family on an Ark;* 1937; gouache. Prints and Photographs Division, Library of Congress, Washington, D.C.

weaves the picturesque, folkloric aspects of Mexico already familiar to North American tourists and patrons of Tamayo's and Rivera's easel and watercolor paintings—popular festivals and customs, colorful native handicrafts, toys, costumes, abundant tropical flora, scenic locales—with more lively contemporary modes of Mexican entertainment—music, dancing, nightlife, resorts—and the chaotic antics of the three cartoon caballeros. Disney animators appropriated many seductive design and color motifs from Mexican artifacts—serapes, piñatas, the pottery of Oaxaca and Tonalá, Tehuana headdresses—abstracting them into the explosive and dazzling animated imagery used throughout. Although the film never refers to ancient indigenous culture, some design elements, particularly the flower petal aureoles enclosing the heads of Donald Duck and a romantic female singer, may ultimately have been inspired by collars surrounding the serpent heads adorning the Temple of Quetzalcoatl at Teotihuacan; also, there even appears to be a fleeting image of a Teotihuacan flower glyph.

One segment of the Mexican sequence, created by Mary Blair, one of the studio artists who accompanied Disney on the Latin tour, features little children participating in a Christmas ritual called "Las Posadas," presented through a series of still watercolor drawings. Blair surely was influenced by the wide-eyed Mexican Indian street urchins of Rivera's easel paintings, whose postures, proportions, features, and coloration ultimately derive from small-scale Aztec figures and West Mexican terra-cottas. Blair, who became Disney's favorite conceptual artist, was heavily influenced by what she saw on the trip, and her art was never the same afterwards. It had a new quality of stylization and a fresh sense of pattern and color during the 1940s and 1950s, which was also expressed in her paintings for the "Small World" sections of the Disney parks.[22]

Conclusion

For the majority of the artists discussed here, Mexican and non-Mexican alike—and certainly for many collectors—form was the determining factor in their attachment to the sculpture of Colima, Jalisco, and Nayarit. With different inflections, these sculptures' synthetic simplification of natural forms into geometric structures was almost Cubistic—clean, compact, hard-edged, rhythmic, and economical, with dynamic curves, planes and hollows—tending toward, but never quite achieving, abstraction. The clay sculpture of the villages of West Mexico appealed to these artists also because of the visual inventiveness it reflected, especially in its decorative surfaces and grotesquerie, and because of its technical proficiency, the vitality of its conventions, and its playfulness and humor. The taste for ancient West Mexican art also coincided with the popularity in the 1920s and 1930s of Edward Weston's pristine close-up photographs of natural objects, many made in Mexico, in which he sought to bring out by means of new technology the abstract forms underlying material reality. And it dovetailed with the fashion for Art Deco, a modern style with recognizable ties to tradition, combining the sleek, smooth, streamlined forms of industrial design with archaistic references.

Similarly, the art of Rivera, Moore, Kahlo, Tamayo, Covarrubias, and Disney, in the period 1930–50, shared an attachment to materiality and to abstraction, a nostalgia for an idealized innocent past combined with a healthy respect for modern technology. Like all modernist artists, they drew inspiration from many diverse sources, among them, the ancient tomb sculpture of West Mexico.

CATALOGUE OF THE EXHIBITION

NOTES TO THE READER

In the following checklist, we have, wherever possible, used the names of geographical locations to designate groups of figures sharing stylistic characteristics and apparently made in workshops within a restricted area. For example, in the vicinity of Comala, Colima, numerous local workshops produced groups of figures. Each of these groups is subtly different from the next, yet these "Comala style" forms have affinities that distinguish them from, say, figures of the "San Sebastián style" of western Jalisco and adjacent parts of Nayarit.

Consistent with the use of place names to designate stylistic clusters, we are dropping certain descriptive terms that may have outlived their usefulness. Thus, instead of using the term "Chinesco," which originally was coined to describe a Nayarit stylistic group with somewhat mongoloid facial features, we are introducing the term "Lagunillas style," which refers to sites in the vicinity of San Pedro Lagunillas at which the sculptures forming that stylistic group are thought to have been made.

In some of the checklist entries below, the reader will find only a geographical term without the word "style" attached because at present there do not seem to be enough related objects to constitute a distinctive, major stylistic grouping. Still other figures have no known place of origin; future archaeological finds or stylistic comparisons may enable us to place them more securely.

Within each stylistic group or cluster in West Mexico, we may suppose that there exist primary, "masterpiece" figures and a whole corpus of replications, derivations, and revivals following in a pattern of canonical hierarchy. At present the locations of regional workshops are unknown, but they may eventually be found through analyses of clays from the figures and from natural deposits. Such detailed studies may also reveal that large workshops with lineages of masters produced a range of related yet distinct figures. Although the sculptural pieces depicted in this catalogue have been chosen for their high level of aesthetic accomplishment and presumably represent the most "courtly" levels of achievement, the present state of archaeological and stylistic studies does not allow us to place these figures with complete certainty in the hierarchy of their respective local stylistic traditions.

In the area embracing southern Jalisco and northern Colima there are also traditions of small-scale distinct figurines coexisting with but stylistically unrelated to the figures of the dominant Comala style. Previously regarded as "Late Formative" in date, figurines of the "pastillage," "teco," and "wrestler" types have recently been found in the context of Late Comala–phase archaeological remains.

Additional archaeological investigations will clarify the dating and sequencing of these figurines.

Finally, it must be noted that all West Mexican styles, on both the "masterpiece" and "popular" levels, exhibit a pattern of mutual borrowings, in some cases appearing to be composites of various traits. Surface finishes and colorings, poses, and the shapes of heads, faces, hands, fingers, ears, limbs, and torsos all suggest travel and exchange between workshops. This idea is supported by the fact that fragments of figures of different styles have often been found in the same tombs, suggesting a pattern of alliances between dominant ruling lineages.

Precise dates or archaeological phases are not always given because this information is in many cases uncertain. The vast majority of the shaft-tomb sculptures in this catalogue date from between 200 B.C. and A.D. 300.

Cat. no. 207

Cat. no. 45

Cat. no. 203

Cat. no. 215

Cat. no. 215

Cat. no. 211

CENTRAL MEXICO

1. Compound vessel; San Pablo, Morelos; 1200/500 B.C.; earthenware. The Saint Louis Art Museum. (Mountjoy essay, fig. 3)

2. Female figure; Tlatilco style; 500/400 B.C.; earthenware. The Art Institute of Chicago, gift of Daniel Michel, 1991.395. (Townsend essay, fig. 14)

COLIMA

3. Necklace; greenstone. Collection of Anthony Patano, Oak Lawn, Ill. (Anawalt essay, fig. 35)

4. Ceremonial earspools; *Spondylus* shell. Collection of Anthony Patano, Oak Lawn, Ill. (Anawalt essay, fig. 32)

5. Earspool attachments; *Spondylus* shell. Collection of Anthony Patano, Oak Lawn, Ill. (Anawalt essay, fig. 32)

6. Seated figure; *Spondylus* shell. Collection of Anthony Patano, Oak Lawn, Ill. (Anawalt essay, fig. 34)

7. Bead necklace and pendant in the form of a large fish eating a small fish; *Spondylus* shell. Collection of Anthony Patano, Oak Lawn, Ill. (Anawalt essay, fig. 31)

8. Pendant in the form of a mythic double-headed creature with serpentine motifs; *Spondylus* shell. Collection of Anthony Patano, Oak Lawn, Ill. (Anawalt essay, fig. 30)

9. Circular pendant with a serpentine motif (necklace); *Spondylus* shell. Collection of Anthony Patano, Oak Lawn, Ill. (Anawalt essay, fig. 33)

10. Figurine pendant; shell. The Metropolitan Museum of Art, New York, purchase, Rogers Fund and gifts in Honor of Carol R. Mayer, 1985. (López and Ramos essay, fig. 12)

11. Figurine pendant; jade. Private collection. (López and Ramos essay, fig. 13)

12. Coatimundi pendant; stone. The Metropolitan Museum of Art, New York, The Michael C. Rockefeller Memorial Collection, purchase, Mrs. Gertrud A. Mellon Gift and Nelson A. Rockefeller Gift, 1970. (Weigand and Beekman essay, fig. 14)

13. Ceremonial club with a human face; stone. Fowler Museum of Cultural History, University of California, Los Angeles. (Pickering and Cabrero essay, fig. 8)

14. *Turbinella* conch shell. Private collection. (Graham essay, fig. 5)

15. Conch shell. Fowler Museum of Cultural History, University of California, Los Angeles. (Mountjoy essay, fig. 10)

16. Group of fourteen heads; shell, jade. Private collection. (Catalogue, p. 288)

17. Necklace; *Spondylus* shell. The Art Institute of Chicago, William and Annabelle McNulty Fund, 1995.195. (Weigand and Beekman essay, fig. 15)

18. Two ceremonial blades; obsidian. The Art Institute of Chicago, through prior acquisitions of Mr. and Mrs. Dave Chapman, Mr. and Mrs. Richard Reed Armstrong, and the Robert A. Waller Fund, 1997.362.1–2. (Townsend essay, fig. 42)

19. Vessel in the form of gourds; Capacha; earthenware. Mint Museum of Art, Charlotte, N.C., gift of Dr. and Mrs. Francis Robicsek. (Mountjoy essay, fig. 2)

20. Ribbed jar; vicinity of Periquillo; earthenware. Private collection. (Catalogue, p. 289)

21. Seated male figure wearing a beaked helmet; Comala style; earthenware. American Museum of Natural History, New York. (Pickering and Cabrero essay, fig. 19)

22. Contortionist; Comala style; earthenware. Private collection. (Townsend, "Introduction," fig. 23)

23. Contortionist; Comala style; earthenware. Private collection. (Townsend essay, fig. 24)

24. Elderly female figure with a cane; Comala style; earthenware. Private collection. (Pickering and Cabrero essay, fig. 22)

25. Female rasp player seated on a stool; Comala style; earthenware. Collection of Mr. and Mrs. Joseph Goldenberg, Los Angeles. (Townsend, "Introduction," fig. 22)

26. Figure of a man bearing a burden of pottery; Comala style; earthenware. Private collection. (Braun essay, fig. 4)

27. Hunchback; Comala style; earthenware. Private collection. (Anawalt essay, fig. 18)

28. Male figure carrying a maguey agave heart with a tumpline; Comala style; earthenware. Private collection. (Butterwick essay, fig. 26)

29. Male figure carrying a vessel with a tumpline; Comala style; earthenware. Private collection, New York. (Schöndube essay, fig. 6)

30. Male figure with a shark headdress; Comala style; earthenware. Private collection. (Furst essay, fig. 30)

31. Model antler with a human head; Comala style; earthenware. Private collection. (Furst essay, fig. 27)

32. Model of a *Strombus* conch shell; Comala style; earthenware. Collection of Barbara and Justin Kerr, New York. (Graham essay, fig. 4)

33. Model of a *teponaztle* drum; Comala style; earthenware. Hudson Museum, University of Maine, Orono, William P. Palmer III Collection. (Furst essay, fig. 23)

34. Seated ithyphallic dwarf; Comala style; earthenware. Private collection. (Catalogue, p. 286)

35. Prisoner; Comala style; earthenware. Private collection. (Townsend essay, fig. 9)

36. Seated chieftain with a conch shell and headdress; Comala style; earthenware. Private collection. (Graham essay, fig. 2)

37. Seated chieftain wearing a headdress with a horn and dog's head; Comala style; earthenware. The Art Institute of Chicago, through prior acquisitions of the Primitive Art Purchase Fund, 1997.363. (Graham essay, fig. 17)

38. Seated drummer; Comala style; earthenware. The University of Iowa Museum of Art, Iowa City, gift of Gerald and Hope Solomons. (Furst essay, fig. 25)

39. Seated dwarf with a bird necklace; Comala style; earthenware. The Cleveland Museum of Art, fiftieth anniversary gift of the Women's Council in honor of the museum's seventy-fifth anniversary. (Furst essay, fig. 18)

40. Seated male figure holding a vat and drinking cup; Comala style; earthenware. Private collection. (Butterwick essay, fig. 17)

41. Seated hunchbacked dwarf; Comala style; earthenware. The Art Institute of Chicago, gifts of Neal Ball, Mrs. Roy Evan Barr, Mr. and Mrs. William D. Berger, Mr. and Mrs. Edwin A. Bergman, Mrs. Leigh B. Block, Hans G. Cahen, Helen Marie Crone Trust, Reverend Richard J. Douaire, Linda Einfeld, Mr. and Mrs. Charles Figeley, Michael Fortino, Merle B. Gordon, Dr. and Mrs. Melvin R. Guttman, Frank B. Hubachek, Mrs. John V. McGuire, Gwendolyn Miller and Herbert Baker, Mr. and Mrs. Howard Miller, Mary Kirk Newcomb in memory of Paulene Kirk, Fred Novy and Edward Pinsel, Meryl Pinsof Platt, Barbara Rose, Anna L. Unizicker, Peter G. Wray, Theodore N. Zekman; restricted gift of Winter and Hirsch; all by exchange; 1988.224. (Pickering and Cabrero essay, fig. 14)

42. Seated male figure wearing a conch-shell headdress; Comala style; earthenware. Utah Museum of Fine Arts, University of Utah, Salt Lake City. (Graham essay, fig. 1)

43. Seated male figure with a horned headdress; Comala style; earthenware. Private collection. (Furst essay, fig. 17)

44. Seated male figure with right arm raised, holding a cup; Comala style; earthenware. Private collection. (Butterwick essay, fig. 28)

45. Sleeping female figure; Comala style; earthenware. Appleton Museum of Art, Ocala, Fla. (Catalogue, p. 283)

46. Standing dancer with animal on helmet; Comala style; earthenware. Private collection. (Catalogue, p. 290)

47. Dancing dogs; Comala style; earthenware. Private collection. (Schöndube essay, fig. 15)

48. Dog wearing a mask with a human face; Comala style; earthenware. Los Angeles County Museum of Art, Los Angeles, The Proctor Stafford Collection, museum purchase with funds provided by Mr. and Mrs. Allan C. Balch. (Furst essay, fig. 26)

49. Sleeping dog; Comala style; earthenware. Collection of Barbara and Justin Kerr, New York. (Braun essay, fig. 19)

50. Coatimundi; Comala style; earthenware. The Miller Family Collection, Chicago. (Schöndube essay, fig. 7)

51. Crab; Comala style; earthenware. Private collection. (Schöndube essay, fig. 10)

52. Duck; Comala style; earthenware. Private collection. (Schöndube essay, fig. 5)

53. Shark swallowing a man; Comala style; earthenware. Private collection. (Furst essay, fig. 29)

54. Old pregnant snarling dog; Comala style; earthenware. Stokes Family Collection, Upper Nyack, N.Y. (Schöndube essay, fig. 16)

55. Snarling dog; Comala style; earthenware. Stokes Family Collection, Upper Nyack, N.Y. (Braun essay, fig. 6)

56. Roasted dog on a platter; Comala style; earthenware. Private collection. (Schöndube essay, fig. 29)

57. Duck; Comala style; earthenware. Private collection. (Braun essay, fig. 25)

58. Turtle; Comala style; earthenware. Private collection. (Schöndube essay, fig. 11)

59. Heron; Comala style; earthenware. Los Angeles County Museum of Art, Los Angeles, The Proctor Stafford Collection, museum purchase with funds provided by Mr. and Mrs. Allan C. Balch. (Valdez essay, fig. 8)

60. Duck; Comala style; earthenware. Fowler Museum of Cultural History, University of California, Los Angeles. (Valdez essay, fig. 7)

61. Prairie dog; Comala style; earthenware. Denver Museum of Natural History. (Schöndube essay, fig. 8)

62. Parrot; Comala style; earthenware. Private collection. (Schöndube essay, fig. 17)

63. Joined ducks; Comala style; earthenware. Private collection. (Schöndube essay, fig. 9)

64. Prisoner; Comala style; earthenware. Collection of Mr. and Mrs. Joseph Goldenberg, Los Angeles. (Townsend essay, fig. 8)

65. "Teardrop" bottle with a dog effigy head; Comala style; earthenware. Hudson Museum, University of Maine, Orono, William P. Palmer III Collection. (Townsend, "Introduction," fig. 27)

66. Bottle with three crayfish supports; Comala style; earthenware. Private collection. (Schöndube essay, fig. 1)

67. Vessel with crayfish; Comala style; earthenware. Private collection. (Schöndube essay, fig. 28)

Cat. no. 209

Cat. no. 111

Cat. no. 101   Cat. no. 34

68. Vessel with armadillos; Comala style; earthenware. The Saint Louis Art Museum, gift of Morton D. May. (Valdez essay, fig. 5)

69. Incised vessel on a four-legged animal support; Comala style; earthenware. Hudson Museum, University of Maine, Orono, William P. Palmer III Collection. (Butterwick essay, fig. 16)

70. Vessel; Comala style; earthenware. Los Angeles County Museum of Art, Los Angeles, The Proctor Stafford Collection, museum purchase with funds provided by Mr. and Mrs. Allan C. Balch. (Townsend, "Introduction," fig. 29)

71. Vessel in the form of an organ cactus; Comala style; earthenware. Los Angeles County Museum of Art, Los Angeles, The Proctor Stafford Collection, museum purchase with funds provided by Mr. and Mrs. Allan C. Balch. (Schöndube essay, fig. 24)

72. Squash vessel with parrot supports; Comala style; earthenware. Private collection. (Schöndube essay, fig. 21)

73. Squash vessel with parrot supports; Comala style; earthenware. Collection of Charles and Marjorie Benton, Evanston, Ill. (Catalogue, p. 288)

74. Vase with iguana supports; Comala style; earthenware. Collection of Barbara and Justin Kerr, New York. (Catalogue, p. 289)

75. Vessel in the form of a section of a *pochotl* (ceiba) tree; Comala style; earthenware. Fowler Museum of Cultural History, University of California, Los Angeles. (Witmore essay, fig. 12)

76. Vessel with crabs; Comala style; earthenware. Private collection. (Schöndube essay, fig. 27)

77. Vessel with *cuahuayote* fruits; Comala style; earthenware. Denver Museum of Natural History. (Schöndube essay, fig. 25)

78. Vessel with parrot legs and a serpentine design; Comala style; earthenware. Private collection. (Catalogue, p. 288)

79. Vessel with trophy heads; Comala style; earthenware. Denver Art Museum. (Townsend essay, fig. 11)

80. Vessel with roasted maguey leaves *(mescal);* Comala style; earthenware. Los Angeles County Museum of Art, Los Angeles, gift of Mrs. Constance McCormick Fearing. (Schöndube essay, fig. 14)

81. Vessel with shrimps; Comala style; earthenware. Fowler Museum of Cultural History, University of California, Los Angeles. (Schöndube essay, fig. 26)

82. Drinking warrior with trophy heads; Comala style; earthenware. Staatliche Museen zu Berlin–Preussischer Kulturbesitz/Museum für Volkerkunde. (Townsend essay, fig. 10)

83. Vessel with squashes; Comala style; earthenware. Private collection. (Schöndube essay, fig. 19)

84. Vessel with *zapotes;* Comala style; earthenware. Fowler Museum of Cultural History, University of California, Los Angeles. (Schöndube essay, fig. 18)

85. *Reclinatorio;* Comala style; earthenware. The Miller Family Collection, Chicago. (Furst essay, fig. 9)

86. *Reclinatorio* with a dog's head in rear; Comala style; earthenware. Collection of Barbara and Justin Kerr, New York. (Furst essay, fig. 8)

87. Burial mask; Comala style; earthenware. Private collection. (The Art Institute of Chicago only.) (Braun essay, fig. 23)

88. Burial mask; Comala phase; greenstone. Private collection, on loan to the Detroit Institute of Arts. (López and Ramos essay, fig. 11)

89. Combat scene with two ballplayers; Comala phase; earthenware. Galerie Mermoz, Paris. (Day essay, fig. 23)

COLIMA/JALISCO

90. Group of conical-headed *"teco"* figurines; Late Comala phase; earthenware. The Art Museum, Princeton University, Princeton, N.J., gift of J. Lionberger Davis, class of 1900. (Mountjoy essay, fig. 8)

91. Male figurine with a finely modeled coiffure; Late Comala phase; earthenware. American Museum of Natural History, New York. (Townsend, "Introduction," fig. 26)

92. Standing male figurine with hands crossed over stomach; Late Comala phase; earthenware. Private collection. (Townsend, "Introduction," fig. 25)

93. Standing male figurine; Late Comala phase; earthenware. Private collection. (Catalogue, p. 287)

94. Standing female figure wearing a skirt; Late Comala phase; earthenware. Private collection. (Pickering and Cabrero essay, fig. 16)

95. Ring of dancers with musicians; Late Comala phase; earthenware. The Saint Louis Art Museum. (Witmore essay, fig. 3)

96. Ring of dancers; Late Comala phase; earthenware. Private collection. (Witmore essay, fig. 4)

97. Dancer wearing a deity headdress; Late Comala phase; earthenware. Hudson Museum, University of Maine, Orono, William P. Palmer III Collection. (Townsend, "Introduction," fig. 12)

98. Phallic dancer with a removable headdress; Late Comala phase; earthenware. Private collection. (Mountjoy essay, fig. 9)

99. Ritual dancer with a crocodile mask; Late Comala phase; earthenware. The Miller Family Collection, Chicago. (Townsend, "Introduction," fig. 11)

100. Three ceremonial dancers; Late Comala phase; earthenware. Private collection. (Mountjoy essay, fig. 6)

101. Standing dancer with a removable headdress; Late Comala phase; earthenware. Private collection. (Catalogue, p. 286)

102. Standing dancer with ritual attire; Late Comala phase; earthenware. Private collection. (Mountjoy essay, fig. 7)

103. Male figurine with detailed coiffure and diaper loincloth; Late Comala phase; earthenware. Stokes Family Collection, Upper Nyack, N.Y. (Pickering and Cabrero essay, fig. 17)

104. Seated male figure with a shoulder cape; Late Comala phase; earthenware. Private collection. (Weigand and Beekman essay, fig. 11)

105. Seated mother with eighty-seven children; Late Comala phase; earthenware. Private collection. (Townsend essay, fig. 18)

106. Standing male holding an *incensario;* vicinity of the Colima volcano; Late Comala phase; earthenware. Private collection. (Townsend, "Introduction," fig. 13)

107. Performer balancing ball on nose; Comala phase; earthenware. Los Angeles County Museum of Art, Los Angeles, The Proctor Stafford Collection, museum purchase with funds provided by Mr. and Mrs. Allan C. Balch. (Townsend, "Introduction," fig. 28)

108. Elephantine female figure holding a vessel with a tumpline; Comala phase; earthenware. Private collection. (Butterwick essay, fig. 13)

COLIMA/MICHOACAN

109. Seated female figure holding a plate; Coahuayana style; earthenware. Private collection. (Townsend essay, fig. 33)

110. Seated female figure holding a plate; Coahuayana style; earthenware. Collection of Saul and Marsha Stanoff, Tarzana, Calif. (Butterwick essay, fig. 12)

111. Grotesque seated female figure; Coahuayana style; earthenware. Fowler Museum of Cultural History, University of California, Los Angeles. (Catalogue, p. 285)

112. Marriage pair seated on stools and holding bowls; Coahuayana style; earthenware. Private collection. (Townsend essay, fig. 31)

113. Female figure with hands on knees; Coahuayana area; earthenware. Private collection. (Townsend, "Introduction," fig. 10)

JALISCO

114. Ceremonial spear point; obsidian. Fowler Museum of Cultural History, University of California, Los Angeles. (Pickering and Cabrero essay, fig. 7)

115. Mirror; obsidian. Natural History Museum of Los Angeles County, Los Angeles. (Mountjoy essay, fig. 11)

116. Seated chieftain; Ameca-Etzatlán style; earthenware. The Kistermann Collection, Aachen, Germany. (Townsend, "Introduction," fig. 8)

117. Seated male figure held by a female figure; Ameca-Etzatlán style; earthenware. Private collection. (Pickering and Cabrero essay, fig. 20)

118. Joined pair; Ameca-Etzatlán style; earthenware. Los Angeles County Museum of Art, Los Angeles, The Proctor Stafford Collection, museum purchase with funds provided by Mr. and Mrs. Allan C. Balch. (Braun essay, fig. 11)

119. Seated male "storyteller" figure; Ameca-Etzatlán style; earthenware. The Art Institute of Chicago, Estate of Ruth Falkenau, 1989.83. (Braun essay, fig. 21)

120. Couple carried on a litter; Ameca-Etzatlán style; earthenware. Private collection. (Butterwick essay, fig. 11)

121. Family group: a) seated female figure nursing a baby; b) gesturing seated chieftain with a young female figure; Ameca-Etzatlán style; earthenware. Private collection. (Braun essay, fig. 17)

122. Seated ballplayer; Ameca-Etzatlán style; earthenware. Private collection. (Day essay, fig. 5)

123. Seated chieftain with female attendants; Ameca-Etzatlán style; earthenware. Private collection. (Butterwick essay, fig. 4)

124. Seated male figure rhythmically gesturing; Ameca-Etzatlán style; earthenware. Los Angeles County Museum of Art, Los Angeles, The Proctor Stafford Collection, museum purchase with funds provided by Mr. and Mrs. Allan C. Balch. (Townsend, "Introduction," fig. 18)

125. Seated chieftain; Ameca-Etzatlán style; earthenware. M.G.N. Collection, Vandoeuvres, Switzerland. (Frontispiece, p. 2)

126. Seated male figure holding a bowl and drinking tube; Ameca-Etzatlán style; earthenware. Galerie Mermoz, Paris. (Butterwick essay, fig. 1)

127. Seated male figure with an upraised weapon in his hand; Ameca-Etzatlán style; earthenware. Private collection. (Weigand and Beekman essay, fig. 10)

128. Seated male pair rhythmically gesturing; Ameca-Etzatlán style; earthenware. Private collection. (Townsend, "Introduction," fig. 9)

129. Seated marriage pair; Ameca-Etzatlán style; earthenware. Private collection. (Townsend essay, fig. 32)

130. Squatting warrior wearing a helmet; Ameca-Etzatlán style; earthenware. Hudson Museum, University of Maine, Orono, William P. Palmer III Collection. (Catalogue, p. 290)

131. Standing ballplayer; Ameca-Etzatlán style; earthenware. Private collection, Barcelona. (Day essay, fig. 8)

132. Standing warrior holding a dart; Ameca-Etzatlán style; earthenware. The Kistermann Collection, Aachen, Germany. (Townsend essay, fig. 5)

133. Standing musician holding a whistle and rattle; Ameca-Etzatlán style; earthenware. Private collection. (Townsend, "Introduction," fig. 19)

134. Standing warrior holding a dart; Ameca-Etzatlán style; earthenware. The Miller Family Collection, Chicago. (Catalogue, p. 290)

135. Standing warrior holding a dart; Ameca-Etzatlán style; earthenware. Private collection. (Catalogue, p. 290)

136. Two standing male warriors with darts; Ameca-Etzatlán style; earthenware. Private collection. (Weigand and Beekman essay, fig. 12)

137. Family group; Ameca-Etzatlán style; earthenware. Private collection. (Townsend essay, fig. 35)

138. Standing warrior holding a dart; Ameca-Etzatlán style; earthenware. Private collection. (Catalogue, p. 290)

139. Figure of a high-ranking matron; Ameca-Etzatlán style; earthenware. Private collection. (Catalogue, p. 287)

140. Standing female figure; San Sebastián style; earthenware. The Art Institute of Chicago, gift of Mr. and Mrs. Joseph Antonow, 1971.888. (Townsend essay, fig. 12)

141. Seated male figure wearing a helmet; San Sebastián style; earthenware. Private collection. (Pickering and Cabrero essay, fig. 18)

142. Seated marriage pair; San Sebastián style; earthenware. The Miller Family Collection, Chicago. (Braun essay, fig. 9)

143. Female figurine; Tala-Tonalá style; earthenware. Denver Art Museum. (Townsend, "Introduction," fig. 20)

144. Elderly female figurine holding a bowl and cane; Tala-Tonalá style; earthenware. Private collection. (Pickering and Cabrero essay, fig. 21)

145. Model of a house; Tala-Tonalá style; earthenware. The Miller Family Collection, Chicago. (Townsend essay, fig. 25)

146. Standing couple; Tala-Tonalá style; earthenware. Galerie Mermoz, Paris. (Townsend essay, fig. 26)

147. Standing couple; Tala-Tonalá style; earthenware. Private collection. (Townsend, "Introduction," fig. 21)

148. Seated marriage pair; Zacatecas style; vicinity of Teocaltiche; earthenware. Denver Art Museum. (Butterwick essay, fig. 9)

149. Marriage pair; Zacatecas style; vicinity of Teocaltiche; earthenware. Collection of Herbert and Paula Molner, Chicago. (Townsend essay, fig. 34)

150. Standing female figure; Arenal style; earthenware. Hudson Museum, University of Maine, Orono, William P. Palmer III Collection. (Braun essay, fig. 15)

151. Standing warrior; Arenal style; earthenware. Los Angeles County Museum of Art, Los Angeles, The Proctor Stafford Collection, museum purchase with funds provided by Mr. and Mrs. Allan C. Balch. (Townsend essay, fig. 6)

152. Shallow bowl with a concentric red and black pattern; vicinity of Etzatlán; earthenware. Private collection. (Weigand and Beekman essay, fig. 4)

153. Bowl with a dotted pattern; vicinity of Huitzilapa; earthenware. Natural History Museum of Los Angeles County, Los Angeles. (Weigand and Beekman essay, fig. 6)

154. Bowl with a grid-and-dot pattern; vicinity of Huitzilapa; earthenware. Natural History Museum of Los Angeles County, Los Angeles. (Weigand and Beekman essay, fig. 5)

155. Bowl with emblematic pseudo-cloisonné designs; earthenware. Private collection. (Weigand and Beekman essay, fig. 18)

156. Bowl with emblematic pseudo-cloisonné designs; earthenware. Private collection. (Weigand and Beekman essay, fig. 19)

Cat. no. 93

Cat. no. 159

Cat. no. 139

Cat. no. 160

Cat. no. 167   Cat. no. 168   Cat. no. 16

MICHOACAN

157. Female figure; El Opeño; earthenware. Stokes Family Collection, Upper Nyack, N.Y. (Mountjoy essay, fig. 1)

158. Seated rotund figure with hands on hips; earthenware. Private collection, New York. (Townsend essay, fig. 16)

159. Elongated figure with hands on hips; earthenware. Private collection. (Catalogue, p. 287)

160. Standing figure wearing a headdress with twin circular motifs; earthenware. Private collection. (Catalogue, p. 287)

MICHOACAN/GUANAJUATO

161. Half-gourd vessel with frog designs; Chupícuaro; earthenware. Fowler Museum of Cultural History, University of California, Los Angeles. (Catalogue, p. 288)

162. Cylindrical tripod vessel; Chupícuaro; earthenware. Private collection. (Butterwick essay, fig. 23)

163. Tray with mammiform legs; Chupícuaro; earthenware. Private collection. (Butterwick essay, fig. 21)

164. Oval-shaped vessel with geometric designs; Chupícuaro; earthenware. Private collection. (Butterwick essay, fig. 24)

165. Vessel with a modeled face and geometric designs; Chupícuaro; earthenware. Fowler Museum of Cultural History, University of California, Los Angeles. (Catalogue, p. 288)

166. Tripod plate with a four-part chevron design; Chupícuaro; earthenware. Private collection. (Butterwick essay, fig. 22)

167. Burial mask with geometric designs; Chupícuaro; earthenware. Private collection. (Catalogue, p. 288)

168. Burial mask with geometric designs; Chupícuaro; earthenware. Private collection. (Catalogue, p. 288)

169. Standing female figure with geometric designs; Chupícuaro; earthenware. Private collection. (Mountjoy essay, fig. 5)

170. Standing female figure with geometric designs; Chupícuaro; earthenware. Fowler Museum of Cultural History, University of California, Los Angeles. (Mountjoy essay, fig. 4)

171. Monumental standing female figure with geometric designs; Chupícuaro; earthenware. Barbier Mueller Museum, Barcelona. (Townsend essay, fig. 15)

NAYARIT

172. Model of a house on a platform; Ixtlán del Río style; earthenware. The Art Institute of Chicago, gift of Ethel and Julian R. Goldsmith, 1991.479. (Butterwick essay, fig. 10)

173. Model of a houselike pavilion on a platform; Ixtlán del Río style; earthenware. Los Angeles County Museum of Art, Los Angeles, The Proctor Stafford Collection, museum purchase with funds provided by Mr. and Mrs. Allan C. Balch. (Butterwick essay, fig. 6)

174. Model of a houselike pavilion on a platform; Ixtlán del Río style; earthenware. Denver Art Museum. (Butterwick essay, fig. 14)

175. Model of a house on a platform; Ixtlán del Río style; earthenware. The Minneapolis Institute of Arts, the John R. VanDerlip Fund. (Butterwick essay, fig. 5)

176. Model of a house on a platform; Ixtlán del Río style; earthenware. Private collection. (Butterwick essay, fig. 8)

Cat. no. 78

Cat. no. 73   Cat. no. 165   Cat. no. 161

177. Model of a ballcourt; Ixtlán del Río style; earthenware. Rijksmuseum voor Volkenkunde, Leiden, The Netherlands. (Day essay, fig. 20)

178. Model of a ballcourt; Ixtlán del Río style; earthenware. Yale University Art Gallery, New Haven. (Day essay, fig. 21)

179. Model of a ballcourt; Ixtlán del Río style; earthenware. Worcester Art Museum, Mass. (Day essay, fig. 22)

180. Model of a ballcourt; Ixtlán del Río style; earthenware. Los Angeles County Museum of Art, Los Angeles, The Proctor Stafford Collection, museum purchase with funds provided by Mr. and Mrs. Allan C. Balch. (Day essay, fig. 1)

181. Model of a pole-climbing ritual; Ixtlán del Río style; earthenware. Yale University Art Gallery, New Haven. (Witmore essay, fig. 10)

182. Model of a tree-climbing ritual; Ixtlán del Río style; earthenware. The Art Institute of Chicago, gift of Ethel and Julian R. Goldsmith, 1990.554.2. (Witmore essay, fig. 13)

183. Model of a circular ceremonial center; Ixtlán del Río style; earthenware. The Art Institute of Chicago, gift of Ethel and Julian R. Goldsmith, 1989.639. (Townsend essay, fig. 2)

184. Model of a circular ceremonial center; Ixtlán del Río style; earthenware. Collection of Alan and Marianne Schwartz, Bloomfield Hills, Mich. (Witmore essay, fig. 1)

185. Model of a funerary scene; Ixtlán del Río style; earthenware. Private collection. (Townsend essay, fig. 38)

186. Model of a *pochotl* tree surrounded by four feasting couples; Ixtlán del Río style; earthenware. Hudson Museum, University of Maine, Orono, William P. Palmer III Collection. (Witmore essay, fig. 11)

187. Funerary cheek-piercing rite; Ixtlán del Río style; earthenware. The Art Institute of Chicago, gift of Ethel and Julian R. Goldsmith, 1997.475. (Townsend essay, fig. 40)

188. Funerary cheek-piercing rite; Ixtlán del Río style; earthenware. Los Angeles County Museum of Art, Los Angeles, The Proctor Stafford Collection, museum purchase with funds provided by Mr. and Mrs. Allan C. Balch. (Townsend essay, fig. 41)

189. Elderly pair; Ixtlán del Río style; earthenware. Private collection. (Furst essay, fig. 11)

190. Standing male figure with a patterned shirt and conical hat; Ixtlán del Río style; earthenware. Los Angeles County Museum of Art, Los Angeles, The Proctor Stafford Collection, museum purchase with funds provided by Mr. and Mrs. Allan C. Balch. (Mountjoy essay, fig. 12)

191. Marriage pair; Ixtlán del Río style; earthenware. The Cleveland Museum of Art, gift of Clara Taplin Rankin. (The Art Institute of Chicago only.) (Weigand and Beekman essay, fig. 13)

192. Marriage pair; Ixtlán del Río style; earthenware. Galerie Mermoz, Paris. (Anawalt essay, fig. 1)

193. Marriage pair; Ixtlán del Río style; earthenware. Private collection. (Townsend essay, fig. 29)

194. Couple with a child; Ixtlán del Río style; earthenware. Private collection. (Anawalt essay, fig. 8)

195. Standing marriage pair; Ixtlán del Río style; earthenware. Private collection. (Butterwick essay, fig. 3)

196. Crouching male figure with a smoking tube and animal visor; Ixtlán del Río style; earthenware. Collection of Mr. and Mrs. Joseph Goldenberg, Los Angeles. (Furst essay, fig. 1)

197. Male figure covered with sores; Ixtlán del Río style; earthenware. Collection of Charles and Marjorie Benton, Evanston, Ill. (Pickering and Cabrero essay, fig. 15)

198. Seated turtle-shell drummer; Ixtlán del Río style; earthenware. American Museum of Natural History, New York. (Townsend, "Introduction," fig. 1)

199. Warrior pair; Ixtlán del Río style; earthenware. Private collection. (Townsend, "Introduction," fig. 14)

200. Seated polychrome female figure with tattoos; Lagunillas style; Bolaños; earthenware. Private collection. (Pickering and Cabrero essay, fig. 5)

201. Kneeling female figure; Lagunillas "A" style; vicinity of Compostela; earthenware. Los Angeles County Museum of Art, Los Angeles, The Proctor Stafford Collection, museum purchase with funds provided by Mr. and Mrs. Allan C. Balch. (Townsend essay, fig. 22)

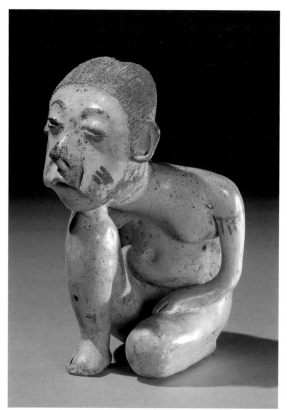
Cat. no. 216

202. Kneeling female figure; Lagunillas "A" style; vicinity of Compostela; earthenware. Stokes Family Collection, Upper Nyack, N.Y. (Townsend essay, fig. 21)

203. Reclining female figure; Lagunillas "B" style; earthenware. The Fine Arts Museums of San Francisco, lent by the Land Collection. (Catalogue, p. 283)

204. Seated male figure holding a cup and an *acocote* gourd sucking tube; Lagunillas "B" style; earthenware. Denver Art Museum. (Butterwick essay, fig. 15)

205. Female figure with an apron "table"; Lagunillas "C" style; earthenware. The Metropolitan Museum of Art, New York, The Michael C. Rockefeller Memorial Collection, bequest of Nelson A. Rockefeller, 1979. (Townsend essay, fig. 19)

206. Seated female figure; Lagunillas "C" style; earthenware. Private collection. (Townsend essay, fig. 13)

207. Seated figure with a striped head; Lagunillas "C" style; earthenware. The University of Iowa Museum of Art, Iowa City, gift of Gerald and Hope Solomons. (Catalogue, p. 283)

Cat. no. 74

Cat. no. 20

Cat. no. 46

Cat. no. 135

Cat. no. 130

Cat. no. 134

Cat. no. 138

208. Seated figure with polychrome face-paint; Lagunillas "C" style; earthenware. Private collection. (Townsend, "Introduction," fig. 17)

209. Standing figure with a painted face and torso; Lagunillas "C" style; earthenware. Private collection. (Catalogue, p. 285)

210. Seated female figure; Lagunillas "C" style; earthenware. Private collection. (Townsend essay, fig. 20)

211. Reclining figure; Lagunillas "E" style; earthenware. Collection of Saul and Marsha Stanoff, Tarzana, Calif. (Catalogue, p. 284)

212. Seated chieftain; Lagunillas "E" style; earthenware. Private collection, Belgium. (The Art Institute of Chicago only.) (Townsend essay, fig. 43)

213. Seated female figure with a "red hand" sign; Lagunillas "E" style; earthenware. Private collection. (Townsend, "Introduction," fig. 16)

214. Seated female figure with a "red hand" sign; Lagunillas "E" style; earthenware. Collection of Saul and Marsha Stanoff, Tarzana, Calif. (Townsend, "Introduction," fig. 15)

215. Seated pair; Lagunillas "E" style; earthenware. Collection of Mr. and Mrs. Morris A. Long, Castle Rock, Colo. (Catalogue, p. 284)

216. Seated elderly male figure with a striped face; Lagunillas "E" style; earthenware. Collection of Barbara and Justin Kerr, New York. (Catalogue, p. 289)

217. Standing female figure; Lagunillas "E" style; earthenware. Denver Art Museum. (Townsend essay, fig. 30b)

218. Standing male figure; Lagunillas "E" style; earthenware. Collection of Mr. and Mrs. Morris A. Long, Castle Rock, Colo. (Townsend essay, fig. 30a)

219. Seated elderly male figure with a black facial design; Lagunillas "E" style; earthenware. Collection of Saul and Marsha Stanoff, Tarzana, Calif. (Pickering and Cabrero essay, fig. 23)

220. Bowl with multiple sets of vertical bands; vicinity of Lagunillas; earthenware. Natural History Museum of Los Angeles County, Los Angeles. (Pickering and Cabrero essay, fig. 10)

221. Bowl with four sets of vertical bands; vicinity of Lagunillas; earthenware. Natural History Museum of Los Angeles County, Los Angeles. (Pickering and Cabrero essay, fig. 11)

222. Plate with a lobed rosette pattern; vicinity of Lagunillas; earthenware. Natural History Museum of Los Angeles County, Los Angeles. (Pickering and Cabrero essay, fig. 9)

TWENTIETH CENTURY

223. Frida Kahlo; *Four Inhabitants of Mexico;* 1938; oil on wood panel. Private collection. (Braun essay, fig. 14)

224. Rufino Tamayo; *Woman with a Birdcage;* 1941; oil on canvas. The Art Institute of Chicago, gift of the Joseph Winterbotham Collection, 1942.57. (Braun essay, fig. 20)

225. Rufino Tamayo; *The Fruit Vendor;* 1943; gouache over graphite on white wove paper. The Art Institute of Chicago, Elizabeth F. Chapman Bequest, 1981.151. (Braun essay, fig. 22)

226. Henry Moore; *Family Group;* 1947; plaster. Art Gallery of Ontario, Toronto, gift of Henry Moore, 1974. (Braun essay, fig. 12)

NOTES

Phil C. Weigand and Christopher S. Beekman, "The Teuchitlán Tradition: Rise of a Statelike Society"

The fieldwork represented in this study was carried out by permission of the Centro Regional de Jalisco of the Instituto Nacional de Antropología e Historia. The authors gratefully acknowledge the support given to research from El Colegio de Michoacán. They would also like to thank Brigitte Boehm de Lameiras, Francisco Ron Siordia, Dolores Soto de Arechavaleta, Joseph Mountjoy, Otto Schöndube, Michael Spence, Jorge Ramos, Lorenza López, Meredith Aronson, Glenn Stuart, Michael Ohnersorgen, Mark Varien, Eduardo Williams, Luis Arias, James Schoenwetter, and express a special thanks to Javier Galván V. and Acelia García de Weigand.

1. Weigand 1993a.
2. See Díaz 1987.
3. See Oliveros 1974, 1992b.
4. Long 1966; Weigand 1985, 1993a, 1996a; Galván 1991; Ramos and López 1996.
5. Von Winning and Hammer 1972.
6. See Ramos and López 1996; and for El Arenal, see Weigand 1993a.
7. Huitzilapa is a type 2 tomb; type 1 tombs measure up to 18–22 meters deep.
8. For El Arenal, see Corona Núñez 1955.
9. For type 3 tombs at Tabachines, see Galván 1991.
10. Ramos and López 1996.
11. Corona Núñez 1955.
12. See Galván 1991, Zepeda 1994.
13. See Southall 1988.
14. Beekman 1996c.
15. For Atemajac, see Galván 1991; Aronson 1993, 1996; Beekman 1996b, 1996c. For the Atoyec–Sayula valley, see Acosta, Ramírez, and Gómez 1996.
16. Beekman 1996b, 1996c.
17. For the Banderas valley, see Mountjoy 1996; for the Río Bolaños gorge, see Kelley 1971; Weigand 1985; Cabrero 1989, 1996; for the Bajío of Guanajuato, see Sanchez and Marmolejo 1990; Cárdenas 1996.
18. Ramos and López led Phil Weigand on a guided tour of Comala in 1996.
19. Algaze 1993.
20. Stuart 1992.
21. Weigand 1994.
22. Weigand 1996a.
23. Soto de Arechavaleta 1982.
24. See also Valdez, Liot, Acosta, and Emphoux 1996.
25. Acosta, Ramírez, and Gómez 1996.
26. For the Río Bolaños canyon, see Kelley 1971 and Cabrero 1996; for Guadalajara, see Galván 1991; for Huitzilapa, see Ramos and López 1996.
27. Jackson 1984.
28. Ibid.
29. Ohnersorgen and Varien 1996.
30. We have kept to a conservative estimate of contemporaneity of fifty percent.
31. Ohnersorgen and Varien 1996 used gravity models for calculating the neighbors that interacted with each other, for areas with formal architecture.
32. On the Maya, see Folan, Kintz, and Fletcher 1983; Ashmore 1981; Culbert 1977; Culbert and Rice 1990. For Teotihuacan, see Millon, Drewitt, and Cowgill 1973; Sanders, Parsons, and Santley 1979.
33. In addition to Mumford 1961, we are thinking here of Handlin and Burchard 1963.
34. Hosler 1988.
35. Pollard 1993.

Lorenza López Mestas Camberos and Jorge Ramos de la Vega, "Excavating the Tomb at Huitzilapa"

The authors wish to acknowledge the assistance of Bruce F. Benz of the Instituto Manantlán de Ecología y la Conservación de la Biodiversidad, Universidad de Guadalajara, for his efforts to identify the organic material present in the Huitzilapa tomb; Robert B. Pickering, for his analysis of the skeletal remains; Gabriela Ulloa, for her drawings in this essay; and Phil Weigand for his consultation throughout our investigation.

1. Weigand 1993a.
2. Service 1962.
3. Sarmiento 1992.
4. Weigand 1993a, p. 67.
5. Weigand 1993a, p. 61.
6. Von Winning 1974; von Winning and Hammer 1972.
7. Eliade 1968, pp. 20–23.
8. López Luján 1993, p. 59.
9. Pickering 1996.
10. P. Furst 1966; Weigand 1993a, p. 53.
11. Sarmiento 1992, p. 116.
12. Robin Fox 1980, p. 46.
13. Robin Fox 1980.
14. Grove and Gillespie 1992a.
15. P. Furst 1966.
16. López Austin 1984, vol. 1, p. 32; 1990, pp. 14–15; 1994, pp. 10–13; Sprajc 1989, pp. 9–14, Williams 1992, p. 49; Townsend 1979.

17. Kirchhoff 1952; Jiménez Moreno 1972, p. 31.
18. P. Furst 1966, pp. 68–69.
19. Saxe 1970b.
20. *Relación de Michoacán* 1977, pp. 219–20.
21. Durán 1967, vol. 1, p. 56.
22. Pickering 1996.
23. Von Winning 1974.
24. Sahagún 1989; vol. 1, p. 220.
25. Townsend 1979; López Austin 1984.
26. López Austin 1984, vol. 1, pp. 58–61.
27. Florescano 1994, p. 127; Townsend 1979, pp. 37–39.
28. Aveni 1991, pp. 266–69.
29. Sprajc 1989, pp. 171–72.
30. Florescano 1993, pp. 13–15.
31. Manzanilla 1994, p. 54.
32. Grove 1981b, p. 64.
33. González 1975, p. 38.
34. P. Furst 1966, pp. 49, 56–57, 63.
35. *Florentine Codex*, vol. 3, p. 39, quoted by González 1975.
36. Galván 1991, p. 246; Girard 1975, pp. 61–62.
37. J. Furst 1982, pp. 207–21.
38. *Codex Borgia*, quoted by Suárez 1974, p. 37.
39. Relación de Michoacán 1977, p. 218; *Florentine Codex*, pl. 57.
40. Villanueva et al. 1996.
41. P. Furst 1966, pp. 157–58, 163.
42. Smith 1984, p. 25ff.
43. Sprajc 1989, p. 118.
44. Weigand 1993a, p. 63.
45. Scarborough and Wilcox 1991.
46. Leyenaar and Parsons 1988.
47. Florescano 1993, p. 19.
48. Manzanilla 1994, p. 55.
49. Castro Leal 1986, p. 27.
50. Gillespie 1991, p. 335.
51. Kan, Meighan, and Nicholson 1970, figs. 123, 127, 129; von Winning 1974, figs. 55–56.
52. Grove and Gillespie 1992b; Sarmiento 1992; Service 1975; Sahlins 1968; Spencer 1987.
53. Grove and Gillespie 1992b, pp. 17–18.
54. Firth 1967; Leach 1954; Godelier 1978; Scarduelli 1988, p. 93.
55. Sprajc 1989, p. 180.
56. Grove and Gillespie 1992b.
57. Sprajc 1989, p. 180.

Robert B. Pickering and Maria Teresa Cabrero, "Mortuary Practices in the Shaft-Tomb Region"

1. Adams 1997. To compound the problem, Adams further implies that even the Tarascans do not measure up to cultural developments in Central Mexico.
2. Kelley 1938, 1945; Scott 1968–73.
3. Cabrero 1995.
4. Especially notable has been the work by Saxe 1970a, Binford 1971, and Brown 1971, and expanded upon more recently by O'Shea 1984 and Beck 1995.
5. Corona Núñez 1955; Long 1966; Oliveras 1974; and Galván 1991.
6. Galván 1991.
7. Corona Núñez 1955.
8. Weigand 1996a; see also P. Furst 1975.
9. Oliveros 1974.
10. Long 1966.
11. Ibid. Since the San Sebastián data was reconstructed by Long rather than observed, this information may not be entirely accurate.
12. Pickering 1996, 1997a, 1997b.
13. Von Winning 1974; von Winning 1987.
14. Bloch 1971; Buikstra 1977, 1979, 1985; Douglass 1969.
15. Perhaps the best description of this type of behavior comes from the Merina of Madagascar; see Bloch 1971.
16. Gill 1971, 1985.
17. P. Furst 1975.

Kristi Butterwick, "Food for the Dead: The West Mexican Art of Feasting"

I am grateful to Barbara Voorhies, Joseph Mountjoy, Peter Furst, Otto Schöndube, Hasso von Winning, Chris Beekman, John E. Clark, Francisco Valdez, Bruce Benz, and William Litzinger, who all helped me to refine my arguments about feasting strategies and *pulque* production in West Mexico. I thank Jane Day, Bob Pickering, and Phil Weigand and Acelia García de Weigand for introducing me to West Mexico, and Jorge Ramos and Lorenza López for facilitating my work at Huitzilapa. The errors invariably are my own.

1. Díaz del Castillo (1956 edition, pp. 209–11).
2. Townsend 1992, pp. 212–15.
3. *Octli* is the Nahuatl term for *pulque*. Agave is the genus that includes hundreds of varieties of the spiky century plant; see Bruman 1940; Gentry 1982.
4. Sahagún 1950–82, book 2 (The Ceremonies), pp. 14, 97.
5. Nicholson 1971, p. 409; for discussions of funerary feasts and Day of the Dead antecedents in Mexico, see Carmichael and Sayer 1992, pp. 27–30; Carrasco 1990, pp. 142–45; Couch 1985; Nutini 1988. For the original description, see Sahagún 1950–82, book 2 (The Ceremonies), pp. 17–18, 111.
6. G. Foster 1948, p. 218; Nutini 1988, pp. 53–76.
7. Coe 1975, p. 193.
8. My discussion of mortuary feasting owes a debt to the scholarly works of Damon 1989; R. Foster 1995; Hayden 1995; Kan 1989; Kirch 1991.
9. My discussion of the economic and political motivations of competitive feasts derives from the scholarly works of Blitz 1993; Brumfiel 1994; Clark and Blake 1994; D'Altroy 1994; Feinman 1995; Friedman and Rowlands 1978; Hayden 1995, 1996; Hayden and Gargett 1990; Sahlins 1968; Spencer 1994.
10. Clark and Blake (1994) argue that population growth is an outcome of social complexity rather than a cause.
11. Gentry 1982, p. 551 ff.
12. Otto Schöndube examines the sculptures of food alone in this volume.
13. Reentz-Budet 1994.
14. In historic times, the Tarahumara, Cora, Huichol, and Tepecan peoples of West Mexico used gourd vessels especially as cups (Lumholtz 1902; Bruman 1940; Mason 1981). Regarding fancy gourd containers, excavations at Ceren, El Salvador, directed by Payson Sheets (1992) uncovered a stack of preserved gourd vessels that had been stuccoed and painted in polychrome designs. The Maya of today use gourd cups in funerary rites (Nash 1970).
15. Karl Taube (1989) identified maize tamales in Maya art using a combination of hieroglyphic and historic sources.
16. I analyzed imagery of feasting, drinking, human figures, personal adornments, and mortuary themes in a study of 82 ceramic architectural models with 590 attached figurines; see Day, Butterwick, and Pickering 1996; Butterwick 1998.
17. Brumfiel 1985; Hastorf 1991.
18. Ekholm 1979.
19. McAnany 1995, p.31.
20. Richard Townsend suggested the Tewa Pueblo as a model of a society practicing dual social organization. Anthropologist Alfonso Ortiz (1969), himself a member of the Tewa Pueblo, describes the tradition.
21. Moore 1995.
22. See Weigand 1974, p. 123; Friedman and Rowlands 1978, p. 221.
23. Pohl and Pohl 1994, pp. 140–41.
24. For discussions on the use of costume to signify social status in pre-Hispanic societies, see (for Mesoamerica) Anawalt 1981, (for South America) Cook 1992 and Rodman 1992, and (for West Mexico) Anawalt 1992, Long 1966, von Winning 1974, and von Winning and Hammer 1972.
25. Ramos and López 1996.
26. P. Furst 1973, 1975.
27. J. Furst 1995; Perrin 1996, p. 408.
28. In a seminal art historical approach, von Winning and Hammer (1972) produced the exhibition catalogue *Anecdotal Sculpture of Ancient West Mexico*. Continued research into the complexities of West Mexican societies, however, has shown that the art is meaningful and symbolic rather than anecdotal: see P. Furst 1973; Dwyer

and Dwyer 1975; Gallagher 1983; Day, Butterwick, and Pickering 1996.

29. Lind 1987. On the Cholula murals, see Luce 1976, Marquina 1971.

30. Fox 1996.

31. Aronson 1993, 1996; Galván 1991; Ramos and López 1996.

32. Aronson 1996, p. 165.

33. Ramos and López 1996, p. 126, table 1. Bruce Benz, an ethnobotanist for the Instituto Manantlán de Ecología of the University of Guadalajara, and of the Botanical Research Institute of Texas, is conducting the analyses.

34. See Craine and Reindorp 1970, pp. 29–47, for Tarascan mortuary feasts; p. 185 for the flagpole ceremony; see also Kelley 1974.

35. Lumholtz 1902. Information regarding his encounters with the Huichol is contained in vol. 2; see pp. 28–30, 242 for feasting references.

36. Ibid., p. 30.

37. Preuss 1996, pp. 120, 126–32. Following in Lumholtz's path, Konrad Theodor Preuss, a German ethnographer, recorded Huichol ceremonies from 1905 to 1907.

38. Lumholtz 1902, vol. 2, p. 29.

39. García de Weigand and Weigand 1992, pp. 228 ff.

40. Silva 1996, pp. 392–94.

41. See Lumholtz 1902, vol. 1, pp. 383–89 for mortuary rituals and feasting. *Tesvino* or *tesgüino* was the name for the ritual brew of Tarahumara, made of fermented corn and/or agave juice.

42. Lumholtz 1902.

43. Merrill 1988, pp. 160–85.

44. G. Foster 1948, p. 219.

45. For accounts of the Tarascan use of *pulque,* see Craine and Reindorp 1970, pp. 203, 13; for historic records, see Bruman 1940; for general pre-Hispanic use, see Gentry 1982; Litzinger 1983; and Parsons and Parsons 1990.

46. Lumholtz 1902, vol. 1, p. 256.

47. Merrill 1988, pp. 175, 178.

48. De Barrios 1971.

49. Litzinger 1983, p. 9; Schele and Freidel 1990, pp. 254–55; Reents-Budet 1994, p. 82; von Winning and Hammer 1972, pp. 36–38.

50. Fox 1996, p. 495.

51. Hayden 1995, p. 63.

52. Kelley 1995; Soto de Arechavaleta 1982.

53. Clark and Blake 1994.

54. McAnany 1995, pp. 32–33.

55. Voorhies 1989.

Christopher L. Witmore, "Sacred Sun Centers"

1. The topic for this study was suggested to me by Joseph B. Mountjoy, and he worked closely with me on the research.

2. Weigand 1985, pp. 66–67.

3. Weigand 1996a.

4. Weigand 1985, pp. 66–67.

5. Chamberlain 1982, p. 183.

6. Ibid.

7. Murie 1981, p. 24.

8. Caso 1938, p. 64; see also Caso 1958.

9. Townsend 1979, p. 37.

10. Ibid.

11. Lumholtz 1900, p. 111.

12. Ibid., p. 26.

13. Ibid., p. 27.

14. Mountjoy 1987, pp. 161–62; Mountjoy 1982a, p. 110.

15. Joseph Mountjoy, personal communication.

16. Weigand 1996a; Kelley 1974.

17. Phil Weigand, personal communication via Richard Townsend; for discussion of the *volador,* see Kelley 1974.

18. Townsend 1979, p. 39.

19. Ibid.

20. Helms 1979, p. 125.

21. Joseph Mountjoy, personal communication.

22. Cohodas 1991.

23. See also Cohodas 1991.

24. Aveni, Hartung, and Kelley 1982, p. 319.

25. Ibid., p. 328.

26. Aveni, Hartung, and Buckingham 1978, p. 52.

27. Aveni and Hartung 1981, pp. 53–57.

28. Weigand 1985, 1992a, 1993b, 1996a.

29. Compania Mexicana de Aerofotos S.A. 1: 40,000 aerial photo of the Teuchitlán area.

Jane Stevenson Day, "The West Mexican Ballgame"

1. Taladoire 1994, p. 10.

2. Oliveros 1974, p. 182.

3. Oliveros 1992a, p. 47.

4. Coe 1965; Castillo 1992.

5. Weigand 1991, 1996a.

6. Von Winning 1974; Kan, Meighan, and Nicholson 1989.

7. Von Winning and Hammer 1972; Day, Butterwick, and Pickering 1996.

8. Ramos and López 1996.

9. Ibid.

10. Gallagher 1983, p. 99, fig. 130; Kan, Meighan, and Nicholson 1989, p. 122, fig. 9.

11. Von Winning 1974.

12. Von Winning and Hammer 1972, pp. 87, 88, figs. 149, 155, 157, 158.

13. Leyenaar and Parsons 1988, fig. 26.

14. P. Furst 1966.

15. Ramos and López 1996.

16. Castro Leal 1992, p. 279.

17. Schöndube 1995.

18. Von Winning and Hammer 1972.

19. Durán 1971.

20. Weigand 1991, 1996a.

21. Uriarte 1992.

22. Wilkerson 1991, p. 60.

23. Solis 1992.

24. Weigand 1991.

25. Braniff 1988, p. 48.

26. Koontz 1994.

27. Weigand 1991.

28. McNeill 1995.

Peter T. Furst, "Shamanic Symbolism, Transformation, and Deities in West Mexican Funerary Art"

1. Covarrubias 1957, p. 87.

2. Rivera told me this during a visit I made to his Mexico city home in 1955.

3. The Mexican ethnologist Roberto Williams García has observed the use of archaeological whistles in a Tepéhua curing rite in Veracruz, Mexico. See Williams García 1963; P. Furst 1967.

4. The conception of the deceased as continuing their lives, albeit on a different plane, also accounts for the representation in some Nayarit house models of below-floor burials as a room below the living floor, sometimes with a dog lying across the threshold, sometimes with people apparently engaged, like those above, in everyday activities. Because these people were not laid out on their backs as would be our dead, the below-floor burials were not recognized as such until relatively recently. That they were in fact sub-floor tombs first occurred to me in the mid-1960s while Richard Rudolph—then chairman of the Department of Oriental Languages at UCLA and a member of my doctoral committee—and I were comparing photographs of architectural models from Han Dynasty tombs in China with house models from Nayarit. Rudolph wondered if I saw the same similarities between them as did Gordon Ekholm, the curator of Middle American Archaeology at the American Museum of Natural History, who had proposed them as evidence for trans-Pacific diffusion. Rudolph attributed them to ideological similarities rather than diffusion; so did I. I incorporated some of these ideas into a public lecture that was later published (P. Furst 1975).

5. I cannot claim this insight as my own. Male figures blowing into a vessel are not uncommon, but their meaning did not become clear to me until I came across an old photograph by Frank

Speck of a Catawba medicine man doing just that (in the archives of the University of Pennsylvania Museum of Archaeology and Anthropology).

6. J. Furst 1978, 1982.

7. Adam 1940.

8. For a discussion of Huichol origins, see P. Furst 1996b.

9. P. Furst 1994.

10. P. Furst 1972, pp. 145–84; P. Furst 1976, pp. 109–33; Myerhoff 1974.

11. Reichel-Dolmatoff 1985.

12. P. Furst 1965b, pp. 29–60.

13. Because the ecstatic trance, often (though by no means always and everywhere) triggered with the assistance of certain plants, is such an important aspect of the shaman's calling, the contributions of ethnobotany and phytochemistry came to be recognized as indispensable to shamanic scholarship. Indeed, ethnobotanists were pioneers among the various specialists working in this area. The groundbreaking field research by ethnobotanist Richard Evans Schultes, longtime director of Harvard's Botanical Museum, in Mexico and Amazonia, beginning in the late 1930s and lasting through much of the second half of the twentieth century, and his numerous scholarly papers and books, deserve special mention. But there are many others, beginning in the mid-nineteenth century with Richard Spruce, without whose ethnobotanical scholarship the ethnology of shamanism would also be much the poorer.

14. See, for example, Reichel-Dolmatoff 1975; Wilbert 1987; Langdon and Baer 1992.

15. Ruíz de Alarcón 1984. As the brother of Juan Ruíz de Alarcón, still celebrated as one of Mexico's and Spain's most distinguished literary figures, and as one of the few seventeenth century clerics to have bothered to learn Nahuatl, the language of the Aztecs and his unfortunate parishioners, Ruíz de Alarcón's words carried considerable weight. For biographical data see Coe and Whittaker 1982.

16. The meaning of *tonalli*, a term related to the Nahuatl-language *tona*, meaning "to make heat or sun," is not easily compressed into a few lines. J. L. McKeever Furst (personal communication) abstracts it as an "animating force that is felt as body heat. It comes and goes from the top of the head, roughly at the position of the anterior fontanelle (i.e., the location of the horn in certain Colima figures). Some people have more of it and can add to it over a lifetime, others less. Those with esoteric knowledge and power have more of it than others; it can leave the body in dreams and at death it leaves for the underworld, the cooling off of the body manifesting its departure and absence." For more details on this complex and sophisticated concept, see López Austin 1988; Ortiz de Montellano 1990; J. L. McKeever Furst 1995.

17. Persistent lobbying by Eastvold helped secure the authorization by Congress, in 1990, of a 7256-acre tract of an ancient lava flow rich in rock art west of Albuquerque, New Mexico, as Petroglyph National Monument, under the aegis of the National Park Service. This area had long been coveted by developers for new housing tracts. In addition to the vast array of petroglyphs inscribed onto its black lava rock, the new national monument is considered sacred and deserving of preservation and protection by at least two pueblos, Laguna and Zia. In their traditions the lava-covered mesa is traversed by spirit trails along which the souls of the dead travel between the Sandia mountain range and the volcanoes.

18. Horcasitas 1953; P. Furst 1993.

19. Zuidema 1977–78.

20. Smith 1997–78.

Mark Graham, "The Iconography of Rulership in Ancient West Mexico"

Initial work on this problem began during a year I spent as a visiting professor in the Department of Art History at the University of Utah, and I want to thank Frank Sanguinetti and his staff at the Utah Museum of Fine Arts for their exceptional support then and since. I am grateful to Mary Miller of Yale University for having included me in a College Art Association meeting in New York where some of these points were discussed.

1. See Kan 1989; Covarrubias 1957; von Winning and Hammer 1972; Kubler 1984; and Adams 1991, respectively.

2. For a time, both Meighan and Nicholson had active research projects in West Mexico; see the extensive bibliography in Kan, Meighan, and Nicholson 1989. Furst, of course, became an influential interpreter of West Mexican art and the pioneering spokesman

for the shamanism-based approach to ancient American art. Probably not unrelated to its academic focus on West Mexico, the Los Angeles area was also a center of the market for West Mexican art, one that developed rapidly in the 1950s and 1960s as sites were stripped and dug on a large scale. There was also considerable museum expertise in Los Angeles. For example, Hasso von Winning, an important and generous source of knowledge and expertise for both the collecting community and the academic community, was at the Southwest Museum.

3. The *locus classicus* for the modern study of shamanism is Mircea Eliade, *Shamanism: Archaic Techniques of Ecstasy* (1964), from the original French edition of 1951. This is a groundbreaking work, widely cited even today, although seldom sufficiently critiqued. It is, for example, very Jungian, and at times any religious or folkloric practice anywhere in the world seems to be grist for the mill of a universal shamanism. From the standpoint of anthropological and historical methodology, many of the conclusions that constitute Eliade's global model of shamanism are weak and poorly argued. For a concise discussion of shamanism by an anthropologist, see Crocker 1985, pp. 3–15; the essay by Langdon in the volume edited by Langdon and Baer (1992); and the essays in the volume edited by Thomas and Humphrey (1994).

4. See P. Furst 1965b, 1965c, 1968, 1973, 1974, and 1975.

5. See Weigand 1985.

6. Furst's study of the ceramic house models is his "House of Darkness and House of Light: Sacred Functions of West Mexican Funerary Art" (P. Furst 1975). This is perhaps the most dazzling demonstration of the compelling rhetorical power of Furst's narrative style. The assumed subtext of Furst's essay is the (then recent) exhibition catalogue by von Winning and Hammer, *Anecdotal Sculpture of Ancient West Mexico* (1972), whose title reveals its connection with the Daily Life model. Furst's work on West Mexico, in particular, deserves a more thorough critical art-historical assessment than it has received up to now.

7. See the essay by Phil Weigand in this volume; Weigand 1993a; and Williams and Weigand 1996.

8. See P. Furst 1975.

9. The point here is not precociousness in the rise of social complexity and inequality, as with the Early and Middle Formative Gulf Coast or Middle Formative Oaxaca, but the normative nature of such developments, a feature of Late Formative and Protoclassic times. For example, discontinuously but more or less simultaneously throughout the Maya regions, similar artifact categories and image configurations were chosen to denote the emergence of superordinate ranks in the Late Formative and Protoclassic periods: temple platforms with planetary masks (Cerros, Belize, and Uaxactun, Guatemala) and three-quarter-view standing figures of "rulers" in association with caves, implements of sacrifice, and cosmic markers (Kaminaljuyú, Guatemala, and Loltun, Yucatán) (see Schele and Freidel 1990; Freidel, Schele, and Parker 1993).

10. See, for example, the review by Gorenstein (1996) in *Latin American Antiquity* of recent volumes on the archaeology of West Mexico written or edited by Williams and Novella, Weigand, and Boehm de Lameiras. See also Gorenstein's introduction to Pollard's (1993) monograph on the Tarascan state, where Gorenstein suggests that the "marginality" of West Mexico derives in part from the adoption of an Aztec-centered evolutionist paradigm that stereotyped much of Mesoamerica and in part from a certain rigidity of mindset of many Mesoamerican archaeologists. As the junior partner in its own set of binary terms, Mesoamerican art history tended to follow and accept Mesoamerican archaeology's priorities and values.

11. See, for example, Miller 1986, p. 56; von Winning 1974, p. 32.

12. Kelly 1980.

13. In traditional formulations of art history's methods or approaches, iconography, as the focus on subject matter, is distinguished from studies of form or style and from connoisseurship, a division commonly acknowledged in the introductory matter of art history survey texts.

14. The spectrum of recent evaluations of the work of Panofsky on iconography is represented by Holly 1984, Preziosi 1989, and Bann 1996. As one would expect, postmodern and poststructuralist critiques of Panofsky have been quite severe, being aimed, among other things, at his interpretative certainty and at his essentially asocial notion of imagery. But such critiques do not significantly erode either the logical merit of Panofsky's analytical method or his insistence on rigorous visual and textual analysis, even if he sometimes failed to meet his own standards. In fact, Panofsky is probably being read more seriously now than a generation ago.

15. See, for example, Panofsky 1955.

16. Kubler 1984, pp. 39–40.

17. Furst 1965b, p. 42.

18. The Colima figure in Utah is unprovenienced, as, of course, are nearly all ceramics from ancient West Mexico. The Utah Museum of Fine Arts at the University of Utah purchased the figure in the 1980s from a California dealer of good reputation. The whereabouts of the figure before its arrival in the United States are unknown.

19. Actual conical elements identical in form to those depicted on many Colima figures' headdresses were discovered in a large multiple burial within the Temple of the Feathered Serpent at Teotihuacan, dated to the Late Formative Miccaotli phase (150–200 A.D.). The context at Teotihuacan did not appear to elucidate the function of the greenstone cones (see Berrin and Pasztory 1993, cat. no. 173).

20. In addition to *S. gigas,* other species and varieties of shells with spires that were used variously as offerings, trumpets, and apparently as headdress elements include *Strombus costatus, Pleuroplaca gigantea, Fasciolara gigantea,* and *Turbinella angulata. T. angulata,* the West Indian chank from the Caribbean and the Gulf of Mexico, is often confused with *Strombus* species that may come from both the Pacific and the Caribbean, and this may be the most common of the so-called conchs represented at Teotihuacan. Shell identifications are based on Abbot and Dance 1983, a standard handbook.

21. Von Winning illustrates as a forgery a seated male figure with what he calls a "spiked headdress," noting it as one of several "iconographic inconsistencies" in the figure (1974, pp. 76–77, fig. 347). After the Utah figure turned up (in the 1980s), however, von Winning accepted its authenticity.

22. See Parsons 1986. A stela is a shaped stone shaft, usually carved in relief, with the image of a ruler or other notable and often with an accompanying hieroglyphic text. (For fuller explanations of this and other terms, see the handbook by Miller and Taube [1993]). Stone monuments from archaeological sites are ordinarily numbered in order of their discovery, so Stela 11 from Kaminaljuyú, Guatemala, referenced in the text, is the eleventh such stone monument discovered at that site. What archaeologists have named the Miraflores-Arenal tradition of stone sculpture embraces sculpture of the southern Maya region of Guatemala and the neighboring Mexican state of Chiapas during the Late Formative period, perhaps 200–100 B.C.; the names Miraflores and Arenal denote local ceramic phases, whose dating (normally by radiocarbon method) allows the stone sculpture in turn to be dated, when found with ceramics of those phases. The Late Formative period in southern Mesoamerica, especially in the regions inhabited by speakers of Mayan languages, was a period during which new ideas about rulership and its cosmic dimensions started to emerge and be given artistic form.

23. Schele and Miller 1986, pp. 119–20.

24. Schele and Freidel 1990.

25. The obverse (the Olmec side) of the Dumbarton Oaks pectoral depicts the same type of headdress gem as that worn by the central figure on La Venta (Tabasco) Altar 4; see de la Fuente 1988, pl. 18 (reversed), figs. 50a–d. Although commonly identified as a pectoral, the arrangement on the La Venta altar suggests that the Dumbarton Oaks piece also might have been worn by its Middle Formative owner(s) as a headdress gem.

26. Among the Maya and some of their neighbors, the sky band was a serpentlike motif that frequently framed or marked the portrayal of notables, playing on the linguistic similarity in most Mayan languages of words for sky and snake. The sky band served to visually express the cosmic dimensions of the ruler. Similarly, in much of Mesoamerica, the iridescent green tail feathers of the quetzal *(Pharomachrus mocinno)* were widely used in noble dress because of the rarity of the feathers themselves (the birds live only in the high, wet cloud forests of Central America) and because of their visual resemblance to jade, the most precious of all natural materials in ancient Mesoamerica, associated intimately with rulership and fertility. See Miller and Taube 1993.

27. Schele and Freidel 1990, pp. 284–85, 408.

28. See Schele and Freidel 1990, pp. 414–15; Schele and Miller 1986. In Mesoamerica, the ritual of bloodletting was strongly associated with the burdens of nobility, for whom the sacrifice of their blood likened them to the gods, and in some archaeological cultures, such as the Maya, bloodletting was a part of accession and other rituals of statecraft. See Miller and Taube 1993, pp. 46–47.

29. Miller and Taube 1993, p. 45.

30. Schele and Freidel 1990, fig. 2.13; Schele 1995, p. 111.

31. Schele and Miller 1986, pp. 308–09.

32. Data on burials at Teotihuacan were compiled by Martha L. Sempowski (see Sempowski and Spence 1994). Sempowski indicated that 19.4 percent (55 of 284) of all burials contained shell, and that whole shells, including conchs, occurred in 7 percent (20 of 284). To the degree that this is a statistically valid sample, the status associations are revealing: shells rarely occurred in children's burials, and adult male burials with shells outnumbered those of females by about two to one, suggesting a congruence of ascribed status and masculine gender or, in other words, high-status males. Sempowski further noted that the Temple of the Feathered Serpent in the Ciudadela is "the one location that is outstanding in terms of the incidence of shell in burials" (Sempowski and Spence 1994, p. 156). The Ciudadela and the Temple of the Feathered Serpent are thought to have been especially associated with the (still little understood) rulership structure of Teotihuacan.

33. According to de la Fuente, Trejo, and Gutiérrez Solana 1988 (see no. 90). The archaeological site of Tula, in the state of Hidalgo, Mexico, is a Terminal Classic and Early Postclassic city and temple-center north of Teotihuacan that inherited some of Teotihuacan's economic power in central Mexico, especially that which derived from the control of economically important raw materials such as obsidian and turquoise.

34. See, for example, Broda 1987.

35. Among the many references to conch shells and their associations in the *Florentine Codex,* see, for example, book 1 ("The Gods"), p. 9; book 2 ("The Ceremonies"), pp. 205, 216; book 3 ("The Origin of the Gods"), pp. 13–14, 65–66; book 8 ("Kings and Lords"), pp. 23–25, 62, 81, and ill. 94; and book 11 ("Earthly Things"), pp. 230–31. References are to the standard English translation by Anderson and Dibble (Sahagún 1950–82).

36. A reference in Durán to the seventh of seven caves of Chicomoztoc (a mythic underworld, the chthonic place of origin of Nahua peoples) suggests that we should take another look at one of the paintings in the Temple of Agriculture at Teotihuacan, where each of three mountains contains seven perfectly rendered *T. angulata* shells. In a copy of the painting, each of the seven shells in each of the three mountains is marked with the three green (i.e., jade) disks that may represent the three hearth stones of the place of cosmic creation. At Teotihuacan, the cave underneath the Pyramid of the Sun has seven lobes or chambers (in groups of two and five), resembling the legendary Chicomoztoc.

37. "Seating" is a simple metaphor with a complex content. At its simplest in this context, "seating" alludes to the notion of occupying or being at rest on an instrument associated with authority, whether it be the woven reed mat or jaguar skin of parts of Mesoamerica or the wood and stone thrones of the Olmec, Maya, and Chibchan peoples. For the various Maya groups, who had similar calendars, even calendrical cycles were said to be "seated," implying apparently their secure placement and readiness to function within the cosmic scheme (see Thompson 1971, pp. 120–21, and Miller and Taube 1993, pp. 110–11, 165–66, on "mat" and "throne"). Ethnographically, it seems clear that the ancient notion of seating is part of the same *très longue durée* notion embodied in the little carved wood stools of the Chibchan, Arawakan, and other tropical forest peoples of Central and South America, for whom the stool is the trance place of the shaman and the meditation place of the priests and chiefs. Throughout tropical America, especially in South America, seating implies stability (emotional and cosmic), balance (especially of cosmic forces), and, essentially, a oneness with the structure of the cosmos.

38. In profile portrayals it is sometimes difficult to distinguish between a nose bead, which is attached by means of a cord through holes in the bead and then through a perforated nasal septum, and nose bars, which are inserted through the nasal septum. But in KJ Stela 11 and the Dumbarton Oaks piece, it is clear that the ornament is a bead, suspended directly under the nose. Many seated Colima figures of the "rulership" type have their septa pierced, apparently for the attachment of jade or greenstone beads. In the other regional traditions of high-status West Mexican ceramic figures, depictions of shell nose and ear ornaments are abundant, and these are perhaps a cognate marker of social and political status. Seated figures with such indicators of status are actually rather uncommon in the Jalisco and Nayarit regional traditions. A systematic analysis of dress and ornament along the lines of Patricia Anawalt's studies of the Aztecs (Anawalt 1981) remains an important task for students of West Mexico.

39. "Three-stone-place" has been tentatively identified by Freidel and Schele (Freidel, Schele, and Parker 1993, pp. 59–122) as the ancient Maya's place of creation, cosmically expressed by three stars in the constellation Orion and prosaically identified with the triangular setting of three stones in the domestic hearth, the latter of course not limited to the Maya of Mexico and Central America. At Teotihuacan, the persistent repetition of conch shells with three marked disks, whatever the material and medium, in contexts that are already construable as creation- and fertility-related, suggests

that this particular notion of creation is not limited to the Maya and that it was not invented by the Maya.

40. Loofs-Wissowa 1991.

41. Chang 1983.

42. Chang 1989.

Francisco Valdez, "The Sayula Basin: Ancient Settlements and Resources"

1. Kan, Meighan, and Nicholson 1970; Linné 1961, pp. 14–19; Miller 1986, pp. 53–59.

2. Kelly 1948.

3. Ibid., p. 67.

4. Ibid., p. 69.

5. Valdez, Liot, and Schöndube 1996.

6. Guffroy and Gómez 1996.

7. Liot 1997.

8. Liot and Valdez 1996.

9. Kelly 1945; Kelly 1949.

10. Kelly 1940–41.

11. Kelly 1948, p. 63.

12. Guffroy 1996, pp. 42–43.

13. Noyola 1994, pp. 66–76; Valdez and Liot 1994.

14. Lorenzo 1964; Aliphat 1988, pp. 145–176.

15. Kelly 1949, 1978, 1980.

16. Meighan 1972.

17. Mountjoy 1983, 1994b, 1995; see also his essay in this volume.

18. On the complexes in the Jalisco highlands, see Galván 1991; on Teuchitlán, see Weigand 1985, 1996b.

19. Schöndube 1980.

20. Long 1966; Kan, Meighan, and Nicholson 1970; Baus Reed Czitrom 1978.

21. Schöndube 1980, pp. 73–206.

22. Weigand 1985, 1993a, 1996a, 1996b; see also his essay in this volume.

23. Schöndube 1980, p. 173.

24. Nelson 1992, p. 361.

25. Valdez 1994; Valdez et al. 1996a, pp. 176–77.

26. Kelly 1980, figs. 18–21.

27. Mountjoy 1994; Mountjoy 1995.

28. Kelly 1949, pp. 115–19.

29. Liot 1995.

30. Liot 1997, pp. 313–320.

31. Kelly 1941–42, appendix 1, pp. 14–15; Noyola 1994, pp. 59–61.

32. Weigand 1996b, pp. 194–99.

33. Beekman 1996a.

Patricia Rieff Anawalt, "They Came To Trade Exquisite Things: Ancient West Mexican-Ecuadorian Contacts"

1. West 1961.

2. The term Mesoamerica defines a specific culture area, a geographic location on the earth's surface inhabited by people who share a similar way of life (see Kirchhoff 1952, p. 23). The concept grew out of the diffusionist thinking of the Boasian school. In the early part of the twentieth century, American anthropologists, led by Franz Boas, became increasingly disillusioned with their nineteenth-century predecessors, the Evolutionists, who believed human cultures moved inexorably upward through sequential evolutionary stages. As the Boasians went out into the field and collected data, they soon found that the grandiose schemes of the Evolutionists, which were based on the accounts of others, often ran afoul of the facts. A part of the Boasian reaction was the belief that human beings were not too inventive; innovations were assumed to have entered cultural inventories through diffusion from an original hearth of invention. The Boasian procedure was to analyze cultures into traits and then trace the movement of those traits through time and space. The area of highest trait concentration was regarded as the most likely center of its invention. In America, this orientation culminated in the elaboration of culture areas, relatively small geographic units based on the contiguous distribution of cultural elements. The culture-area concept continues to be a useful device for summing up the diagnostic cultural features of a specific location, although the emphasis of American anthropological theory is no longer so strongly on diffusion. Nonetheless, diffusionist studies—particularly trans-Pacific diffusionist studies—continue to stimulate lively debate (see Meggers 1992, p. 30).

3. See, for example, Long 1967; Long and Taylor 1966; Noguera 1942, 1971; Oliveros 1974; Smith 1977–78.

4. Gallagher 1983; Kan, Meighan, and Nicholson 1989; von Winning 1974.

5. Weigand 1985, 1992a.

6. Andresen 1977–78; Kelly 1974, 1980.

7. Meighan 1969.

8. Hosler 1988, 1994; Mountjoy 1969.

9. See, for example, Coe 1960; Evans and Meggers 1966; Green and Lowe 1967; Grove 1981a, p. 391, 1982; Lathrap 1966; Lowe 1975; Paulsen 1977; Steward Anthropological Society 1977–78.

10. Anawalt 1981, 1990, 1992, in press (a), in press (b).

11. Beals 1969; Brand 1943, 1971; Chadwick 1971; Freddolino 1973; Pollard 1972, 1993; Warren 1985.

12. Freddolino 1973, p. 1.

13. Durán 1967, vol. 2, p. 30; Sahagún 1950–82, book 10, pp. 188–89.

14. The forty-four colored drawings of the *Relación de Michoacán* provide the Tarascan clothing data. With the exception of two obvious colonial introductions—a European-style shawl (*Relación de Michoacán* 1956, p. 2133, pl.38) and robe (*Relación de Michoacán* 1956, p. 100, pl. 13)—the garments illustrated are unique in Late Postclassic Mesoamerica.

15. See, for example, *Codex Telleriano-Remensis* 1964, folio 25v; Durán 1967, vol. 2, p. 30; Sahagún 1950–82, book 10, p. 189.

16. *Lienzo de Tlaxcala* 1892, p. 52.

17. Beaumont 1932, vol. 3, p. 122.

18. See, for example, *Historia Tolteca Chichimeca* 1976, folio 2r, MS 54–58, p. 6; folio 7v, MS 51–53, p. 13; *Codex Telleriano-Remensis* 1964, folios 25v–28v.

19. Willey 1966, figs. 4-1, 4-2.

20. Chadwick 1971, p. 657.

21. Kan, Meighan, and Nicholson 1989, p. 69.

22. Von Winning and Stendahl 1968, p. 67.

23. Smith 1977–78, p. 186.

24. Lathrap 1975, p. 30.

25. Contact-period stirrup jars with long, slender spouts and stirrups serving as handles are known as "basket-handled" vessels (Christopher Donnan, personal communication, 1990). Such ceramics are depicted three times in the *Relación* (fig. 6, this essay, and *Relación de Michoacán* 1956, p. 218, pl. 39; p. 251, pl. 44). Similar bottle shapes have been found in Ecuador (d'Harcourt 1942, pl. 4, fig. 6).

26. Lathrap 1975, pp. 33–34.

27. Kelly 1974; 1980, pp. 34–35, 37.

28. Lapiner 1966.

29. Lapiner (1966, pl. 5 caption) refers to the pendant worn by many of the Los Esteros male figures as a curved shell. The Denver Art Museum has a similar piece in its collection (no. 1972:142) that appears to be carved from a conch (Robert Stroessner, Latin American Curator, personal communication, June 1989). This shell may be *Strombus*, a marine mollusk that lives in tropical, intertidal waters close to shore. *Strombus*—together with *Spondylus*—was an Ecuadorian export to the Andean high cultures for use in religious rituals (Paulsen 1974).

30. Hosler 1994, p. 185.

31. Ibid.

32. *Cyanocorax dickeyi* and *Cyanocorax mysticalis* are so close physically that many ornithologists think they should be classed as the same species. The painted jay is a darker blue and has a slightly larger body and crest than the white-tailed jay, but to an extent well within the limits of normal variation in the white-tailed species (Haemig 1979, p. 81).

33. Haemig 1979.

34. Cordy-Collins 1994.

35. Lathrap 1975, p. 25.

36. Jijón y Caamaño 1941.

37. Edwards 1965, 1969.

38. Norton 1986, p. 136.

39. Oviedo y Valdes 1945.

40. Samanos 1844.

41. Davidson 1980, p. 32.

42. Cordy-Colllins 1989, p. 396.

43. Hosler 1994, p. 103.

Joseph B. Mountjoy, "The Evolution of Complex Societies in West Mexico: A Comparative Perspective"

1. Personal communication, Dept. de Registro, I.N.A.H., 1997.
2. I owe the number of radiocarbon dates in West Mexico to personal communication with Christopher Beekman, 1996; for Tlaxcala and Puebla, see García 1989; for Teotihuacan, see Rattray 1991.
3. Aveleyra 1956; Solorzano 1980.
4. MacNeish, et al. 1972.
5. Hardy 1994.
6. Mountjoy, in press.
7. Mountjoy 1982b.
8. Mountjoy 1970.
9. Mountjoy 1994.
10. Oliveros 1974.
11. Kelly 1980.
12. Oliveros and Paredes 1993.
13. Noguera 1942; Oliveros 1974.
14. Mountjoy 1974; Mountjoy and Claassen 1989.
15. Champion et al. 1984.
16. Kan, Meighan, and Nicholson 1989.
17. Meighan 1969.
18. Bruhns 1994.
19. Donnan 1978.
20. P. Furst 1974.
21. Nicholson 1971.
22. Donnan 1978.
23. Piña Chán and Oi 1982; Pollard 1997.
24. Barbour 1996.
25. Corona Núñez 1972.
26. Chadwick 1971; Jarquin and Martínez 1998.
27. Nelson 1990.
28. Kelley 1976.
29. Hers 1989.
30. Ibid.; Kelley 1990.
31. Childe 1950.
32. Grove 1997.
33. Weigand 1996b.
34. Ibid.
35. Webb 1982.
36. Ohnersorgen and Varien 1996.
37. Bense 1994.
38. Knight, in press.
39. Whalen and Minnis 1996.
40. Ibid.
41. Kristiansen 1991.
42. Childe 1950.
43. Cabrera 1986.
44. Mellaart 1967.
45. Trumbold et al. 1993; Glascock, Sergio, and Neff 1997.
46. Weigand 1992b.
47. Hers 1996; fieldwork by Mountjoy and Otto Schöndube in Jalisco, 1997.
48. Carneiro 1970.
49. Marcus and Flannery 1996, p. 157.
50. Nelson 1995.
51. Earle 1991, p. 1.
52. Ibid., p. 4.
53. Kristiansen 1991; Drennan 1991.

Barbara Braun, "West Mexican Art And Modernist Artists"

1. Goldwater 1967 (first published as *Primitivism in Modern Painting* in 1938).
2. My own *Pre-Columbian Art and the Post-Columbian World* (Braun 1993) was the first comprehensive study of the subject.
3. Medioni and Pinto 1941. West Mexican material was pursued most avidly in the United States on the West Coast by members of the Hollywood movie colony. The actor Charles Laughton had one of the most important collections.
4. Salvador Toscano, Paul Kirchhoff, and Daniel Rubín de la Borbolla contributed articles to the catalogue, which illustrated more than 150 objects and focused further aesthetic and archaeological attention on this area. Toscano's article was one of the first to distinguish between Tarascan art and the ancient art of Colima and Nayarit, Rubín de la Borbolla's article concerned the Tarascans and the state of Michoacán, and Kirchhoff's was a stylistic and typological analysis of the costumes and ornaments seen on West Mexican figural sculptures. See Kan, Meighan, and Nicholson 1989, p. 15.
5. For a discussion of Rivera's beliefs about the continuity of the pre-Hispanic in modern Mexican forms, see Braun 1993, pp. 186–215.
6. The mural is organized on the basis of the Aztec polarities and the theme of death and rebirth, familiar from Rivera's earlier murals and signaled here by the dualistic life-death mask from Tlatilco reproduced at the bottom of its central axis. The right side of the bifurcated composition portrays the world of pre-Columbian medicine; the left, that of modern Mexico. Beneath the goddess Tlazolteotl is a panel illustrating the great variety of medicinal plants administered by Aztec sorcerer-curers, which Rivera copied from a colonial herbarium.
7. Brown 1986, pp. 145–52, 155.
8. Goldman 1977, p. 114; Brown 1986, p. 155. See also Klein 1986.
9. Gallagher 1983, p. 35. Citing a Cora creation myth of considerable age recounted by von Winning, Gallagher further suggests that for ancient West Mexicans, the dog represented a powerful being associated not only with the underworld but also with the creation of mankind.
10. See Lowe 1991, pp. 40–43, for an insightful discussion of this painting. Lowe's book is an extremely thoughtful and penetrating analysis of Kahlo as an artist.
11. Herrera 1983, p. 17.
12. Lowe 1991, pp. 48–50. As Lowe points out, this painting is one of several in which Kahlo reinvented important moments of her personal history, mapping her life cycle.
13. See Herrera 1983, pp. 210, 378, fig. 49. Herrera points out that in 1938 Kahlo painted a self-portrait with such a dog, *Escuincle Dog and Me,* now lost but documented in a photograph, which she illustrates. According to Herrera, Kahlo's features deliberately match that of the dog in this self-portrait.
14. See Sherwood 1937, p. 41.
15. John Canemaker, personal communication, August 5, 1997. Canemaker is a professor of animation at New York University and author of *Before the Animation Begins: The Art and Lives of Disney Inspirational Sketch Artists* (1997) and other titles about Disney and animation.
16. Canemaker 1997.
17. Schickel 1997, pp. 181–89.
18. David Smith, archivist, the Disney Studios, personal communication, August 5, 1997.
19. See "Frank Lloyd Wright: A Vision of Maya Temples" in Braun 1993, pp. 137–85.
20. I am grateful to John Canemaker for sending me a copy of Charlot's lectures at the Disney training program. Charlot was a fluent, astute, and prolific art writer. Among his many books and articles are *Art from the Mayans to Disney* (1939) and *An Artist on Art* (1972), in the latter of which a chapter, "From Altamira to Disney," refers to certain aspects of Maya graphic and mural art as precursors of Disney animation. Canemaker also made available Charlot's article, "But Is it Art? A Disney Disquisition" (1939), in which the author defends animation as a true art form, characterizing cartoons as "great murals that move [and] are pets of the people."
21. They also had the advantage of removing Disney from the scene of a bitter labor dispute in his studio, which was resolved in his absence. For information about these trips and their results, see Schickel 1997, pp. 263–81; Shales 1982; and, especially, Smoodin 1994, pp. 131–81.
22. John Canemaker, personal communication, August 5, 1997; Canemaker 1997 includes a chapter on Mary Blair (pp. 115–43).

BIBLIOGRAPHY

Abbot, Tucker R., and S. Peter Dance. 1983. *Compendium of Seashells.* New York: E. P. Dutton.

Acosta N., Rosario, Susana Ramírez U., and Luis Gómez G. 1996. Desarrollo Sociocultural de la Cuenca de Sayula durante la Epoca Prehispanica. Paper presented at the IV Coloquio Internacional de Occidentalistas, ORSTOM, Guadalajara.

Adam, Leonhard. 1940. *Primitive Art.* London: Pelikan Books.

Adams, R. E. W. 1991. *Prehistoric Mesoamerica.* Rev. ed. Norman: University of Oklahoma Press.

Adams, R. E. W. 1997. *Ancient Civilizations of the New World.* Boulder: Westview Press.

Algaze, Guillermo. 1993. Expansionary Dynamics of Some Early Pristine States. *American Anthropologist* 95, no. 2, pp. 304–33.

Aliphat, Mario. 1988. La Cuenca Zacoalco-Sayula: Ocupación humana durante el pleistoceno final en el occidente de México. In *Orígenes del Hombre Americano,* ed. A. González Jácome, pp. 145–76. México, D.F.: S.F.P.

Anawalt, Patricia. 1981. *Indian Clothing Before Cortés: Mesoamerican Costumes from the Codices.* Norman: University of Oklahoma Press.

Anawalt, Patricia Rieff. 1990. The Emperors' Cloak: Aztec Pomp, Toltec Circumstance. *American Antiquity* 55, no. 2, pp. 291–307.

Anawalt, Patricia Rieff. 1992. Ancient Cultural Contacts Between Ecuador, West Mexico, and the American Southwest: Clothing Similarities. *Latin American Antiquity* 3, no. 2, pp. 114–29.

Anawalt, Patricia Rieff. In press (a). Mesoamerican Clothing. In *The Archaeology of Ancient Mexico and Central America: An Encyclopedia,* ed. Susan Evans. New York: Garland Publishing.

Anawalt, Patricia Rieff. In press (b). Three Thousand Years of Mesoamerican Clothing. In *Homenaje to Doris Heyden,* ed. Maria Rodriguez-Shadow. México, D.F.

Anawalt, Patricia Rieff. 1997. "Traders of the Ecuadorian Littoral." *Archaeology* 50, no. 6, pp. 48–52.

Andresen, John M. 1977–78. Stirrup-Spouts in the New World: A Distributional Study. In Steward Anthopological Society 1977–78, pp. 205–30.

Aronson, Meredith Alexandra. 1993. Technological Change: West Mexican Mortuary Ceramics. Ph.D. diss., University of Arizona, Tucson.

Aronson, Meredith Alexandra. 1996. Technological Change: Ceramic Mortuary Technology in the Valley of Atemajac from the Late Formative to the Classic Periods. *Ancient Mesoamerica* 7, no. 1, pp. 163–70.

Ashmore, Wendy, ed. 1981. *Lowland Maya Settlement Patterns.* Tucson: University of New Mexico Press.

Aveleyra, Luís. 1956. The Second Mammoth and Associated Artifacts at Santa Isabel Iztapan, Mexico. *American Anthropologist* 22, pp. 12–28.

Aveni, Anthony F. 1991. *Observadores del cielo en el México antiguo.* México, D.F.: Fondo de Cultura Económica.

Aveni, Anthony F., Horst Hartung, and B. Buckingham. 1978. The Pecked Cross Symbol in Ancient Mesoamerica. *Science* 202, no. 4365, pp. 266–84.

Aveni, Anthony F., and H. Hartung. 1981. The Observation of the Sun at the Time of Passage through the Zenith in Mesoamerica. *Archaeoastronomy* 3, pp. 51–69.

Aveni, Anthony F., Horst Hartung, and J. Charles Kelley. 1982. Alta Vista (Chalchihuites), Astronomical Implications of a Mesoamerican Ceremonial Outpost at the Tropic of Cancer. *American Antiquity* 47, no. 2, pp. 316–35.

Bann, Stephen. 1996. Meaning/Interpretation. In *Critical Terms for Art History,* ed. Robert S. Nelson and Richard Schiff, pp. 87–100. Chicago: University of Chicago Press.

Barbour, Warren T. 1996. The Grammar of Teotihuacan Figurines. Paper presented at the sixty-first annual meeting of the Society for American Archaeology, New Orleans.

Baus Reed Czitrom, Carolyn. 1978. *Figurillas sólidas de estilo Colima: Una tipología.* México, D.F.: I.N.A.H.

Beals, Ralph L. 1969. The Tarascans. In Wauchope 1964–76, vol. 8, pp. 725–73.

Beaumont, Friar Pablo. 1932. *Crónica de Michoacán.* 3 vols. México, D.F.: Talleres Gráficos de la Nación.

Beck, L. A. 1995. *Regional Approaches to Mortuary Analysis.* New York: Plenum Press.

Becker, Michael Joseph. 1975. Moieties in Ancient Mesoamerica. *American Indian Quarterly* 2, no. 3, pp. 217–36.

Becker, Michael Joseph. 1975. Moieties In Ancient Mesoamerica, Part II. *American Indian Quarterly* 2, no. 4, pp. 315–30.

Beekman, Christopher S. 1996a. El complejo El Grillo del centro de Jalisco: una revisión de su cronología y significado. In Williams and Weigand 1996, pp. 247–93.

Beekman, Christopher S. 1996b. The Long-Term Evolution of a Political Boundary: Archaeological Research in Jalisco, Mexico. Ph.D. diss., Vanderbilt University.

Beekman, Christopher S. 1996c. Political Boundaries and Political Structure: The Limits of the Teuchitlán Tradition. *Ancient Mesoamerica* 7, no. 1, pp. 135–47.

Bell, Betty, ed. 1974. *The Archaeology of West Mexico.* Ajijic, Jalisco: Sociedad de Estudios Avanzados del Occidente de México.

Bense, Judith A. 1994. *Archaeology of the Southeastern United States.* New York: Academic Press.

Benz, Bruce, and Karen Laitner de Benz. 1996. Relaciones temporales y estilisticas de la cerámica de los complejos Morett y Tuxcacuesco del Occidente de México. Paper presented at the IV Coloquio Internacional de Occidentalistas, ORSTOM, Guadalajara.

Berrin, Kathleen, and Esther Pasztory, eds. 1993. *Teotihuacan: Art from the City of the Gods.* New York: Thames and Hudson and The Fine Arts Museums of San Francisco.

Binford, Lewis. 1971. Mortuary Practices: Their Study and Their Potential. In *Approaches to the Social Dimensions of Mortuary Practices,* ed. J. A. Brown, pp. 6–29. Memoirs of the Society for American Archaeology, vol. 25.

Blitz, John H. 1993. Big Pots for Big Shots: Feasting and Storage in a Mississippian Community. *American Antiquity* 58, no. 1, pp. 80–95.

Bloch, M. 1971. *Placing the Dead*. London: Seminar Press.

Brand, Donald D. 1943. An Historical Sketch of Anthropology and Geography in the Tarascan Region: Part I. *New Mexico Anthropologist* 6–7, no. 2, pp. 37–108.

Brand, Donald D. 1971. Ethnohistoric Synthesis of Western Mexico. In Wauchope 1964–76, vol. 11, pp. 632–56.

Braniff, Beatriz. 1988. A proposito de el ulama en el norte de Mexico. *Arqueologia* 3, pp. 47–94. México, D.F.: I.N.A.H.

Braun, Barbara. 1993. *Pre-Columbian Art and the Post-Columbian World: Ancient American Sources of Modern Art*. New York: Harry N. Abrams.

Broda, Johanna. 1987. The Provenience of the Offerings: Tribute and *Cosmovisión*. In *The Aztec Templo Mayor*, ed. Elizabeth Hill Boone, pp. 211–56. Washington, D.C.: Dumbarton Oaks and Trustees for Harvard Unversity.

Brown, Betty Ann. 1986. The Past Idealized: Diego Rivera's Use of Pre-Columbian Imagery. In *Diego Rivera: A Retrospective*. New York and London.

Brown, J. A. 1971. Introduction. In *Approaches to the Social Dimensions of Mortuary Practices*, ed. J. A. Brown, pp. 1–5. Memoirs of the Society for American Archaeology, no. 25. Washington, D.C.: Society for American Archaeology.

Bruhns, Karen O. 1994. *Ancient South America*. Cambridge: Cambridge University Press.

Bruman, Henry J. 1940. *Aboriginal Drink Areas in New Spain*. Ph.D. diss., University of California, Berkeley.

Brumfiel, Elizabeth M. 1985. Weaving and Cooking in Aztec Mexico. In *Engendering Archaeology*, ed. Joan M. Gero and Margaret W. Conkey, pp. 224–54. Oxford: Blackwell Press.

Brumfiel, Elizabeth M. 1994. Factional Competition and Political Development in the New World: An Introduction. In Brumfiel and Fox 1994, pp. 3–14.

Brumfiel, Elizabeth M., and John W. Fox. 1994. *Factional competition and political development in the New World*. Cambridge: Cambridge University Press.

Buikstra, J. E. 1977. Biocultural Dimensions of Archaeological Study: A Regional Perspective. In *Biocultural Adaptations in Prehistoric America*. Athens: University of Georgia Press.

Buikstra, J. E. 1979. Human Skeletal Remains: Excavation, Analysis, Interpretation. *American Anthropologist* 81, no. 6, pp. 447–48.

Buikstra, J. E. 1985. Paleodemography: Critiques and Controversies. *American Anthropologist* 87, no. 6, pp. 316–33.

Bunzel, Ruth. 1932. Zuni Katcinas. In *47th Annual Report of the Bureau of American Ethnology*. Washington, D.C.: Smithsonian Institution.

Bushnell, Geoffrey. 1965. *Ancient Arts of the Americas*. London

Butterwick, Kristi. 1998. Ritual Consumption and Ancestor Worship in Ancient West Mexico. Ph.D. diss., University of Colorado, Boulder.

Cabrera C., Ruben. 1986. La verificación de algunos de los resultados del Mapping Project en recientes excavaciones en Teotihuacán. *Revista Mexicana de Estudios Antropológicos* 32, pp. 127–46.

Cabrero G., Maria Teresa. 1989. *Civilizacion en el Norte de Mexico. Arqueología de la Cañada del Río Bolaños (Zacatecas y Jalisco)*. México, D.F.: Universidad Nacional Autonoma de México.

Cabrero G., Maria Teresa. 1995. *La muerte en el Occidente del Mexico prehispanico*. Mexico, D.F.: Universidad Nacional Autonoma de México.

Cabrero G., Maria Teresa. 1996. Algunas Consideraciones de Caracter Socio-economico de la Cultura Bolaños. Paper presented at the IV Coloquio Internacional de Occidentalistas, ORSTOM, Guadalajara.

Canemaker, John. 1997. *Before the Animation Begins: The Art and Lives of Disney Inspirational Sketch Artists*. New York: Hyperion.

Cárdenas, Efrain. 1996. La Arquitectura de Patio Hundido y las Estructuras Circulares en el Bajio. Evidencias de un Desarrollo Local y de un Intercambio Cultural. Paper presented at the XXIV Mesa Redonda de la Sociedad Mexicana de Antropología, Tepic.

Carmichael, Elizabeth, and Chlöe Sayer. 1992. *The Skeleton at the Feast: The Day of the Dead in Mexico*. Austin: University of Texas Press and British Museum Press.

Carneiro, Robert. 1970. A Theory of the Origin of the State. *Science* 169, pp. 733–38.

Carrasco, David. 1990. *Religions of Mesoamerica: Cosmovisión and Ceremonial Centers*. New York: Harper and Row.

Caso, Alfonzo. 1938. *Trece Obras Maestras de Arqueologia Mexicana*. Detroit: Ethridge Books.

Caso, Alfonzo. 1958. *The Aztecs: People of the Sun*. Norman: University of Oklahoma Press.

Castillo, Patricia Ochoa. 1992. La pelota prehispánica y el origen del juego en el altiplano central. In Museu Etnològic 1992, pp. 26–38.

Castro Leal, Marcia. 1986. *El juego de pelota*. México, D.F.: I.N.A.H.

Castro Leal, Marcia. 1992. El juego de pelota en la costa del golfo, inicio y culminacion del rito. In Museu Etnològic 1992, pp. 76–91.

Chadwick, Robert. 1971. Archaeological Synthesis of Michoacán and Adjacent Regions. In Wauchope 1964–76, vol. II, pp. 657–91.

Chamberlain, Von Del. 1982. The Pawnee Earth Lodge as an Observatory. In *Archeoastronomy in the New World*, ed. Anthony Aveni. Cambridge: Cambridge University Press.

Champion, Timothy, C. Gamble, S. Shennan, and A. Whittle. 1984. *Prehistoric Europe*. London: Academic Press.

Chang, Kwang-chih. 1983. *Art, Myth, and Ritual: The Path to Political Authority in Ancient China*. Cambridge: Harvard University Press.

Chang, Kwang-chih. 1989. Ancient China and Its Anthropological Significance. In *Archaeological Thought in America*, ed. C. C. Lamberg-Karlovsky, pp. 155–66. New York: Cambridge University Press.

Charlot, Jean. 1972. *An Artist on Art*. 2 vols. Honolulu: University of Hawaii Press.

Charlot, Jean. 1939. *Art from the Mayans to Disney*. New York and London: Sheed and Ward.

Charlot, Jean. 1939. But Is It Art? A Disney Disquisition. *American Scholar* 8, no. 3 (July 1939), pp. 260–70.

Childe, V. Gordon. 1950. The Urban Revolution. *Town Planning Review*, pp. 3–17.

Clark, John E., and Michael Blake. 1994. The Power of Prestige: Competitive Generosity and the Emergence of Rank Societies in Lowland Mesoamerica. In Brumfiel and Fox 1994, pp. 17–30.

Codex Telleriano-Remensis: Antigüedades de México, basdadas en la recopilación de Lord Kingsborough. 1964. Vol. 1, ed. José Corona Núñez, pp. 151–337. México, D.F.: Secretaria de Hacienda y Crédito Público.

Coe, Michael D. 1960. Archaeological Linkages with North and South America at La Victoria, Guatemala. *American Anthropologist* 62, no. 3, pp. 363–93.

Coe, Michael. 1965. *The Jaguar's Children: Preclassic Central Mexico*. New York.

Coe, Michael D. 1975. Death and the Afterlife in Pre-Columbian America: Closing Remarks. In *Death and the Afterlife in Pre-Columbian America*, ed. Elizabeth P. Benson, pp. 191–96. Washington, D.C.: Dumbarton Oaks.

Coe, Michael D., and Gordon Whittaker. 1982. *Aztec Sorcerers in Seventeenth-Century Mexico: The Treatise on Superstitions by Hernando Ruíz de Alarcón*. Albany: Institute for Mesoamerican Studies, Publication 7.

Cohen, Ronald, and E. R. Service. *Origins of the State: The Anthropology of Political Evolution*. Philadelphia.

Cohodas, Marvin. 1991. Ballgame Imagery of the Maya Lowlands: History and Iconography. In Scarborough and Wilcox 1991, pp. 251–88.

Cook, Anita G. 1992. The Stone Ancestors: Idioms of Imperial Attire and Rank among Huari Figurines. *Latin American Antiquity* 3, no. 4, pp. 341–64.

Cordy-Collins, Alana. 1989. Fonga Sigde, Shell Purveyor to the Chimú Kings. In *Dumbarton Oaks Conference on the Northern Dynasties: Kingdom and Statecraft in Chimor*, ed. Michael E. Moseley and Alana Cordy-Collins, pp. 393–417. Washington, D.C.: Dumbarton Oaks.

Cordy-Collins, Alana. 1994. An Unshaggy Dog Story. *Natural History* 103, no. 2, pp. 34–41.

Corona Núñez, José. 1955. *Tumba de El Arenal, Jalisco*. México, D.F.: I.N.A.H.

Corona Núñez, José. 1972. Los teotihuacanos en el Occidente de México. In *Teotihuacan*, XI Mesa Redonda de la Sociedad Mexicana de Antropología, pp. 253–56. México, D.F.

Couch, Christopher. 1985. The Festival Cycle of the Aztec Codex Borbonicus. BAR International Series 270.

Covarrubias, Miguel. 1957. *Indian Art of Mexico and Central America*. New York.

Craine, Eugene R., and Reginald C. Reindorp., trans. and eds. 1970. *The Chronicles of Michoacán*. Norman: University of Oklahoma Press. Originally written from 1539 to 1541 by Fray Martin de Jesus de la Coruna.

Crocker, Jon Christopher. 1985. *Vital Souls: Bororo Cosmology, Natural Symbolism, and Shamanism*. Tucson: University of Arizona Press.

Culbert, T. Patrick. 1977. Early Maya Development at Tikal, Guatemala. In *The Origins of Maya Civilization,* ed. Richard Adams, pp. 27–43. Tucson: University of New Mexico Press.

Culbert, T. Patrick, and D. S. Rice., eds. 1990. *Precolumbian Population History in the Maya Lowlands.* Albuquerque: University of New Mexico Press.

D'Altroy, Terrence N. 1994. Factions and Political Development in the Central Andes. In Brumfiel and Fox 1994, pp. 171–88.

Damon, Frederick H. 1989. Introduction. In *Death Rituals and Life in the Societies of the Kula Ring,* ed. Frederick H. Damon and Roy Wagner, pp. 3–22. DeKalb: Northern Illinois University Press.

Davidson, Judith R. 1980. The *Spondylus* Shell in Chimú Iconography. Master's thesis, California State University, Northridge.

D'Harcourt, Raoul. 1942. Archéologie de la Province d'Esmeraldas (Equateur). *Journal de la Société des Americanistes* 34, pp. 61–200.

Day, Jane S., Kristi Butterwick, and Robert Pickering. 1996. Archaeological Interpretations of West Mexican Ceramic Art from the Late Preclassic Period. *Ancient Mesoamerica* 7, no. 1, pp. 149–62.

De Barrios, Virginia Bottorff. 1971. *A Guide to Tequila, Mezcal and Pulque.* México, D.F.: Editorial Minutiae Mexicana.

De la Fuente, Beatríz, Silvia Trejo, and Nelly Gutiérrez Solana. 1988. *Escultura en piedra de Tula: Catálogo.* México, D.F.: U.N.A.M.

Díaz, Clara. 1987. *El Occidente de Mexico.* México, D.F.: García Valadez Editores.

Díaz del Castillo, Bernal. 1956. *The Discovery and Conquest of Mexico,* trans. A. P. Maudslay. New York: Farrar, Strauss and Cudahy.

Disselhoff, H. D. 1932. Note sur le résultat de quelques fouilles archéologiques faites à Colima (Mexique). *Revista del Instituto de Etnología de la Universidad Nacional de Tucumán* 2, pp. 525–38.

Disselhoff, H. D. 1936. Trachtstücke und Geräte der Bewohner des alten Colima. *Baessler-Archiv* 19, pp. 16–21.

Disselhoff, H. D. 1960. Notizen zur Archäologie Westmexicos. *Ethnologica* 2, pp. 542–47.

Dixon, Keith A. 1963. "The Interamerican Diffusion of a Cooking Technique: The Culinary Shoe-Pot." *American Anthropologist* 65, no. 3, pp. 593–619.

Dixon, Keith A. 1976. "Shoe-Pots, Patojos and the Principle of Whimsy." *American Antiquity* 41, no. 3, pp. 386–91.

Donnan, Christopher B. 1978. *Moche Art of Peru.* Los Angeles: Museum of Cultural History, University of California.

Douglass, W. A. 1969. *Death in Murelaga.* Seattle: University of Washington Press.

Drennan, Robert D. 1991. Pre-Hispanic Chiefdom Trajectories in Mesoamerica, Central America, and Northern South America. In *Chiefdoms: Power, Economy, and Ideology,* ed. T. Earle, pp. 263–87.

Durán, Diego. 1967. *Historia de las indias de Nueva España e islas de la tierra firme,* ed. Angel María Garibay K. México, D.F.: Editorial Porrua.

Durán, Diego. 1971. *Book of the Gods and Rites and the Ancient Calendar,* trans. and ed. Fernando Horcasitas and Doris Hayden. Norman: University of Oklahoma Press.

Dwyer, Jane, and Edward B. Dwyer. 1975. *Fire, Earth and Water: Sculpture from the Land Collection of Mesoamerican Art.* San Francisco: The Fine Arts Museums of San Francisco.

Earle, Timothy. 1991. The Evolution of Chiefdoms. In *Chiefdoms: Power, Economy, and Ideology,* ed. T. Earle, pp. 1–15.

Edwards, Clinton R. 1965. Aboriginal Watercraft on the Pacific Coast of South America. *Ibero Americana* 47. Berkeley: University of California Press.

Edwards, Clinton R. 1969. Possibilities of Pre-Columbian Maritime Contacts among New World Civilizations. In Kelley and Riley 1969, pp. 3–10.

Ekholm, Susanna. 1979. The Lagartero Figurines. In *Maya Archaeology and Ethnohistory,* ed. Norman Hammond and Gordon R. Willey, pp. 172–88. Austin: University of Texas Press.

Eliade, Mircea. 1964. *Shamanism: Archaic Techniques of Ecstasy,* trans. Willard R. Trask. Princeton: Princeton University Press.

Eliade, Mircea. 1965. *Rites and Symbols of Initiation,* trans. Willard R. Trask. New York: Harper and Row.

Eliade, Mircea. 1968. *El mito del eterno retorno.* Buenos Aires: Emecé Editores.

Eliade, Mircea. 1970. *Patterns in Comparative Religion,* trans. Rosemary Sheed. New York: World Publishing.

Evans, Clifford, and Betty J. Meggers. 1966. Mesoamerica and Ecuador. In Wauchope 1964–76, vol. 4, pp. 243–64.

Feinman, Gary M. 1995. The Emergence of Inequality: A Focus on Strategies and Processes. In *Foundations of Social Inequality,* ed.

T. Douglas Price and Gary M. Feinman, pp. 255–80. New York: Plenum Press.

Fernández, Rodolfo, and Daria Deraga. 1992. La Cuenca de Sayula y el proceso civilizatorio del occidente Mexicano. In *Origen y Desarrollo de la Civilizacíon en el Occidente de México,* ed. Brigitte Boehm de Lameiras and Phil C. Weigand, pp. 307–18. Zamora: El Colegio de Michoacán.

Firth, Raymond W. 1967. *Tikopia Ritual and Belief.* London: Allen and Unwin.

Florescano, Enrique. 1993. *El mito de Quetzalcóatl.* México, D.F.: Fondo de Cultura Económica.

Florescano, Enrique. 1994. *Memoria Mexicana.* México, D.F.: Fondo de Cultura Económica.

Folan, William, Ellen Kintz, and Loraine Fletcher. 1983. *Coba: A Classic Maya Metropolis.* New York: Academic Press.

Foster, George M. 1948. *Empire's Children: The People of Tzintzuntzan.* Smithsonian Institution, Institute of Social Anthropology, no. 6. México: Imprenta Nuevo Mundo.

Foster, Robert J. 1995. *Social Reproduction and History in Melanesia.* Cambridge: Cambridge University Press.

Foster, Michael S., and Phil C. Weigand, eds. 1985. *The Archaeology of West And Northwest Mesoamerica.* Boulder: Westview Press.

Fox, John Gerard. 1996. Playing with Power: Ballcourts and Political Ritual in Southern Mesoamerica. *Current Anthropology* 37, no. 3, pp. 483–509.

Fox, Robin. 1980. *Kinship and Marriage: An Anthropological Perspective.* Harmondsworth: Penguin.

Freddolino, Marie Kimball. 1973. An Investigation into the 'Pre-Tarascan' Cultures of Zacapu, Michoacán, Mexico. Ph.D. diss. Ann Arbor: University Microfilms International.

Freidel, David, Linda Schele, and Joy Parker. 1993. *Maya Cosmos: Three Thousand Years on the Shaman's Path.* New York: William Morrow.

Fried, Morton. 1967. *The Evolution of Political Society.* New York.

Friedman, J., and Rowlands, M. J., eds. 1978. Notes towards an Epigenetic Model of the Evolution of "Civilization." In *The Evolution of Social Systems,* pp. 201–76. Pittsburgh: University of Pittsburgh Press.

Furst, Jill Leslie. 1978. *Codex Vindobonensis Mexicanus I: A Commentary.* Albany: Institute for Mesoamerican Studies, State University of New York at Albany.

Furst, Jill Leslie. 1982. Skeletonization in Mixtec Art: a Reevaluation. In *The Art and Iconography of Late Postclassic Central Mexico,* ed. Elizabeth Boone, pp. 207–25. Washington, D.C.: Dumbarton Oaks.

Furst, Jill L. McKeever. 1995. *The Natural History of the Soul in Ancient Mexico.* New Haven: Yale University Press.

Furst, Peter T. 1965a. Radiocarbon Dates from a Tomb in Mexico. *Science* 147, pp. 612–13.

Furst, Peter T. 1965b. West Mexican Tomb Sculpture as Evidence for Shamanism in Prehispanic America. *Antropológica* 15, pp. 29–80.

Furst, Peter T. 1965c. West Mexico, the Caribbean, and Northern South America: Some Problems in New World Interrelationships. *Antropológica* 14, pp. 1–37.

Furst, Peter T. 1966. Shaft Tombs, Shell Trumpets, and Shamanism: A Culture-Historical Approach to Problems in West Mexican Archaeology. Ph.D. diss., University of California, Los Angeles.

Furst, Peter T. 1967. Huichol Conceptions of the Soul. *Folklore Americas* 26, no. 2, pp. 39–106. Los Angeles: Center for the Study of Comparative Folklore and Mythology, University of California, Los Angeles.

Furst, Peter T. 1968. The Olmec Were-Jaguar Motif in the Light of Ethnographic Reality. In *Dumbarton Oaks Conference on the Olmec,* ed. Elizabeth P. Benson, pp. 143– 78. Washington, D.C.: Dumbarton Oaks.

Furst, Peter T., ed. 1972. *Flesh of the Gods: The Ritual Use of Hallucinogens.* New York: Praeger Publishers.

Furst, Peter. 1973. West Mexican Art: Secular or Sacred? In *The Iconography of Middle American Sculpture,* ed. Dudley T. Easby, Jr., pp. 98–133. New York: The Metropolitan Museum of Art.

Furst, Peter T. 1974. Ethnographic Analogy in the Interpretation of West Mexican Art. In Bell 1974, pp. 132–46.

Furst, Peter T. 1975. House of Darkness and House of Light: Sacred Functions of West Mexican Funerary Art. In *Death and the Afterlife in Pre-Columbian America,* pp. 33–68, ed. Elizabeth P. Benson. Washington, D.C.: Dumbarton Oaks.

Furst, Peter T. 1976. *Hallucinogens and Culture.* San Francisco: Chandler and Sharp.

Furst, Peter T., ed. 1990. *Flesh of the Gods: The Ritual Use of Hallucinogens.* Rev. ed. Prospect Heights, Ill.: Waveland Press.

Furst, Peter T. 1993. Huichol Cosmogony: How the World was Destroyed by a Flood and Dog Woman Gave Birth to the Human Race. In *South- and Meso-American Native Spirituality,* ed. Gary Gossen in collaboration with Miguel León-Portilla, pp. 303–23. New York: Crossroad.

Furst, Peter T. 1994. The Maiden Who Ground Herself: Myths of the Origin of Maize from the Sierra Madre Occidental. *Latin American Indian Literatures Journal* 10, no. 2, pp. 101–55.

Furst, Peter T. 1996a. Huichol Conceptions of the Soul. *Folklore Americas* 26, no. 2, pp. 39–106.

Furst, Peter T. 1996b. Myth as History, History as Myth. In Schaefer and Furst 1996, pp. 26–60.

Gallagher, Jackie. 1983. *Companions of the Dead: Ceramic Tomb Sculpture from Ancient West Mexico.* Los Angeles: Museum of Cultural History, University of California, Los Angeles.

Galván Villegas, Luis Javier. 1991. *Las tumbas de tiro del Valle de Atemajac, Jalisco.* México, D.F.: I.N.A.H.

Ganot R., Jaime, and Alejandro Peschard F. 1997. *Aztatlan: Apuntes para la historia y arqueología del Estado de Durango.* Durango: Secretaria de Educacion, Cultura y Deporte.

García, C. Angel. 1989. El Formativo en Tlaxcala-Puebla. In *El Preclásico o Formativo, avances y perspectivas,* ed. M. Carmona M., pp. 161–93. México, D.F.

García de Weigand, Celia, and Phil C. Weigand. 1992. Muere y luto entre los huicholes del Occidente de México. In *Ensayos sobre el gran nayar entre Coras, Huicholes y Tepehuanos,* ed. Phil C. Weigand, pp. 215–32. Zamora: El Colegio de Michoacán.

Gennep, Arnold van. 1960. *The Rites of Passage,* trans. Monika Vizedom and Gabrielle L. Caffee. Chicago: University of Chicago Press.

Gentry, Howard Scott. 1982. *Agaves of Continental North America.* Tucson: University of Arizona Press.

Giles, S. and J. Stewart. 1989. *The Art of Ruins: Adela Breton and the Temples of Mexico.* Bristol: City of Bristol Museum and Art Gallery.

Gill, G. W. 1971. The Prehistoric Inhabitants of Northern Coastal Nayarit: Skeletal Analysis and Description of Burials. Ph.D. diss., University of Kansas.

Gill, G. W. 1977. Manifestation of a Conceptual Artistic Ideal within a Prehistoric Culture. *American Antiquity* 42, no. 1, pp. 101–10.

Gill, G. W. 1985. Cultural Implications of Artificially Modified Human Remains from Northwestern Mexico. In Foster and Weigand 1985, pp. 193–215.

Gillespie, Susan D. 1991. Ballgames and Boundaries. In Scarborough and Wilcox 1991, pp. 317–45.

Girard, Rafael. 1975. La tumba de tiro en el área maya. In *Balance y perspectiva de la antropología de Mesoamérica y del Norte de México,* XIII Mesa Redonda, vol. 2, pp. 61–74. México, D.F.: Sociedad Mexicana de Antropología.

Glascock, Michael D., R. Sergio H., and H. Neff. 1997. Hydration and Source Analysis of Obsidian from Excavated Archaeological Contexts in the Municipality of Puerto Vallarta, Jalisco, Mexico. Report of the University of Missouri Research Reactor Center. Columbia.

Godelier, Maurice. 1978. La part idéelle du réel. Essai sur l'idéologique. *L'Home* 18, pp. 3–4.

Goldman, Shifra. 1977. *Contemporary Mexican Painting in a Time of Change.* Austin: University of Texas Press.

Goldwater, Robert J. 1967. *Primitivism in Modern Art.* New York: Vintage Books.

González T., Yólotl. 1975. El culto a los muertos entre los Mexica. *Boletín INAH,* 2nd series, 14.

Gorenstein, Shirley. 1996. Review of *Arqueología del occidente del México,* ed. Eduardo Williams and R. Novella; *Evolución de una civilización prehispánica: arqueología de Jalisco, Nayarit y Zacatecas,* by Phil C. Weigand; and *El Michoacán antiguo,* ed. Brigitte Boehm de Lameiras. *Latin American Antiquity* 7, no. 1, pp. 88–91.

Green, Dee F., and Gareth W. Lowe. 1967. Altamira and Padre Pidra, Early Preclassic Sites in Chiapas, Mexico. *Papers of the New World Archaeological Foundation* 15. Provo.

Grimes, Joseph E., and T. Hinton. 1969. The Huichol and Cora. In Wauchope 1964–76, vol. 8, pp. 192–813.

Grove, David C. 1981a. The Formative Period and the Evolution of Complex Culture. In *Supplement to The Handbook of Middle American Indians,* ed. Victoria Reifler Brickler, pp. 373–91. Austin: University of Texas Press.

Grove, David C. 1981b. Olmec Monuments: Mutilation as a Clue to Meaning. In *The Olmec and Their Neighbors,* ed. Elizabeth P. Benson. Washington, D.C.: Dumbarton Oaks.

Grove, David C. 1982. The Mesoamerican Formative and South American Influences. *Primer Simposio de Correclaciones Antropológicas Andino-Mesoamericano, July 25–31, 1971,* ed. Jorge G. Marcos and Presley Norton Escuela. Guayaquil.

Grove, David C. 1997. Olmec Archaeology: A Half Century of Research and Its Accomplishments. *Journal of World Prehistory* 11, no. 1, pp. 51–73.

Grove, David C., and Susan D. Gillespie. 1992a. Archaeological Indicators of Formative Period Elites: A Perspective from Central Mexico. In *Mesoamerican Elites: An Archaeological Assessment,* ed. Diane Z. Chase and Arlen F. Chase, pp. 191–205. Norman: University of Oklahoma Press.

Grove, David C., and Susan D. Gillespie. 1992b. Ideology and Evolution at the Pre-State Level: Formative Period Mesoamerica. In *Ideology and Pre-Columbian Civilizations,* ed. Arthur K. Demarest and Geoffrey W. Conrad, pp. 15–36. Santa Fe: School of American Research Press.

Guffroy, Jean. 1996. Cerritos Colorados: un sitio con arquitectura monumental en la Cuenca de Sayula, Jalisco. *Estudios del Hombre* 3, pp. 37–64.

Guffroy, Jean, and Luis Gómez Gastélum. 1996. Cerritos Colorados, un sitio del Clásico Tardío en la Cuenca de Sayula, Jalisco. In Williams and Weigand 1996, pp. 395–426.

Haemig, Paul D. 1979. Secret of the Painted Jay. *Biotropica* 11, no. 2, pp. 81–87.

Handlin, Oscar, and John Burchard., eds. 1963. *The Historian and the City.* Cambridge: M.I.T. Press.

Hardy, Karen. 1994. Colecciones líticas de superficie del Occidente de México. In *Arqueología del Occidente de México,* ed. E. Williams and R. Novela, pp. 123–38. Zamora: El Colegio de Michoacán.

Hastorf, Christine A. 1991. Gender, Space, and Food in Prehistory. *Engendering Archaeology,* ed. Joan M. Gero and Margaret W. Conkey, pp. 132–62. Oxford: Basil Blackwell.

Hayden, Brian. 1995. Pathways to Power. In *Foundations of Social Inequality,* ed. T. Douglas Price and Gary M. Feinman, pp. 15–86. New York: Plenum Press.

Hayden, Brian. 1996. Thresholds of Power in Emergent Complex Societies. In *Emergent Complexity,* ed. Jeanne E. Arnold, pp. 50–58. Ann Arbor: International Monographs in Prehistory.

Hayden, Brian, and Rob Gargett. 1990. Big Man, Big Heart? A Mesoamerican View of the Emergence of Complex Society. *Ancient Mesoamerica* 1, pp. 3–20.

Helms, Mary W. 1979. *Ancient Panama: Chiefs in Search of Power.* Austin: University of Texas Press.

Herrera, Hayden. 1983. *Frida: A Biography of Frida Kahlo.* New York: Harper and Row.

Hers, Marie-Areti. 1989. *Los toltecas en tierras chichimecas.* México, D.F.: U.N.A.M.

Hers, Marie-Areti. 1996. Cronología arqueológica de Durango, Sinaloa y Zacatecas. Paper presented at the symposium Cronología Historiográfica de Occidente. I.N.A.H and Universidad de Colima.

Hirth, Kenneth G. 1992. Interregional Exchange as Elite Behavior: An Evolutionary Perspective. In *Mesoamerican Elites: An Archaeological Assessment,* ed. Diane Z. Chase and Arlen F. Chase, pp. 18–29. Norman: University of Oklahoma Press.

Historia Tolteca Chichimeca. 1976. Ed. Paul Kirchhoff, Lina Odena Guemes, and Luis Reyes García. México, D.F.: I.N.A.H.

Holly, Michael Ann. 1984. *Panofsky and the Foundations of Art History.* Ithaca: Cornell University Press.

Horcasitas, Fernando. 1953. An Analysis of the Deluge Myth in Mesoamerica. Master's thesis, Centro de Estudios Universitarios, Mexico City College.

Hosler, Dorothy. 1988. Ancient West Mexican Metallurgy: South and Central American Origins and West Mexican Transformations. *American Anthropologist* 90, no. 4, pp. 832–55.

Hosler, Dorothy. 1994. *The Sounds and Colors of Power: The Sacred Metallurgical Technology of Ancient West Mexico.* Cambridge: Massachusetts Institute of Technology Press.

Jackson, John B. 1984. *Discovering the Vernacular Landscape.* New Haven: Yale University Press.

Jarquin, Ana Maria, and E. Martinez. 1998. La cerámica prehispánica del sitio de La Compana, Colima. Lecture presented at the International Symposium on Prehispanic West Mexican Ceramics, Guadalajara.

Jijón y Caamaño, Jacinto. 1941. *El Ecuador interandino y occidental antes de la conquista Castellana.* 4 vols. Quito: Editorial Ecuatoriana.

Jiménez Moreno, Wigberto. 1972. Estratigrafia y tipología religiosas. In *Religión en Mesoamérica,* ed. Jaime Litvak and Noemi Castillo, pp. 31–36. México, D.F.: Sociedad Mexicana de Antropología.

Kan, Michael. 1989. The Pre-Columbian Art of West Mexico: Nayarit, Jalisco, Colima. In Kan, Meighan, and Nicholson 1989, pp. 13–27.

Kan, Michael, Clement W. Meighan, and H. B. Nicholson. 1970. *Sculpture of Ancient West Mexico: Nayarit, Jalisco, Colima.* Los Angeles: Los Angeles County Museum of Art.

Kan, Michael, Clement Meighan, and H. B. Nicholson. 1989. *Sculpture of Ancient West Mexico: Nayarit, Jalisco, Colima.* 2nd ed. Los Angeles and Albuquerque: Los Angeles County Museum of Art and University of New Mexico Press.

Kan, Sergei. 1989. *Symbolic Immortality.* Washington, D.C.: Smithsonian Institution Press.

Kelley, J. Charles. 1971. Archaeology of the Northern Frontier: Zacatecas and Durango. In Wauchope 1964–76, vol. 11, pp. 768–801.

Kelley, J. Charles. 1974. Speculations on the Culture History of Northwestern Mesoamerica. In Bell 1974.

Kelley, J. Charles. 1976. Alta Vista: Outpost of Mesoamerican Empire on the Tropic of Cancer. In *Las Fronteras de Mesoamérica,* XIV Mesa Redonda de la Sociedad Mexicana de Antropología, pp. 21–40. Tegucigalpa.

Kelley, J. Charles. 1990. The Classic Epoch in the Chalchihuites Culture of the State of Zacatecas. In *La Epoca Clásica: Nuevos Hallazgos, Nuevas Ideas,* ed. A. Cardos de Méndez, pp. 11–14. México, D.F.: I.N.A.H. and Museo Nacional de Antropología.

Kelley, J. Charles. 1995. Trade Goods, Traders and Status in Northwestern Greater Mesoamerica. In *The Gran Chichimeca: Essays on the Archaeology and Ethnohistory of Northern Mesoamerica,* ed. Jonathan E. Reyman, pp. 102–45. Aldershot, Hampshire: Avebury Press.

Kelley, J. Charles, and Carroll L. Riley, eds. 1969. *Pre-Columbian Contact within Nuclear America.* Carbondale: University Museum, Southern Illinois University.

Kelly, Isabel. 1938. Excavations at Chametla, Sinaloa. *Ibero-Americana* 14. Berkeley: University of California Press.

Kelly, Isabel. 1945. Excavations at Culiacán, Sinaloa. *Ibero-Americana* 25. Berkeley: University of California Press.

Kelly, Isabel. 1940–41. A Surface Reconnaissance of the Sayula-Zacoalco Basins. Unpublished ms.

Kelly, Isabel. 1945. The Archaeology of the Autlán-Tuxcacuesco Area of Jalisco: I. Autlán Zone. *Ibero-americana.* 27. Berkeley: University of California Press.

Kelly, Isabel. 1948. Ceramic Provinces of Northwest Mexico. In *El Occidente de México,* IV Reunión de Mesa Redonda sobre Problemas Antropológicos de México y Centro América, pp. 55–71. México, D.F.: Sociedad Mexicana de Antropología.

Kelly, Isabel. 1949. The Archaeology of the Autlán-Tuxcacuesco Area of Jalisco. II: The Tuxcacuesco-Zapotitlán Zone. *Ibero-Americana.* 27. Berkeley: University of California Press.

Kelly, Isabel. 1974. Stirrup Pots from Colima: Some Implications. In Bell 1974, pp. 206–11.

Kelly, Isabel. 1978. Seven Colima Tombs: An Interpretation of Ceramic Content. In *Studies in Ancient Mesoamerica,* vol. 3, ed. John Graham, pp. 1–26. Berkeley: University of California Archaeological Research Facility.

Kelly, Isabel. 1980. *Ceramic Sequence in Colima: Capacha, an Early Phase.* Anthropological Papers of the University of Arizona, no. 37. Tucson: University of Arizona Press.

Kirch, Patrick. 1991. Chiefship and Competitive Involution: The Marquesas Islands of Eastern Polynesia. In *Chiefdoms: Power, Economy, and Ideology,* ed. Timothy Earle, pp. 119–45. Cambridge: Cambridge University Press.

Kirchhoff, Paul. 1943. Mesoamérica. *Acta Americana* 1, pp. 92–107.

Kirchhoff, Paul. 1952. Mesoamerica: Its Geographic Limits, Ethnic Composition and Cultural Characteristics. In *Heritage of Conquest,* ed. Sol Tax, pp. 17–30. New York: Macmillan.

Klein, Cecelia. 1986. Masking Empire. *Art History* 9, no. 2 (June 1986).

Knight, Vernon J., Jr. In press. Moundville as a Diagrammatic Ceremonial Center. In *Studies in Moundville Archaeology,* ed. Vernon J. Knight, Jr., and V. P. Steponaitis. Washington, D.C.: Smithsonian Institution Press.

Koontz, Rex. 1994. The Iconography of El Tajín, Vera Cruz, Mexico. Ph.D. diss., University of Texas, Austin.

Kristiansen, Kristian. 1991. Chiefdoms, States, and Systems of Social Evolution. In *Chiefdoms: Power, Economy, and Ideology,* ed. T. Earle, pp. 16–43. Cambridge: Cambridge University Press.

Kubler, George. 1984. *The Art and Architecture of Ancient America.* Harmondsworth: Penguin.

Langdon, E. Jean Matteson, and Gerhard Baer, eds. 1992. *Portals of Power: Shamanism in South America.* Albuquerque: University of New Mexico Press.

Lapiner, Alan. 1966. *Ancient Sculpture of Ecuador.* Denver: Denver Art Museum and Arts of the Four Quarters, Ltd.

Lapiner, Alan. 1976. *Pre-Columbian Art of South America.* New York: Harry N. Abrams.

Lathrap, Donald W. 1966. Relationships between Mesoamerica and the Andean Areas. In Wauchope 1964–76, vol. 4, pp. 265–76.

Lathrap, Donald W. 1975. *Ancient Ecuador: Culture, Clay, and Creativity, 3000–300 B.C.* Chicago: Field Museum of Natural History.

Leach, Edmund R. 1954. *Political Systems of Highland Burma.* London: Bell.

Leyenaar, Ted J. J., and Lee A. Parsons. 1988. *Ulama: The Ballgame of the Mayas and Aztecs, 2000 B.C.–A.D. 2000.* Leiden: Spruyt, Van Mantgem and De Does.

Lienzo de Tlaxcala. 1892. In *Antigüedades Mexicanas,* ed. Alfred Chavero. México, D.F.: Publicadeas por la Junta Colombina de México, Secretaría de Fomento.

Lind, Michael. 1987. *The Sociocultural Dimensions of Mixtec Ceramics.* Nashville: Vanderbilt University Publications in Anthropology.

Linné, Sigvald. 1961. Lí Art du Mexique et de lí Amerique Central. In *Amerique Précolombienne, Les Hautes Civilisations du Nouveau Monde,* ed. H. D. Disselhoff and Sigvald Linné, pp. 5–133. Paris: Editions Alvin Michael.

Liot, Catherine. 1995. Evidencias arqueológicas de producción de sal en la Cuenca de Sayula (Jalisco): relación con el medio físico, estudio de tecnología. In *La sal en México,* ed. Juan Carlos Reyes, pp. 1–32. Colima: Universidad de Colima.

Liot, Catherine. 1997. Les Salines Prehispaniques du Bassin de Sayula (Jalisco, Mexique): Milieu et Techniques. Ph.D. diss., University of Paris.

Liot, Catherine, and Francisco Valdez. 1996. El Comercio prehispánico de la sal en Sayula (Jalisco). Paper presented at the II National Conference, Mérida, Yucatan.

Litzinger, William Joseph. 1983. The Ethnobiology of Alcoholic Beverage Production by the Lacandon, Tarahumara, and Other Aboriginal Mesoamerican Peoples. Ph.D. diss., University of Colorado, Boulder.

Long, Stanley Vernon. 1966. Archaeology of the Municipio of Etzatlán, Jalisco. Ph.D. diss., University of California, Los Angeles.

Long, Stanley. 1967. Formas y distribución de tumbas de pozo con camara lateral. *Razón y Fabula* 1, pp. 1–15.

Long, Stanley, and R. E. Taylor. 1966. Chronology of a West Mexican Shaft-Tomb. *Nature* 212, no. 5062, pp. 651–52.

Loofs-Wissowa, Helmut. 1991. Dongson Drums: Instruments of Shamanism or Regalia? *Arts Asiatiques* 46, pp. 39–49.

López Austin, Alfredo. 1984. *Cuerpo humano e ideólogía: Las concepciones de los antiguos nahuas.* 2nd ed. 2 vols. México, D.F.: U.N.A.M., Instituto de Investigaciones Antropológicas.

López Austin, Alfredo. 1988. *The Human Body and Ideology: Concepts of the Ancient Nahuas.* 2 vols. Salt Lake City: University of Utah Press.

López Austin, Alfredo. 1990. *Los mitos del tlacuache: Caminos de la mitología mesoamericana.* México, D.F.: Alianza Editorial.

López Austin, Alfredo. 1994. Tamoanchan y Tlalocan. México, D.F.: Fondo de Cultura Económica.

López Luján, Leonardo. 1993. *Las ofrendas del Templo Mayor de Tenochtlan.* México, D.F.: I.N.A.H.

López Mestas C., Lorenza, Jorge Ramos, and Robert Pickering. 1996. Culto funerario y organización social en las tradición Teuchitlán durante el Formativo tardió. Paper presented at the IV Coloquio Internacional de Occidentalistas, ORSTOM, Guadalajara.

Lorenzo, José Luis. 1964. Dos Puntas Acanaladas de la Región de Chapala. *Boletín INAH,* 1st series, 17, pp. 1–6.

Lowe, Gareth W. 1975. The Early Preclassic Barra Phase of Altamira, Chiapas. *Papers of the New World Archaeological Foundation* 38, ed. Jorge G. Marcos. Provo.

Lowe, Sarah M. 1991. *Frida Kahlo.* New York: Universe.

Luce, Ann Raymond. 1976. Quetzalcoatl and the Bebedores Murals at Cholula. Thesis, University of Colorado, Boulder.

Lumholtz, Carl. 1900. Symbolism of the Huichol Indians. In *Memoirs of the American Museum of Natural History,* vol. 3. New York: American Museum of Natural History.

Lumholtz, Carl S. 1902. *Unknown Mexico.* London: Macmillan and Co., and New York: C. Scribner's Sons.

MacNeish, Richard S., M. L. Fowler, A. García C., F. A. Peterson, A. Nelken-Terner, and J. A. Neely. 1972. Excavations and Reconnaissance. In *The Prehistory of the Tehuacan Valley,* vol. 5, ed. R. S. MacNeish. Austin: University of Texas Press.

Maltin, Leonard. 1980. *Of Mice and Magic: A History of American Animated Cartoons.* New York.

Manzanilla, Linda. 1994. Geografía sagrada e inframundo en Teotihuacan. In *Antropológicas,* pp. 53–65. México, D.F.: Instituto de Investigaciones Antropológicas.

Marcus, Joyce, and Kent V. Flannery. 1996. *Zapotec Civilization: How Urban Society Evolved in Mexico's Oaxaca Valley.* London: Thames and Hudson.

Marquina, Ignacio. 1971. La Pintura en Cholula. *Artes de Mexico* 140, pp. 25–40.

Mason, James A. 1981. The Ceremonialism of the Tepecan Indians of Azqueltán, Jalisco. In *Themes of Indigenous Acculturation in Northwest Mexico,* ed. Thomas Hinton and Phil C. Weigand, pp. 62–76. Tucson: University of Arizona Press.

McAnany, Patricia A. 1995. *Living with the Ancestors.* Austin: University of Texas Press.

McKeever Furst, Jill L. 1995. *The Natural History of the Soul in Ancient Mexico.* New Haven: Yale University Press.

McNeill, William. 1995. *Keeping Together in Time.* Cambridge: Harvard University Press.

Medioni, Gilbert, and Marie Therese Pinto. 1941. *Art in Ancient Mexico: Selected and Photographed from the Collection of Diego Rivera.* New York: Oxford University Press.

Meggers, Betty J. 1992. Jamon-Valdivia Similarities: Convergence or Contact? *NEARA Journal* 27, pp. 23–32.

Meighan, Clement W. 1969. Cultural Similarities between Western Mexico and Andean Regions. In Kelley and Riley 1969, pp. 11–25.

Meighan, Clement W. 1972. Archaeology of the Morret Site, Colima. Publications in Anthropology, no. 7. Los Angeles: University of California Press.

Mellaart, James. 1967. *Catal Huyuk: A Neolithic Town in Anatolia.* London: Thames and Hudson.

Merrill, William L. 1988. *Rarámuri Souls: Knowledge and Social Process in Northern Mexico.* Washington, D.C.: Smithsonian Institution Press.

Miller, Mary Ellen. 1986. *The Art of Mesoamerica from Olmec to Aztec.* London: Thames and Hudson.

Miller, Mary. 1988. The Boys in the Bonampak Band. In *Maya Iconography,* ed. E. Benson and G. Griffin, pp. 318–30. Princeton: Princeton University Press.

Miller, Mary, and Karl Taube. 1993. *The Gods and Symbols of Ancient Mexico and the Maya: An Illustrated Dictionary of Mesoamerican Religion.* New York: Thames and Hudson.

Millon, René, Bruce Drewitt, and George Cowgill. 1973. *Urbanization at Teotihuacan, Mexico.* Austin: University of Texas Press.

Moore, Jerry D. 1995. The Archaeology of Dual Organization in Andean South America: A Theoretical Review and Case Study. *Latin American Antiquity* 6, no. 2, pp. 165–81.

Mountjoy, Joseph B. 1969. On the Origin of West Mexican Metallurgy. In Kelley and Riley 1969, pp. 26–42.

Mountjoy, Joseph B. 1970. Prehispanic Culture History and Cultural Contact on the Southern Coast of Nayarit, Mexico. Ph.D. diss., Southern Illinois University.

Mountjoy, Joseph B. 1974. San Blas Complex Ecology. In Bell 1974, pp. 106–19.

Mountjoy, Joseph B. 1982a. An Interpretation of the Pictographs at La Pena Pintada, Jalisco, Mexico. *American Antiquity* 47, no. 1, pp. 110–25.

Mountjoy, Joseph B. 1982b. *El Proyecto Tomatlán de Salvamento Arqueológico: fondo etnohistórico y arqueológico, desarrollo del proyecto, estudios de la superficie.* México, D.F.: I.N.A.H.

Mountjoy, Joseph B. 1983. Nuevos hallazgos sobre la habitación. Formativo Medio en San Blas, Nayarit. Paper presented at the XVIII Round Table (Western Mexico), Sociedad Mexicana de Antropología, Taxco.

Mountjoy, Joseph B. 1987. Antiquity, Interpretation, and Stylistic Evolution of Petroglyphs in West Mexico. *American Antiquity* 52, no. 1, pp. 161–74.

Mountjoy, Joseph B. 1994a. Capacha: Una cultura enigmática del Occidente de México. *Arqueología Mexicana* 2, no. 9, pp. 39–42.

Mountjoy, Joseph B. In press. El desarrollo de cultura indígena en la costa de Jalisco. In *Arqueología del Occidente de México.* Colima: University of Colima.

Mountjoy, Joseph B. 1994. Las tres transformaciones más importantes en la habitación indígena de la costa del Occidente de México. In *Transformaciones Mayores en el Occidente de Mèxico,* ed. R. Avila Palafox, pp. 217–24. Guadalajara.

Mountjoy, Joseph B. 1995. Análisis cronológico de la cerámica del Formativo, excavada en el sitio de La Pintada, Jalisco. In

Arqueología del norte y del occidente de México, ed. Barbro Dahgren and Dolores Soto de Arachavaleta, pp. 115–29. México, D.F.: U.N.A.M.

Mountjoy, Joseph B. 1996. Cálculos de la población prehispánica en la cuenca del Río Tomatlán. *Estudios del Hombre.* 3, pp. 173–94.

Mountjoy, Joseph B., and C. Claassen. 1989. Seasonality and Diet of Middle Formative People on the Central Coast of Nayarit, Mexico. Paper presented at the 88th Annual Meeting of the American Anthropological Association, Washington, D.C.

Mountjoy, Joseph B., R. E. Taylor, and L. Feldman. 1972. Matanchen Complex: New Radiocarbon Dates on Early Coastal Adaptation in West Mexico. *Science* 175, pp. 1242–43.

Mountjoy, Joseph B., and P. C. Weigand. 1975. The Prehispanic Settlement Zone at Teuchitlán, Jalisco. Paper presented at the International Congress of Americanists, Cordoba.

Mumford, Lewis. 1961. *The City in History. Its Origins, Its Transformations, and Its Prospects.* New York: Harcourt, Brace and World.

Murie, James R. 1981. Ceremonies of the Pawnee, Part 1: The Shiri. *Smithsonian Contributions to Anthropology,* no. 27. Washington, D.C.: Smithsonian Institution Press.

Museu Etnològic. 1992. *El juego de pelota en el México precolombino.* Exh. cat. Barcelona: Fundació Folch/Ajuntament de Barcelona.

Myerhoff, Barbara G. 1974. *Peyote Hunt: The Sacred Journey of the Huichols.* Ithaca: Cornell University Press.

Nash, June. 1970. *In the Eyes of the Ancestors.* New Haven: Yale University Press.

Nelson, Ben A. 1990. Observaciones acerca de la presencia tolteca en La Quemada, Zacatecas. In *Mesoamerica y Norte de México: Siglo IX–XII,* ed. F. Sodi M., pp. 521–39. México, D.F.: I.N.A.H. and Museo Nacional de Antropología.

Nelson, Ben. 1992. El maguey y el nopal en la economía de subsistencia de La Quemada, Zacatecas. In *Origen y Desarrollo de la Civilización en el Occidente de México,* ed. Brigitte Boehm de Lameiras and Phil C. Weigand, pp. 359–82. Zamora: El Colegio de Michoacán.

Nelson, Ben A. 1995. Complexity, Hierarchy, and Scale: A Controlled Comparison Between Chaco Canyon, New Mexico, and La Quemada, Zacatecas. *American Antiquity* 60, no. 4, pp. 597–618.

Nicholson, Henry B. 1971. Religion in Pre-Hispanic Central Mexico. In Wauchope 1964–76, vol. 10, pp. 395–446.

Noguera, Eduardo. 1942. Exploraciones en El Opeño, Michoacán. *XXVII Congreso Internacional de Americanistas* 1, pp. 574–86. México, D.F.

Noguera, Eduardo. 1971. Nuevas exploraciones en El Opeño. *Anales de Antropología* 8, pp. 83–100.

Norton, Presley. 1986. El Señorio de Salangone y la Liga de Mercaderes: El Cartel Spondylus-Balsa. In *Arqueología y Etnohistoria del Sur de Colombia y Norte del Ecuador,* ed. José Alcina Franch and Segundo Moreno Yánez, pp. 131–43. Guayaquil: Banco Central del Ecuador.

Noyola, Andrés. 1994. Análisis preliminar de la cerámica del Fraccionamiento San Juan, Atoyac, Jalisco. In *Contribuciones a la arqueología y etnohistoria del Occidente de México,* ed. Eduardo Williams, pp. 55–91. Zamora: El Colegio de Michoacán.

Nutini, Hugo G. 1988. *Todos Santos in Rural Tlaxcala: A Syncretic, Expressive, and Symbolic Analysis of the Cult of the Dead.* Princeton: Princeton University Press.

Ohnersorgen, Michael A., and M. D. Varien. 1996. Formal Architecture and Settlement Organization in Ancient West Mexico. *Ancient Mesoamerica* 7, no. 1, pp. 103–20.

Oliveros, Jose Arturo. 1974. Nuevas exploraciones en El Opeño, Michoacán. In Bell 1974, pp. 182–201.

Oliveros, Jose Arturo. 1992a. Apuntes sobre origenes y desarrollo del juego de pelota. In *El juego de pelota en mesoamerica,* ed. Maria Teresa Uriarte, pp. 39–54. México, D.F.: Siglo veintiuno editores.

Oliveros, Jose Arturo. 1992b. El Valle Zamora-Jacoma: Un proyecto arqueológico en Michoacán. In *Origen y Desarrollo de la Civilizacíon en el Occidente de México,* ed. Brigitte Boehm de Lameiras and Phil C. Weigand, pp. 239–49. Zamora: El Colegio de Michoacán.

Oliveros, Jose Arturo, and Magdalena de los Ríos Paredes. 1993. La Cronología de El Opeño, Michoacán. *Arqueología,* no. 9–10, pp. 45–58.

Ortiz, Alfonso. 1969. *The Tewa World.* Chicago: University of Chicago Press.

Ortiz de Montellano, Bernard. 1990. *Aztec Medicine, Health, and Nutrition.* New Brunswick: Rutgers University Press.

O'Shea, J. M. 1984. *Mortuary Variability: An Archaeological Perspective.* New York: Academic Press.

Oviedo y Valdes, Gonzalo Fernandez de. 1945. *Historia general y natural de las Indias, Islas y Tierra-Firme del mar Oceano,* vol. 11. Asunción: Editorial Guarania.

Palafox, Ricardo Avila, ed. 1989. *El Occidente de México: Arqueología, Historia, Antropología.* Guadalajara.

Panofsky, Erwin. 1955. Iconography and Iconology: An Introduction to the Study of Renaissance Art. In *Meaning in the Visual Arts,* pp. 26–54. New York: Doubleday.

Parsons, Jeffrey R., and Mary H. Parsons. 1990. *Maguey Utilization in Highland Central Mexico.* Ann Arbor: Museum of Anthropology, University of Michigan.

Parsons, Lee A. 1986. The Origins of Maya Art: Monumental Stone Sculpture of Kaminaljuyú, Guatemala, and the Southern Pacific Coast. *Studies in Pre-Columbian Art and Archaeology* 28. Washington, D.C.: Dumbarton Oaks and Trustees for Harvard University.

Paulsen, Allison C. 1974. The Thorny Oyster and the Voice of God: *Spondylus* and *Strombus* in Andean Prehistory. *American Antiquity* 39, no. 1, pp. 597–607.

Paulsen, Allison C. 1977. Patterns of Maritime Trade between South Coastal Ecuador and Western Mesoamerica, 1500 B.C.–A.D. 600. In *The Sea in the Pre-Columbian World,* ed. Elizabeth P. Benson, pp. 141–60. Washington, D.C.: Dumbarton Oaks.

Perrin, Michel. 1996. The Urukáme, A Crystallization of the Soul: Death and Memory. In Schaefer and Furst 1996, pp. 403–28.

Pickering, R. B. 1996. Paper presented at the sixty-first annual meeting of the Society for American Archaeology, New Orleans.

Pickering, R. B. 1997a. Discovering the Occidente. *Archaeology* 50, no. 6, pp. 42–46.

Pickering, R. B. 1997b. Maggots, Graves, and Scholars. *Archaeology* 50, no. 6, pp. 46–47.

Piña Chan, Román, and Kuniakí Oi. 1982. *Exploraciones Arqueológicas en Tingambato, Michoacán.* México, D.F.: I.N.A.H.

Pohl, Mary E. D., and John M. D. Pohl. 1994. Cycles of Conflict: Political Factionalism in the Maya Lowlands. In Brumfiel and Fox 1994, pp. 138–57.

Pollard, Helen Perlstein. 1972. Pre-Hispanic Urbanism at Tzintzuntzan, Michoacán. Ph.D. diss. Ann Arbor: University Microfilms International.

Pollard, Helen P. 1993. *Taríacuri's Legacy: The Prehispanic Tarascan State.* Norman: University of Oklahoma Press.

Pollard, Helen P. 1997. Recent Research in West Mexican Archaeology. *Journal of Archaeological Research* 5, no. 4, pp. 345–84.

Preuss, Konrad Theodor. 1996. Konrad Theodor Preuss (1869–1938) on the Huichols. In Schaefer and Furst 1996, pp. 88–136.

Preziosi, Donald. 1989. *Rethinking Art History: Meditations on a Coy Science.* New Haven: Yale University Press.

Ramos de la Vega, Jorge, and M. Lorenza López Mestas Camberos. 1996. Datos preliminares sobre el descubrimiento de una tumba de tiro en el sitio de Huitzilapa, Jalisco. *Ancient Mesoamerica* 7, no. 1, pp. 121–34.

Rattray, Evelyn C. 1991. Fechamientos por radiocarbono en Teotihuacan. *Arqueología,* pp. 3–18. México, D.F.: I.N.A.H.

Reents-Budet, Dorie. 1994. *Painting the Maya Universe: Royal Ceramics of the Classic Period.* Durham, N.C.: Duke University Press.

Reichel-Dolmatoff, Gerardo. 1975. *The Shaman and the Jaguar: A Study of Narcotic Drugs among the Indians of Colombia.* Philadelphia: Temple University Press.

Reichel-Dolmatoff, Gerardo. 1985. *Los Kogi, Una Tribu de la Sierra Nevada de Santa Marta, Colombia.* 2 vols. Bogotá: Procultura.

Relación de Michoacán. 1956. Ed. José Tudela, José Núñez, and Paul Kirchhoff. Madrid: Aguila.

Relación de Michoacán. 1977. *Relación de las ceremonias y ritos y población y gobierno de los indios de la Provincia de Michoacán (1541),* ed. José Tudelas. México, D.F.: Balsal Editores.

Rodman, Amy Oakland. 1992. Textiles and Ethnicity: Tiwanaku in San Pedro de Atacama, North Chile. *Latin American Antiquity* 3, no. 4, pp. 316–40.

Roediger, Virginia More. 1941. *Ceremonial Costumes of the Pueblo Indians: Their Evolution, Fabrication, and Significance in the Prayer Drama.* Berkeley.

Ruíz de Alarcón, Hernando. 1984. *Treatise on the Heathen Superstitions that Today Live among the Indians Native to this New Spain, 1629,* trans. J. Richard Andrews and Ross Hassig. Norman: University of Oklahoma Press.

Sahagún, Bernardino de. 1950–82. *Florentine Codex: General History of the Things of New Spain,* ed. Arthur J. O. Anderson and Charles E. Dibble. 12 vols. Santa Fe: School of American Research and Salt Lake City: University of Utah Press.

Sahagún, Bernardino de. 1989. Historia general de las cosas de Nueva España. 2nd ed. México, D.F.: Consejo Nacional para la Cultura y las Artes and Alianza Editorial.

Sahlins, Marshall D. 1968. *Tribesmen.* Englewood Cliffs, N.J.: Prentice Hall.

Samanos, Juan de. 1844. Relación de los primeros descubrimientos de Francisco Pizarro y Diego de Almagro, sacada del códice número CXX de la Biblioteca Imperial de Viena. In *Colección de documentos inéditos para la historia de España* V, pp. 193–201. Madrid.

Sanchez, Sergio, and E. G. Marmolejo. 1990. Algunas Apreciaciones sobre el Clasico en el Bajio Central, Guanajuato. In *La Epoca Clasica: Nuevos Hallazgos, Nuevas Ideas,* ed. Amalia Cardos de Mendez, pp. 267–78. México, D.F.: Museo Nacional de Antropologia and I.N.A.H.

Sanders, William, Jeffery Parsons, and Robert Santley. 1979. *The Basin of Mexico.* New York: Academic Press.

Sarmiento Fradera, Griselda. 1992. *Las primeras sociedades jerárquicas.* México, D.F.: I.N.A.H.

Saxe, A. 1970a. Social Dimensions of Mortuary Practices. Ph.D. diss., University of Michigan.

Saxe, A. 1970b. Social Dimensions of Mortuary Practices in a Mesolithic Population from Wadi Halfa, Sudan. *American Antiquity* 25, pp. 39–57.

Scarborough, Vernon L., and David R. Wilcox, eds. 1991. *The Mesoamerican Ballgame.* Tucson: University of Arizona Press.

Scarduelli, Pietro. 1988. *Dioses, espíritus, ancestros: Elementos para la comprensión de sistemas rituales.* México, D.F.: Fondo de Cultura Económica.

Schaefer, Stacy B., and Peter T. Furst. 1996. *People of the Peyote: Huichol Indian History, Religion, and Survival.* Albuquerque: University of New Mexico Press.

Schele, Linda. 1995. The Olmec Mountain and Tree of Creation in Mesoamerican Cosmology. In *The Olmec World: Ritual and Rulership,* ed. Elizabeth P. Benson, pp. 105–17. Princeton.

Schele, Linda, and David Freidel. 1990. *A Forest of Kings.* New York: William Morrow.

Schele, Linda, and Mary Ellen Miller. 1986. *The Blood of Kings: Dynasty and Ritual in Maya Art.* Fort Worth: Kimbell Art Museum and Sotheby's Publications.

Schickel, Richard. 1997. *The Disney Version: The Life, Times, Art, and Commerce of Walt Disney.* 3rd ed. Chicago: John R. Dee Publisher.

Schöndube, Otto. 1980. Epoca prehispánica. In *Historia de Jalisco,* vol. 1, ed. José Maria Muriá, pp. 113–257. Guadalajara: Gobierno del Estado de Jalisco.

Schöndube, Otto. 1995. Identification of Plants and Animals on West Mexico Ceramics. Paper presented at the Denver Museum of Natural History, October 12–15, 1995.

Schöndube, Otto, and Sara Ladrón de Guevara. 1990. *Bibliografía arqueológica del Occidente de México.* Guadalajara: Editorial Universidad de Guadalajara.

Scott, S. 1968–73. *Archaeological Reconnaissance and Excavations in the Marismas Nacionales, Sinaloa and Nayarit, Mexico.* Parts 1–7. Buffalo: State University of New York.

Scott, Stuart D. 1985. Core Versus Marginal Mesoamerica: A Coastal West Mexican Perspective. In Foster and Weigand 1985, pp. 181–91.

Sempowski, Martha L., and Michael Spence. 1994. *Mortuary Practices and Skeletal Remains at Teotihuacan.* Vol. 3 of *Urbanization at Teotihuacan, Mexico,* ed. René Millon. Salt Lake City: University of Utah Press.

Service, Elman R. 1962. *Primitive Social Organization: An Evolutionary Perspective.* New York: Random House.

Service, Elman R. 1975. *Origins of the State and Civilization.* New York: Norton.

Shales, Richard. 1982. *Donald Duck Joins Up: The Walt Disney Studio During World War II.* Ann Arbor: UMI Research Press.

Sheets, Payson D. 1992. *The Ceren Site: A Prehistoric Village Buried by Volcanic Ash in Central America.* Fort Worth: Harcourt Brace Javanovich.

Sherwood, Lydia E. 1937. The Eternal Road-Company. *Vogue,* June 15, 1937, pp. 40–41, 87.

Silva, Ramón Medina. 1996. A Huichol Soul Travels to the Land of the Dead. In Schaefer and Furst 1996, pp. 389–402.

Smith, Michael E. 1977–78. A Model for the Diffusion of the Shaft-Tomb Complex from South America to West Mexico. In Steward Anthropological Society 1977–78, pp. 179–205.

Smith, Virginia G. 1984. *Izapa Relief Carving: Form, Content, Rules for Design, and Role in Mesoamerican Art History and Archaeology.* Washington, D.C.: Dumbarton Oaks.

Smoodin, Eric. 1994. *Disney Discourse: Producing the Magic Kingdom.* New York and London: Routledge.

Solis, Felipe. 1992. El sagrado juego de pelota en la capital de los Mexicas. In Museu Etnológic 1992, pp. 76–91.

Solórzano, Federico A. 1980. Prehistoria. In *Historia de Jalisco,* vol. 1, ed. José Maria Muriá, pp. 89–110. Guadalajara: Gobierno del Estado de Jalisco.

Soto de Arechavaleta, Dolores. 1982. Análisis de la Tecnología de Producción de Taller de Obsidiana de Guachimontón, Teuchitlán, Jalisco. Ph.D. diss., Escuela Nacional de Antropología e Historia, México, D.F.

Southall, Aidan. 1988. The Segmentary State in Africa and Asia. *Comparative Studies of Society and History* 30, pp. 52–82.

Spencer, Charles S. 1987. Rethinking the Chiefdom. In *Chiefdoms in the Americas,* ed. Robert D. Drennan and Carlos A. Uribe. Lanham, Md.: University Press of America.

Spencer, Charles S. 1994. Factional Ascendance, Dimensions of Leadership, and the Development of Centralized Authority. In Brumfiel and Fox 1994, pp. 31–43.

Sprajc, Ivan. 1989. *Venus, lluvia y maíz: Simbolismo y astronomía en la cosmovisión mesoamericana.* Thesis, Escuela Nacional de Antropología e Historia, México, D.F.

Steward Anthropological Society. 1977–78. *Prehistoric Contacts Between Mesoamerica and South America: New Data and Interpretations. Journal of the Steward Anthropological Society* 9, nos. 1–2.

Stuart, Glenn. 1992. Better Loams and Gardens. The Archaeological Potential of Palynological Research on Chinampas. Highland Lake Areas of Jalisco, Mexico. Unpublished ms.

Suárez, Lourdes. 1974. *Técnicas prehispánicas en los objetos de concha.* México, D.F.: I.N.A.H.

Taladoire, Eric. 1994. El Juego de Pelota Precolombino. *Arqueológia Mexicana* 2, no. 9, p. 10.

Taube, Karl A. 1989. The Maize Tamale in Classic Maya Diet, Epigraphy, and Art. *American Antiquity* 54, no. 1, pp. 31–51.

Thomas, Nicholas, and Caroline Humphrey, eds. 1994. *Shamanism, History, and the State.* Ann Arbor: University of Michigan Press.

Thompson, J. Eric S. 1971. *Maya Hieroglyphic Writing: An Introduction.* 3rd ed. Norman: University of Oklahoma Press.

Titiv, Mischa. 1950. The Religion of the Hopi Indians. In *Forgotten Religions,* ed. Vergilius Ferm. New York: Philosophical Library.

Toscano, Salvador, and Federico Canessi. 1946. *Arte Precolombino del Occidente de México.* México, D.F.: Secretaria de Educacion Publica.

Townsend, Richard F. 1979. *State and Cosmos in the Art of Tenochtitlan.* Washington, D.C.: Dumbarton Oaks.

Townsend, Richard F. 1987. Coronation at Tenochtitlan. In *The Aztec Templo Mayor.* Washington, D.C.: Dumbarton Oaks.

Townsend, Richard F. 1992. *The Aztecs.* London: Thames and Hudson.

Trombold, Charles D., J. F. Luhr, T. Hasenaka, and M. Glascock. 1993. Chemical Characteristics of Obsidian from Archaeological Sites in Western Mexico and the Tequila Source Area. *Ancient Mesoamerica* 4, pp. 255–70.

Uriarte, Maria Teresa. 1992. El juego de pelota en los murales de Tepantitla en Teotihuacan. In *El juego de pelota en mesoamerica,* ed. Maria Teresa Uriarte, pp. 113–42. México, D.F.: Siglo veintiuno editores.

Valdez, Francisco. 1994. Tumbas de Tiro en Usmajac (Jalisco): Hacia una reorientación de la temática. *Trace* 25, pp. 92–111.

Valdez, Francisco. 1996. Tiempo, espacio y cultura en la Cuenca de Sayula. *Estudios del Hombre* 3, pp. 15–35.

Valdez, Francisco, Catherine Liot, Rosario Acosta, and Jean Pierre Emphoux. 1996. The Sayula Basin: Lifeways and Salt Flats of Central Jalisco. *Ancient Mesoamerica* 7, no. 1, pp. 171–86.

Valdez, Francisco, Catherine Liot, and Otto Schöndube. 1996. Recursos naturales y su uso en las cuencas lacustres del Sur de Jalisco. El Caso de Sayula. In Williams and Weigand 1996, pp. 325–66.

Villanueva, Gerardo, Jimena Manrique, and Lorenza López Mestas. 1996. Especies marinas ofrendadas en la tumba de tiro de Huitzilapa. Paper presented at the IV Coloquio Internacional de Occidentalistas, ORSTOM, Guadalajara.

Vogt, Evon. 1969. *Zinacantán.* Cambridge: Harvard University Press.

Von Winning, Hasso. 1974. *The Shaft Tomb Figures of West Mexico.* Southwest Museum Papers, no. 24. Los Angeles: Southwest Museum.

Von Winning, Hasso. 1987. *Portrayal of Pathological Symptoms in Pre-Columbian Mexico.* Carbondale: The Pearson Museum, Southern Illinois University School of Medicine.

Von Winning, Hasso, and Olga Hammer. 1972. *Anecdotal Sculpture of Ancient West Mexico.* Los Angeles: Ethnic Arts Council of Los Angeles.

Von Winning, Hasso, and Alfred Stendahl. 1968. *Pre-Columbian Art of Mexico and Central America.* New York: Harry N. Abrams.

Voorhies, Barbara, ed,. 1989. *Ancient Trade and Tribute: Economies of the Soconusco Region of Mesoamerica.* Salt Lake City: University of Utah Press.

Warren, J. Benedict. 1985. *The Conquest of Michoacán.* Norman: University of Oklahoma Press.

Wauchope. Robert, ed. 1964–76. *Handbook of Middle American Indians.* 16 vols. Austin: University of Texas Press.

Webb, Clarence H. 1982. The Poverty Point Culture. In *Geoscience and Man,* vol. 17. 2nd ed. rev. Baton Rouge: Louisiana State University Press.

Weigand, Phil C. 1974. The Ahualulco Site and Shaft-Tomb Complex of the Etzatlán Area. In Bell 1974, pp. 120–31.

Weigand, Phil C. 1985. Evidence for Complex Societies during the Western Mesoamerican Classic Period. In Foster and Weigand 1985, pp. 47–91.

Weigand, Phil C. 1989. Architecture and Settlement Patterns within the Western Mesoamerican Formative Tradition. In *El Preclasico o Formativo,* ed. Martha Carmona Macias, pp. 39–64. México, D.F.

Weigand, Phil C. 1991. The Western Mesoamerican *Tlachco:* A Two-Thousand-Year Perspective. In Scarborough and Wilcox 1991, pp. 73–86.

Weigand, Phil C. 1992a. Central Mexico's Influences in Jalisco and Nayarit during the Classic Period. In *Resources, Power, and International Interaction,* ed. E. Schorlman and P. Urban, pp. 221–32. New York: Plenum Press.

Weigand, Phil C. 1992b. Ehecatl: ¿Primer dios supremo del Occidente? In *Origen y Desarrollo en el Occidente de México,* ed. Brigitte Boehm de Lameiras and Phil C. Weigand, pp. 205–37. Zamora: El Colegio de Michoacán.

Weigand, Phil C. 1993a. *Evolución de una civilización prehispánica: Arqueología de Jalisco, Nayarit, y Zacatecas.* Zamora: El Colegio de Michoacán.

Weigand, Phil C. 1993b. The Evolution and Decline of a Core of Civilization: The Teuchitlán Tradition and the Archaeology of Jalisco. Paper for the Centro de Estudios Antropológicos Colegio de Michoacán and the Anthropology Museum of Northern Arizona.

Weigand, Phil C. 1994. Obras Hidráulicas a Gran Escala en el Occidente de Mesoamerica. In *Contribuciones a la Arqueología y Etnohistoria del Occidente de Mexico,* ed. Eduardo Williams, pp. 227–77. Zamora: El Colegio de Michoacán.

Weigand, Phil C. 1996a. The Architecture of the Teuchitlán Tradition of the Occidente of Mesoamerica. *Ancient Mesoamerica* 7, no. 1, pp. 91–102.

Weigand, Phil C. 1996b. La evolución y ocaso de un núcleo de civilización: La Tradición Teuchitlán y la arqueología de Jalisco. In Williams and Weigand 1996, pp. 185–245.

West, Robert C. 1961. Aboriginal Sea Navigation between Middle and South America. *American Anthropologist* 63, no. 1, pp. 133–35.

Whalen, Michael E., and P. E. Minnis. 1996. Ball Courts and Political Centralization in the Casas Grandes Region. *American Antiquity* 61, pp. 732–46.

Wilbert, Johannes. 1987. *Tobacco and Shamanism in South America.* New Haven: Yale University Press.

Wilkerson, S. Jeffrey K. 1991. And Then They Were Sacrificed: The Ritual Ballgame of Northeastern Mesoamerica through Time and Space. In Scarborough and Wilcox 1991, pp. 45–72.

Willey, Gordon. 1966. *An Introduction to American Archaeology,* ed. David M. Schneider. Vol. I: North and Middle America. Prentice-Hall, Inc., Englewood Cliffs, New Jersey.

Williams García, Roberto. 1963. *Los Tepéhuas.* Jalapa: Universidad Veracruzana, Instituto de Antropología.

Williams, Eduardo. 1992. *Las piedras sagradas: Escultura prehispánica del Occidente de México.* México, D.F.: El Colegio de Michoacán.

Williams, Eduardo, and Phil C. Weigand, eds. 1996. *Las cuencas del Occidente de México (Epoca prehispánica).* Zamora: El Colegio de Michoacán.

Yoffee, Norman. 1993. Too Many Chiefs? (or, Safe Texts for the '90s). In *Archaeological Theory: Who Sets the Agenda,* ed. Norman Yoffee and Andrew Sherratt, pp. 60–78. Cambridge: Cambridge University Press.

Zepeda, Gabriela. 1994. *Ixtlán: Ciudad del Viento.* México, D.F.: I.N.A.H.

Zuidema, T. R. 1997–78. Shaft-Tombs and the Inca Empire. In Steward Anthropological Society 1977–78, pp. 133–77.

CONTRIBUTORS

Richard F. Townsend, Curator in the Department of African and Amerindian Art at The Art Institute of Chicago, is a scholar specializing in Mesoamerican art and cultural history. He received his Ph.D. in the history of art in 1975 from Harvard University and has taught at the University of Nebraska and the University of Texas. His publications include *The Aztecs* (1992) and *The Ancient Americas: Art from Sacred Landscapes* (1992).

Patricia Rieff Anawalt is the Director of the Center for the Study of Regional Dress at the Fowler Museum of Cultural History at the University of California, Los Angeles. Her areas of specialization include the history of pre-Hispanic, Spanish colonial, and present-day Mexican and Central American textiles and costumes; the prehistory and contemporary history of the cultures of middle America; and Mesoamerican ethnohistory. Among her many books and articles is *Indian Clothing before Cortes: Mesoamerican Costumes from the Codices* (1990).

Christopher S. Beekman is Visiting Assistant Professor of Anthropology at Indiana University–Purdue University at Fort Wayne. He received his Ph.D. from Vanderbilt University in 1997. His archaeological research in Mesoamerica has encompassed studies of boundaries, political organization, migration and ethnicity, and chronology.

Barbara Braun is an independent scholar with a Ph.D. in art history and archaeology from Columbia University. She has been a curator of pre-Columbian art at Dumbarton Oaks in Washington, D.C., and has taught pre-Columbian and modern art at various universities. Her publications include *Pre-Columbian Art and the Post-Columbian World*. She is president of Barbara Braun Associates, Inc., a literary agency in New York City.

Kristi Butterwick received her Ph.D. in 1998 from the University of Colorado. She has participated in several archaeological excavations in Mexico, Guatemala, and the United States and produced several teaching and educational programs and videos on the subject of Mesoamerican archaeology. She is now investigating the nature of sociopolitical complexity among West Mexican societies during the Late Formative period.

Maria Teresa Cabrero is a research archaeologist at the Instituto des Investigaciones Antropológicos at the Universidad Nacional Autonoma de México in Mexico City. She has conducted extensive fieldwork in West Mexico and has a special interest in the mortuary practices of the shaft-tomb cultures. Her publications include *La muerte en el Occidente del México prehispanico* (1995).

Jane Stevenson Day retired in 1997 as Chief Curator at the Denver Museum of Natural History and Curator of Latin American Archaeology in the museum's Department of Anthropology. She is an adjunct professor of archaeology at the University of Colorado at Denver and at the University of Denver. She has lectured and published extensively on the archaeology of Central America and produced numerous exhibitions. She is the coeditor (with Gary Seaman) of *Ancient Traditions: Shamanism in Central Asia and the Americas* (1994).

Peter T. Furst is Research Associate at the University of Pennsylvania Museum of Archaeology and Anthropology, Adjunct Professor in the university's Department of Anthropology, and a member of its Latin American Studies faculty. He has extensive field research experience in Mexico, Central America, and northern South America. His scholarly interests include art, iconography, mythology, shamanism, ethnobotany, and belief systems in the ancient Americas, particularly West Mexico. He is the author and coauthor of numerous books and articles, including (with Stacy B. Scheafer) *People of the Peyote: Huichol Indian History, Religion, and Survival* (1996).

Mark Miller Graham is Associate Professor of Art History at Auburn University. He received his Ph.D. in pre-Columbian art history from the University of California, Los Angeles, in 1985. He has published articles and lectured widely in the fields of art history and archaeology. One of his primary fields of interest is in what anthropologists term the Intermediate Area, which ranges from Costa Rica to Colombia.

Lorenza López Mestas Camberos is a research archaeologist at the Jalisco center of the Instituto Nacional de Antropología e Historia. She has conducted extensive archaeological salvage work and regional surveying in West Mexico and is one of the principal excavators of the Huitzilapa tomb. She is currently directing an archaeological project in the valley of Cihuatlán and conducting a survey of highland Jalisco.

Joseph B. Mountjoy is an archaeologist and professor of anthropology. For the last twenty-five years, he has taught at the University of North Carolina at Greensboro. He has done extensive fieldwork in the West Mexico, including mapping sites and establishing chronologies in the coastal areas. Among his numerous books, monographs, articles, and reviews is *El Proyecto Tomatlán de Salvamento Arqueológico: fondo etnohistórico y arqueológico, desarrollo del proyecto, estudios de la superficie* (1982).

Robert B. Pickering is a physical anthropologist and the head of the Department of Anthropology at the Denver Museum of Natural History. His major interests include forensic anthropology, mortuary behavior studies, and museum studies. He worked closely with Jorge Ramos and Lorenza López on the skeletal materials recovered from the Huitzilapa tomb. His publications include the forthcoming book *The Shaft-Tomb Cultures of Ancient West Mexico*.

Jorge Ramos de la Vega is an investigative archaeologist at the Jalisco center of the Instituto Nacional de Antropología e Historia. He has conducted several archaeological salvage projects in West Mexico and is one of the principal excavators of the Huitzilapa tomb. He is currently surveying the archaeological sites of highland Jalisco and conducting studies of Formative-period sites in the region of Huitzilapa, Jalisco, and Ortices, Colima.

Otto Schöndube, Curator of Archaeology at the Regional Museum of Guadalajara, is a field archaeologist specializing in material remains. He is a native of the West Mexican region and has a detailed knowledge of its flora and fauna. He is the author of numerous articles on the history and archaeology of Jalisco and Colima.

Francisco Valdez is an archaeologist at L'Institut Français de Recherche Scientifique pour le Développement en Coopération (ORSTOM). He was formerly at the Museo del Banco Central del Ecuador and directed archaeological projects at the coastal site of La Tolita. He has published several books and articles on Ecuadorian and West Mexican art and archaeology, among them *Signos amerindios: 5,000 Años de arte precolombino en Ecuador* (1992).

Phil C. Weigand is President of the Council of Ethnohistory at the Colegio de Michoacán and a Research Professor at its Centro de Estudios Antropológicos. His projects have been focused upon the ethnography, ethnohistory, and archaeology of Jalisco, Nayarit, and Zacatecas. Over the past twenty-five years, he has documented and published numerous articles defining the Teuchitlán tradition. He is the principal formulator of the theory of complex societies in the West Mexico region. Among his numerous articles and books is *Evolución de una civilización prehispánica: Arqueología de Jalisco, Nayarit y Zacatecas* (1993).

Christopher L. Witmore is currently working on a master's degree in landscape archaeology at the University of Sheffield in England. He recently served as co-director of paleobotanical and geological operations for the Mochlos Excavation in Crete with the University of North Carolina at Greensboro and the Greek Archaeological Service.

Photography Credits

Richard F. Townsend, "Introduction: Renewing the Inquiry in Ancient West Mexico"
1, 9, 10, 12, 13, 17, 19, 21, 23, 24, 26, 27: photos © by Justin Kerr; 2, 4: from Graciela Romandia de Cantu, *Adela Breton: Una Artista Británica en México, 1894–1908* (1993); 3, 5, 6: photos by Richard F. Townsend; 7: photo by Otto Schondube; 8: courtesy of the Kistermann Collection; 11: photo by Michael Tropea; 14, 15, 22, 25, 30: photos © by Douglas M. Parker Studio; 16: Tucson Museum of Art; 18, 28, 29: Los Angeles County Museum of Art; 20: photo © by Dirk Bakker.

Phil C. Weigand and Christopher S. Beekman, "The Teuchitlán Tradition: Rise of a Statelike Society"
1, 17a, 21: photos by Richard F. Townsend; 2, 7–9, 16, 17b: drawings by Gigi Bayliss after Phil Weigand; 3: map by Christopher Beekman after Phil Weigand; 4: photo © by Douglas M. Parker Studio; 5, 6: Natural History Museum of Los Angeles County; 10, 11, 18, 19: photos © by Dirk Bakker; 12, 14, 20: photos © by Justin Kerr; 13: The Cleveland Museum of Art; 15: The Art Institute of Chicago; 22: reconstruction drawing by Michael Guran, Project Architect.

Lorenza López Mestas Camberos and Jorge Ramos de la Vega, "Excavating the Tomb at Huitzilapa"
1, 2, 7, 9, 10, 15–19: courtesy of the Huitzilapa Project, INAH; composite image for fig. 9 realized by Rob McAleavy, Denver Museum of Natural History; 3–6, 8: drawings by Gabriela Ulloa, courtesy of the Huitzilapa Project, INAH; 11: photo © by Dirk Bakker; 12: photo by Dave Marlow; 13: photo © by Justin Kerr; 14: from *Codex Magliabechiano*, complete color facsimile edition of Academische Druck u. Verlagsanstalt (1970).

Robert B. Pickering and Maria Teresa Cabrero, "Mortuary Practices in the Shaft-Tomb Region"
1, 12: drawings by Gabriela Ulloa, courtesy of the Huitzilapa Project, INAH; 2, 13: photos by Robert Pickering; 3: drawings by Gigi Bayliss; 4: courtesy of Maria Teresa Cabrero and Carlos López Cruz; 5, 15, 18, 20: photos © by Dirk Bakker; 6: chart by Robert Pickering and Maria Teresa Cabrero; 7, 8: Fowler Museum of Cultural History, University of California, Los Angeles; 9–11: Natural History Museum of Los Angeles County; 14: The Art Institute of Chicago; 16, 19, 21, 22: photos © by Justin Kerr; 17: photo © by John Taylor; 23: photo © by Douglas M. Parker Studio.

Kristi Butterwick, "Food for the Dead: The West Mexican Art of Feasting"
1: courtesy of Galerie Mermoz; 2, 25: photos by Richard F. Townsend; 3, 12, 21–24: photos © by Douglas M. Parker Studio; 4, 7, 16, 26: photos © by Justin Kerr; 5: The Minneapolis Institute of Arts; 6: Los Angeles County Museum of Art; 8, 9, 11, 14, 15, 17, 28: photos © by Dirk Bakker; 10: The Art Institute of Chicago; 13: photo by Robert M. Hashimoto; 18: from *Codex Nuttall*, complete color facsimile edition of Academische Druck u. Verlagsanstalt (1987); 19: from *Artes de Mexico* 140 (1971), watercolor by Ignacio Marquina; 20: Fowler Museum of Cultural History, University of California, Los Angeles; 27: from *Codex Borbonicus*, complete color facsimile edition of Academische Druck u. Verlagsanstalt (1974).

Richard F. Townsend, "Before Gods, Before Kings"
1: photo by Charles D. Townsend; 2, 12, 14, 40, 42: The Art Institute of Chicago; 3: after Orozco y Berra, 1877; 4, 23, 37: from *Codex Borbonicus*, complete color facsimile edition of Academische Druck u. Verlagsanstalt (1974); 5: courtesy of the Kistermann Collection; 6, 22, 41: Los Angeles County Museum of Art; 7, 36: Bodleian Library, Oxford University; 8, 27, 33: photos © by Douglas M. Parker Studio; 9, 16, 19, 29, 31, 32, 35, 38: photos © by Justin Kerr; 10: photo by Dietrich Graf; 11, 13, 18, 30a–b, 34: photos © by Dirk Bakker; 15: photo by P. A. Ferrazzini; 17: photo by Michael Cavanagh and Kevin Montague, Indiana University Art Museum; 20: photo by Dave Marlow; 21: photo © by John Taylor; 24: from *Codex Borgia*, Codes Vaticanus mess. 1. Color facsimile edition of Academische Druck u. Verlagsanstalt (1976); 25: photo by

Michael Tropea; 26: courtesy of Galerie Mermoz; 28a: drawing by Sarah Guernsey after Hasso von Winning and Olga Hammer, *Anecdotal Sculpture of Ancient West Mexico* (1972); 28b: drawing by Gigi Bayliss after von Winning and Hammer (1972); 39: from von Winning and Hammer, (1972); 43: photo by Hughes du Bois.

Christopher L. Witmore, "Sacred Sun Centers"
1: photo by Dirk Bakker; 2: site plan and elevation by Michael Alexander Guran, Project Architect, after Phil Weigand; 3: The Saint Louis Art Museum; 4: photo © by Douglas M. Parker Studio; 5: from Earl H. Morris, Jean Charlot, and Ann Axtell Morris, *The Temple of the Warriors at Chichén Itzá* (1931); 6: photo © The British Museum; 7: drawing by Joseph Cochand; 8: Liverpool Museum; 9a–d: from *Memoirs of the American Museum of Natural History* (1900); 10: Yale University Art Gallery; 11: photo © by Justin Kerr; 12: Fowler Museum of Cultural History, University of California, Los Angeles; 13: The Art Institute of Chicago; 14, 15: photos by Thomas Holien; 16: photo by Dr. Jaime Ganot R. and Dr. Alejandro Peshard F.

Jane Stevenson Day, "The West Mexican Ballgame"
1, 10: Los Angeles County Museum of Art; 2: from *Codex Borbonicus*, complete color facsimile edition of Academische Druck u. Verlagsanstalt (1974); 3: photo by Richard F. Townsend; 4, 6, 9–15, 18: drawings by Gigi Bayliss; 5, 22: photos © by Justin Kerr; 7, 23: courtesy of Galerie Mermoz; 8: photo © 1994 Sotheby's, Inc.; 16: photo © by Dirk Bakker; 17, 19: photos by Jane Day; 20: photo by Gishaaver; 21: Yale University Art Gallery.

Peter T. Furst, "Shamanic Symbolism, Transformation, and Deities in West Mexican Funerary Art"
1, 17: photos © by Douglas M. Parker Studio; 2–7, 10, 13–16, 19–21, 24, 28: photos by Peter Furst; 8, 11, 23, 29: photos © by Justin Kerr; 9: photo by Michael Tropea; 12: courtesy of Ron Messick Fine Arts, Santa Fe, N.M.; 18: The Cleveland Museum of Art; 22, 27, 30: photos © by Dirk Bakker; 25: The University of Iowa Museum of Art; 26: Los Angeles County Museum of Art.

Mark Miller Graham, "The Iconography of Rulership in Ancient West Mexico"
1: Utah Museum of Fine Arts, University of Utah; 2: photo © by Dirk Bakker; 3, 16: Los Angeles County Museum of Art; 4: photo © by Justin Kerr; 5: photo © by Douglas M. Parker Studio; 6: drawing by Gigi Bayliss; 7a–b, 14: Dumbarton Oaks, Washington D.C.; 7c–d, 11–13, 15: from Linda Schele and Mary Ellen Miller, *The Blood of Kings: Dynasty and Ritual in Maya Art* (1986), drawings by Linda Schele; 8: from Ignacio Marquina, *Arquitectura Prehispanica* (1964); 9: from Eduardo Matos Moctezuma, *Teotihuacán: The City of Gods* (1990); 10: photo by Richard F. Townsend; 17: The Art Institute of Chicago.

Otto Schöndube, "Natural Resources and Human Settlements in Ancient West Mexico"
1, 5, 6, 10, 11, 15, 28: photos © by Justin Kerr; 2–4, 12, 13, 20: photos by Richard F. Townsend; 7: photo by Michael Tropea; 8, 17, 25: photos © by Dirk Bakker; 9, 19, 21, 27, 29: photos © by Douglas M. Parker Studio; 14, 24: Los Angeles County Museum of Art; 16: photo © by John Taylor; 18, 26: Fowler Museum of Cultural History, University of California, Los Angeles; 22, 23: photos by Otto Schöndube.

Francisco Valdez, "The Sayula Basin: Ancient Settlements and Resources"
1–3, 6: photos by Francisco Valdez; 4: chart by Francisco Valdez; 5: The Saint Louis Art Museum; 7: Fowler Museum of Cultural History, University of California, Los Angeles; 8: Los Angeles County Museum of Art; 9: photo by Richard F. Townsend; 10: chronological chart by Francisco Valdez; 11: map by Francisco Valdez; 12, 14: drawings by Francisco Valdez; 13: plan by Francisco Valdez.

Patricia Rieff Anawalt, "They Came to Trade Exquisite Things: Ancient West Mexican–Ecuadorian Contacts"
1: courtesy of Galerie Mermoz; 2: Mapping Specialists; 3, 29: Bodleian Library, Oxford University; 4–7, 23: from *Relación de Michoacán*, color facsimile edition, Balsal Edi-

tores (1977); 8: photo © by Douglas M. Parker Studio; 9: from Alan Lapiner, *Pre-Columbian Art of South America* (1976); 10, 11: courtesy of Thomas Cummins; 12: from *Arte Precolombiano de Ecuador* (1977); 13: Denver Art Museum; 14, 15, 22a–b: drawings by Gigi Bayliss; 16, 30–35: photos © by Dirk Bakker; 17: from Samuel Kirkland Lothrop, *Coclé: An Archeological Study of Central Panama* (1937); 18: photo © by Justin Kerr; 19, 20: courtesy of Museo del Banco Central, Guayaquil; 21: The Art Institute of Chicago; 24: from Dorothy Hosler, *The Sounds and Colors of Power* (1994); 25: from *Biotropica* 11, 2 (1979); 26: courtesy of Museo Arqueológico del Banco del Pacífico; 27: courtesy of Museo Naval, Madrid, Spain; 28: photo by Don Cole.

Joseph B. Mountjoy, "The Evolution of Complex Societies in West Mexico: A Comparative Perspective"
1: photo © by John Taylor; 2: Mint Museum of Art; 3: The Saint Louis Art Museum; 4, 10: Fowler Museum of Cultural History, University of California, Los Angeles; 5: photo © by Douglas M. Parker Studio; 6, 9: photos © by Justin Kerr; 7: photo © by Dirk Bakker; 8: The Art Museum, Princeton University; 11: Natural History Museum of Los Angeles County; 12: Los Angeles County Museum of Art; 13: from Daniel Schávelzon, *La Piramide de Cuicuilco* (1983), drawing by Daniel Schávelzon (1980), after an original by INAH (1978); 14: photo by Richard F. Townsend; 15, 16: photos by Thomas Holien; 17: from Carlos Nebel, *Viaje pintoresco y arqueológico sobre la parte mas interesante de la Republica Mexicana* (1963); 18: photo by Junius Bird, Bayou Macon, Louisiana, © American Museum of Natural History, New York; 19: from Jon L. Gibson, *The Earthen Face of Civilization: Mapping and Testing at Poverty Point, 1983* (1984); 20: courtesy of Vernon J. Knight, University of Alabama.

Barbara Braun, "West Mexican Art and Modernist Artists"
1, 2: photos by Dirk Bakker, © Estate of Diego Rivera/ Licensed by VAGA, New York, N.Y.; 3: photo by Bob Schalkwijk, © Estate of Diego Rivera/ Licensed by VAGA, New York, N.Y.; 4, 15, 17, 19, 23, 25: photos © by Justin Kerr; 5: San Francisco Museum of Modern Art, © Estate of Diego Rivera/ Licensed by VAGA, New York, N.Y.; 6: photo © by John Taylor; 7, 8: from *Mural Painting of the Mexican Revolution: 1921–1960* (1960), © Estate of Diego Rivera/ Licensed by VAGA, New York, N.Y.; 9: photo by Michael Tropea; 10: The Museum of Modern Art, New York, © 1998; 11: Los Angeles County Museum of Art; 12: Art Gallery of Ontario; 13, 18: from Carlos Monsiváis and Rafael Vázquez Bayod, *Frida Kahlo: Una Vida, Una Obra* (1992), © Estate of Frida Kahlo/ Licensed by VAGA, New York, N.Y.; 14: courtesy of Sotheby's, New York, © Estate of Frida Kahlo/ Licensed by VAGA, New York, N.Y.; 16: from *Frida Kahlo: La Casa Azul* (1993), © Estate of Frida Kahlo/ Licensed by VAGA, New York, N.Y.; 20, 22: The Art Institute of Chicago, reproduced with permission of Fundacion Olga y Rufino Tamayo; 21: The Art Institute of Chicago; 24: The Museum of Modern Art, New York, © 1998; reproduced with permission of Fundacion Olga y Rufino Tamayo; 26: from Sylvia Navarette, *Artist y Explorador: Miguel Covarrubias* (1993); this illustration originally appeared in *Vogue*, 1937; 27: © Disney Enterprises, Inc.
All works by Diego Rivera and Frida Kahlo are reproduced with permission of Instituto Nacional de Bellas Artes y Literatura.

Catalogue of the Exhibition
16: photo by Robert Hashimoto; 20, 34, 209, 219: photos © by Douglas M. Parker Studio; 45: Appleton Museum of Art; 46, 74, 78, 130, 135, 138, 139, 159, 160, 167, 168, 216: photos © by Justin Kerr; 73, 93, 101, 215: photos © by Dirk Bakker; 111, 161, 165: Fowler Museum of Cultural History, University of California, Los Angeles; 134: photo by Michael Tropea; 203: The Fine Arts Museum of San Francisco; 207: The University of Iowa Museum of Art.